Voice Over!
Seiyu Academy

10

Vol.**10**
Story & Art by
Maki Minami

TECHNICAL ADVISORS
Yoichi Kato, Kaori Kagami, Ayumi Hashidate,
Ayako Harino and Touko Fujitani

Voice Over! Seiyu Academy

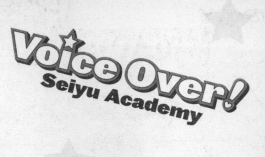

Vol. 10

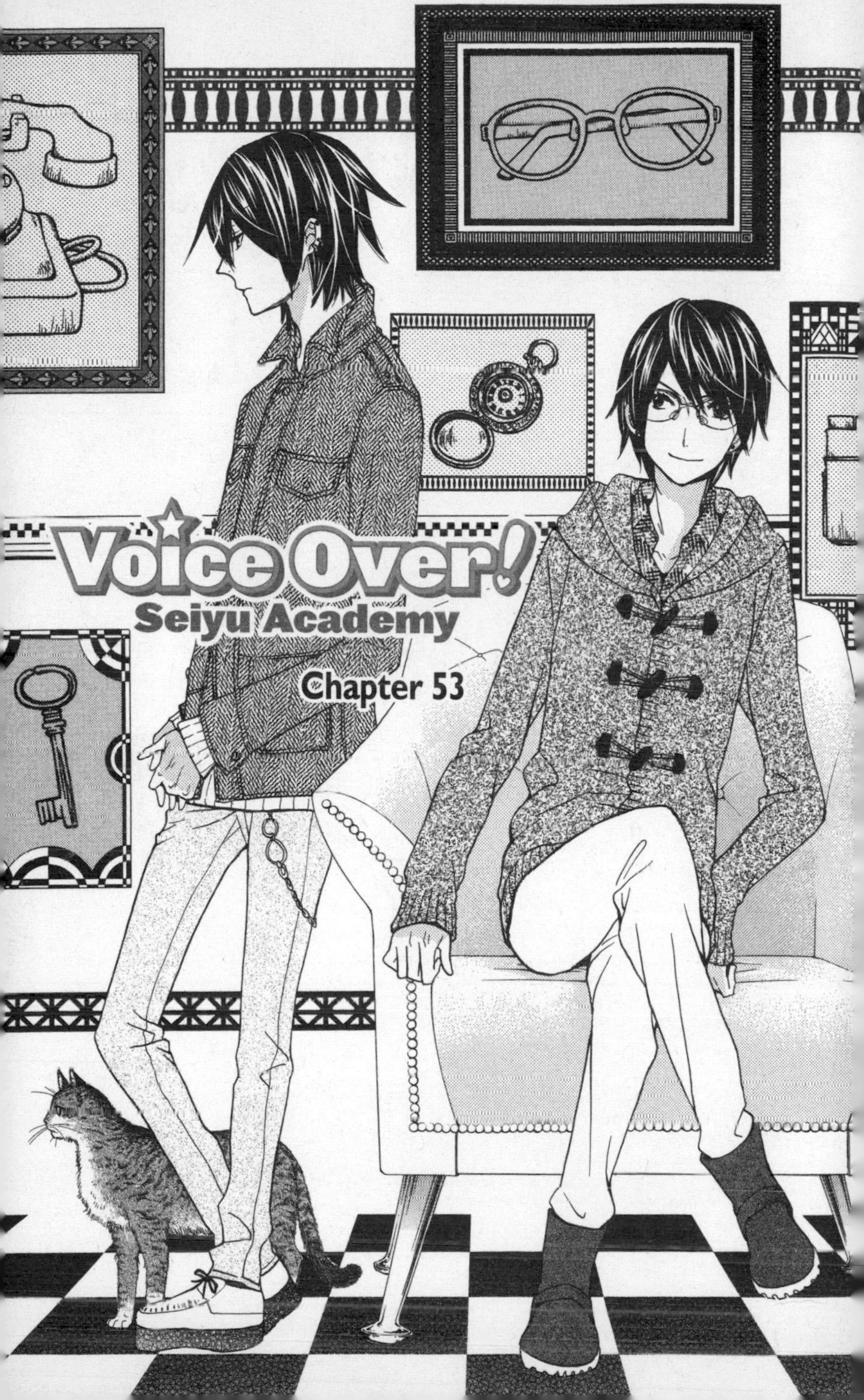
Voice Over!
Seiyu Academy
Chapter 53

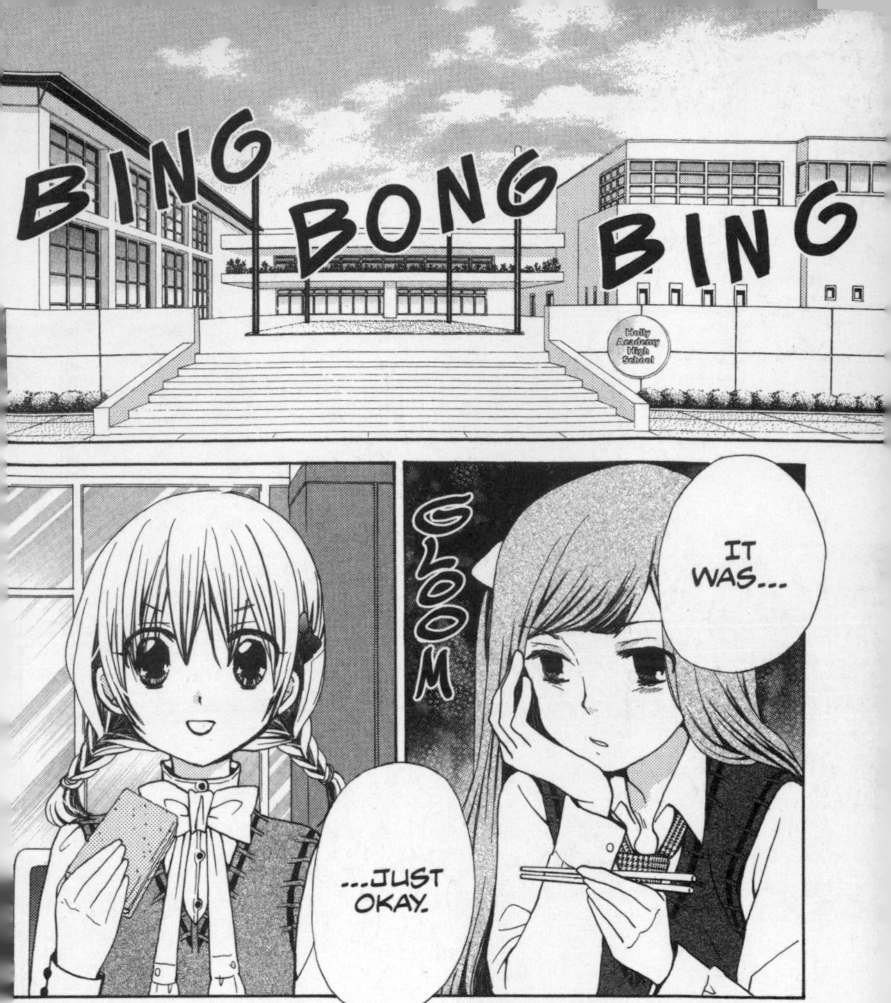
BING
BONG
BING
Holly Academy High School
GLOOM
IT WAS...
...JUST OKAY.

• Cover & Various Things •

• The cover this time shows Senri and Shiro engaged in *Octalia* cosplay! I changed the overall color scheme this time.

My assistant I-san, who is illustrating the anime scenes, drew the title page illustration!!

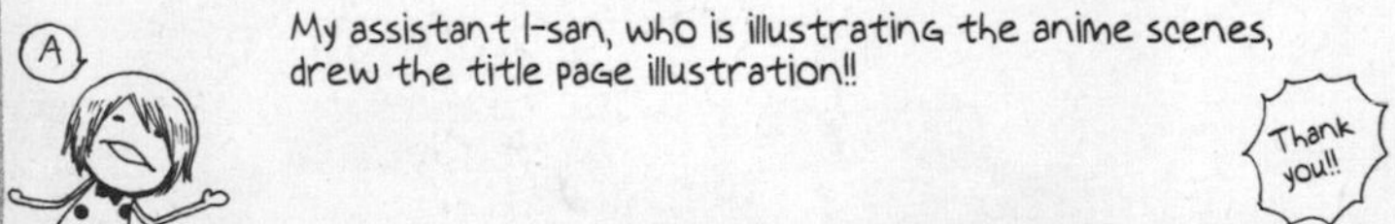
A
Thank you!!

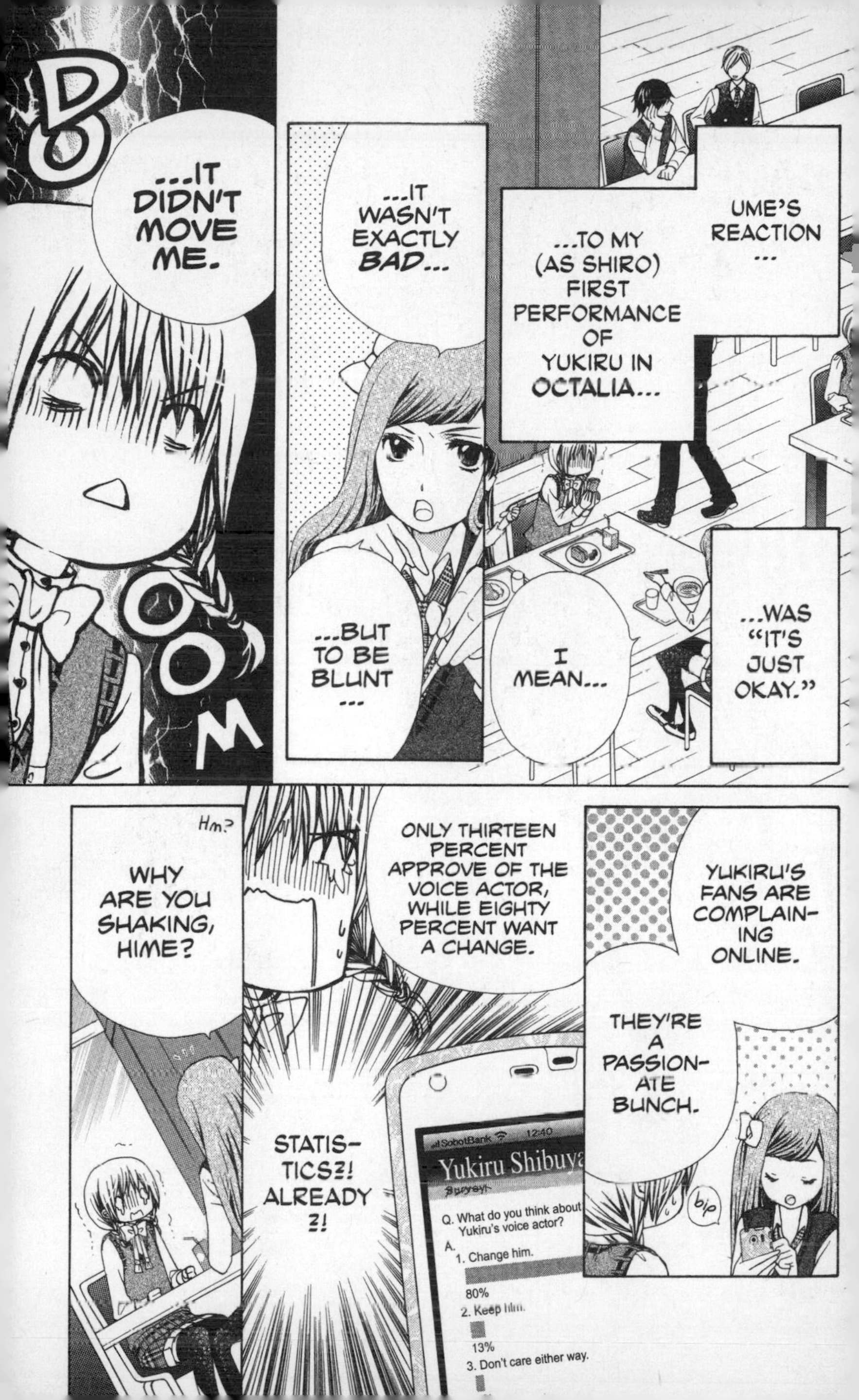
UME'S REACTION...
...TO MY (AS SHIRO) FIRST PERFORMANCE OF YUKIRU IN OCTALIA...
...WAS "IT'S JUST OKAY."
I MEAN...
...IT WASN'T EXACTLY BAD...
...BUT TO BE BLUNT...
...IT DIDN'T MOVE ME.
DOOOM
YUKIRU'S FANS ARE COMPLAINING ONLINE.
THEY'RE A PASSIONATE BUNCH.
bip
ONLY THIRTEEN PERCENT APPROVE OF THE VOICE ACTOR, WHILE EIGHTY PERCENT WANT A CHANGE.
STATISTICS?! ALREADY?!
SobotBank 12:40
Yukiru Shibuya
Q. What do you think about Yukiru's voice actor?
A.
1. Change him.
80%
2. Keep him.
13%
3. Don't care either way.
Hm?
WHY ARE YOU SHAKING, HIME?

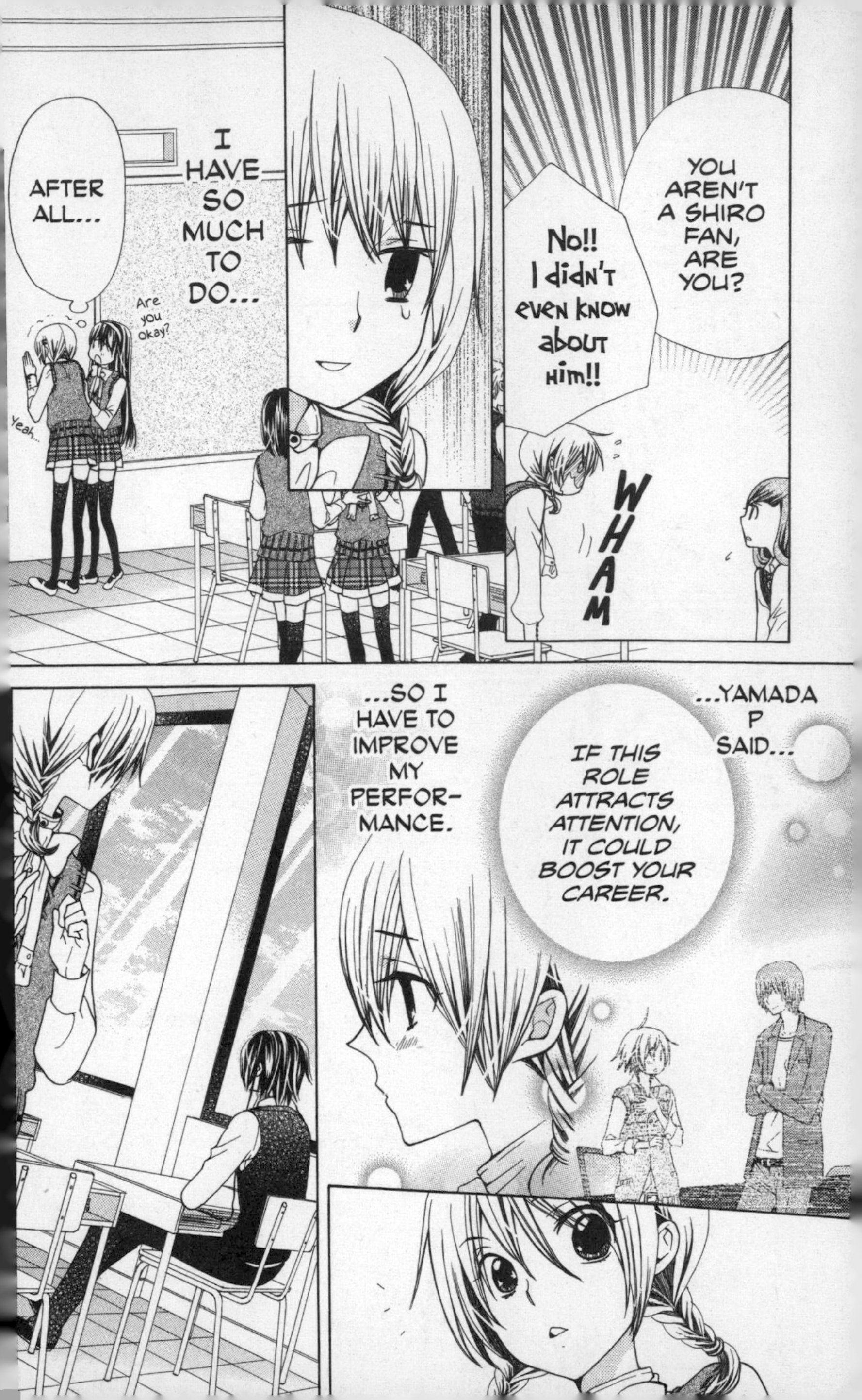
YOU AREN'T A SHIRO FAN, ARE YOU?
No!! I didn't even know about him!!
WHAM
I HAVE SO MUCH TO DO...
AFTER ALL...
Are you okay?
Yeah...
...YAMADA P SAID...
IF THIS ROLE ATTRACTS ATTENTION, IT COULD BOOST YOUR CAREER.
...SO I HAVE TO IMPROVE MY PERFORMANCE.

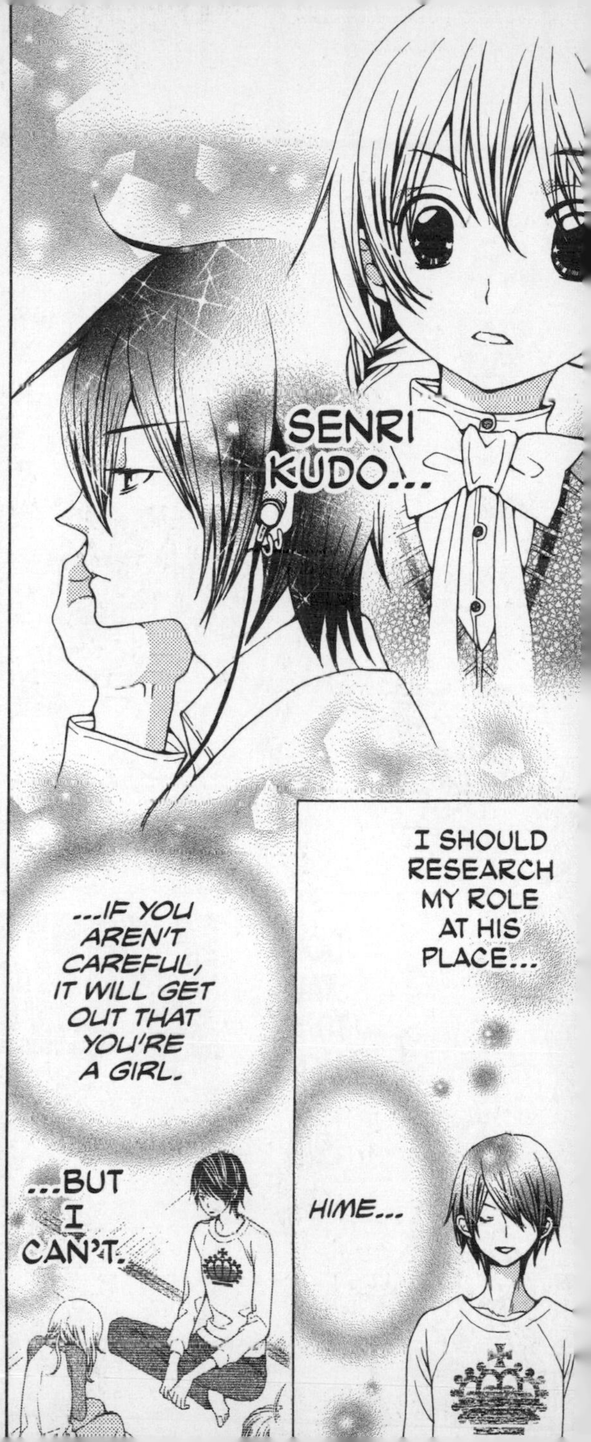
SENRI KUDO...
I SHOULD RESEARCH MY ROLE AT HIS PLACE...
HIME...
...IF YOU AREN'T CAREFUL, IT WILL GET OUT THAT YOU'RE A GIRL.
...BUT I CAN'T.

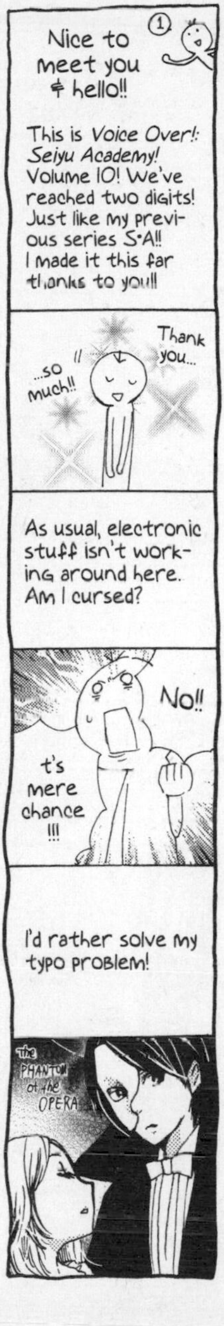
1
Nice to meet you & hello!!
This is *Voice Over!: Seiyu Academy!* Volume 10! We've reached two digits! Just like my previous series S•A!! I made it this far thanks to you!!
Thank you...
...so much!!
As usual, electronic stuff isn't working around here. Am I cursed?
No!!
t's mere chance !!!
I'd rather solve my typo problem!
The PHANTOM of the OPERA

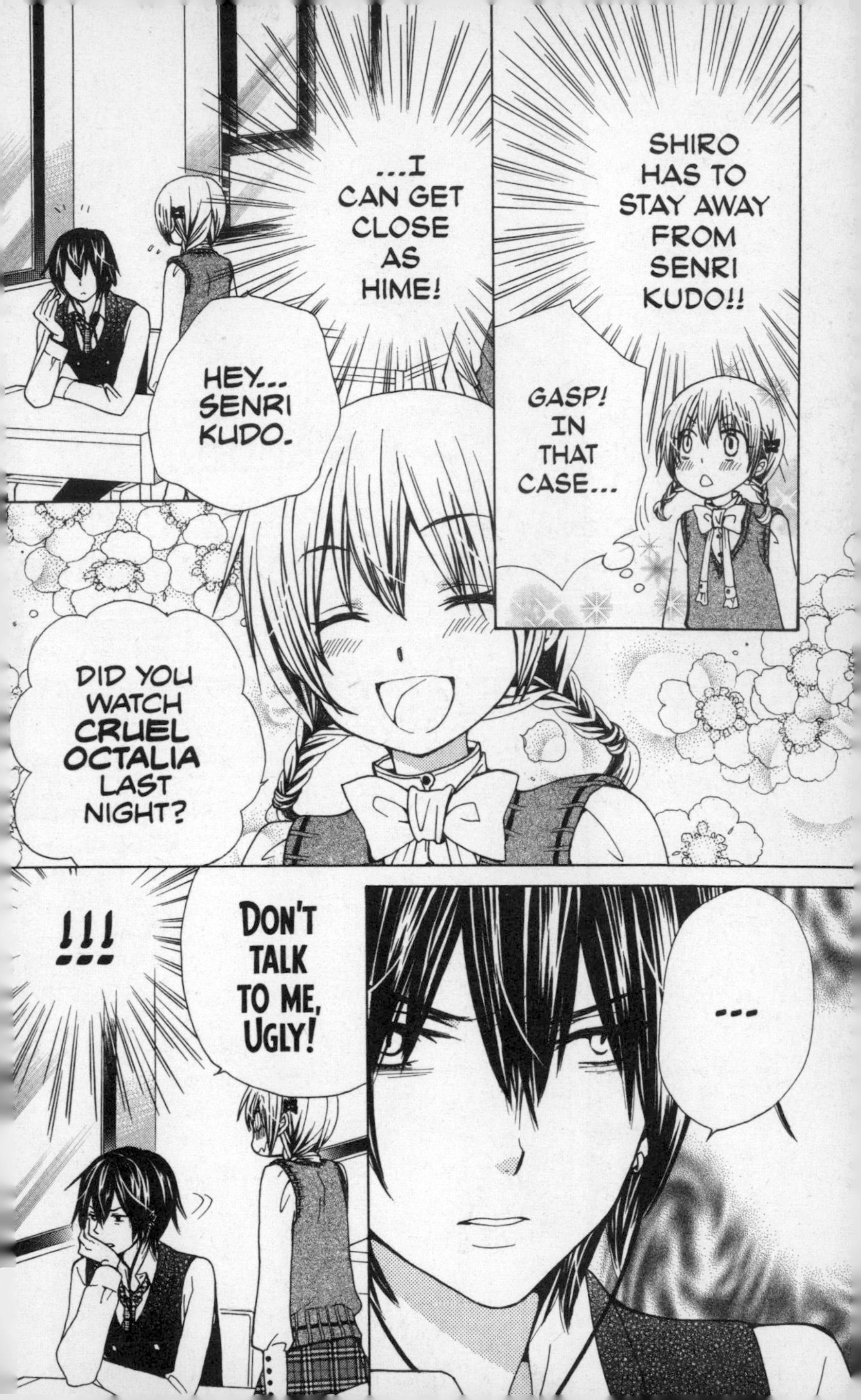
SHIRO HAS TO STAY AWAY FROM SENRI KUDO!!
GASP! IN THAT CASE...
...I CAN GET CLOSE AS HIME!
HEY... SENRI KUDO.
DID YOU WATCH CRUEL OCTALIA LAST NIGHT?
...
DON'T TALK TO ME, UGLY!
!!!

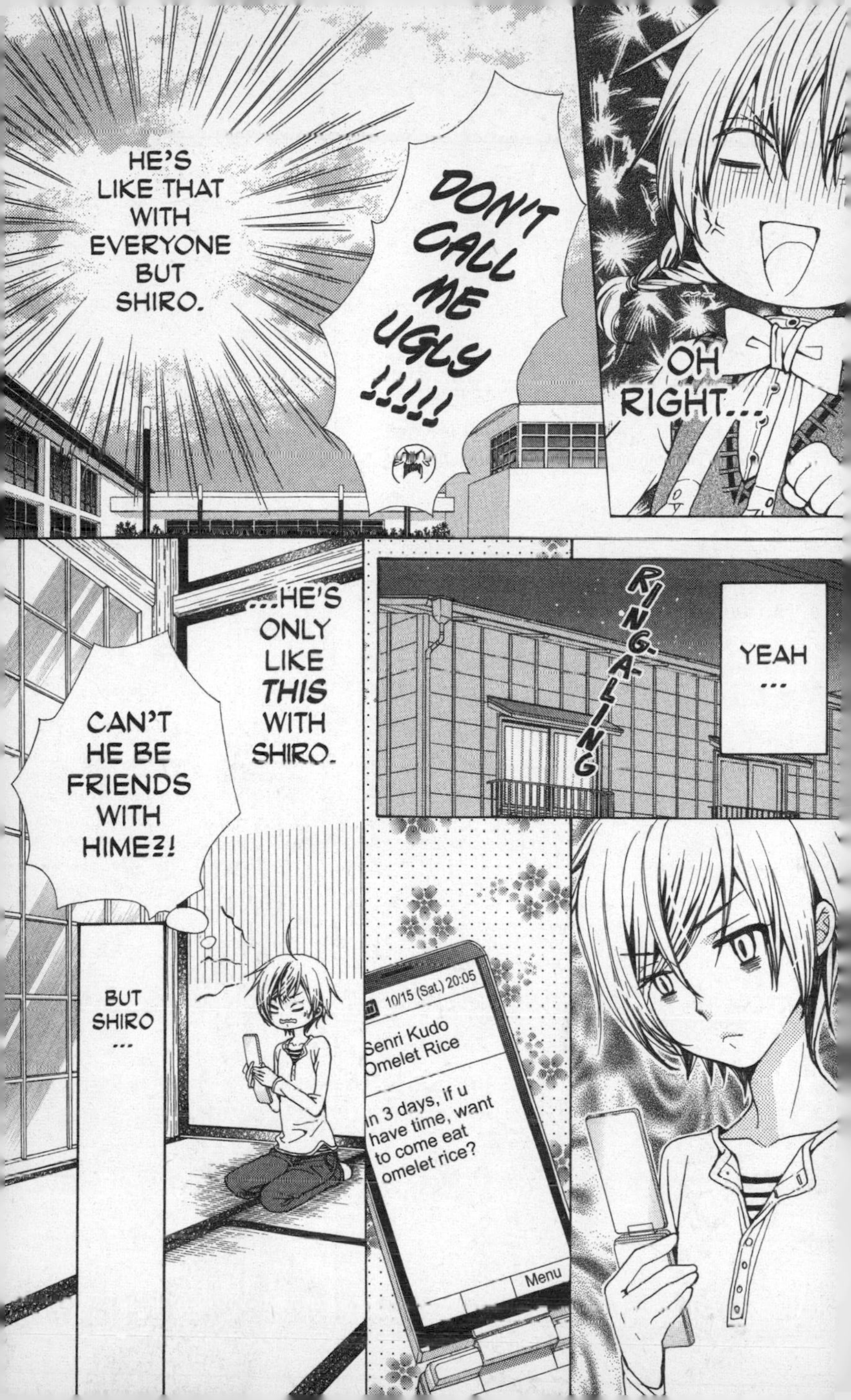
OH RIGHT...
DON'T CALL ME UGLY!!!!!
HE'S LIKE THAT WITH EVERYONE BUT SHIRO.
YEAH...
RING-A-LING
10/15 (Sat.) 20:05
Senri Kudo
Omelet Rice
In 3 days, if u have time, want to come eat omelet rice?
Menu
...HE'S ONLY LIKE THIS WITH SHIRO.
CAN'T HE BE FRIENDS WITH HIME?!
BUT SHIRO...

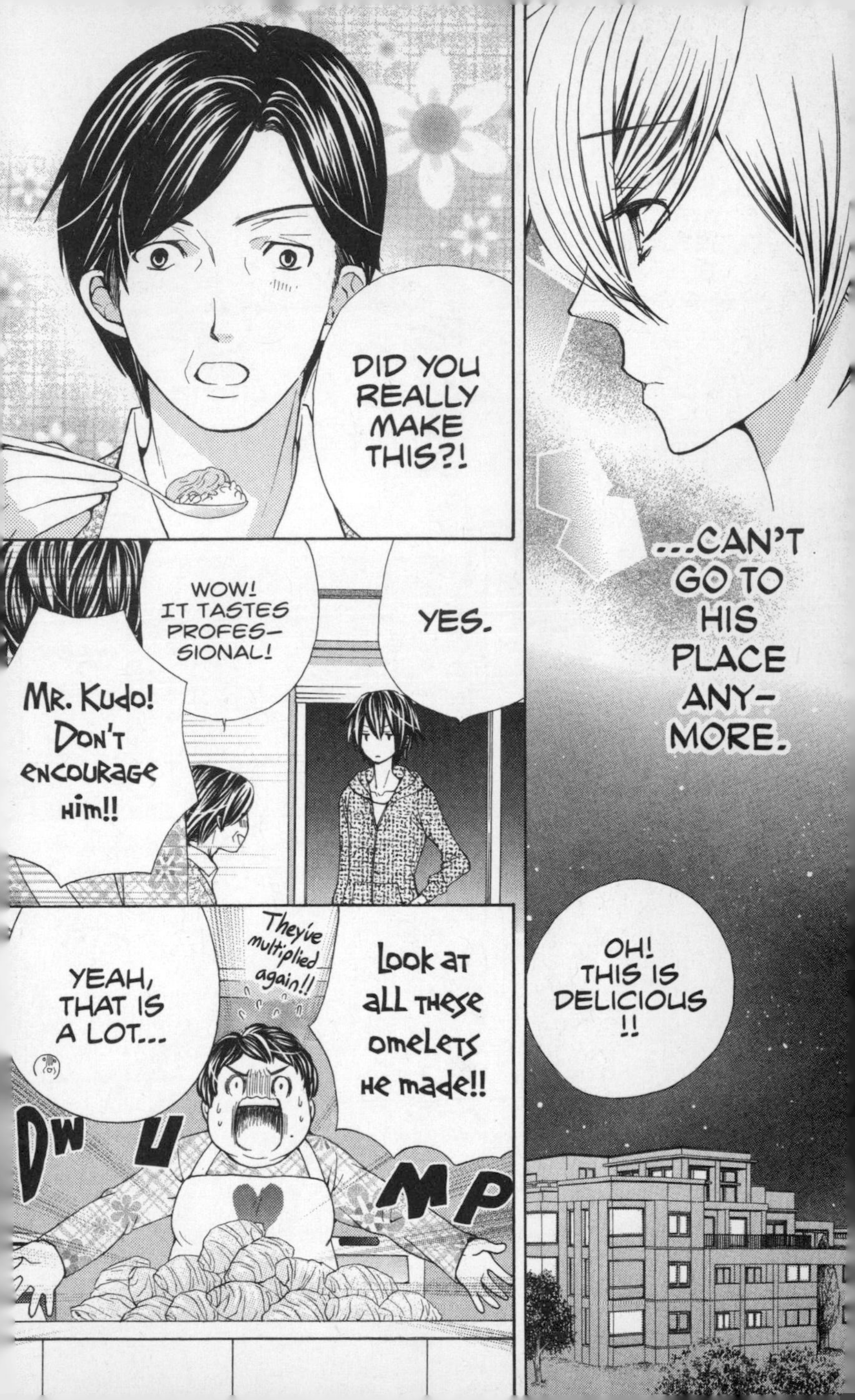
...CAN'T GO TO HIS PLACE ANYMORE.
OH! THIS IS DELICIOUS!!
DID YOU REALLY MAKE THIS?!
YES.
WOW! IT TASTES PROFES-SIONAL!
Mr. Kudo! Don't encourage him!!
Look at all these omelets he made!!
They've multiplied again!!
YEAH, THAT IS A LOT...
DWUMP

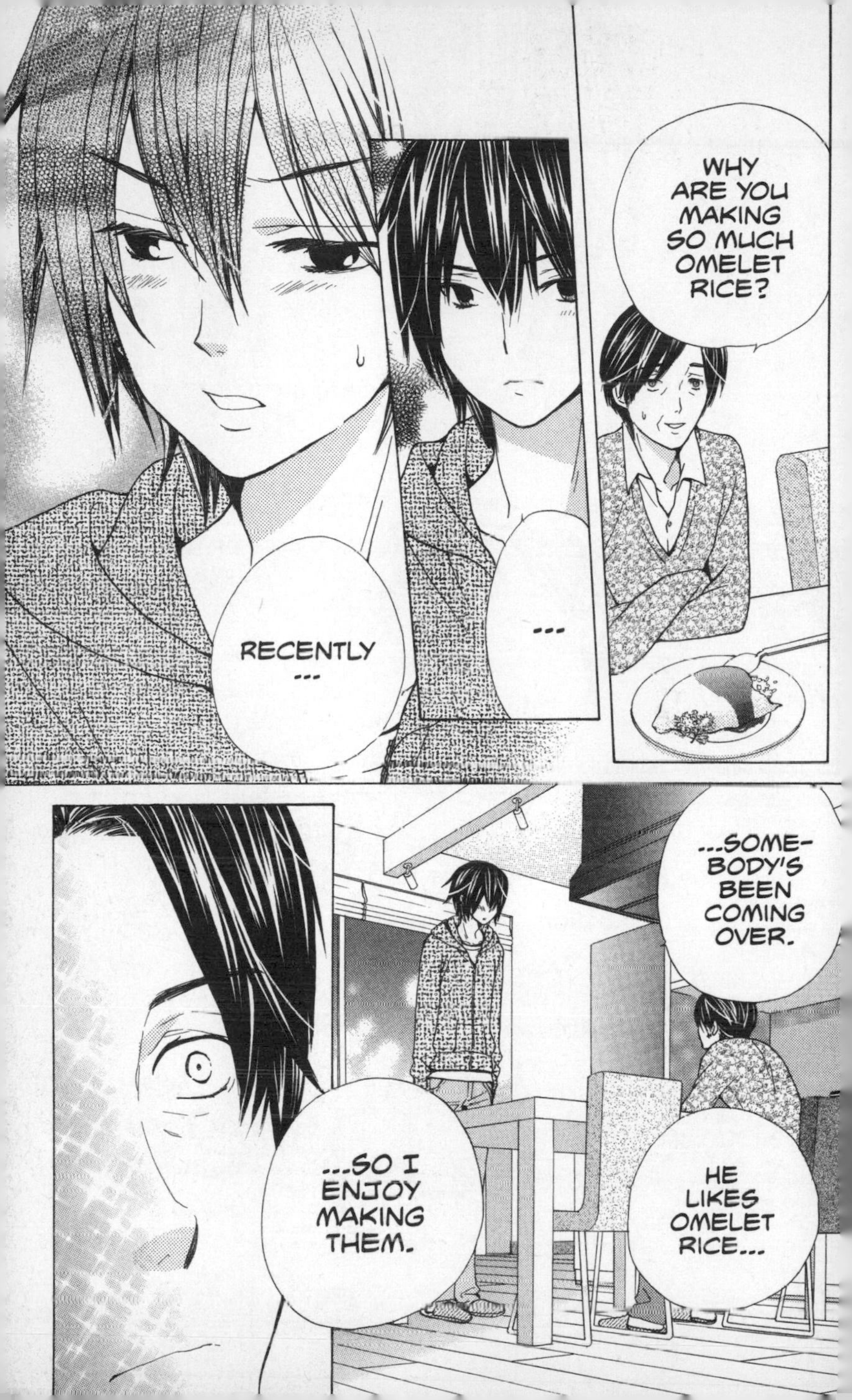
WHY ARE YOU MAKING SO MUCH OMELET RICE?
...
RECENTLY...
...SOMEBODY'S BEEN COMING OVER.
HE LIKES OMELET RICE...
...SO I ENJOY MAKING THEM.

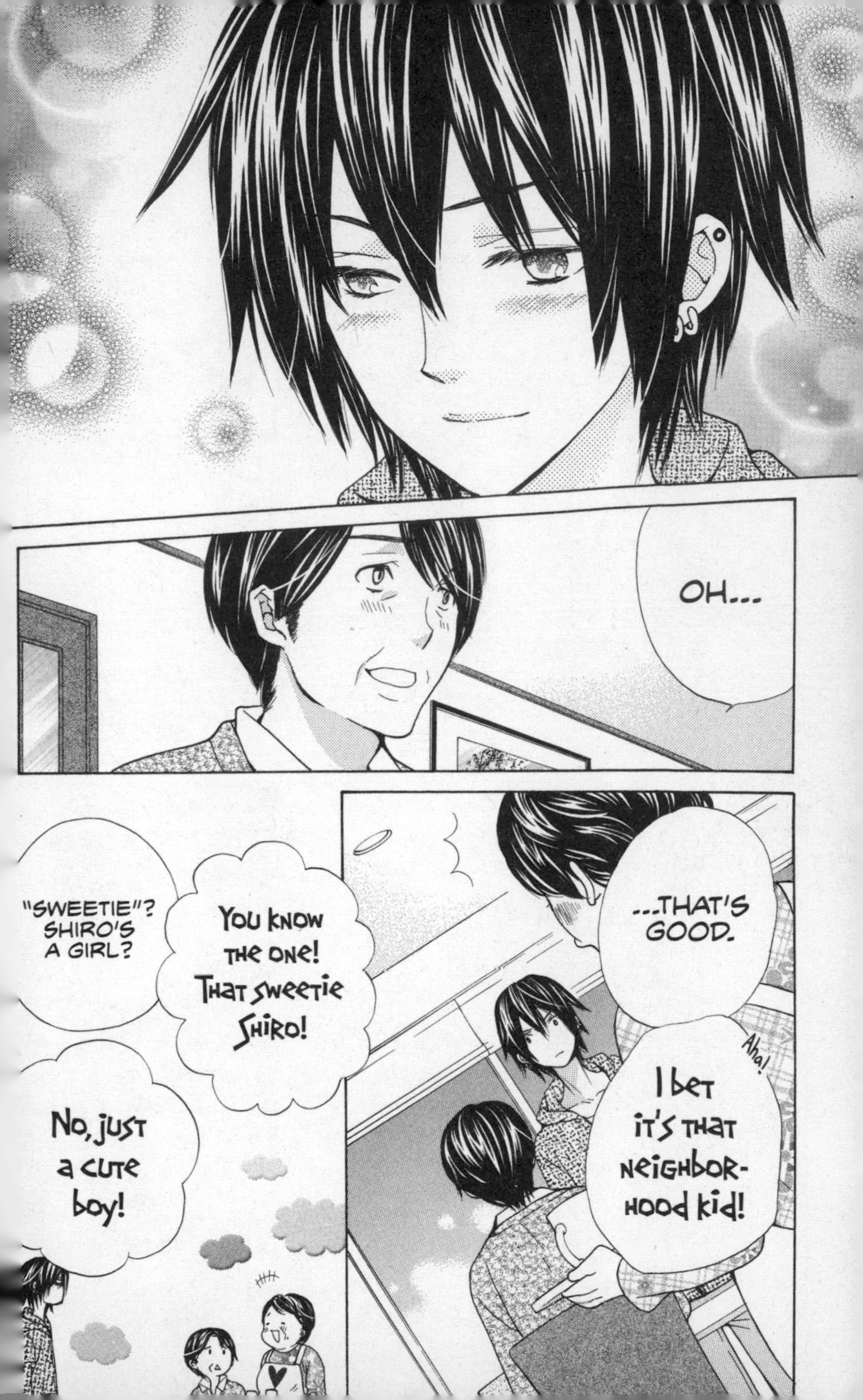
OH...
...THAT'S GOOD.
Aha!
I bet it's that neighbor-hood kid!
You know the one! That sweetie Shiro!
"SWEETIE"? SHIRO'S A GIRL?
No, just a cute boy!

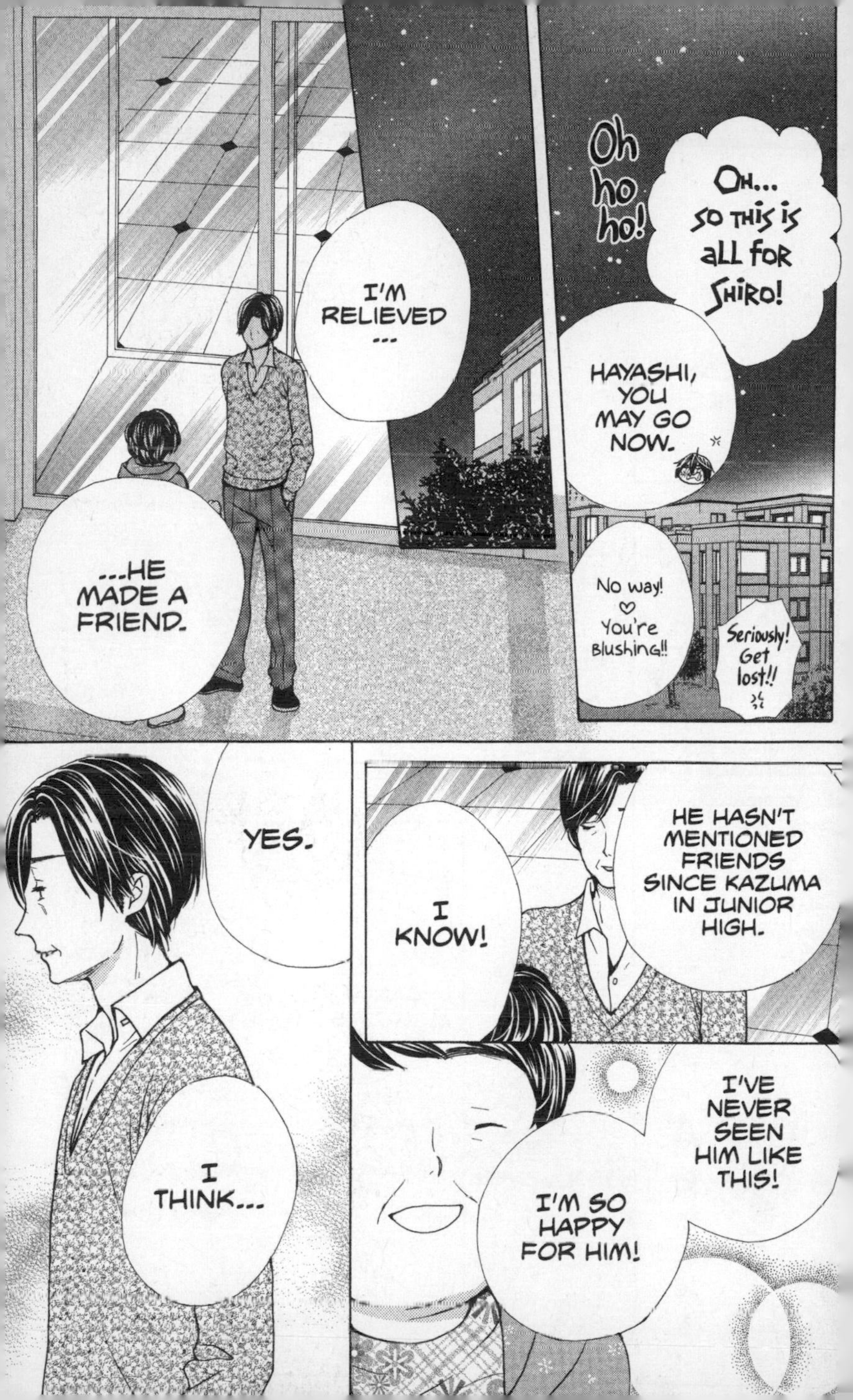
OH... SO THIS IS ALL FOR SHIRO!
Oh ho ho!
HAYASHI, YOU MAY GO NOW.
No way! ♡ You're blushing!!
Seriously! Get lost!!
I'M RELIEVED...
...HE MADE A FRIEND.
HE HASN'T MENTIONED FRIENDS SINCE KAZUMA IN JUNIOR HIGH.
I KNOW!
I'VE NEVER SEEN HIM LIKE THIS!
I'M SO HAPPY FOR HIM!
YES.
I THINK...

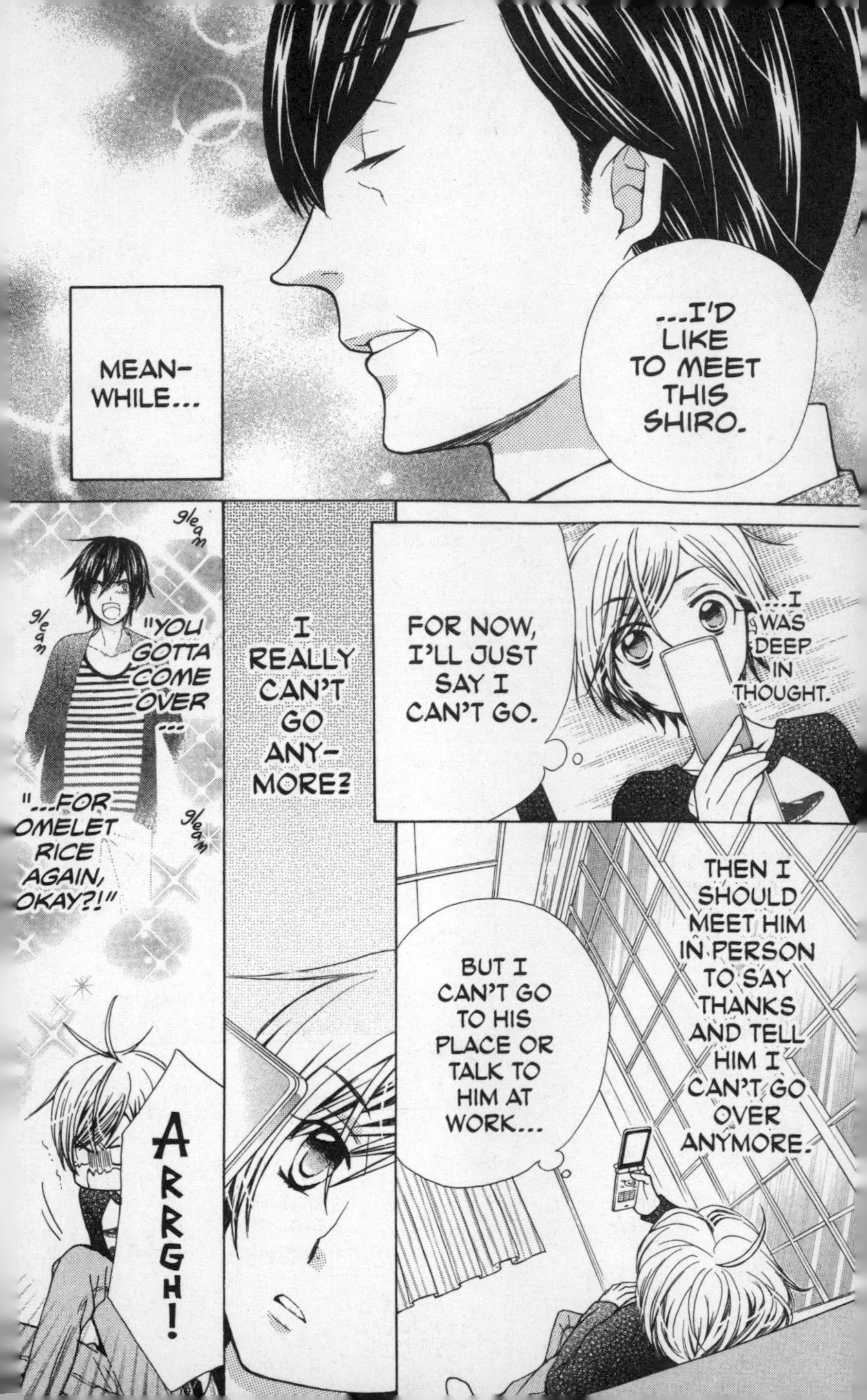
...I'D LIKE TO MEET THIS SHIRO.
MEANWHILE...
...I WAS DEEP IN THOUGHT.
FOR NOW, I'LL JUST SAY I CAN'T GO.
THEN I SHOULD MEET HIM IN PERSON TO SAY THANKS AND TELL HIM I CAN'T GO OVER ANYMORE.
BUT I CAN'T GO TO HIS PLACE OR TALK TO HIM AT WORK...
I REALLY CAN'T GO ANYMORE?
gleam
gleam
"YOU GOTTA COME OVER...
"...FOR OMELET RICE AGAIN, OKAY?!"
gleam
ARRGH!

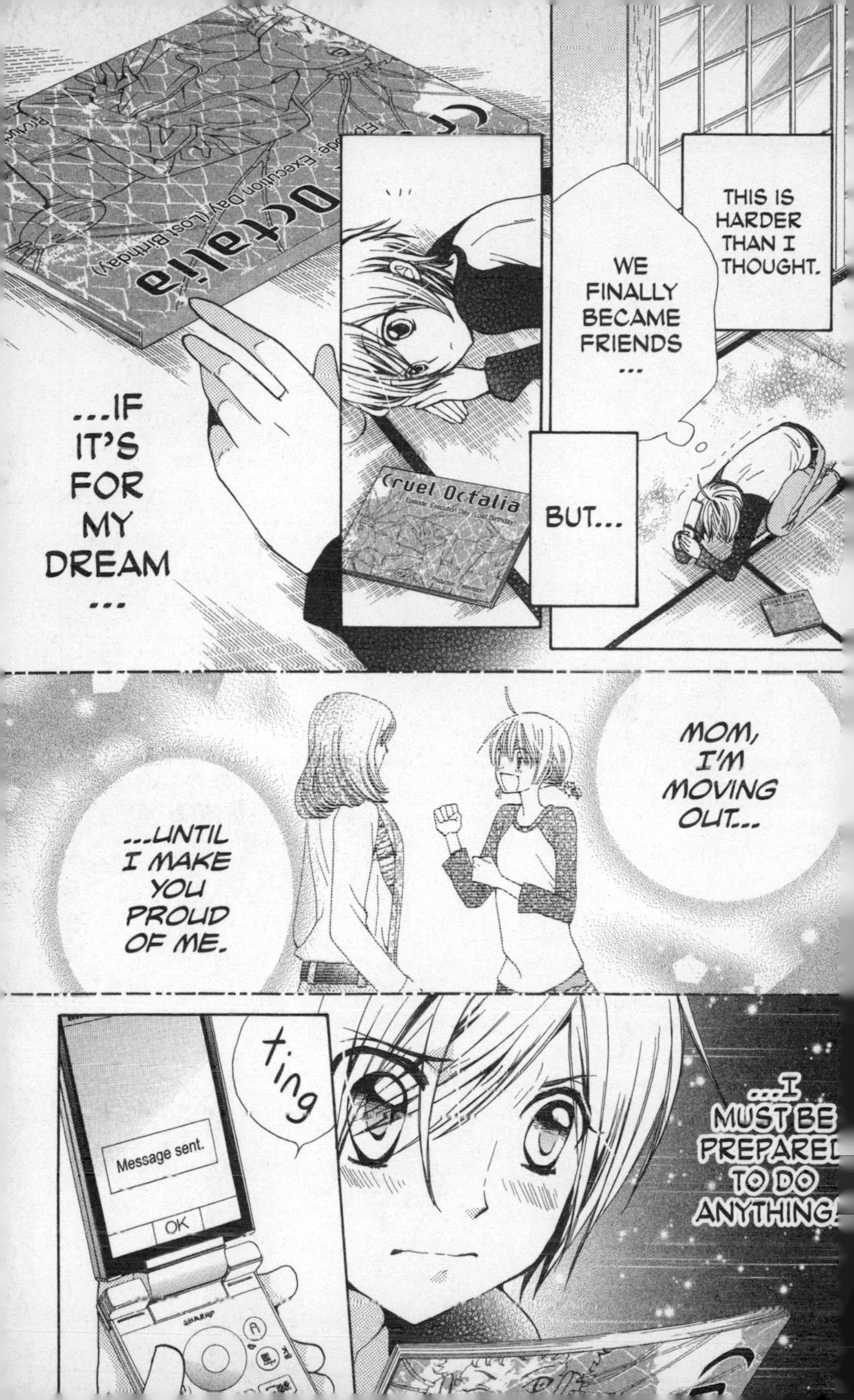
THIS IS HARDER THAN I THOUGHT.
WE FINALLY BECAME FRIENDS...
BUT...
Cruel Octalia
Episode: Execution Day (Lost Birthday)
...IF IT'S FOR MY DREAM...
MOM, I'M MOVING OUT...
...UNTIL I MAKE YOU PROUD OF ME.
...I MUST BE PREPARED TO DO ANYTHING.
ting
Message sent.
OK

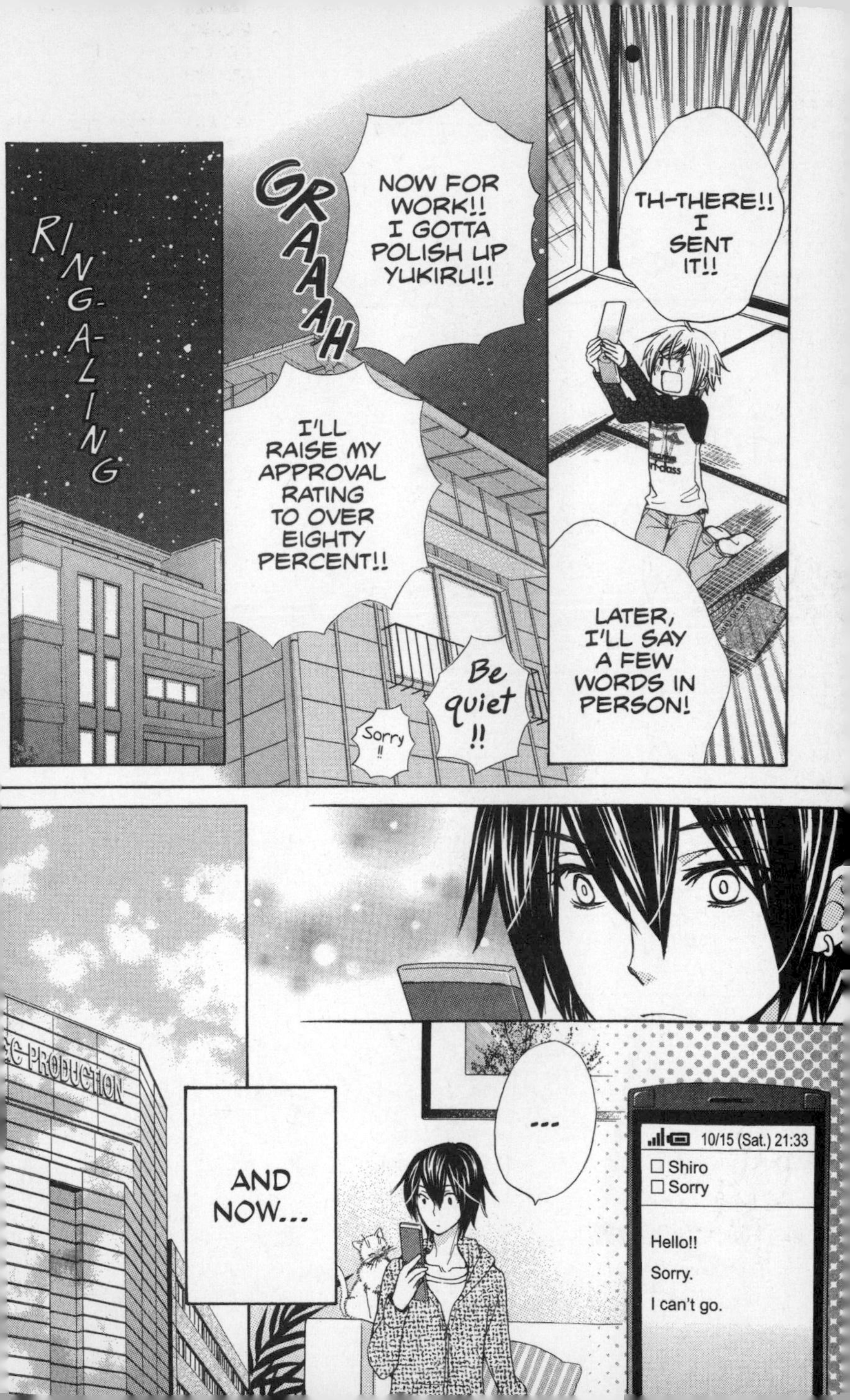
TH-THERE!! I SENT IT!!
LATER, I'LL SAY A FEW WORDS IN PERSON!
GRAAAAH
NOW FOR WORK!! I GOTTA POLISH UP YUKIRU!!
I'LL RAISE MY APPROVAL RATING TO OVER EIGHTY PERCENT!!
Be quiet!!
Sorry!!
RING-A-LING
10/15 (Sat.) 21:33
☐ Shiro
☐ Sorry
Hello!!
Sorry.
I can't go.
...
AND NOW...
PRODUCTION

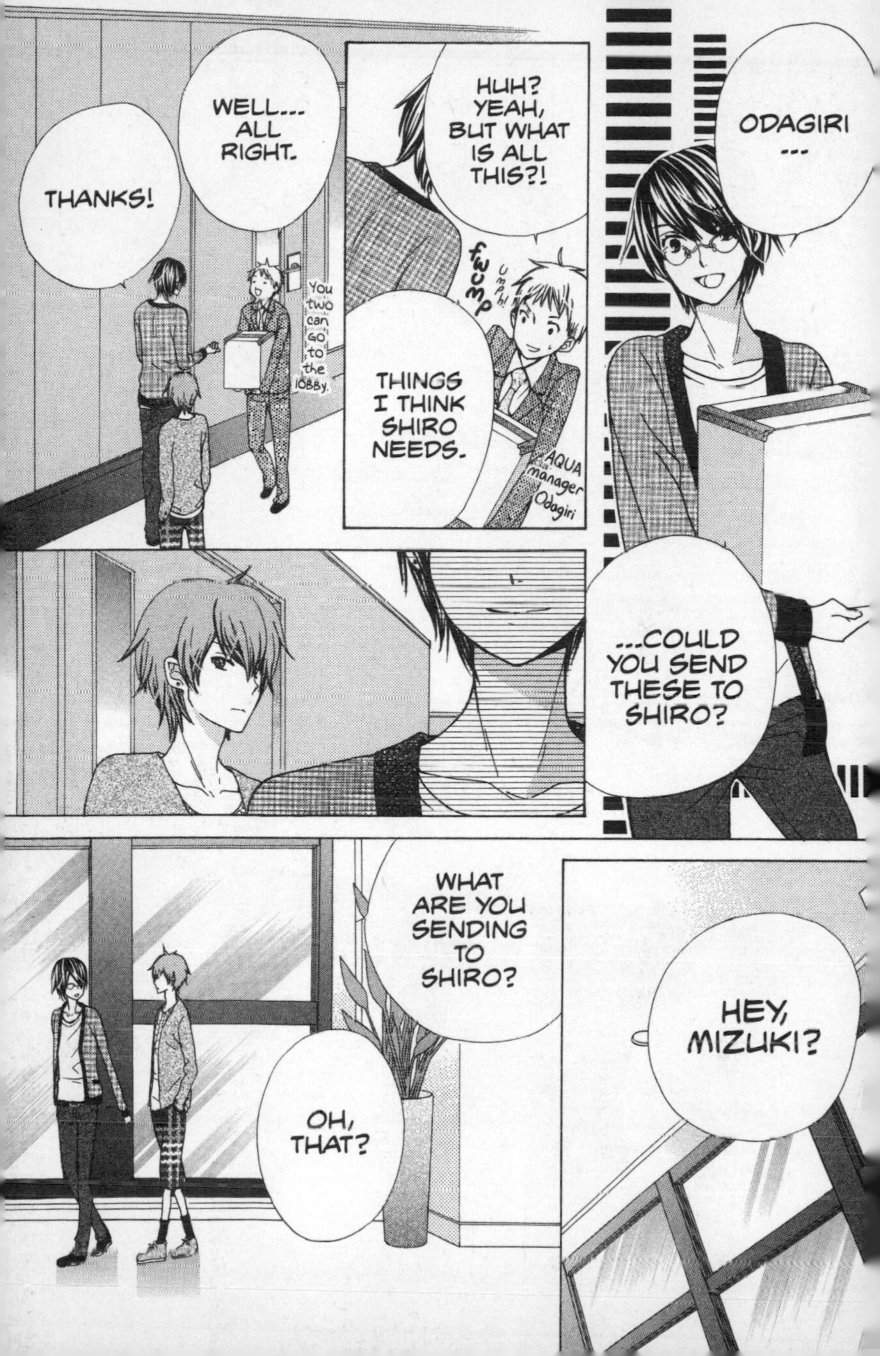
ODAGIRI...
...COULD YOU SEND THESE TO SHIRO?
HUH? YEAH, BUT WHAT IS ALL THIS?!
fwump
Umph!
THINGS I THINK SHIRO NEEDS.
AQUA manager Odagiri
WELL... ALL RIGHT.
THANKS!
You two can GO to the lobby.
HEY, MIZUKI?
WHAT ARE YOU SENDING TO SHIRO?
OH, THAT?

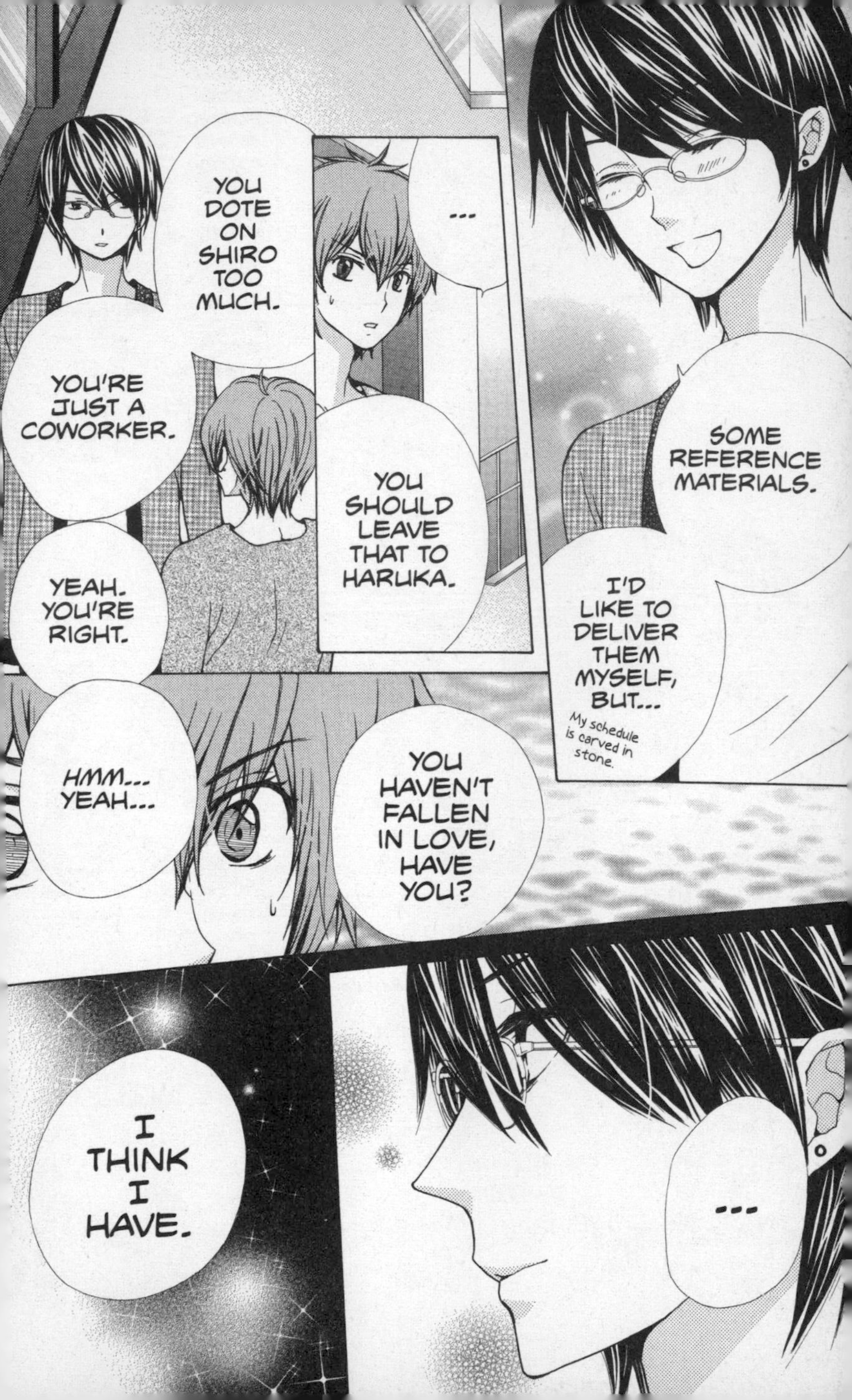
SOME REFERENCE MATERIALS.
I'D LIKE TO DELIVER THEM MYSELF, BUT...
My schedule is carved in stone.
...
YOU SHOULD LEAVE THAT TO HARUKA.
YOU DOTE ON SHIRO TOO MUCH.
YOU'RE JUST A COWORKER.
YEAH. YOU'RE RIGHT.
YOU HAVEN'T FALLEN IN LOVE, HAVE YOU?
HMM... YEAH...
...
I THINK I HAVE.

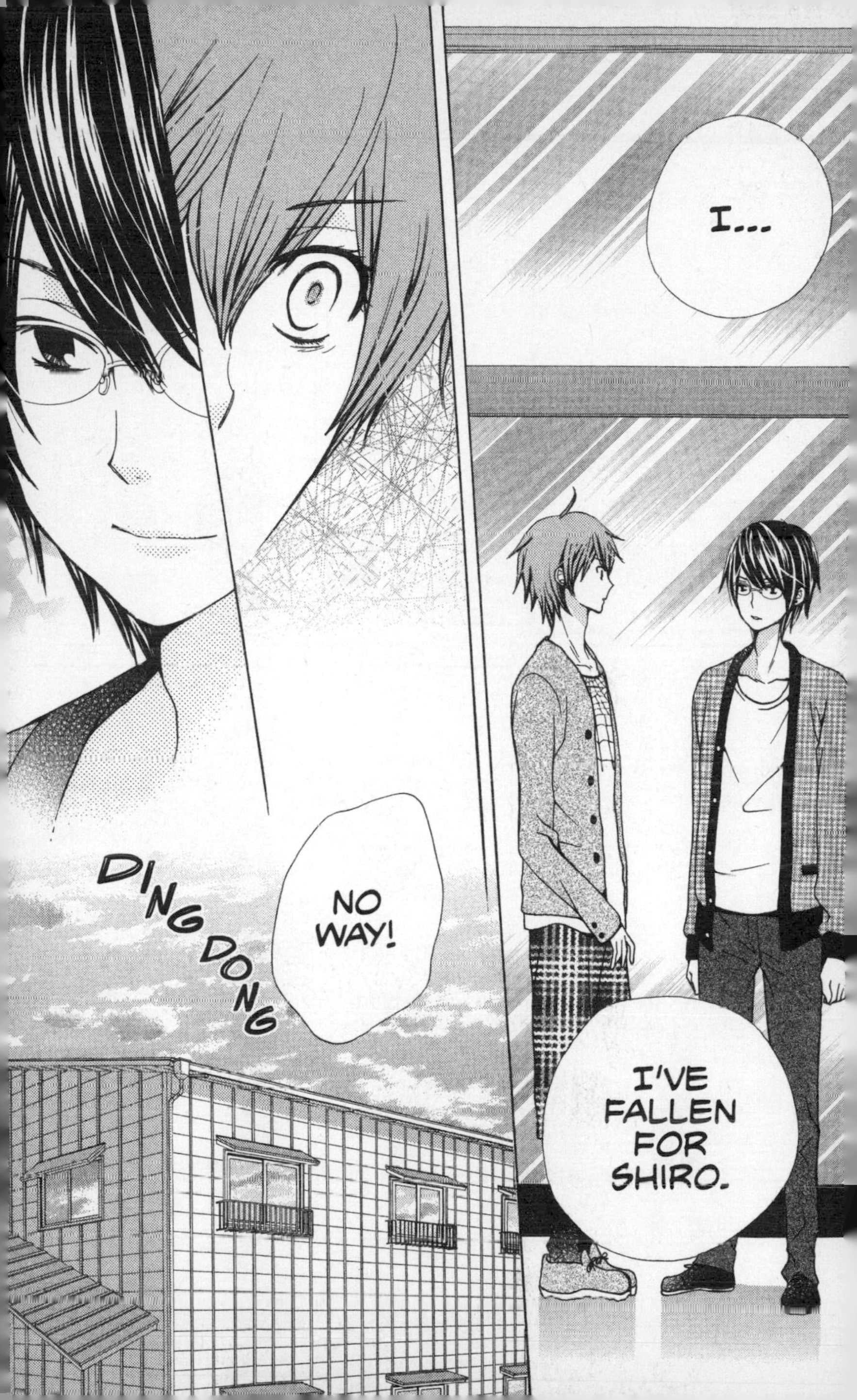
I...
I'VE FALLEN FOR SHIRO.
NO WAY!
DING DONG

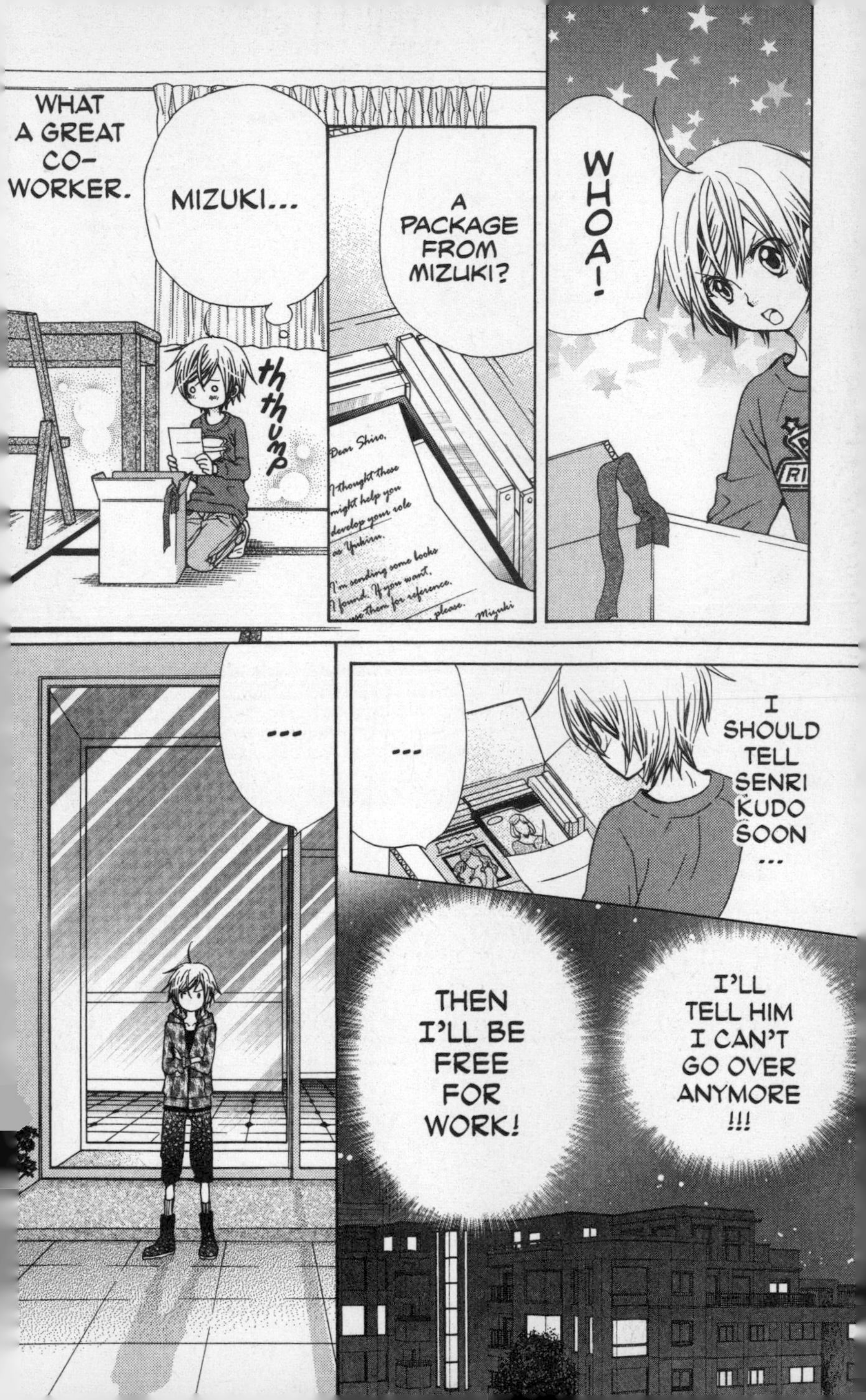
WHOA!
A PACKAGE FROM MIZUKI?
Dear Shiro,
I thought these might help you develop your role as Yukiru.
I'm sending some books I found. If you want,
se them for reference.
please.
Mizuki
MIZUKI...
th thump
WHAT A GREAT CO-WORKER.
I SHOULD TELL SENRI KUDO SOON...
...
I'LL TELL HIM I CAN'T GO OVER ANYMORE!!!
THEN I'LL BE FREE FOR WORK!
...

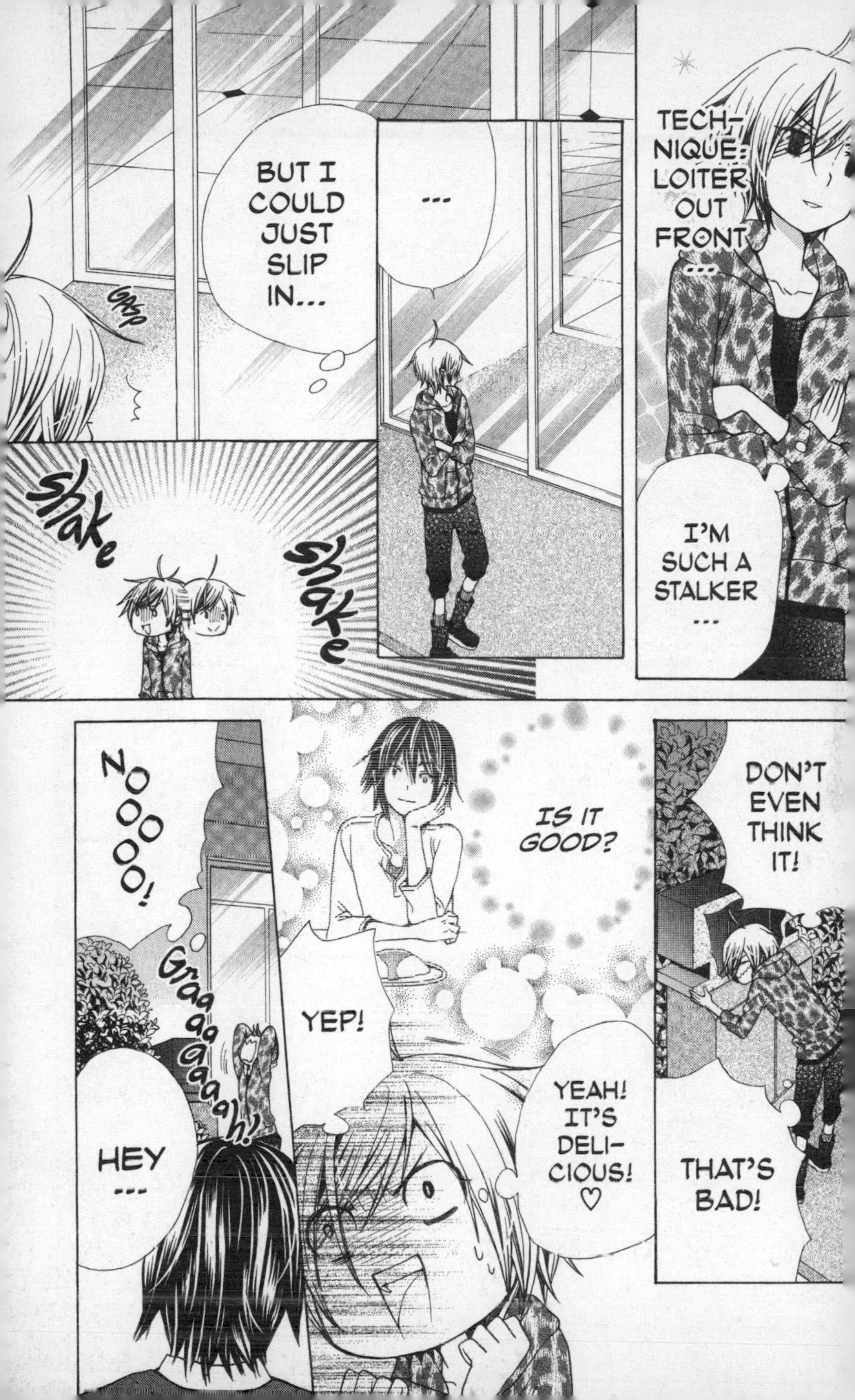

TECH-NIQUE: LOITER OUT FRONT...
I'M SUCH A STALKER...
...
BUT I COULD JUST SLIP IN...
GASP
shake
shake
DON'T EVEN THINK IT!
THAT'S BAD!
IS IT GOOD?
YEAH! IT'S DELICIOUS! ♡
YEP!
NOOOOO!
Graaaaaaaah!
HEY...

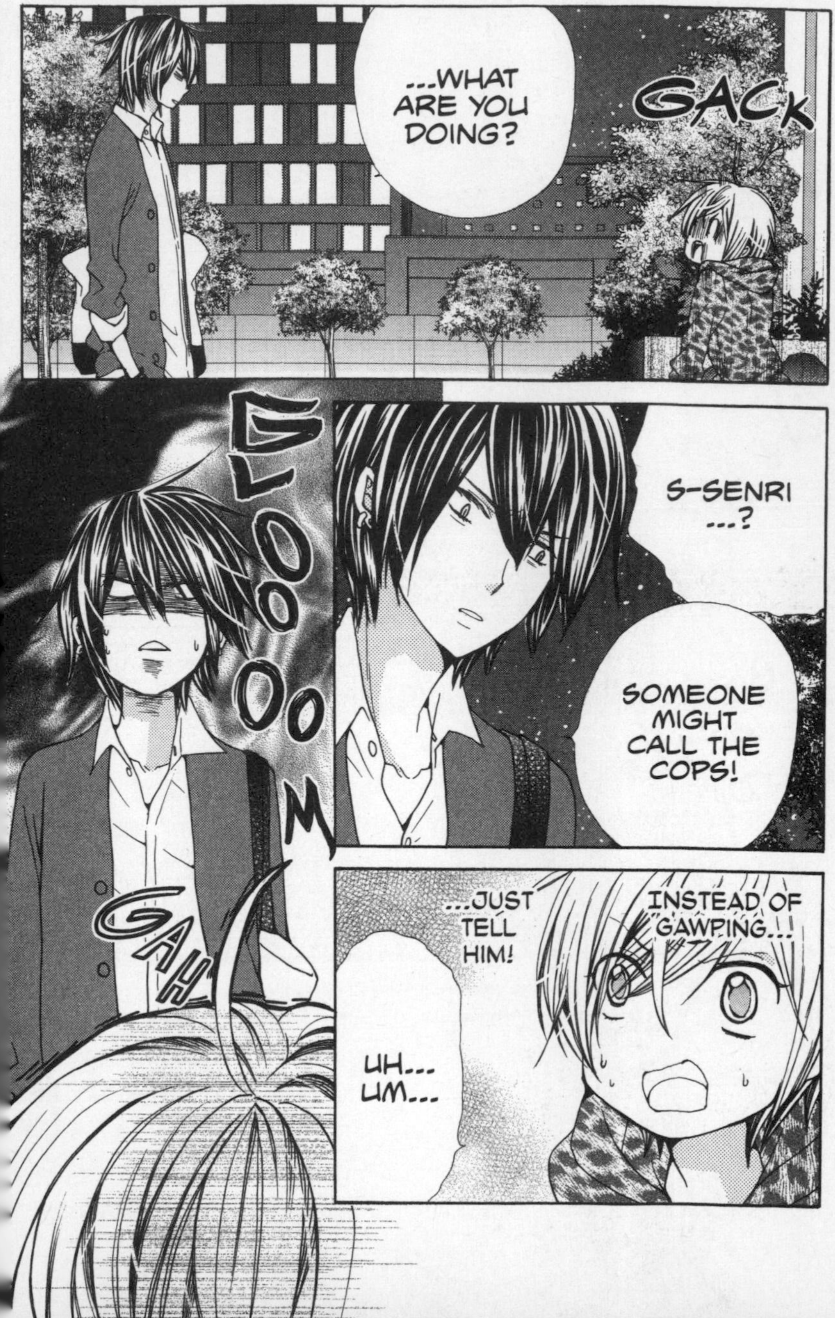

GACK
...WHAT ARE YOU DOING?
S-SENRI ...?
SOMEONE MIGHT CALL THE COPS!
INSTEAD OF "GAWPING"...
...JUST TELL HIM!
UH... UM...
GLOOOOM
GAH

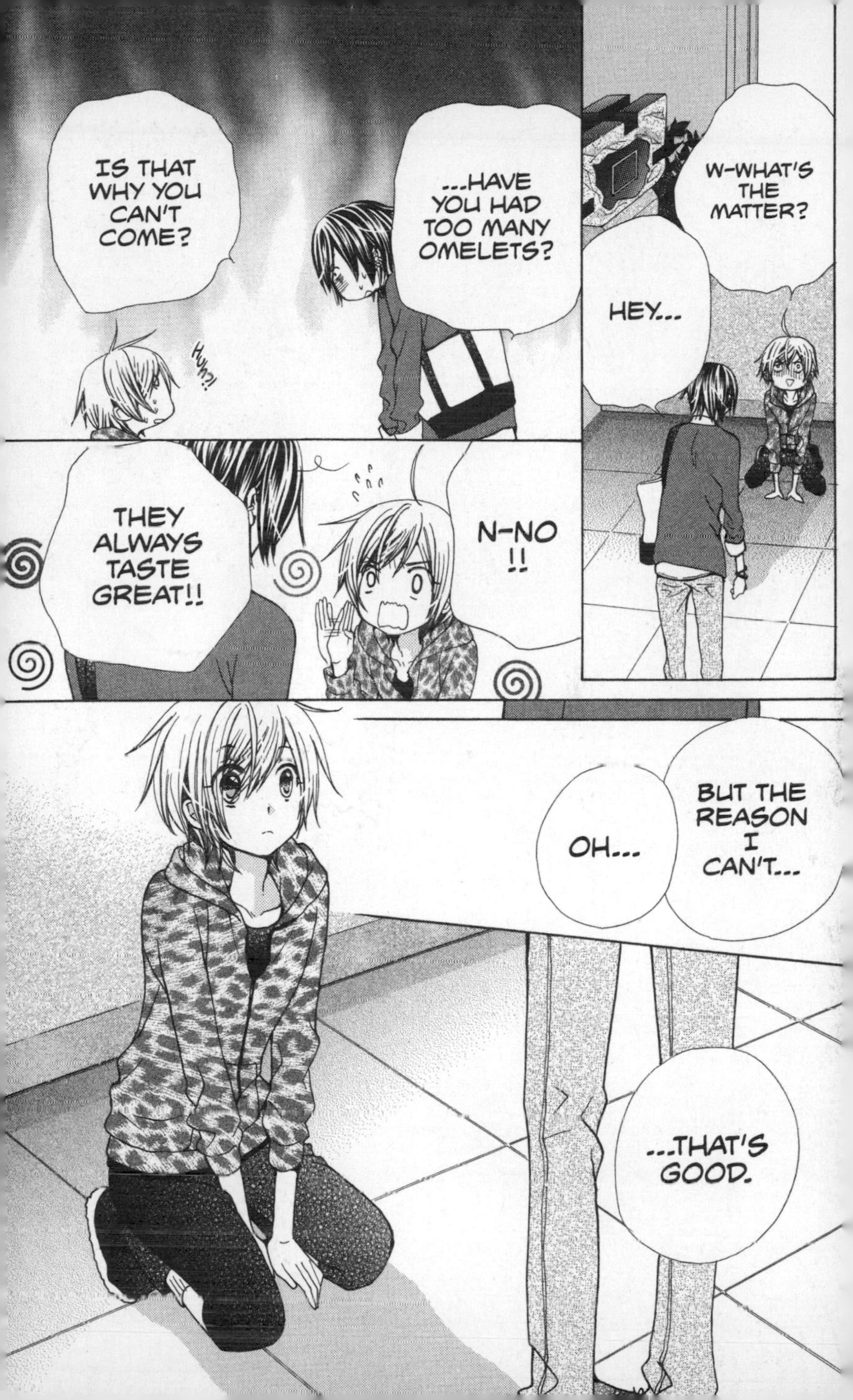
W-WHAT'S THE MATTER?
HEY...
...HAVE YOU HAD TOO MANY OMELETS?
IS THAT WHY YOU CAN'T COME?
HUH?!
N-NO!!
THEY ALWAYS TASTE GREAT!!
BUT THE REASON I CAN'T...
OH...
...THAT'S GOOD.

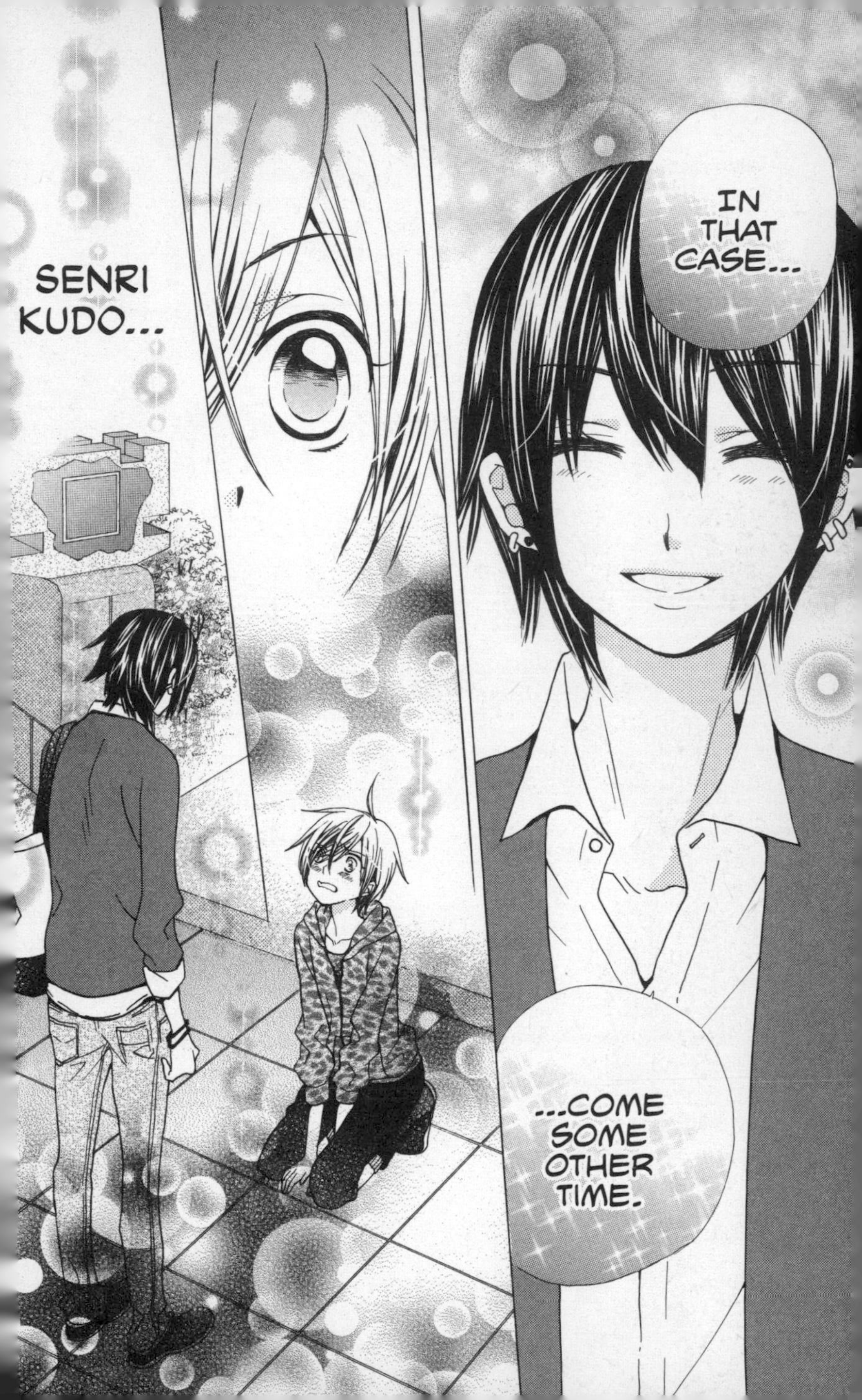
IN THAT CASE...
...COME SOME OTHER TIME.
SENRI KUDO...

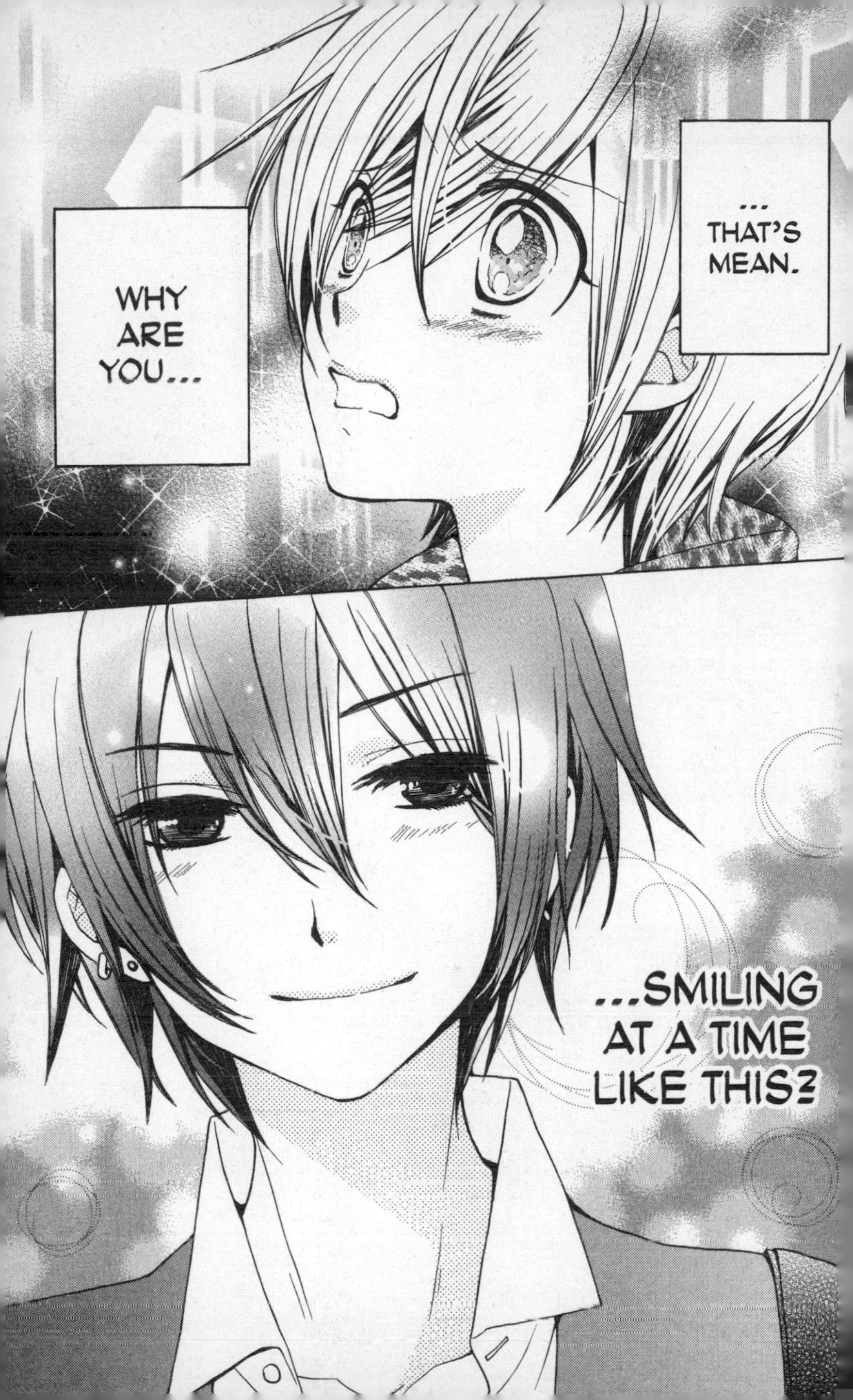
...THAT'S MEAN.
WHY ARE YOU...
...SMILING AT A TIME LIKE THIS?

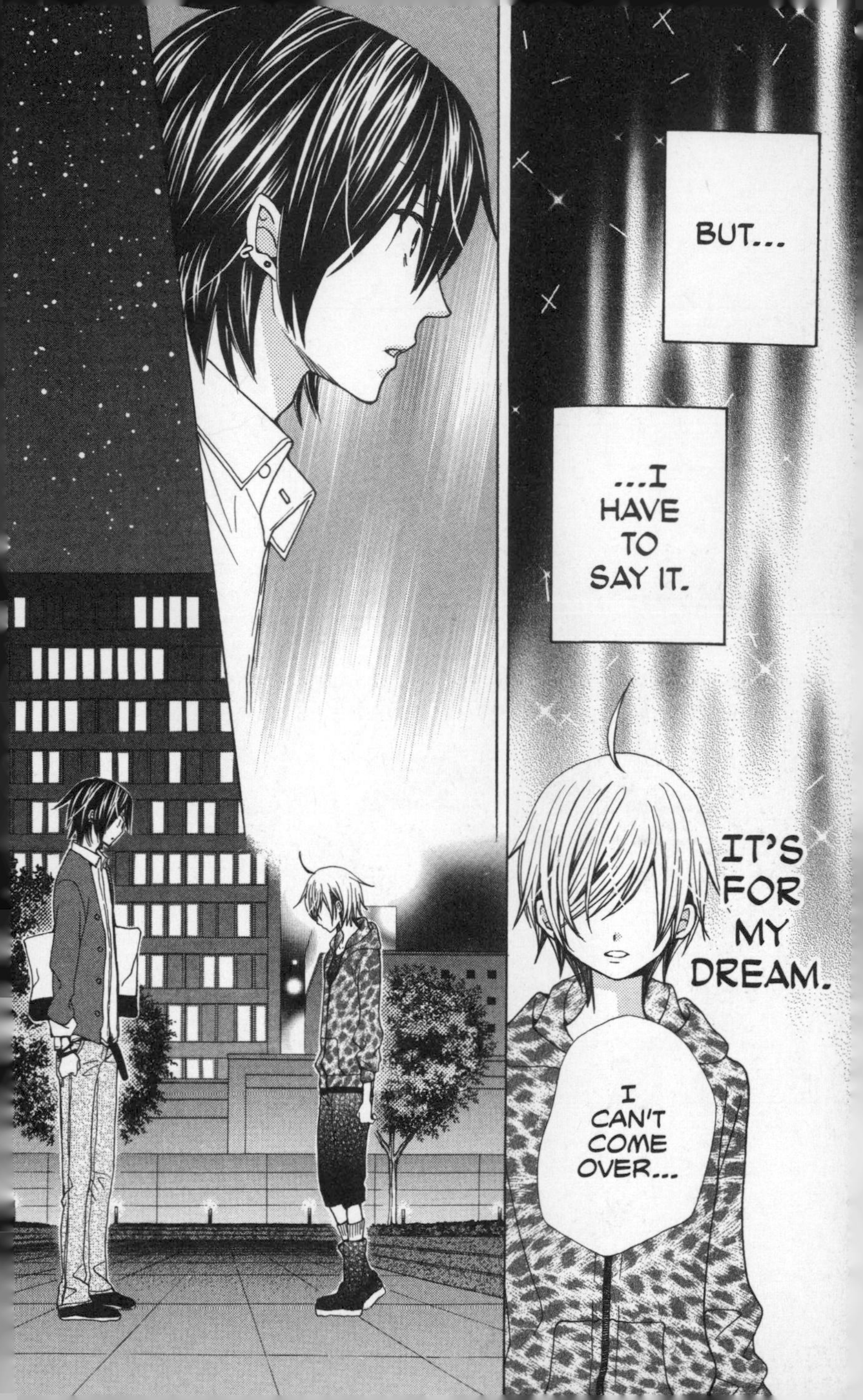
BUT...
...I HAVE TO SAY IT.
IT'S FOR MY DREAM.
I CAN'T COME OVER...

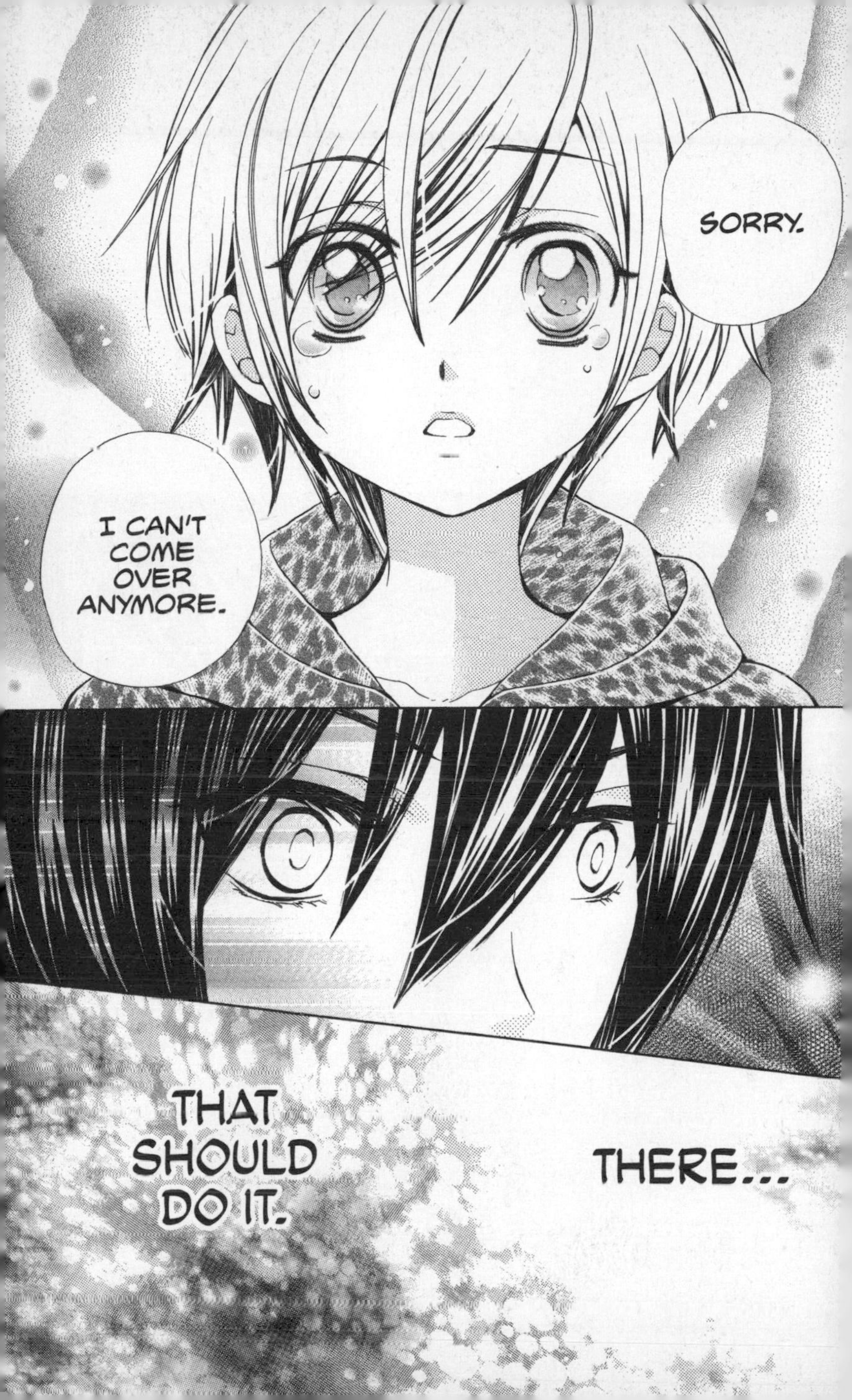
SORRY.
I CAN'T COME OVER ANYMORE.
THERE...
THAT SHOULD DO IT.

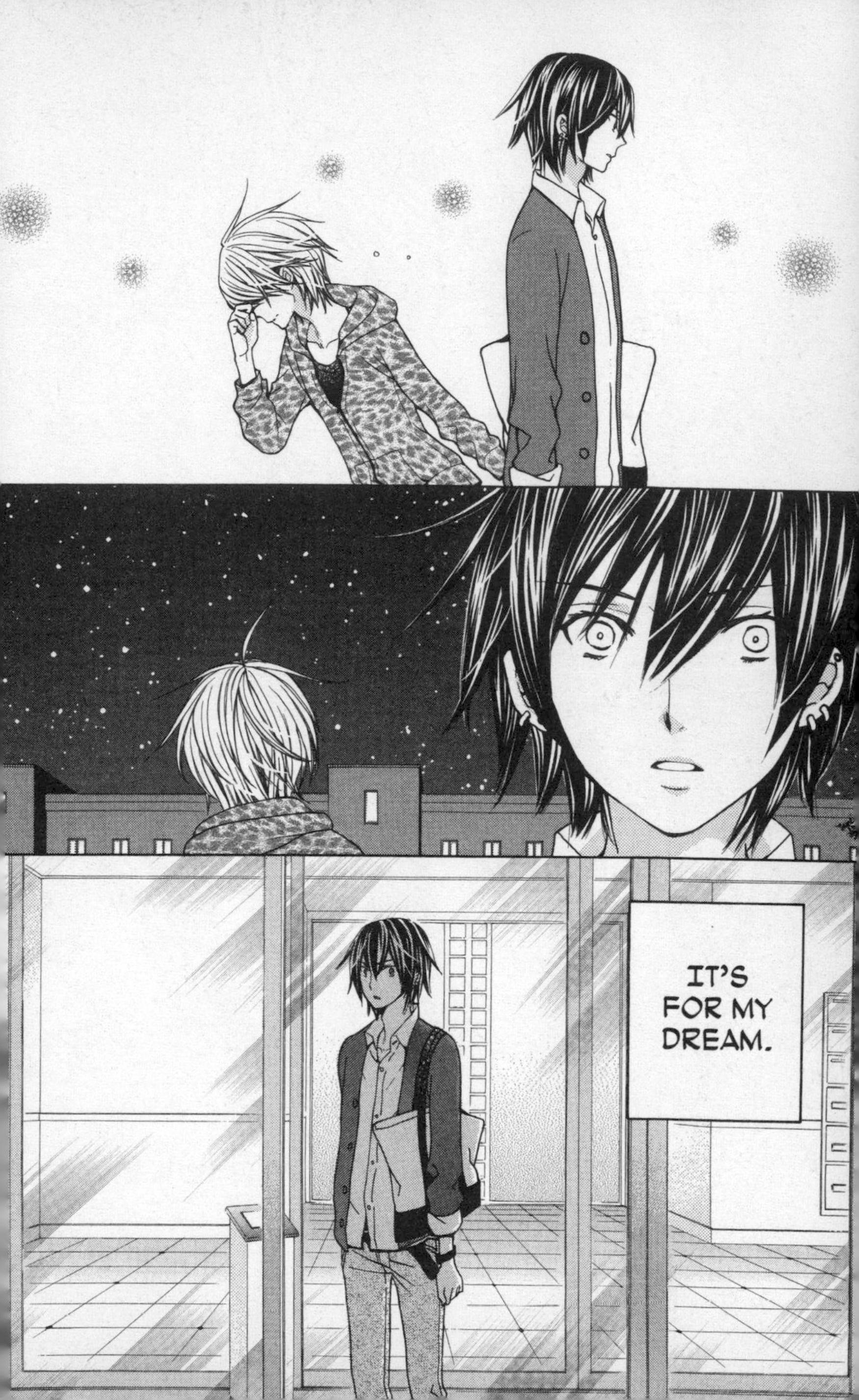
IT'S
FOR MY
DREAM.

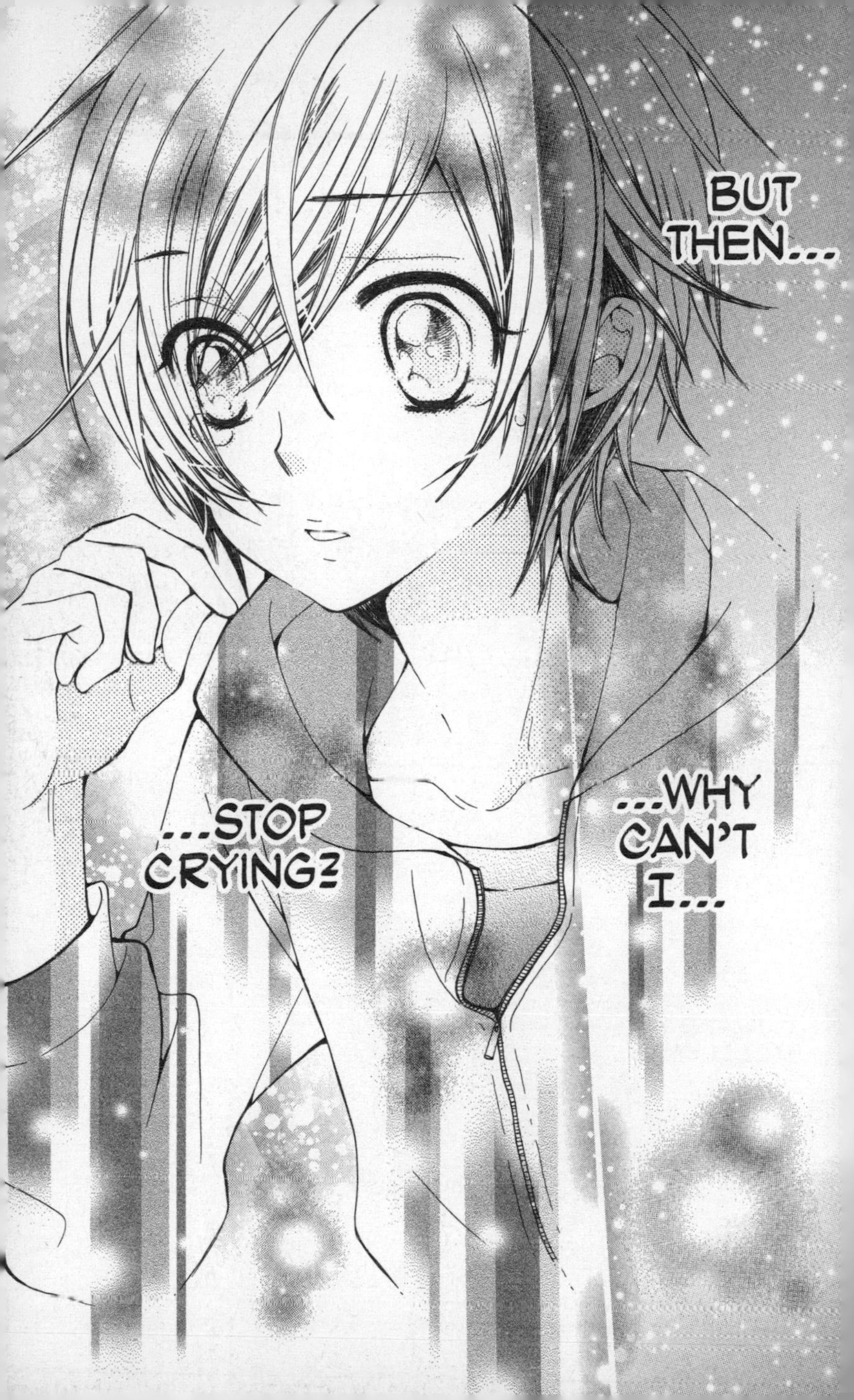
BUT THEN...
...WHY CAN'T I...
...STOP CRYING?

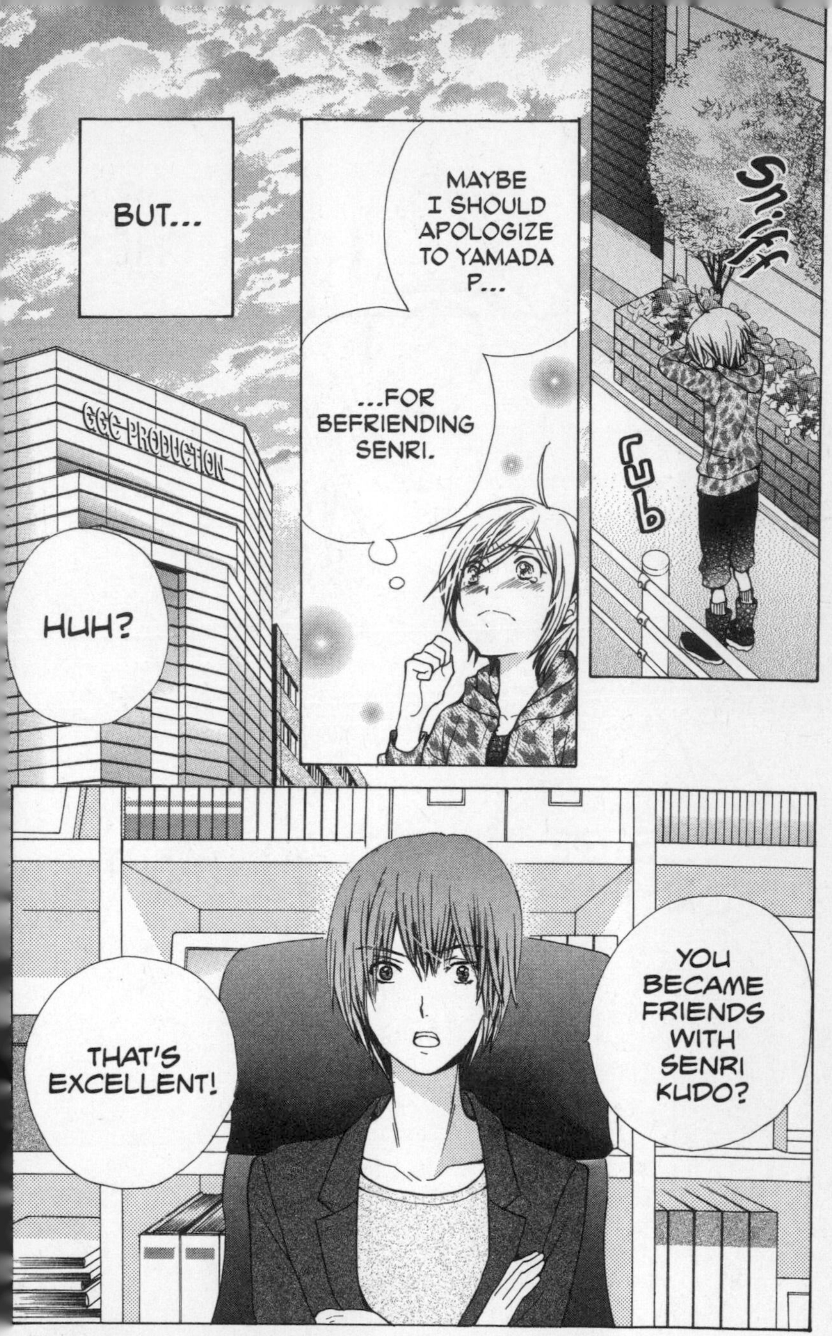
SNIFF
RUB
MAYBE I SHOULD APOLOGIZE TO YAMADA P...
...FOR BEFRIENDING SENRI.
BUT...
GGC PRODUCTION
HUH?
YOU BECAME FRIENDS WITH SENRI KUDO?
THAT'S EXCELLENT!

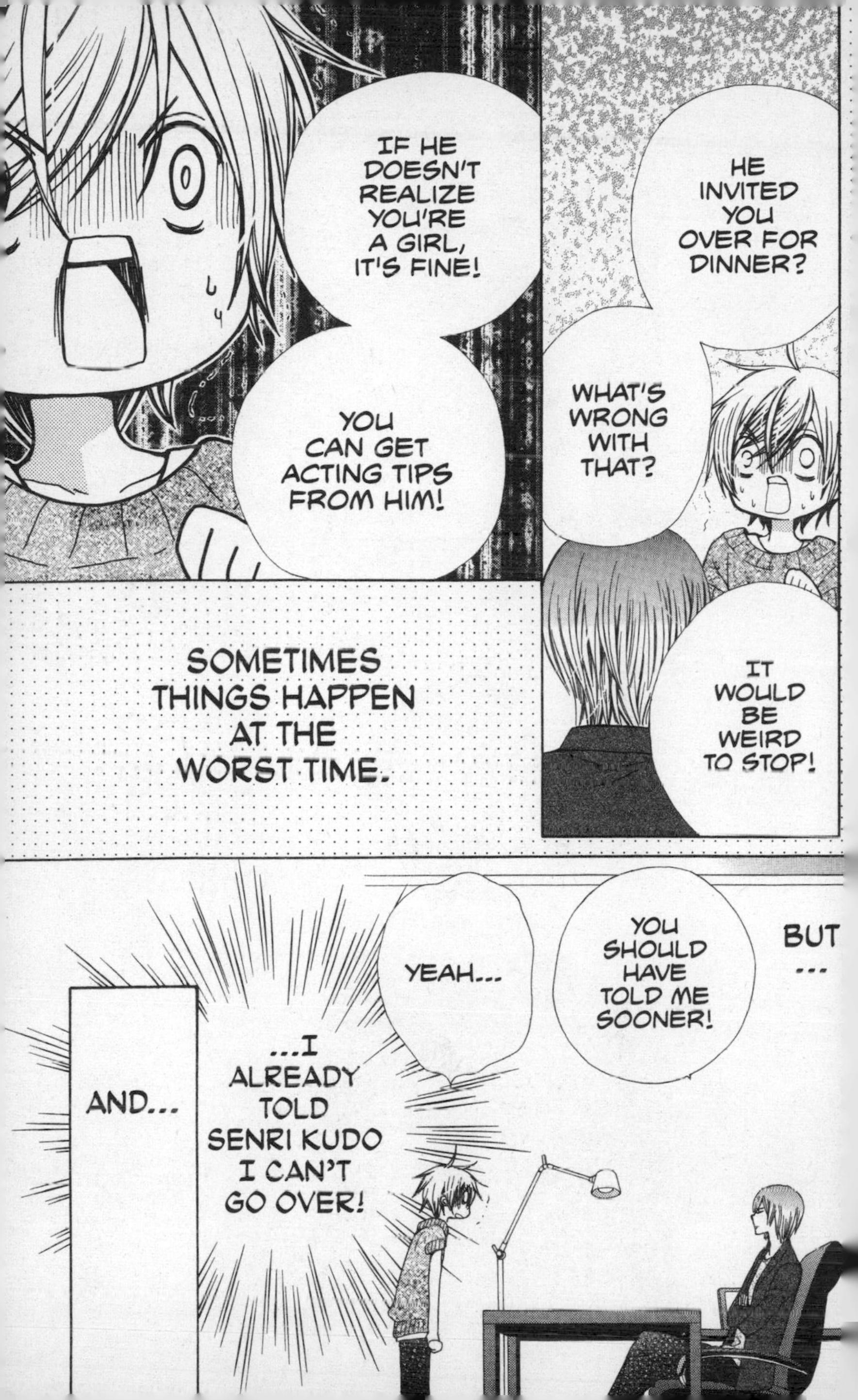
HE INVITED YOU OVER FOR DINNER?
WHAT'S WRONG WITH THAT?
IT WOULD BE WEIRD TO STOP!
IF HE DOESN'T REALIZE YOU'RE A GIRL, IT'S FINE!
YOU CAN GET ACTING TIPS FROM HIM!
SOMETIMES THINGS HAPPEN AT THE WORST TIME.
BUT ...
YOU SHOULD HAVE TOLD ME SOONER!
YEAH...
...I ALREADY TOLD SENRI KUDO I CAN'T GO OVER!
AND...

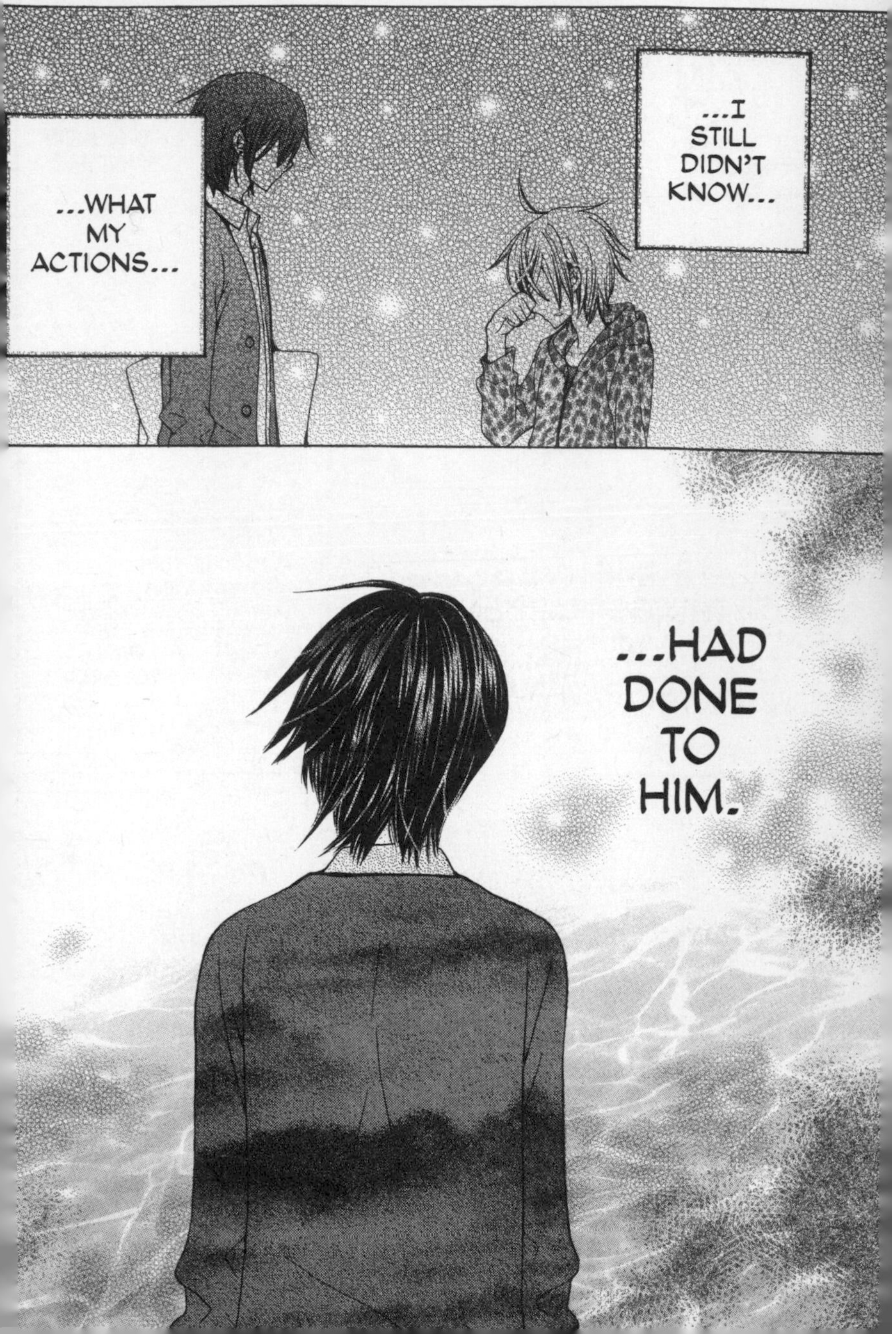
...I STILL DIDN'T KNOW...
...WHAT MY ACTIONS...
...HAD DONE TO HIM.

Chapter 54

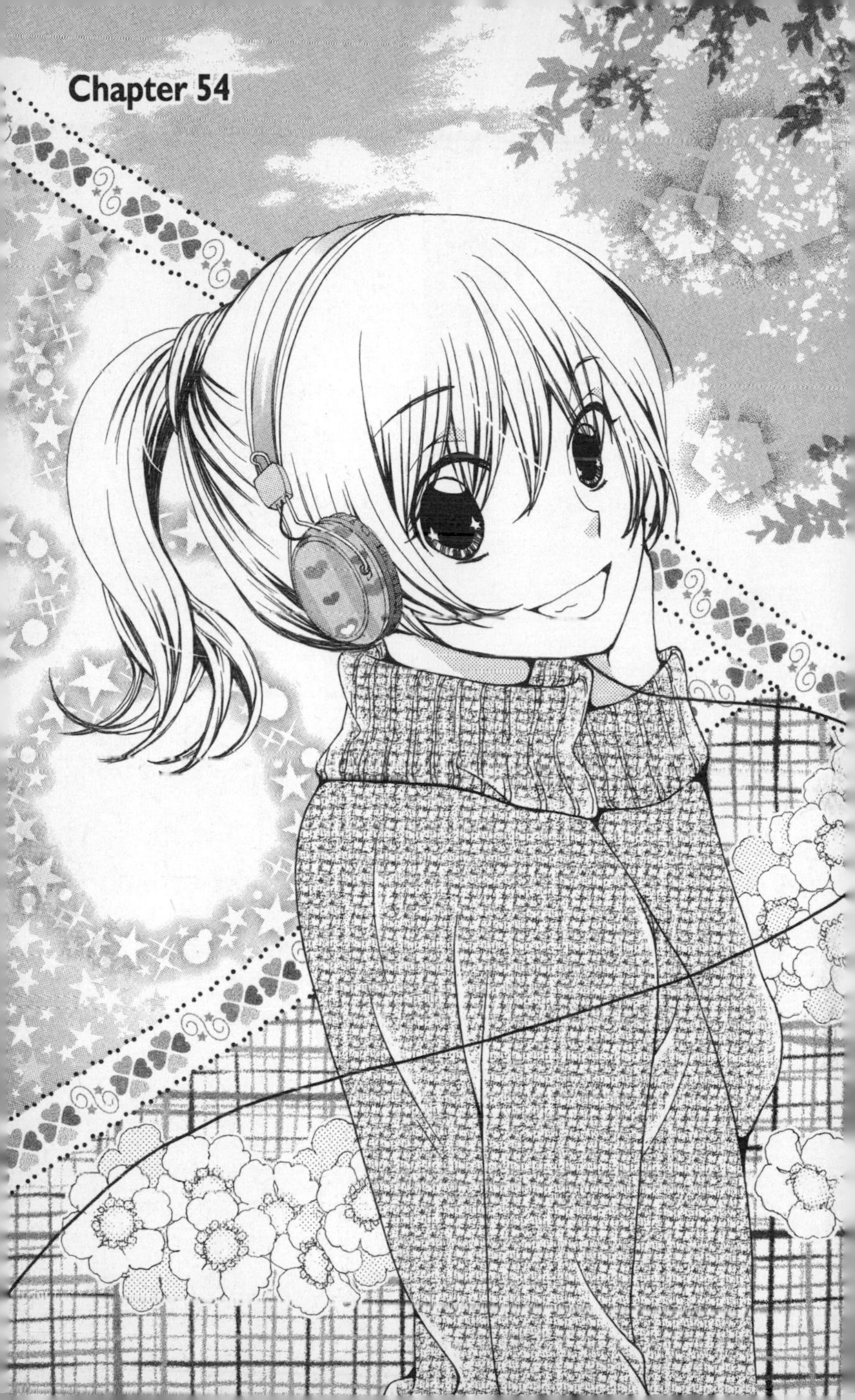

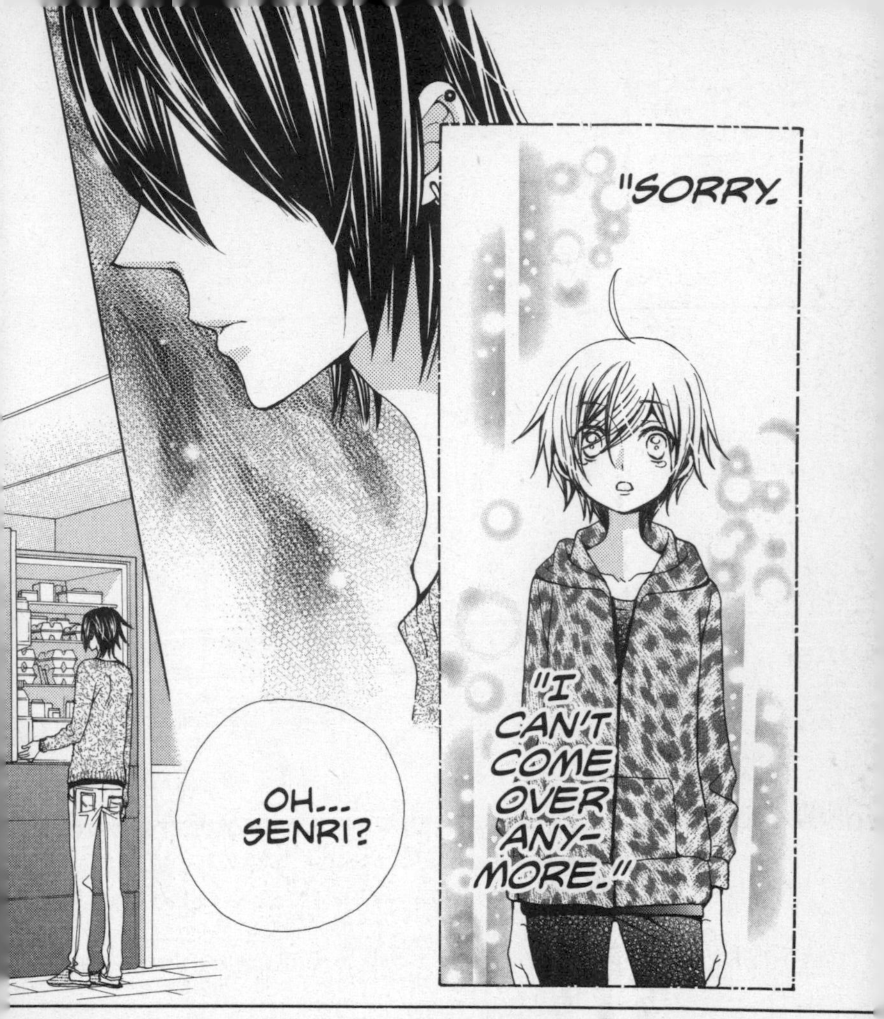
"SORRY.
"I CAN'T COME OVER ANY-MORE."
OH... SENRI?

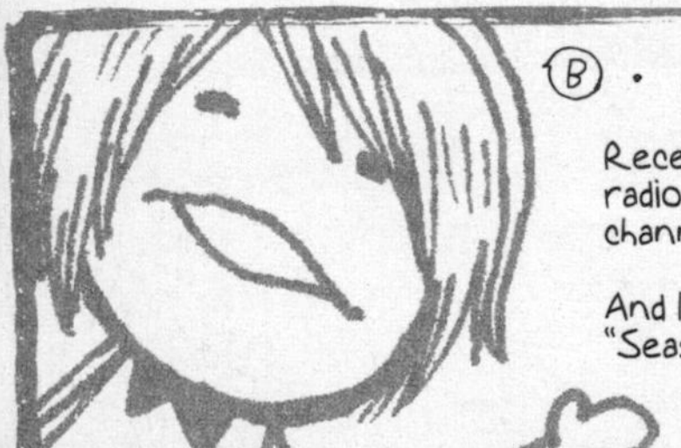

Ⓑ • Music at Work

Recently, I've mostly been listening to the radio. I love Radiko, which provides various channels with a clear sound. I recommend it!!

And I've been listening like crazy to "Season of Love" from the musical *Rent*!

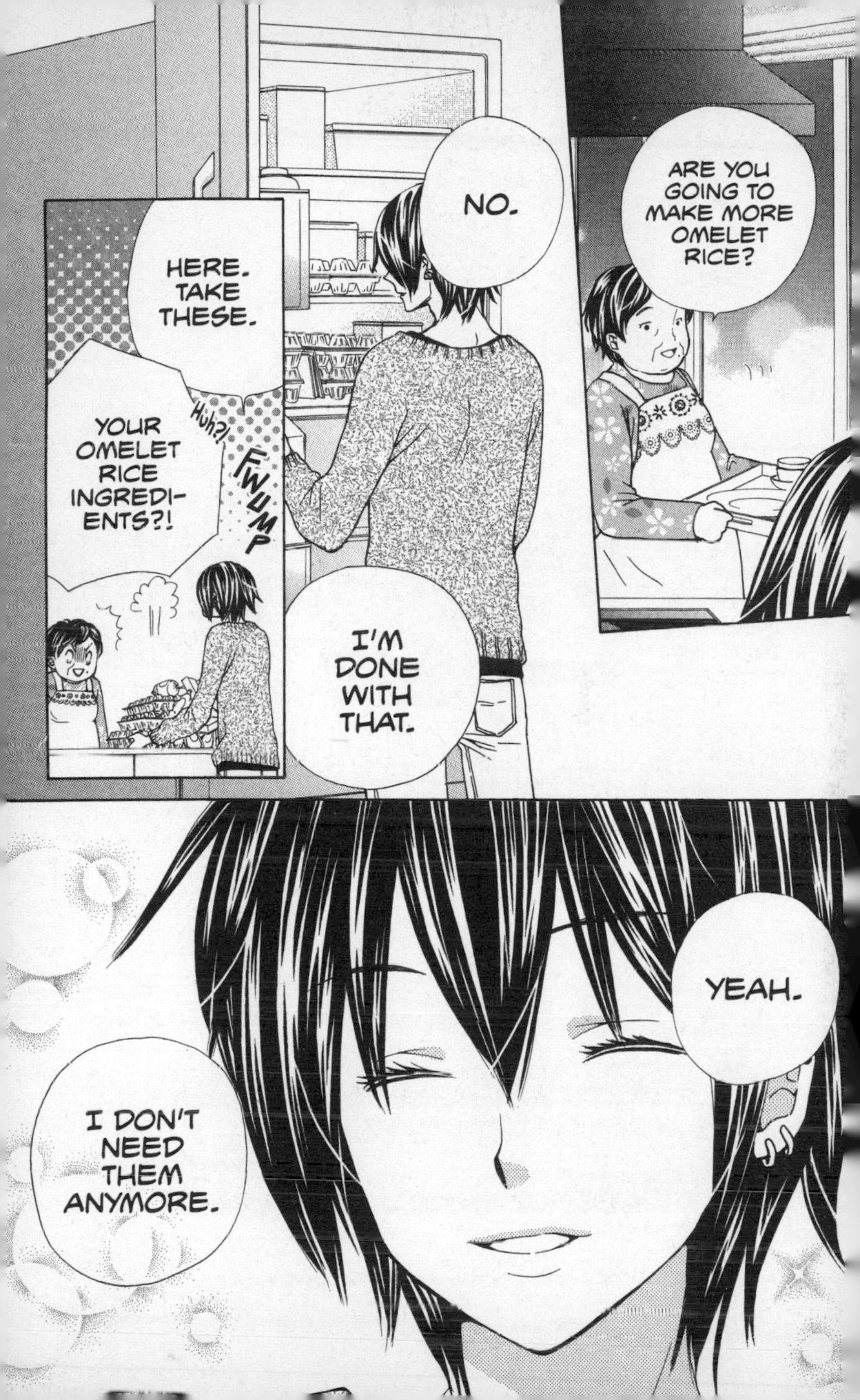
ARE YOU GOING TO MAKE MORE OMELET RICE?
NO.
I'M DONE WITH THAT.
HERE. TAKE THESE.
Huh?!
FWUMP
YOUR OMELET RICE INGREDIENTS?!
YEAH.
I DON'T NEED THEM ANYMORE.

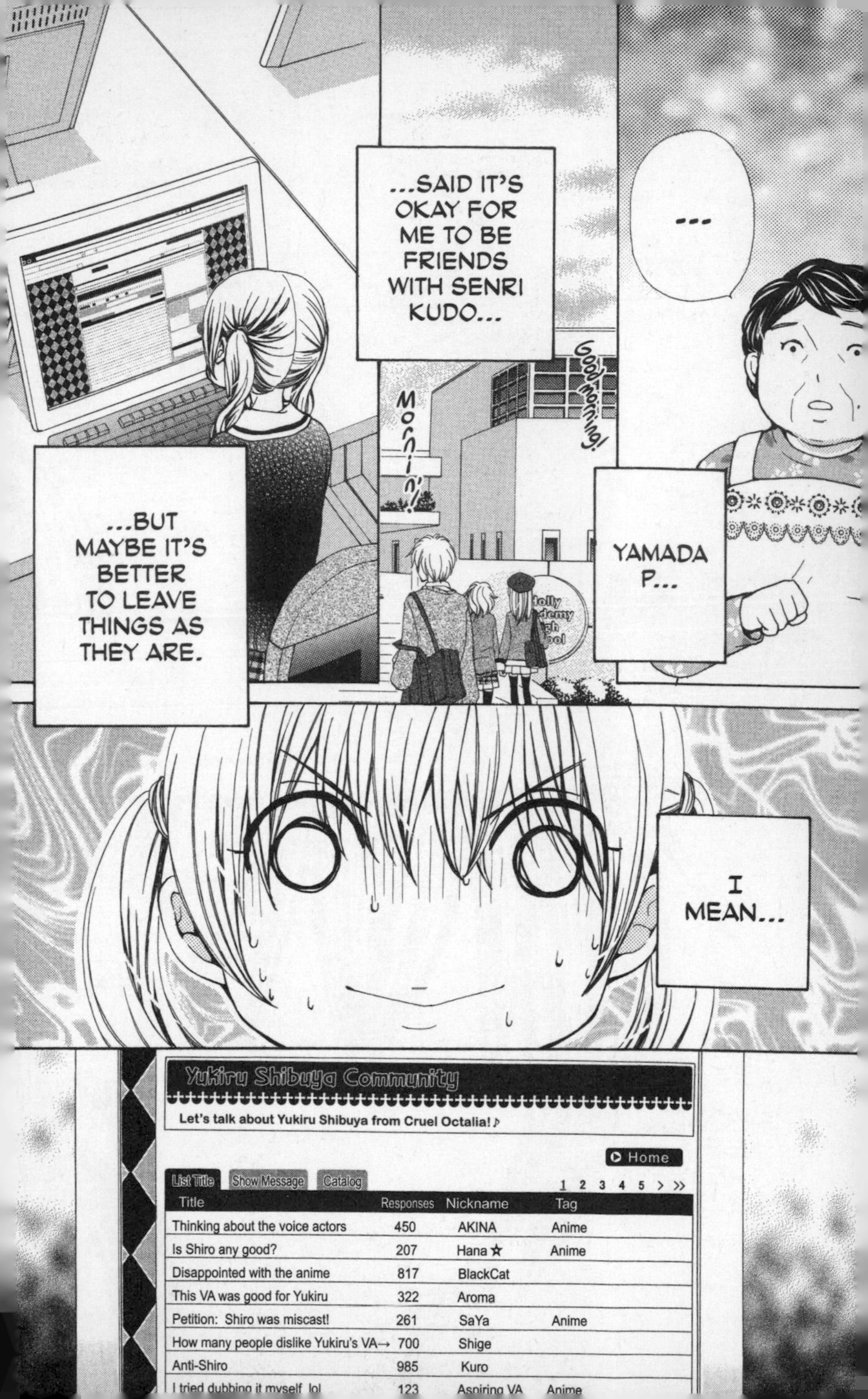
...
YAMADA P...
...SAID IT'S OKAY FOR ME TO BE FRIENDS WITH SENRI KUDO...
Good morning!
Mornin'!
...BUT MAYBE IT'S BETTER TO LEAVE THINGS AS THEY ARE.
I MEAN...
Yukiru Shibuya Community
Let's talk about Yukiru Shibuya from Cruel Octalia! ♪
Home
List Title
Show Message
Catalog
1 2 3 4 5 > >>
Title Responses Nickname Tag
Thinking about the voice actors 450 AKINA Anime
Is Shiro any good? 207 Hana ☆ Anime
Disappointed with the anime 817 BlackCat
This VA was good for Yukiru 322 Aroma
Petition: Shiro was miscast! 261 SaYa Anime
How many people dislike Yukiru's VA→ 700 Shige
Anti-Shiro 985 Kuro
I tried dubbing it myself lol 123 Aspiring VA Anime

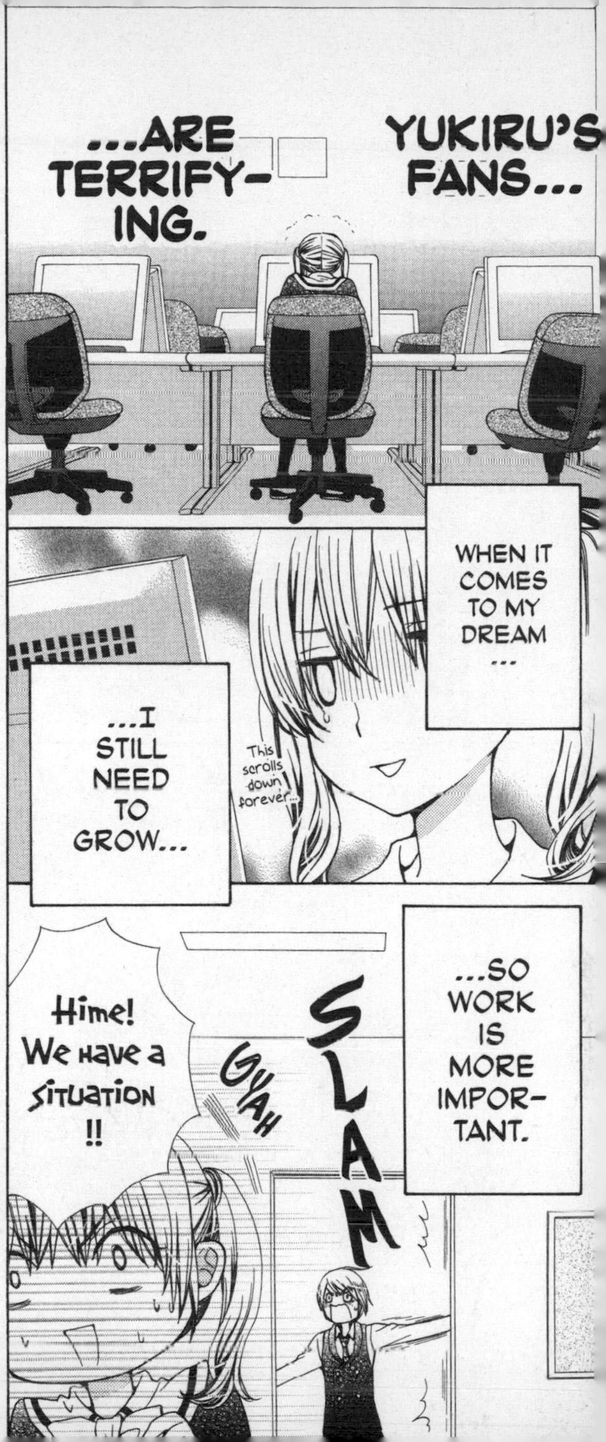
YUKIRU'S FANS...
...ARE TERRIFY-ING.
WHEN IT COMES TO MY DREAM...
This scrolls down forever...
...I STILL NEED TO GROW...
...SO WORK IS MORE IMPOR-TANT.
SLAM
GYAH
Hime! We have a situation!!

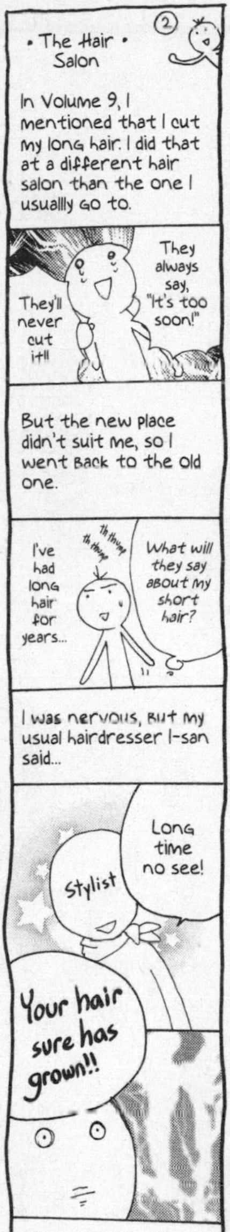
• The Hair • Salon
②
In Volume 9, I mentioned that I cut my long hair. I did that at a different hair salon than the one I usuallly go to.
They always say, "It's too soon!"
They'll never cut it!!
But the new place didn't suit me, so I went back to the old one.
What will they say about my short hair?
th thump th thump
I've had long hair for years...
I was nervous, but my usual hairdresser I-san said...
Long time no see!
Stylist
Your hair sure has grown!!
I shouldn't have worried...

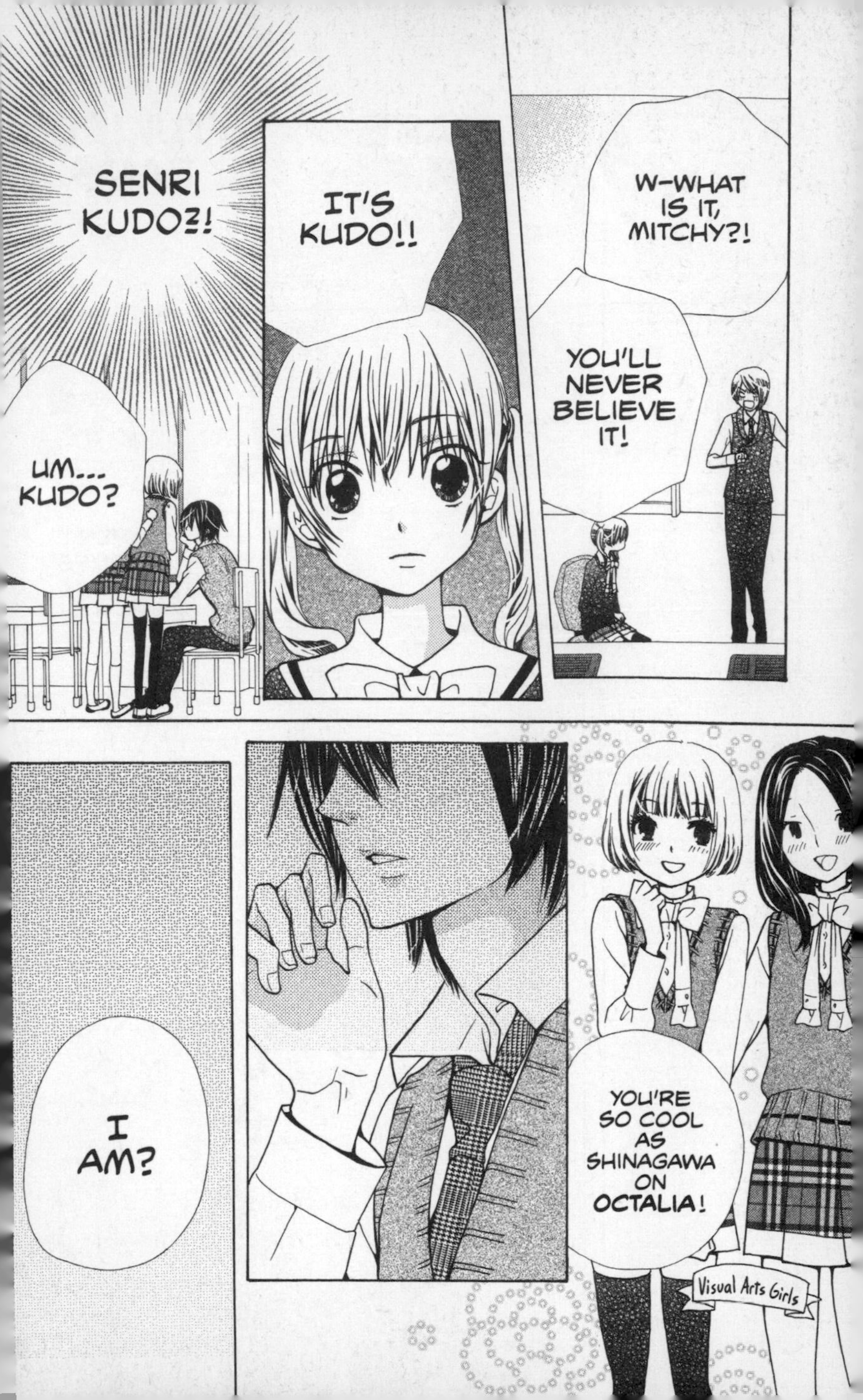
W-WHAT IS IT, MITCHY?!
YOU'LL NEVER BELIEVE IT!
IT'S KUDO!!
SENRI KUDO?!
UM... KUDO?
YOU'RE SO COOL AS SHINAGAWA ON OCTALIA!
Visual Arts Girls
I AM?

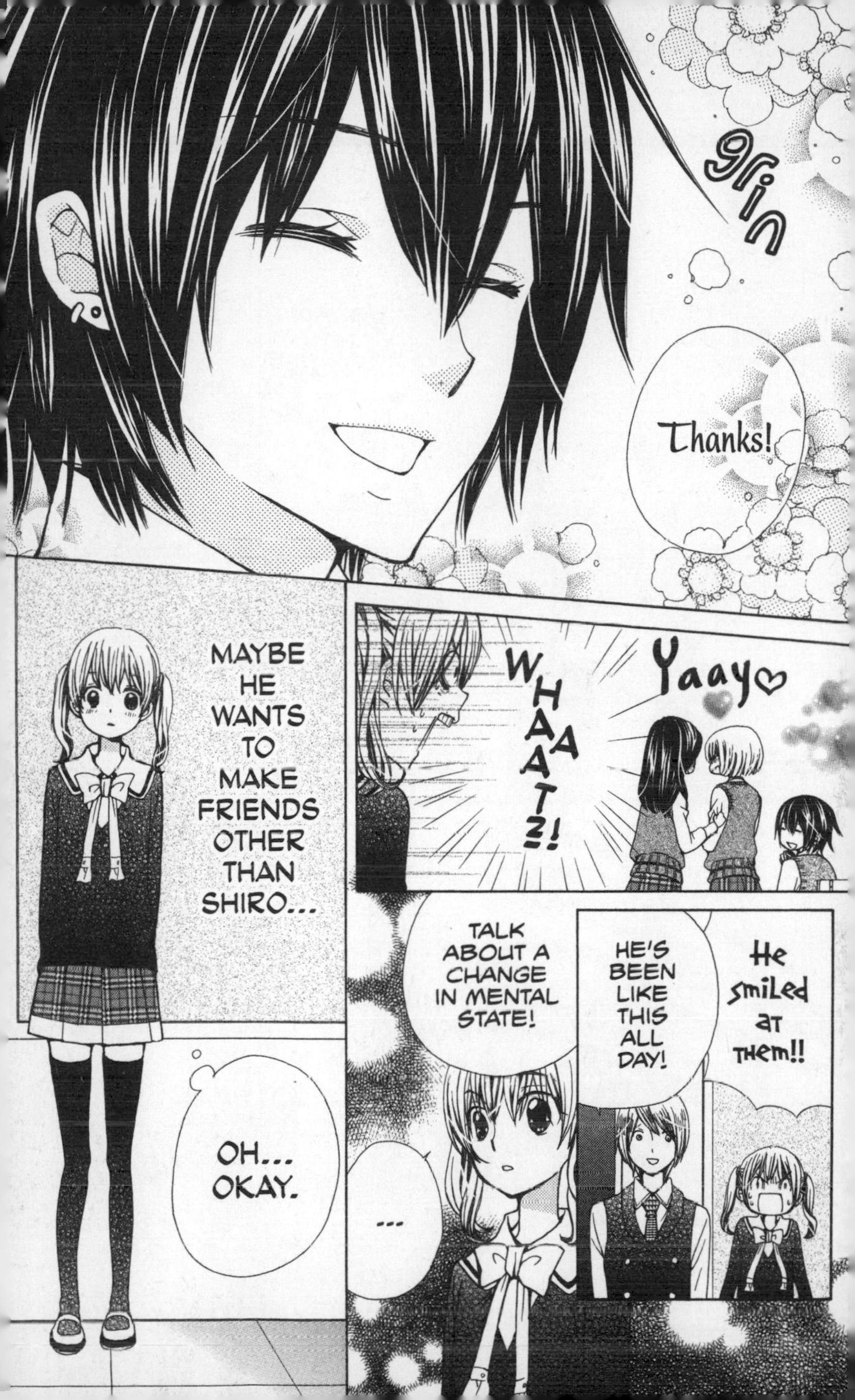
grin
Thanks!
Yaay♡
WHAAATZ!
MAYBE HE WANTS TO MAKE FRIENDS OTHER THAN SHIRO...
He smiled at them!!
HE'S BEEN LIKE THIS ALL DAY!
TALK ABOUT A CHANGE IN MENTAL STATE!
...
OH... OKAY.

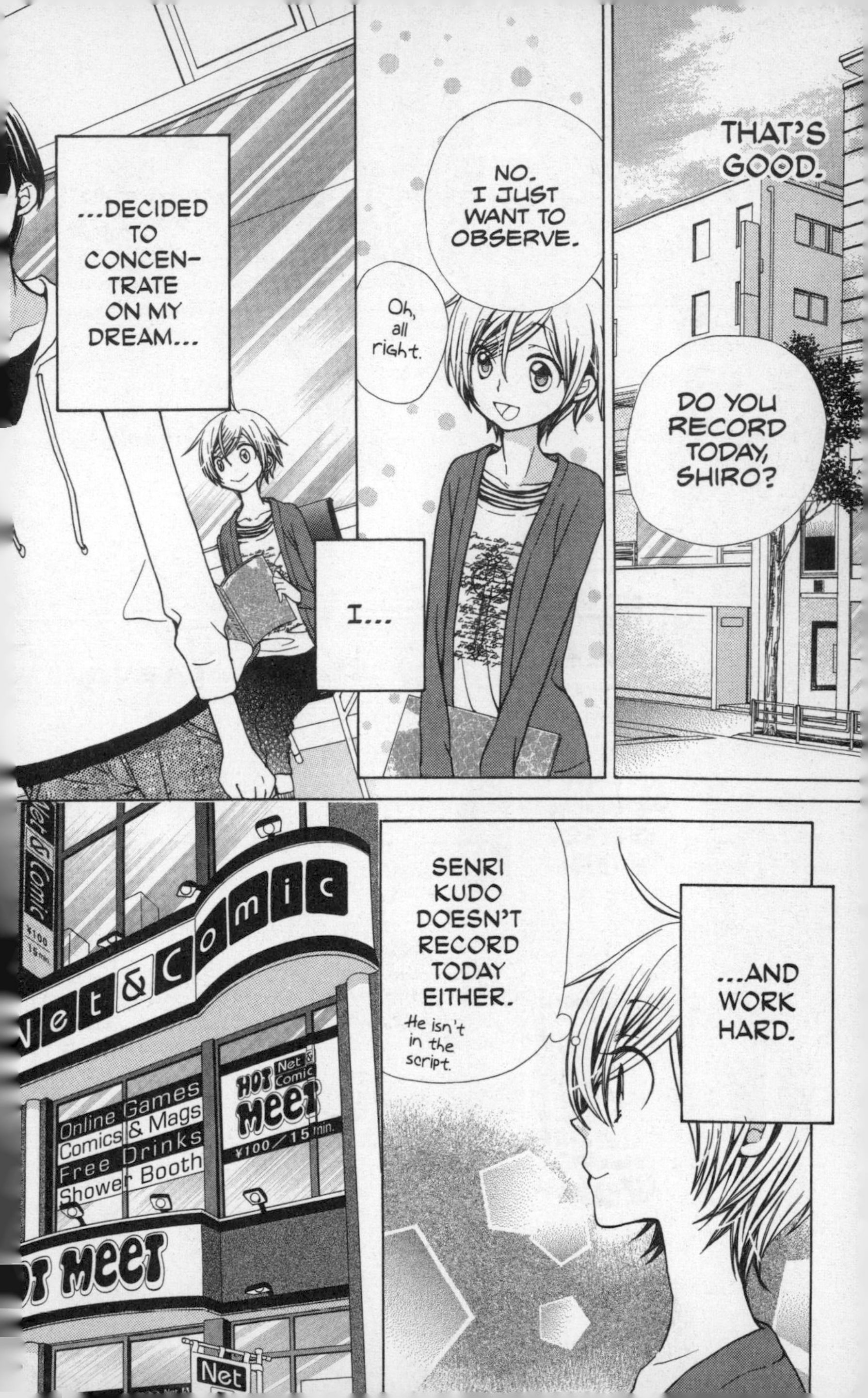
THAT'S GOOD.
DO YOU RECORD TODAY, SHIRO?
NO. I JUST WANT TO OBSERVE.
Oh, all right.
I...
...DECIDED TO CONCEN-TRATE ON MY DREAM...
...AND WORK HARD.
SENRI KUDO DOESN'T RECORD TODAY EITHER.
He isn't in the script.
Net & Comic
Net & Comic ¥100 15 min.
HOT Net & Comic Meet ¥100／15 min.
Online Games
Comics & Mags
Free Drinks
Shower Booth
OT Meet
Net

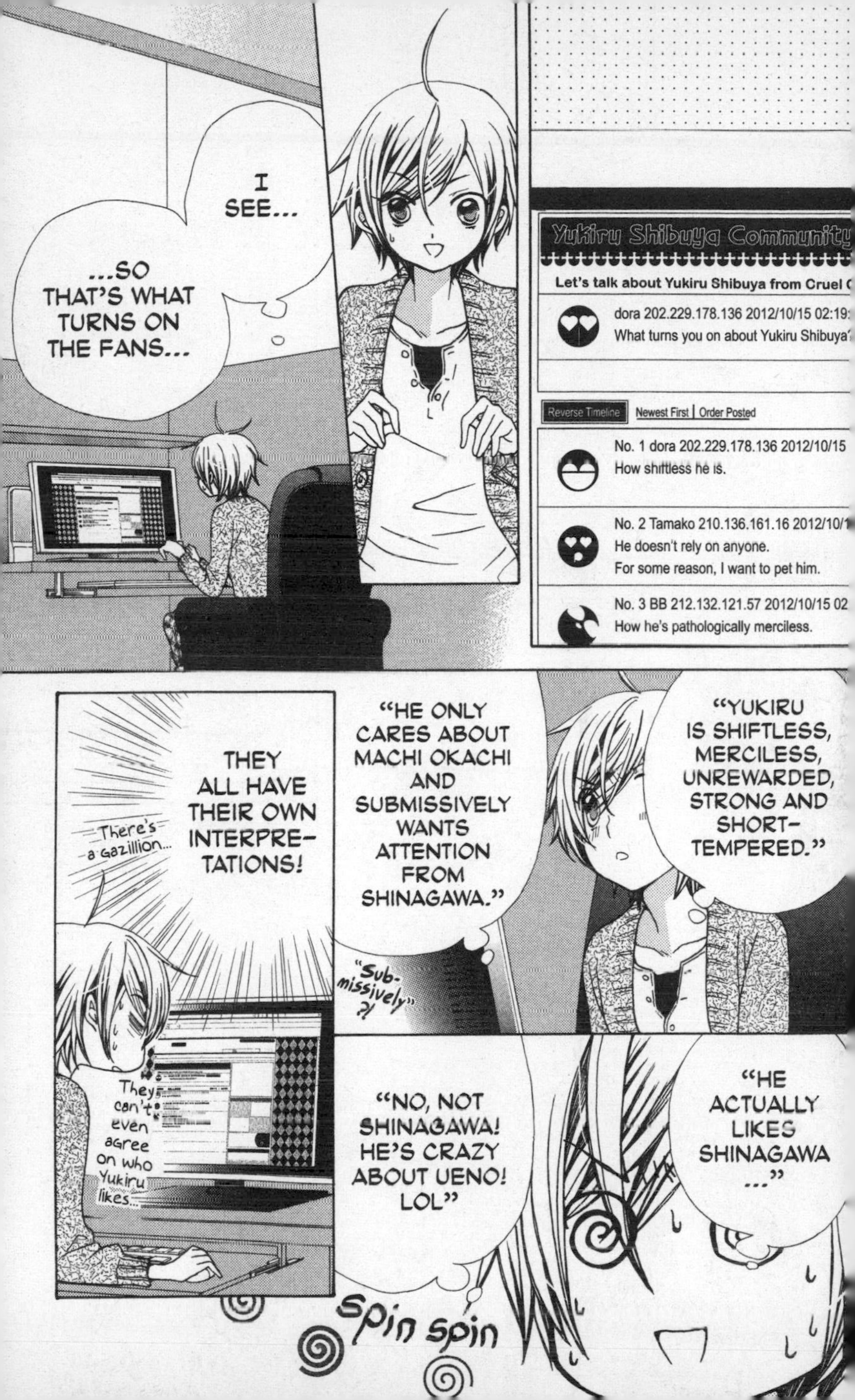
Yukiru Shibuya Community
Let's talk about Yukiru Shibuya from Cruel C
dora 202.229.178.136 2012/10/15 02:19
What turns you on about Yukiru Shibuya?
Reverse Timeline
Newest First | Order Posted
No. 1 dora 202.229.178.136 2012/10/15
How shiftless he is.
No. 2 Tamako 210.136.161.16 2012/10/1
He doesn't rely on anyone.
For some reason, I want to pet him.
No. 3 BB 212.132.121.57 2012/10/15 02
How he's pathologically merciless.
I SEE...
...SO THAT'S WHAT TURNS ON THE FANS...
"YUKIRU IS SHIFTLESS, MERCILESS, UNREWARDED, STRONG AND SHORT-TEMPERED."
"HE ONLY CARES ABOUT MACHI OKACHI AND SUBMISSIVELY WANTS ATTENTION FROM SHINAGAWA."
"Submissively"?!
"HE ACTUALLY LIKES SHINAGAWA..."
"NO, NOT SHINAGAWA! HE'S CRAZY ABOUT UENO! LOL"
Spin spin
There's a gazillion...
THEY ALL HAVE THEIR OWN INTERPRE-TATIONS!
They can't even agree on who Yukiru likes...

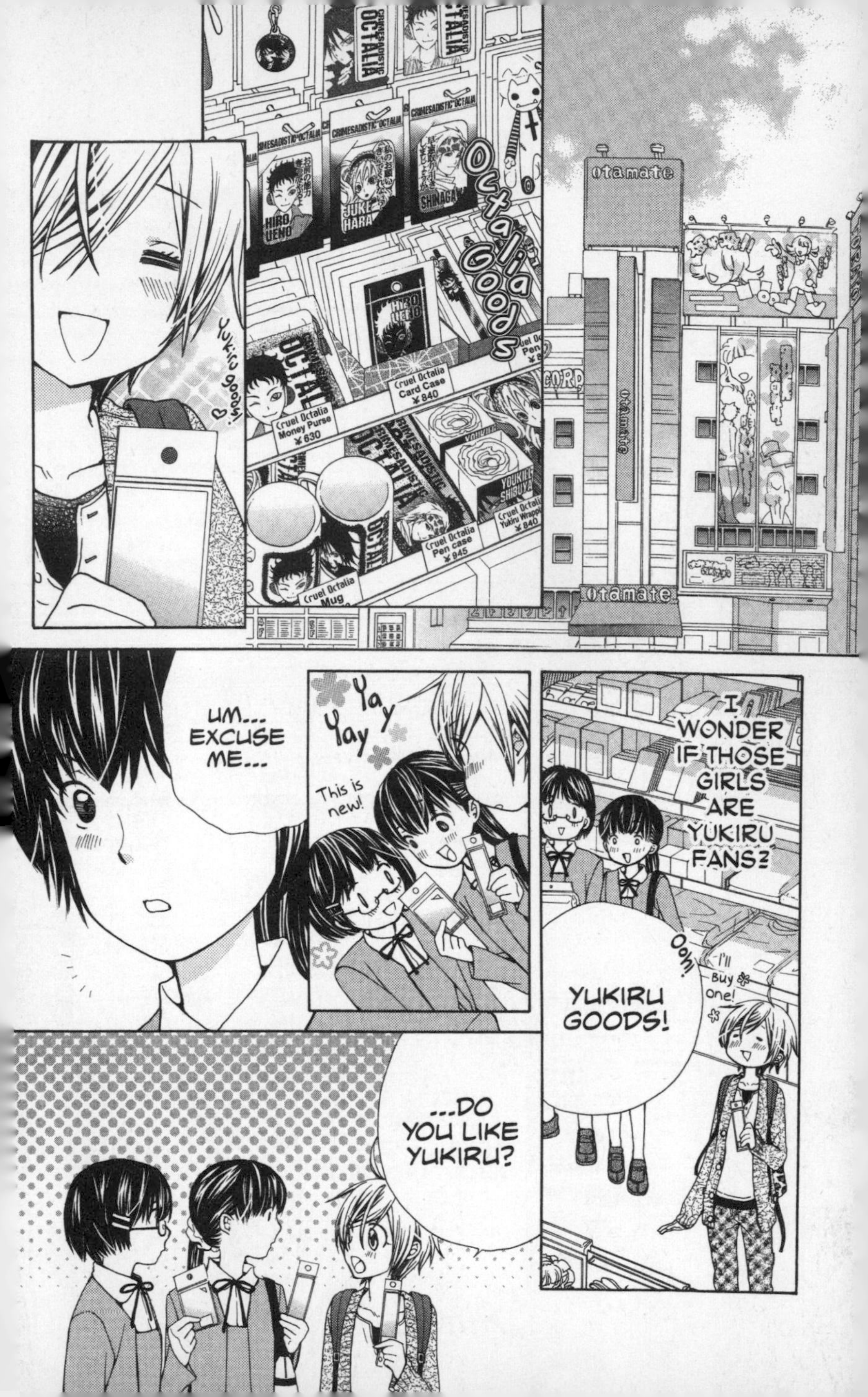
otamate
CRIMESADISTIC OCTALIA
HIRO UENO
JUKE HARA
SHINAGAWA
Octalia Goods
Cruel Octalia Card Case ¥840
Cruel Octalia Money Purse ¥630
Cruel Octalia Pen case ¥945
Cruel Octalia Mug
Yukiru goods!
I WONDER IF THOSE GIRLS ARE YUKIRU FANS?
Ooh!
YUKIRU GOODS!
I'll Buy One!
Yay Yay
This is new!
UM... EXCUSE ME...
...DO YOU LIKE YUKIRU?

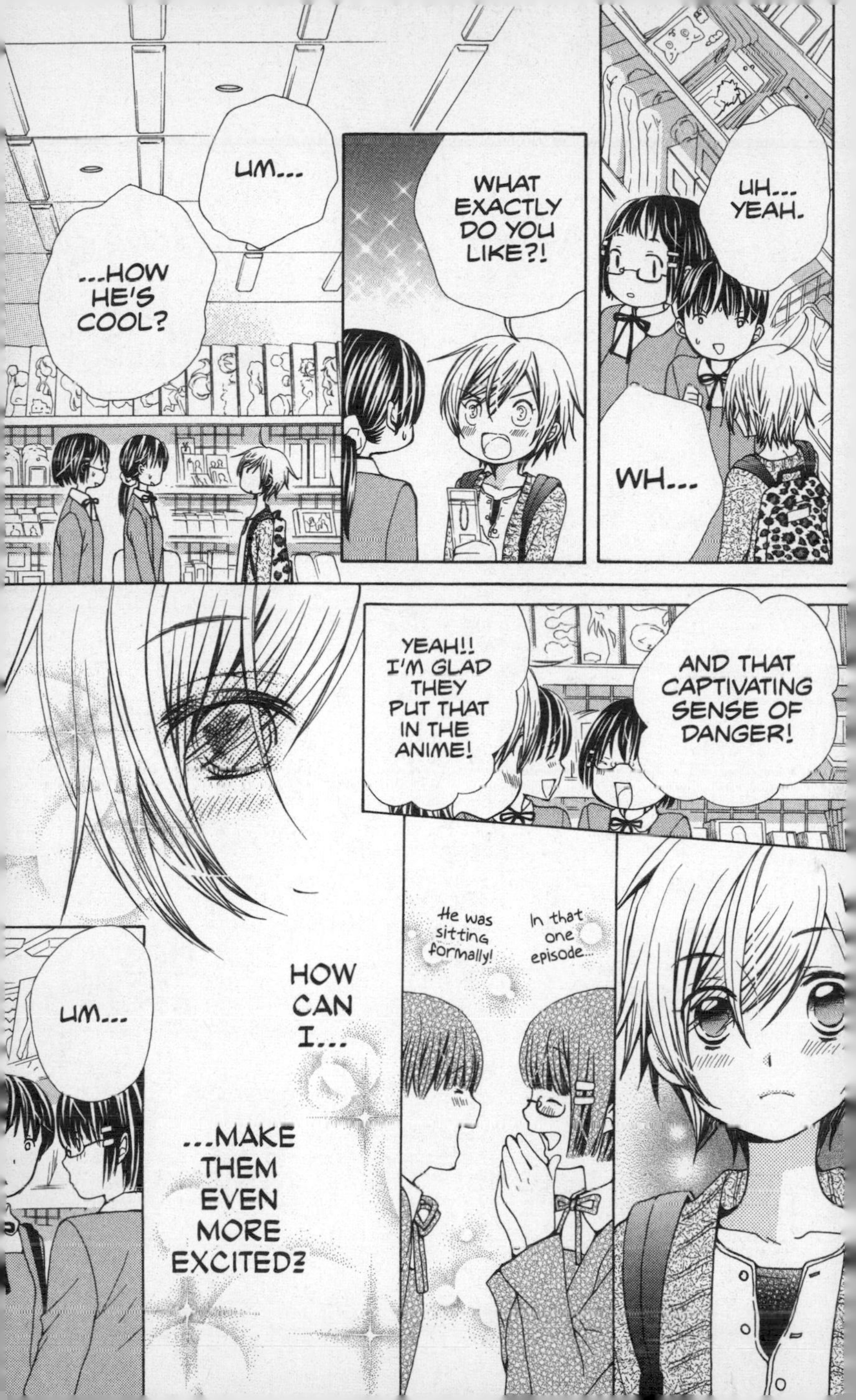
UH... YEAH.
WH...
WHAT EXACTLY DO YOU LIKE?!
UM...
...HOW HE'S COOL?
AND THAT CAPTIVATING SENSE OF DANGER!
YEAH!! I'M GLAD THEY PUT THAT IN THE ANIME!
In that one episode...
He was sitting formally!
HOW CAN I...
...MAKE THEM EVEN MORE EXCITED?
UM...

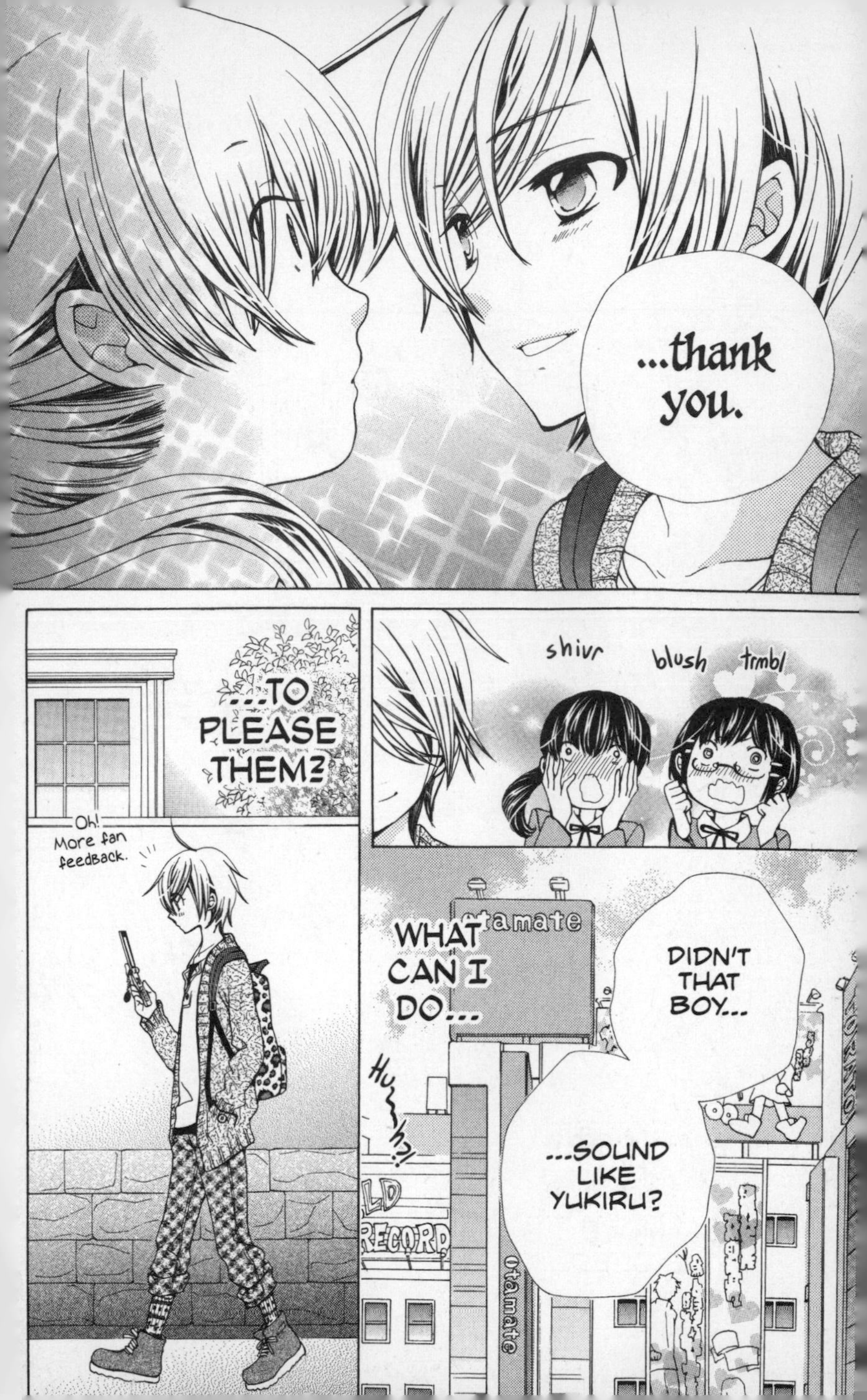
...thank you.
shivr
blush
trmbl
...TO PLEASE THEM?
DIDN'T THAT BOY...
WHAT CAN I DO...
Hu-h?!
...SOUND LIKE YUKIRU?
Oh! More fan feedback.

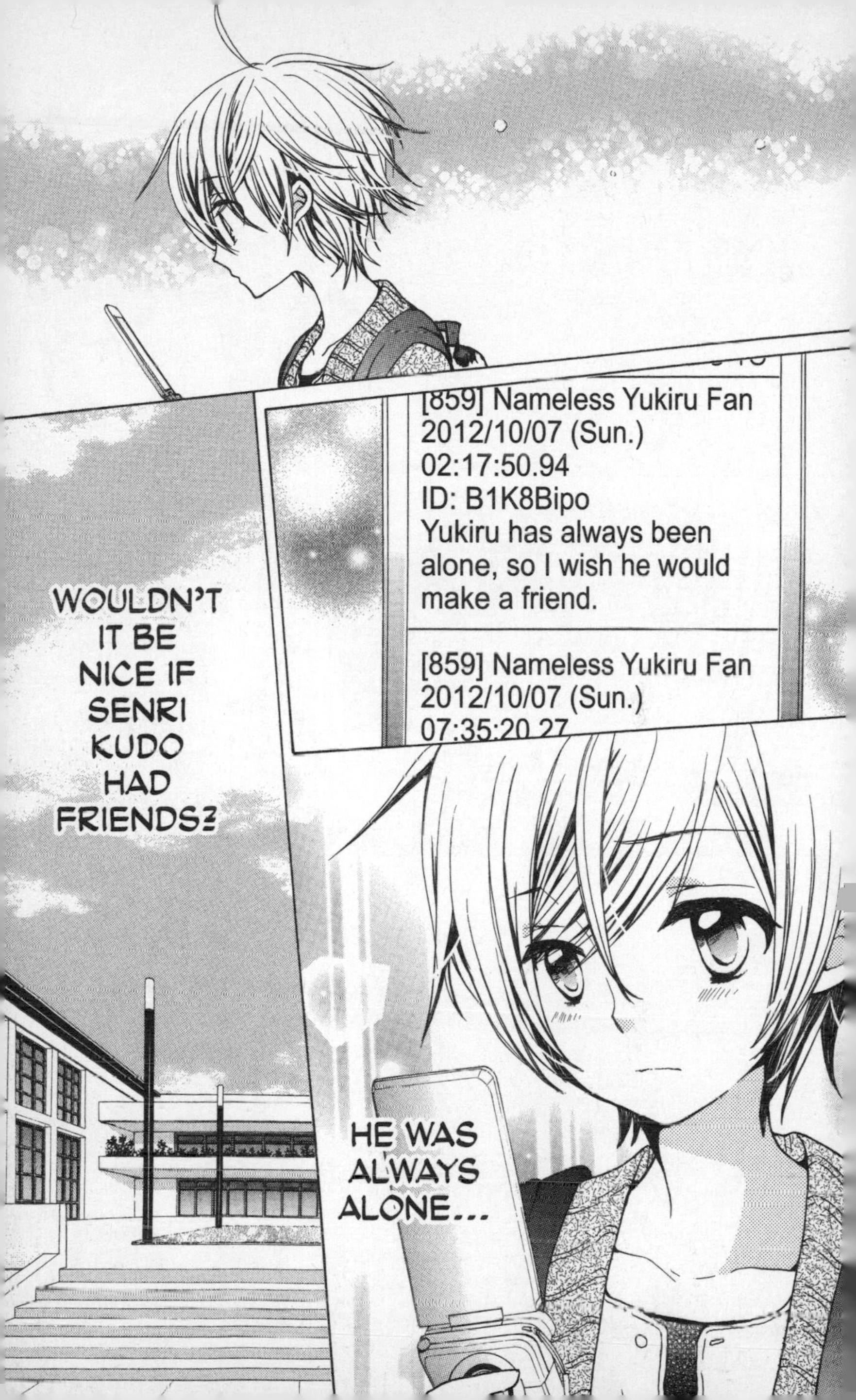
[859] Nameless Yukiru Fan
2012/10/07 (Sun.)
02:17:50.94
ID: B1K8Bipo
Yukiru has always been alone, so I wish he would make a friend.
[859] Nameless Yukiru Fan
2012/10/07 (Sun.)
07:35:20.27
HE WAS ALWAYS ALONE...
WOULDN'T IT BE NICE IF SENRI KUDO HAD FRIENDS?

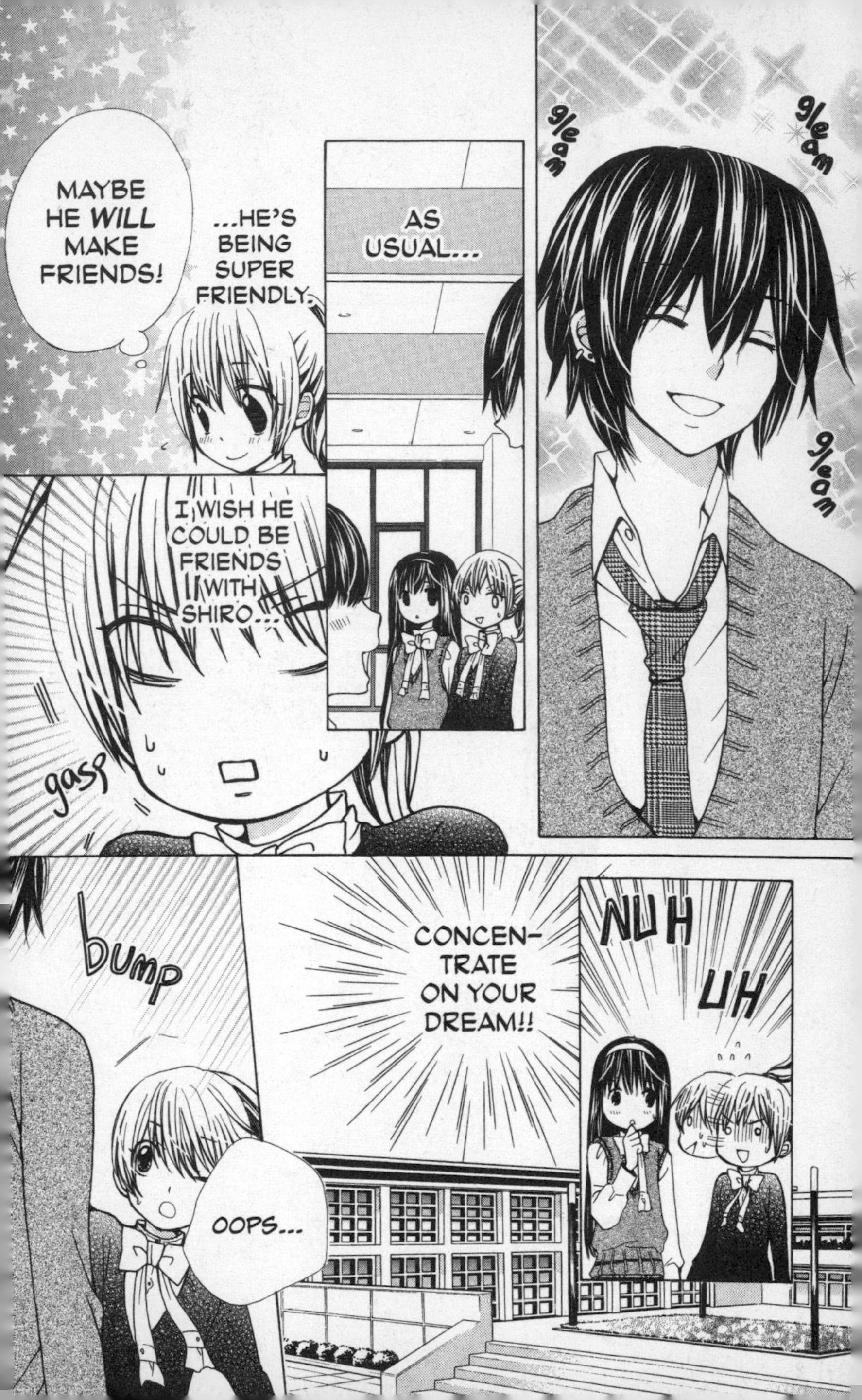
gleam
gleam
gleam
AS USUAL...
...HE'S BEING SUPER FRIENDLY.
MAYBE HE *WILL* MAKE FRIENDS!
I WISH HE COULD BE FRIENDS WITH SHIRO...
gasp
NUH UH
CONCEN-TRATE ON YOUR DREAM!!
bump
OOPS...

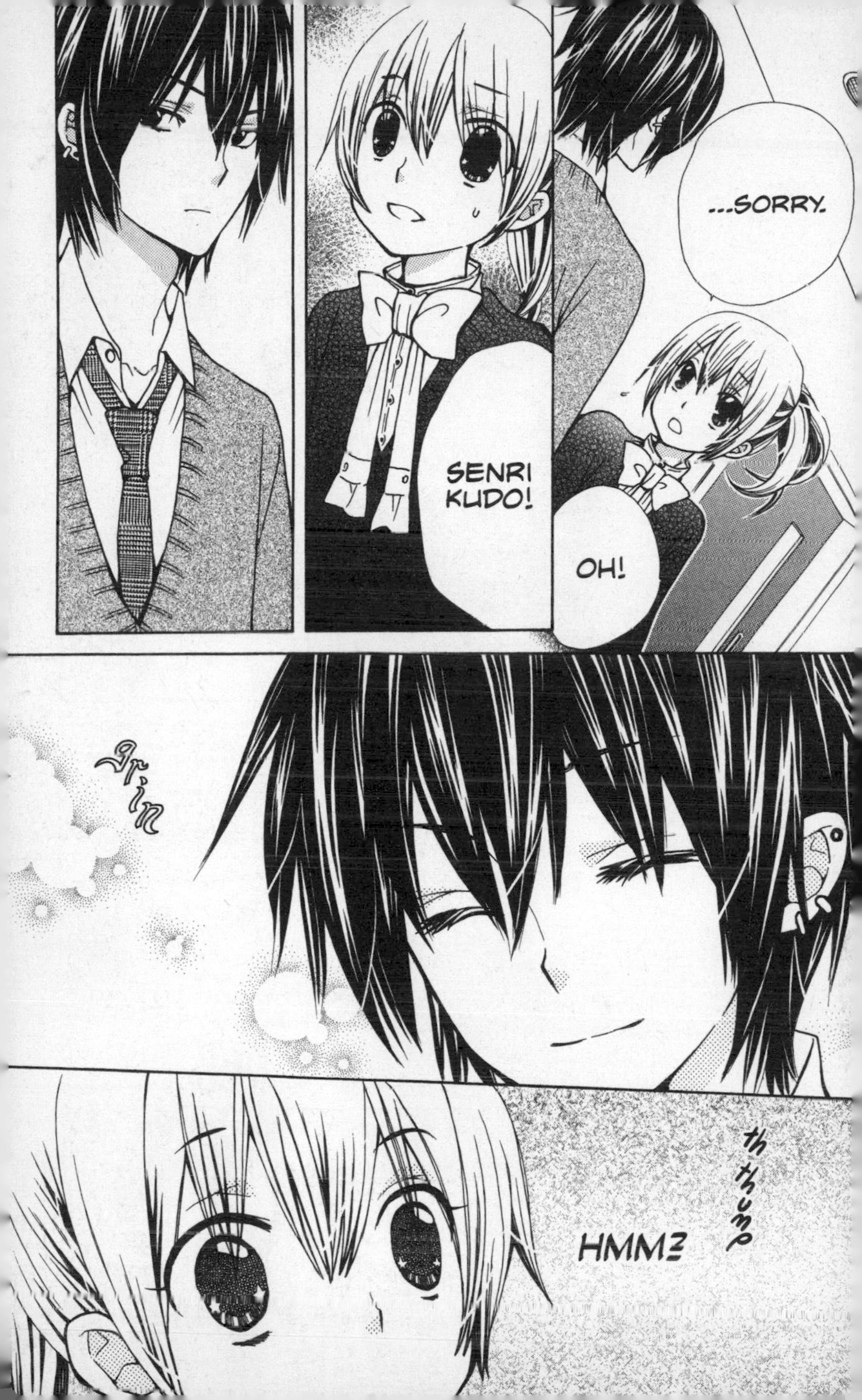
...SORRY.
OH!
SENRI KUDO!
grin
th thump
HMM?

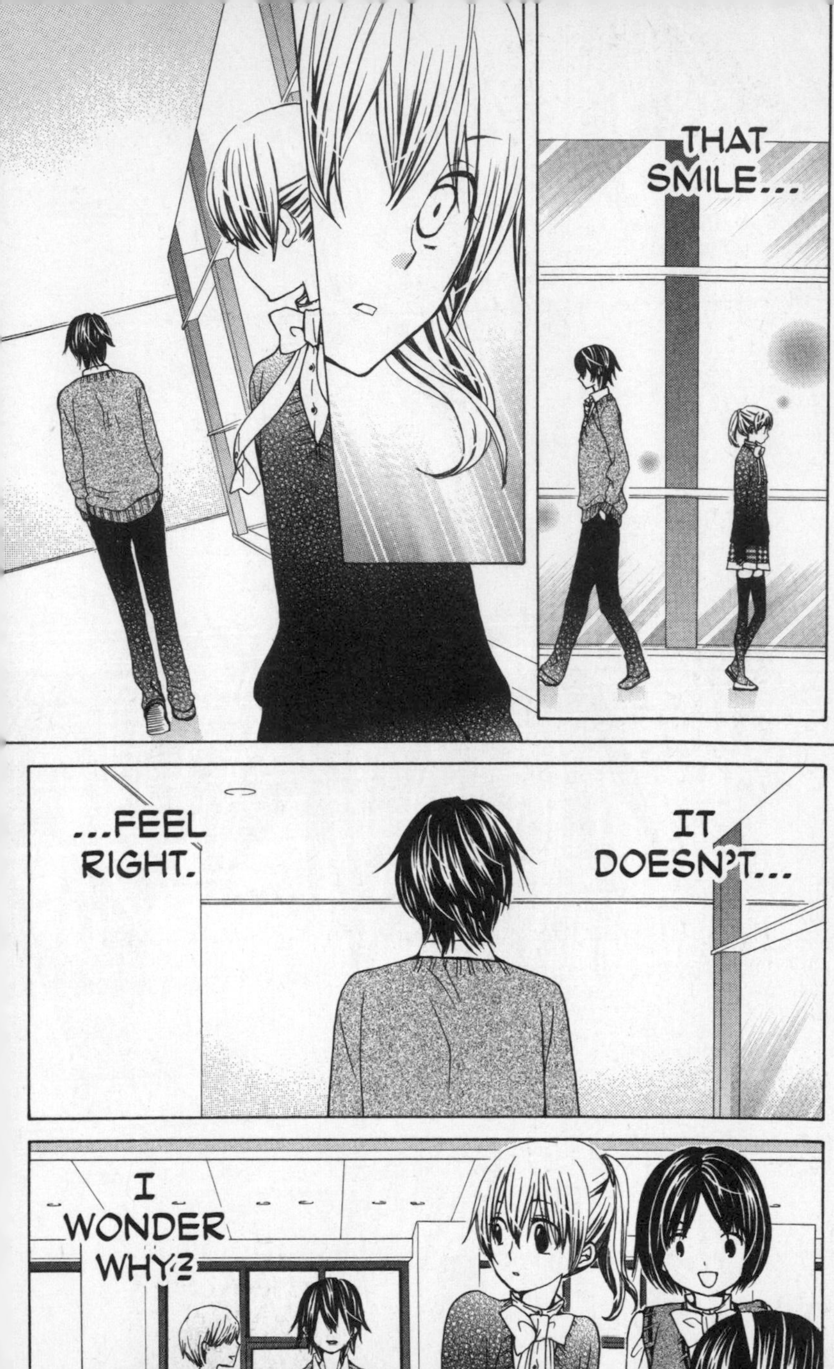
THAT SMILE...
IT DOESN'T...
...FEEL RIGHT.
I WONDER WHY?

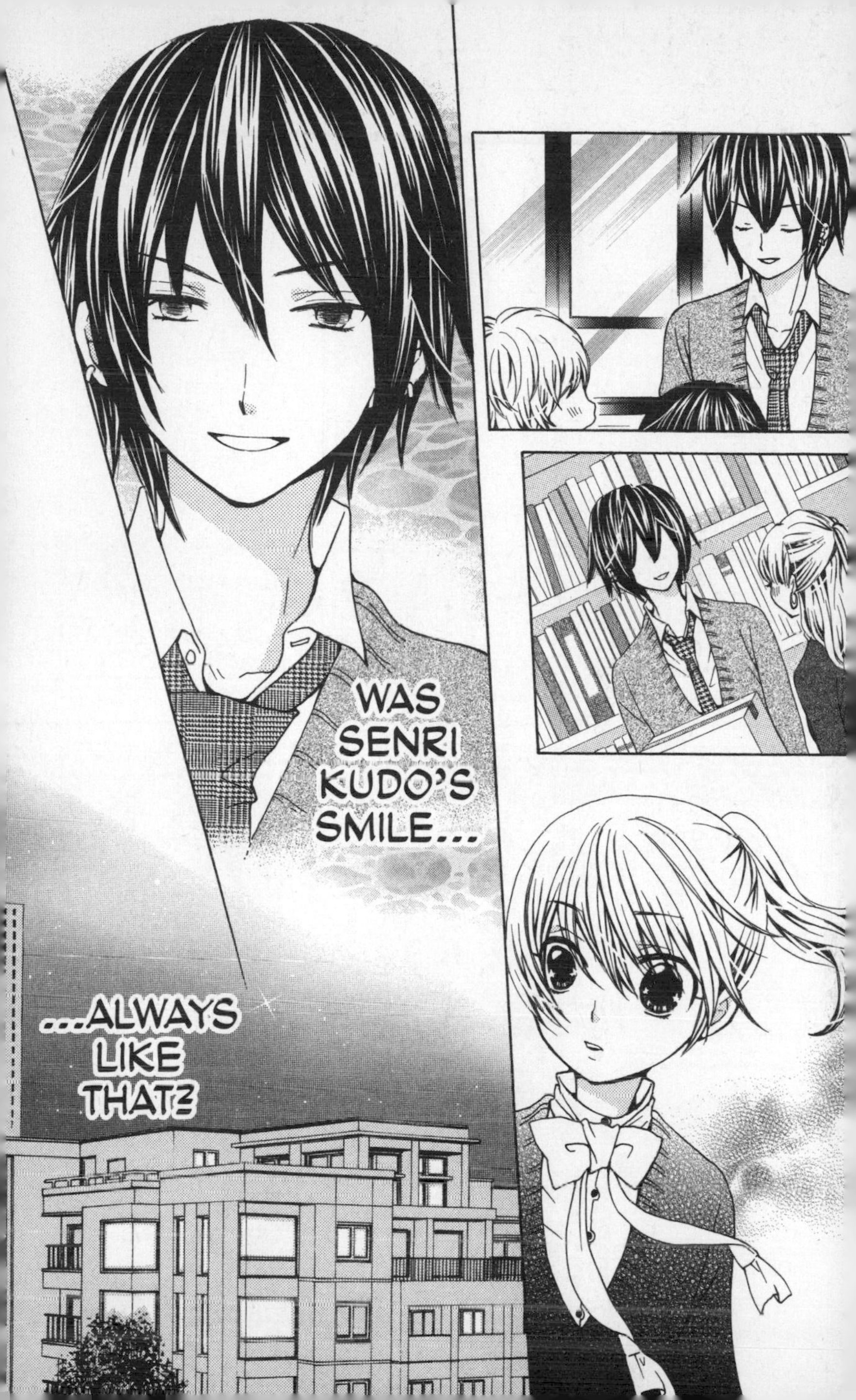
WAS SENRI KUDO'S SMILE...
...ALWAYS LIKE THAT?

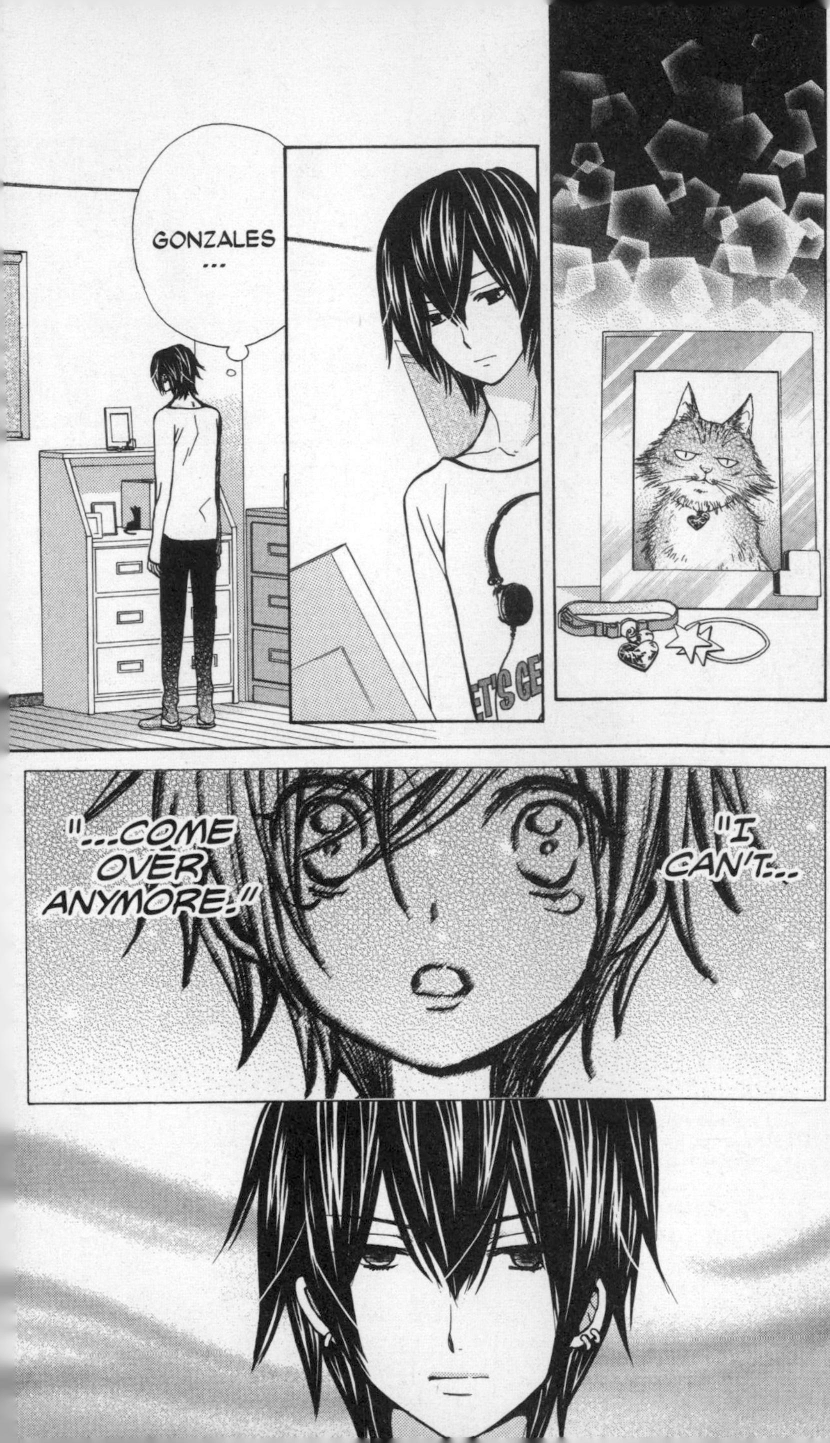
GONZALES ...
"I CAN'T...
"...COME OVER ANYMORE...!!"

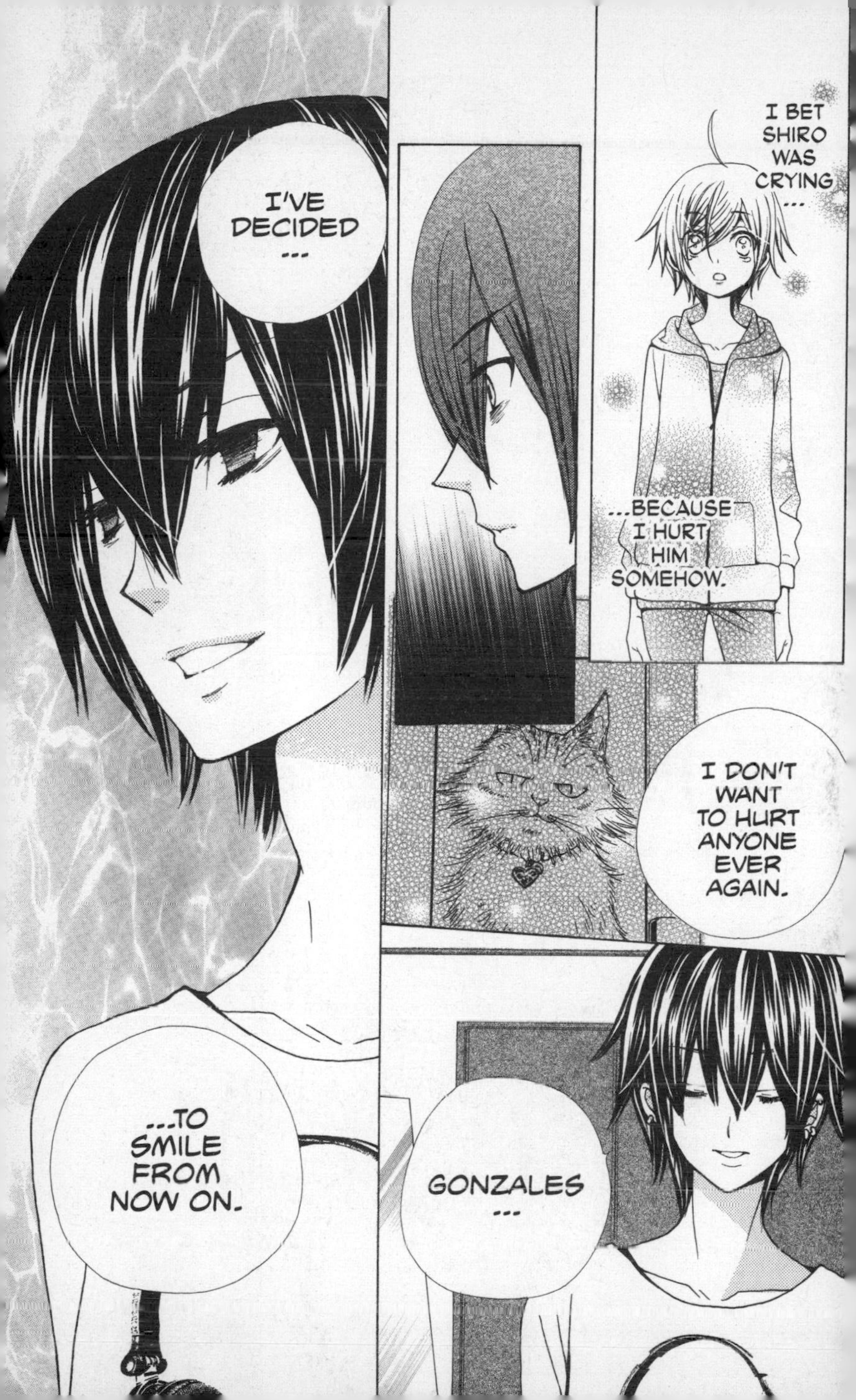
I BET SHIRO WAS CRYING...
...BECAUSE I HURT HIM SOMEHOW.
I DON'T WANT TO HURT ANYONE EVER AGAIN.
GONZALES...
I'VE DECIDED...
...TO SMILE FROM NOW ON.

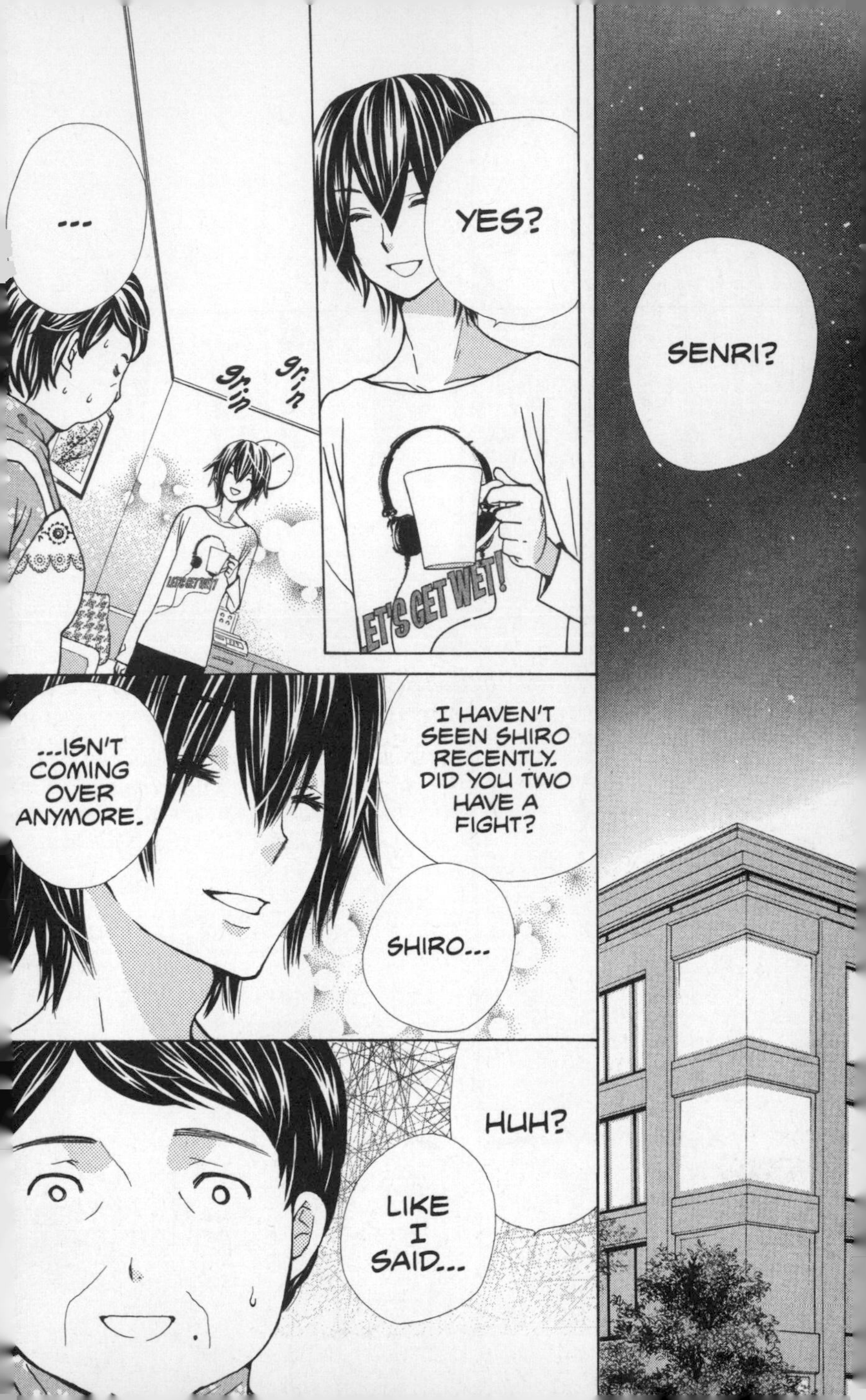
SENRI?
YES?
LET'S GET WET!
...
gr.in
gr.in
I HAVEN'T SEEN SHIRO RECENTLY. DID YOU TWO HAVE A FIGHT?
SHIRO...
...ISN'T COMING OVER ANYMORE.
HUH?
LIKE I SAID...

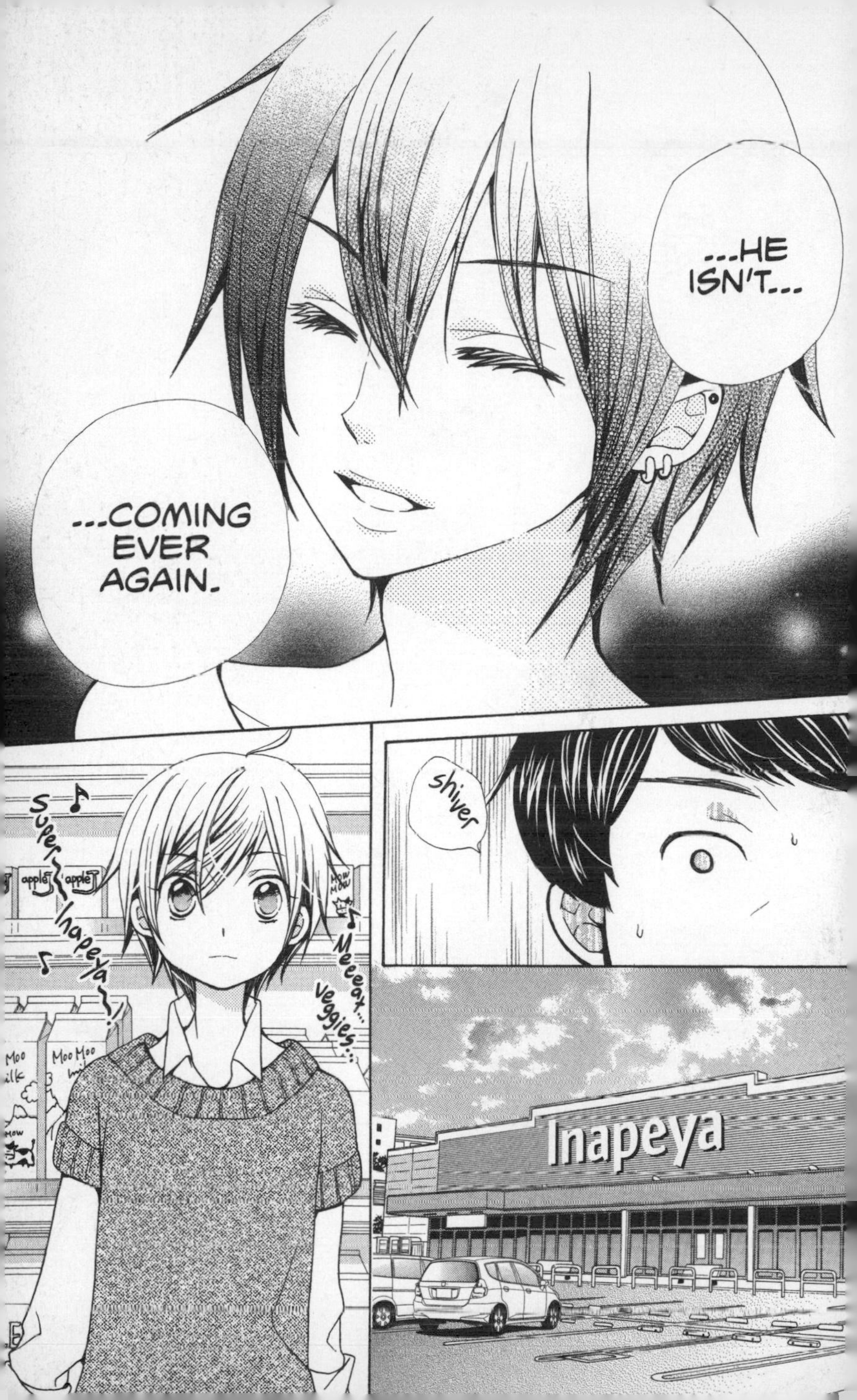
...HE ISN'T...
...COMING EVER AGAIN.
shiver
Inapeya
Super~ Inapeya~!
Meeeat... veggies...
apple
apple
MOW MOW

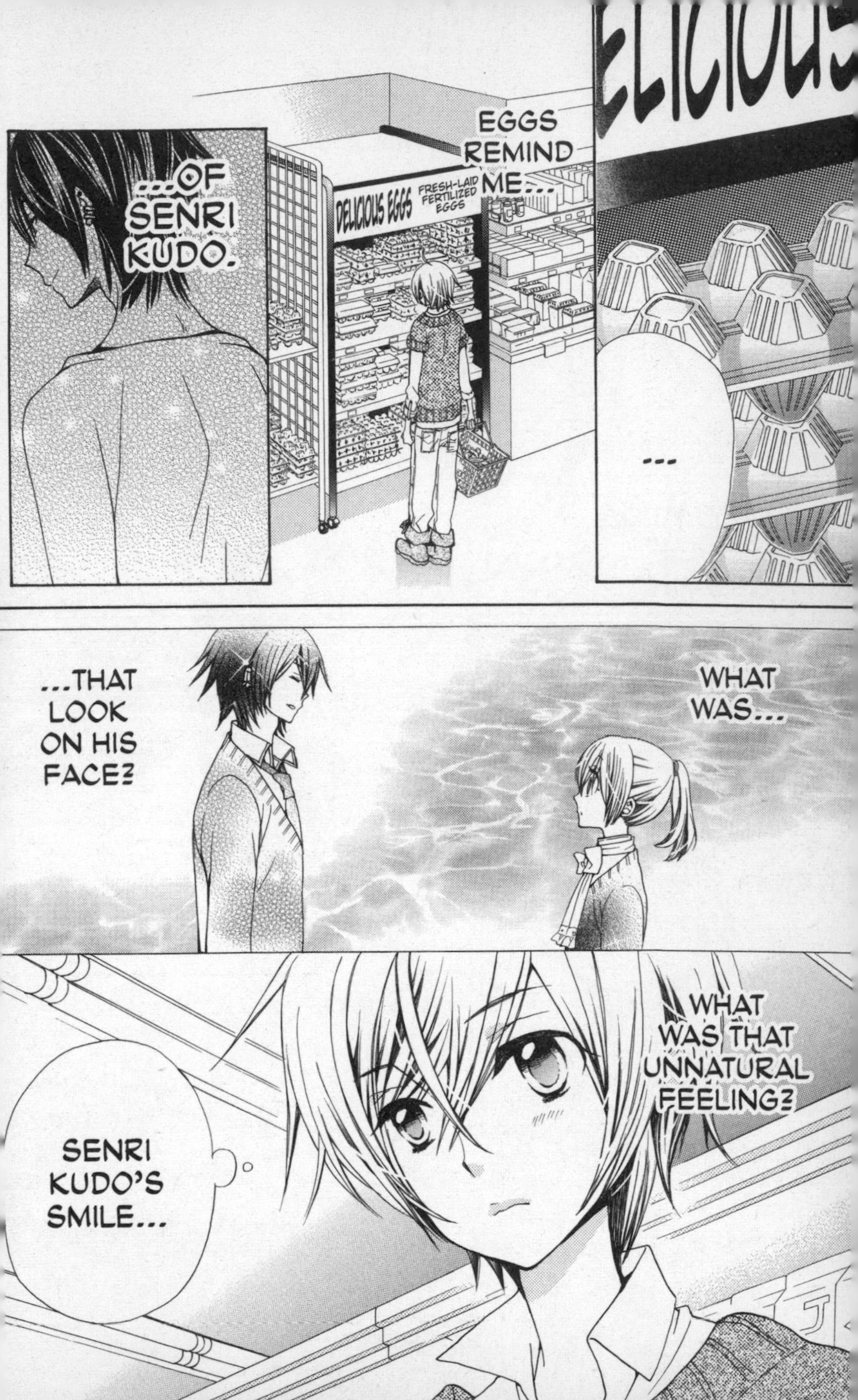
...
EGGS REMIND ME...
DELICIOUS EGGS
FRESH-LAID FERTILIZED EGGS
...OF SENRI KUDO.
WHAT WAS...
...THAT LOOK ON HIS FACE?
WHAT WAS THAT UNNATURAL FEELING?
SENRI KUDO'S SMILE...

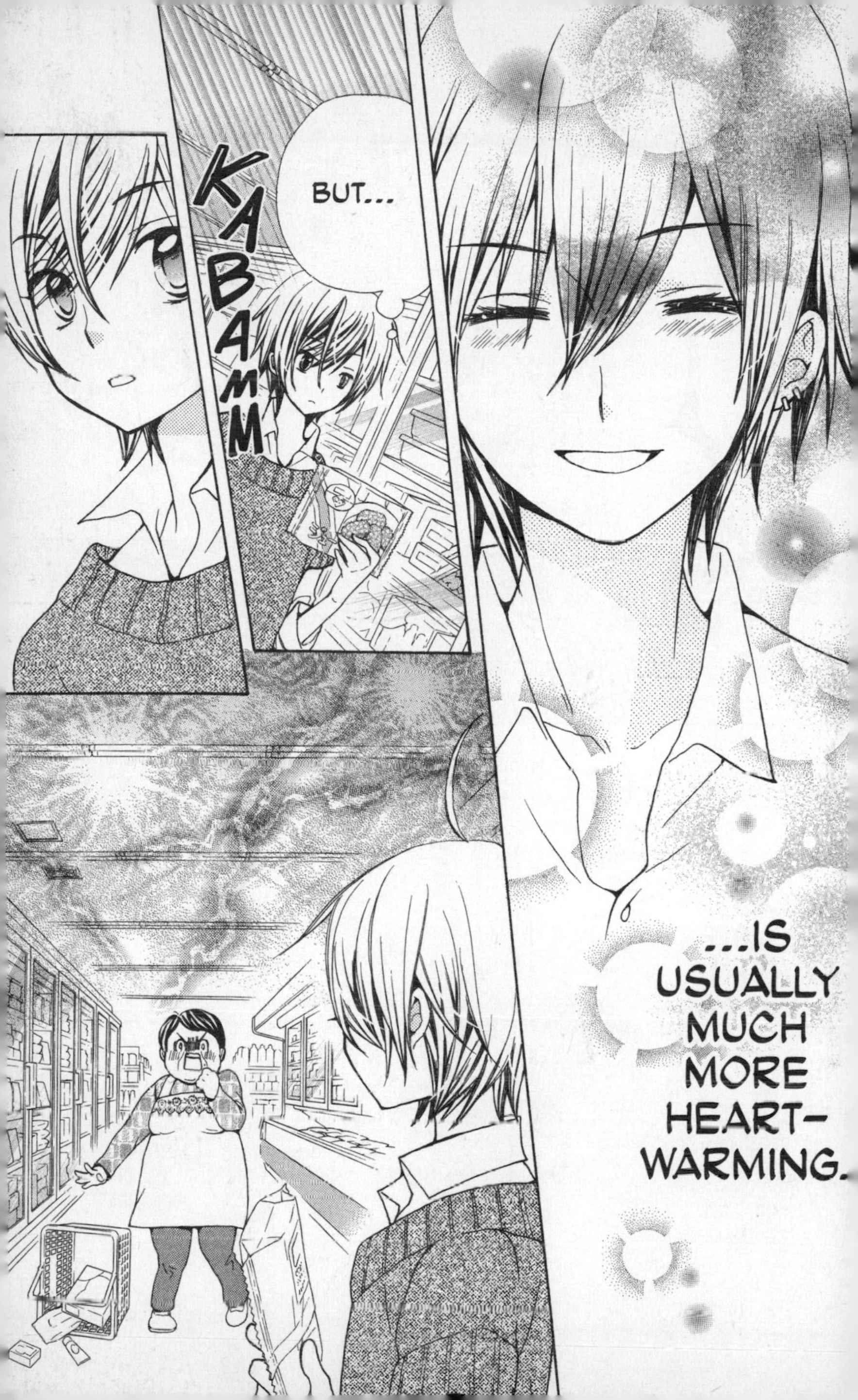
...IS USUALLY MUCH MORE HEART-WARMING.
BUT...
KABAMMM

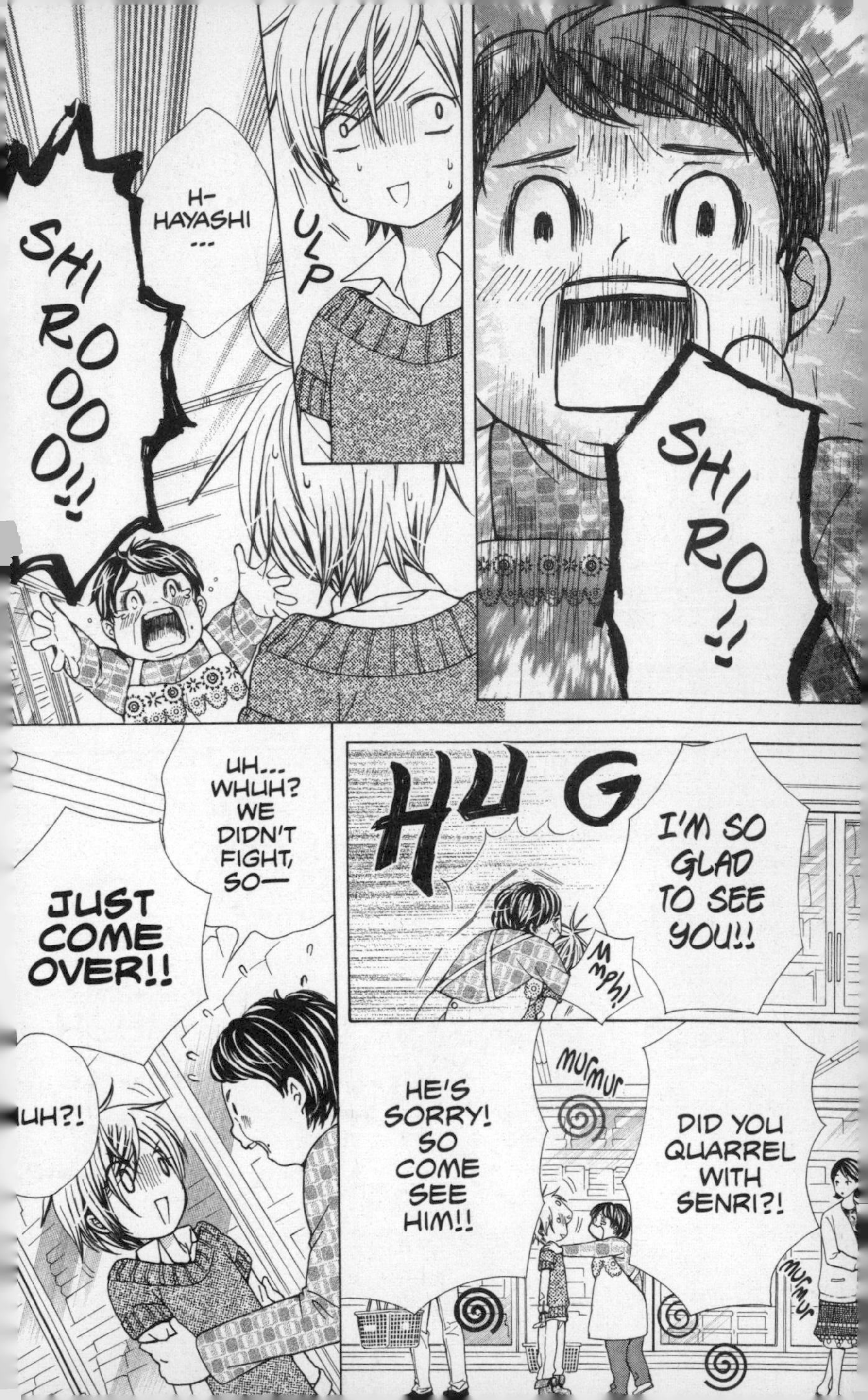
SHIRO!!
ULP
H-HAYASHI...
SHIROOOOO!!
HUG
I'M SO GLAD TO SEE YOU!!
Mmph!
murmur
DID YOU QUARREL WITH SENRI?!
HE'S SORRY! SO COME SEE HIM!!
murmur
UH... WHUH? WE DIDN'T FIGHT, SO—
JUST COME OVER!!
UH?!

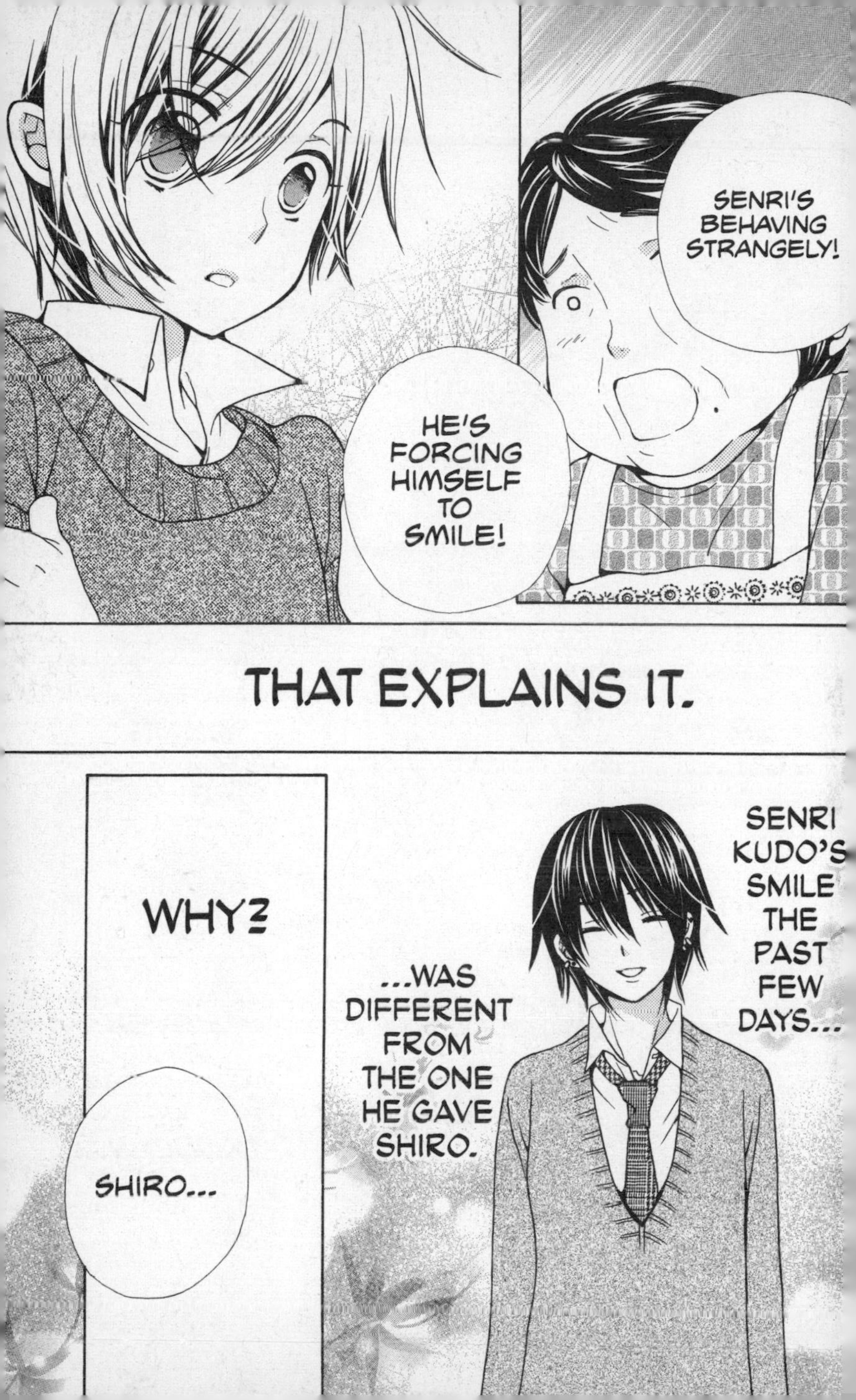
SENRI'S BEHAVING STRANGELY!
HE'S FORCING HIMSELF TO SMILE!
THAT EXPLAINS IT.
SENRI KUDO'S SMILE THE PAST FEW DAYS...
...WAS DIFFERENT FROM THE ONE HE GAVE SHIRO.
WHY?
SHIRO...

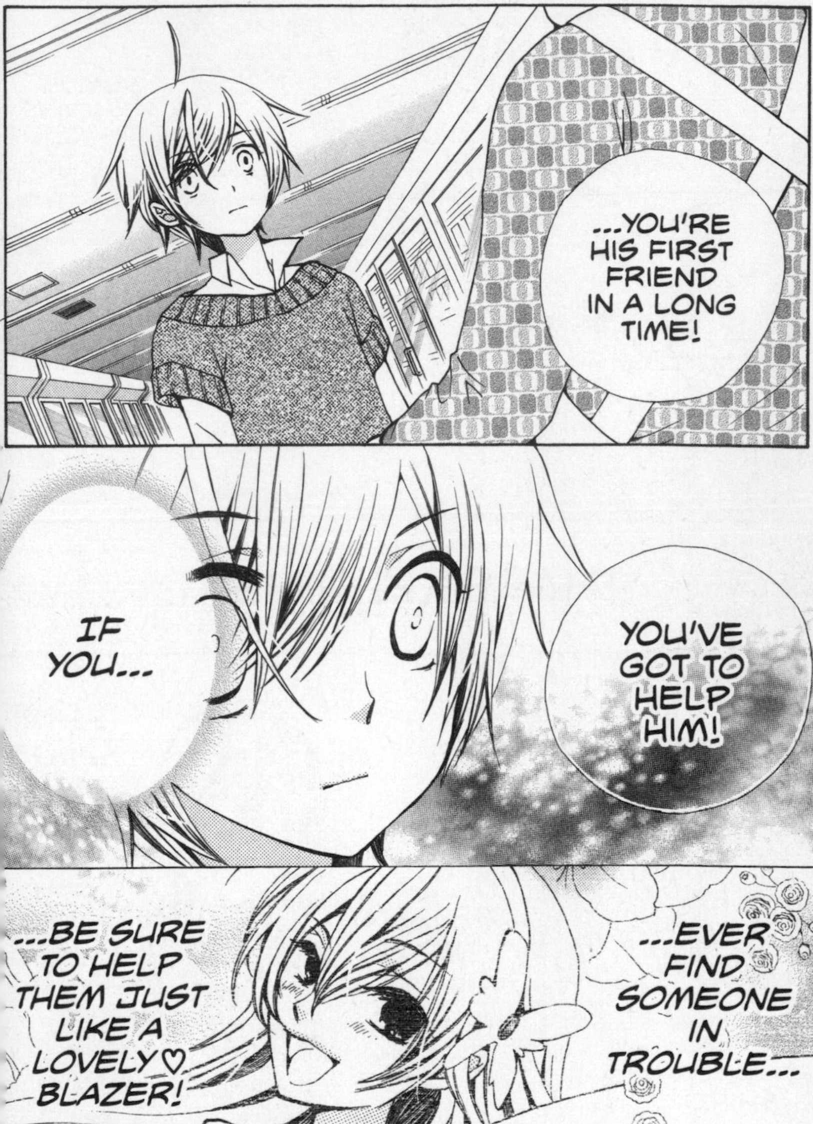
...YOU'RE HIS FIRST FRIEND IN A LONG TIME!
YOU'VE GOT TO HELP HIM!
IF YOU...
...EVER FIND SOMEONE IN TROUBLE...
...BE SURE TO HELP THEM JUST LIKE A LOVELY♡ BLAZER!

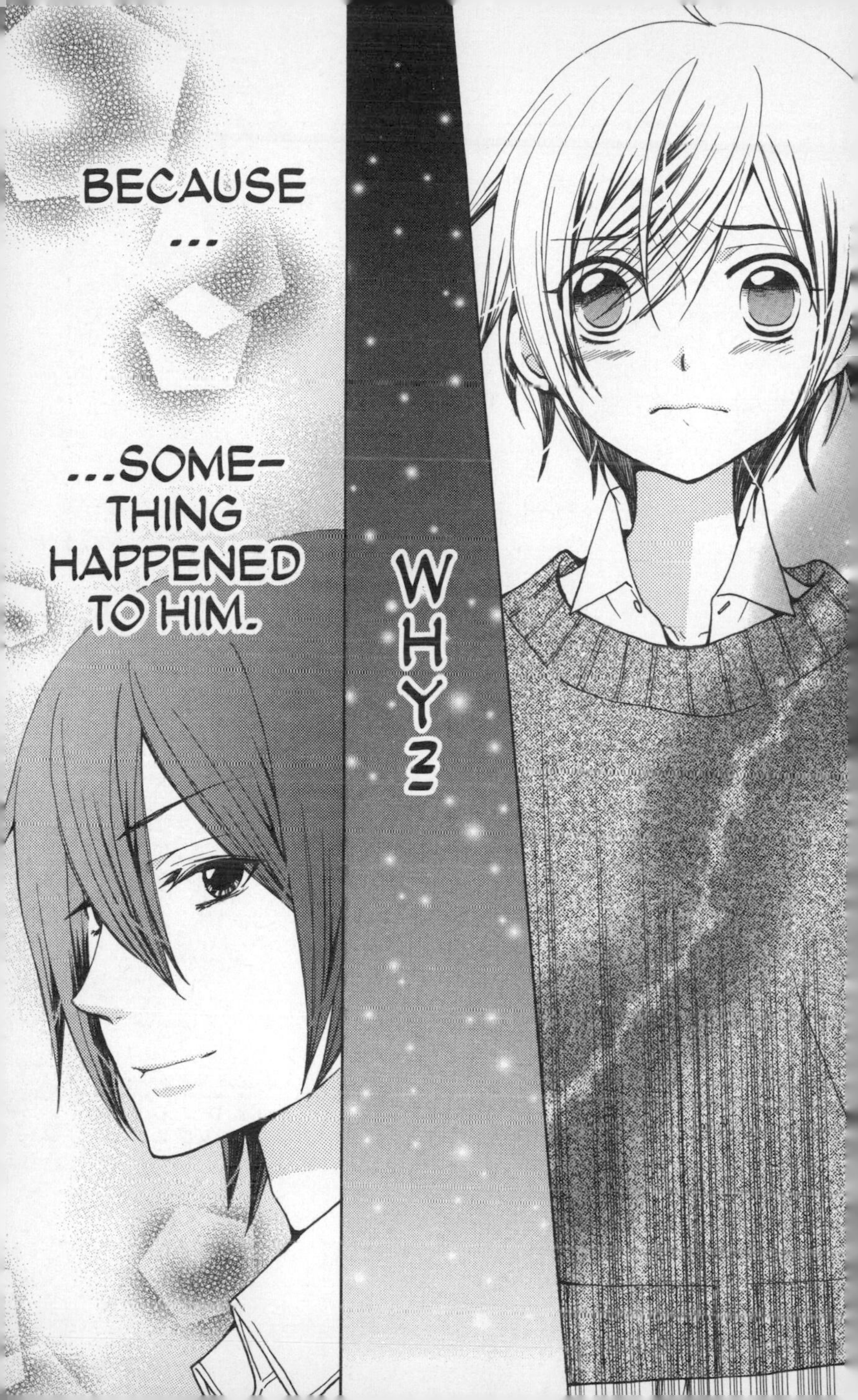
WHY?
BECAUSE...
...SOME-THING HAPPENED TO HIM.

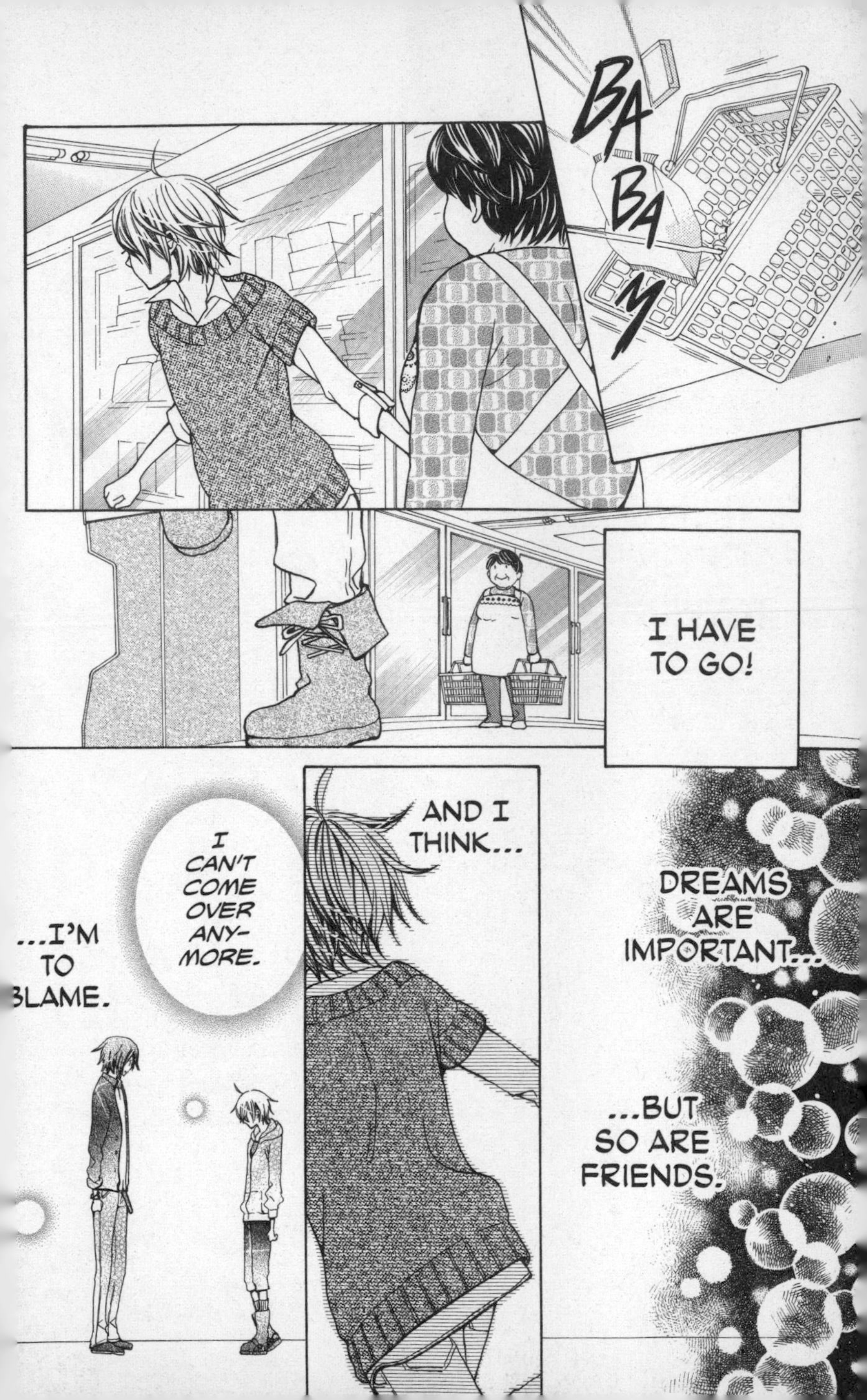
BA BA M
I HAVE TO GO!
DREAMS ARE IMPORTANT...
...BUT SO ARE FRIENDS.
AND I THINK...
I CAN'T COME OVER ANYMORE.
...I'M TO BLAME.

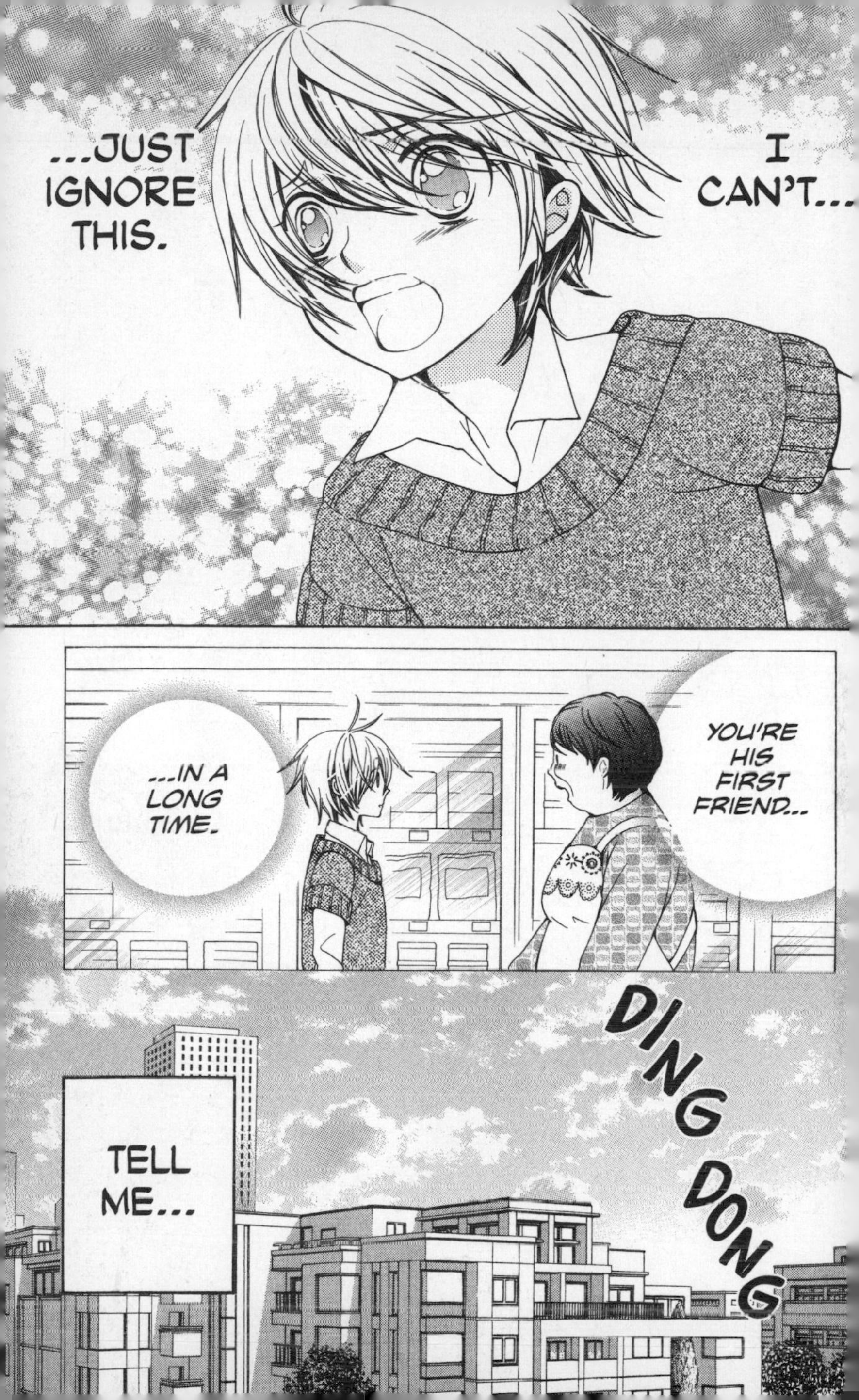
I CAN'T...
...JUST IGNORE THIS.
YOU'RE HIS FIRST FRIEND...
...IN A LONG TIME.
DING DONG
TELL ME...

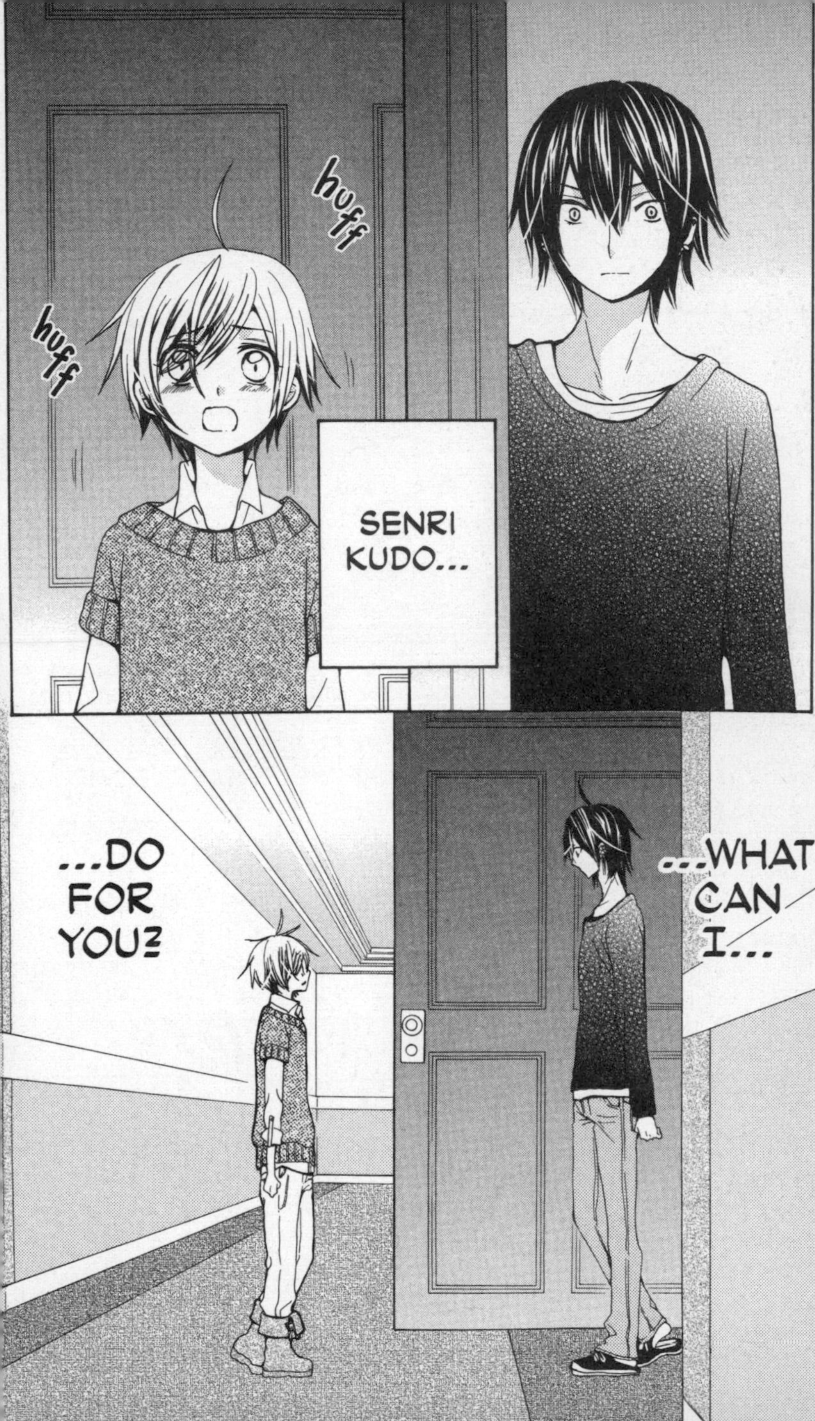
huff
huff
SENRI KUDO...
...WHAT CAN I...
...DO FOR YOU?

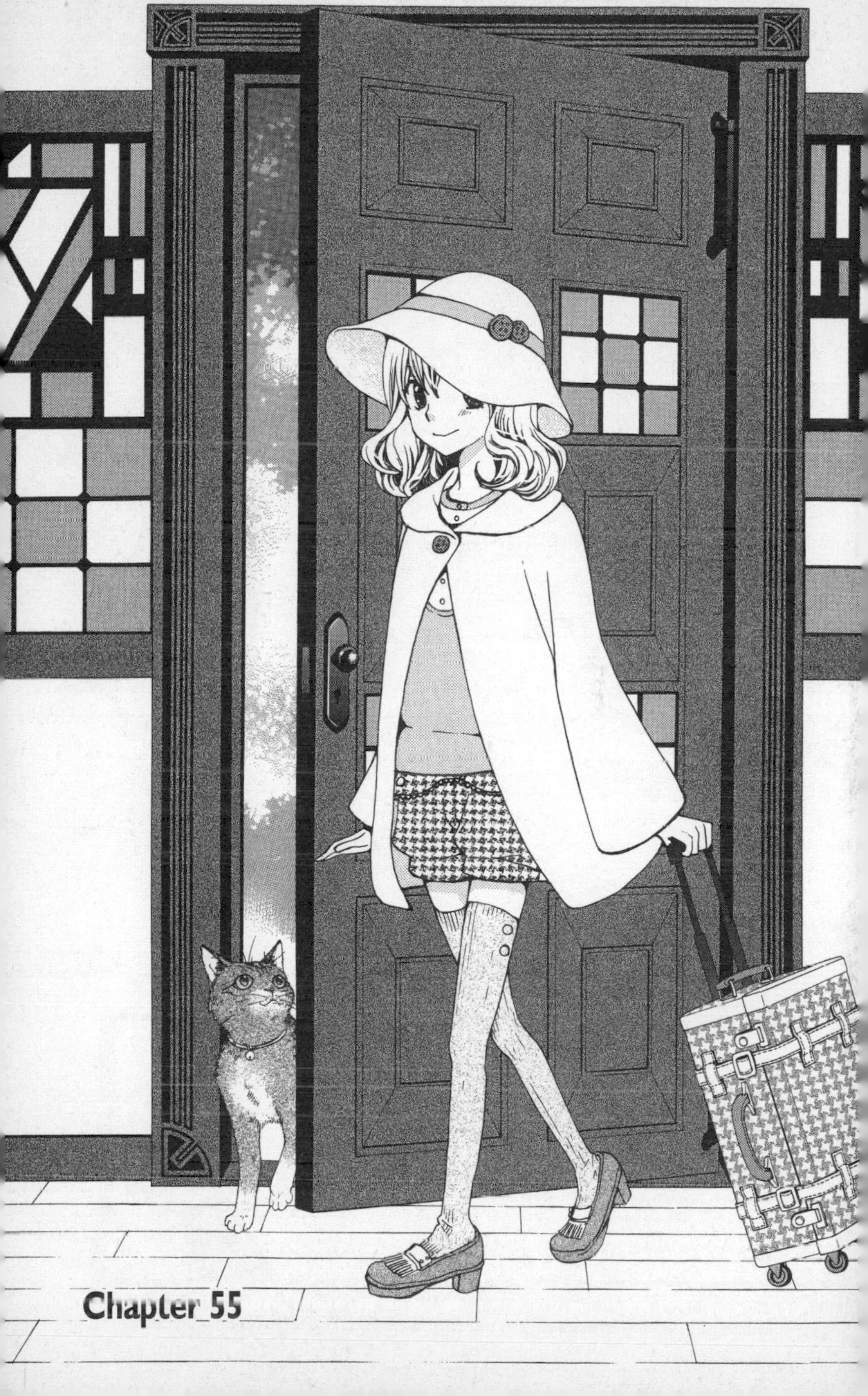
Chapter 55

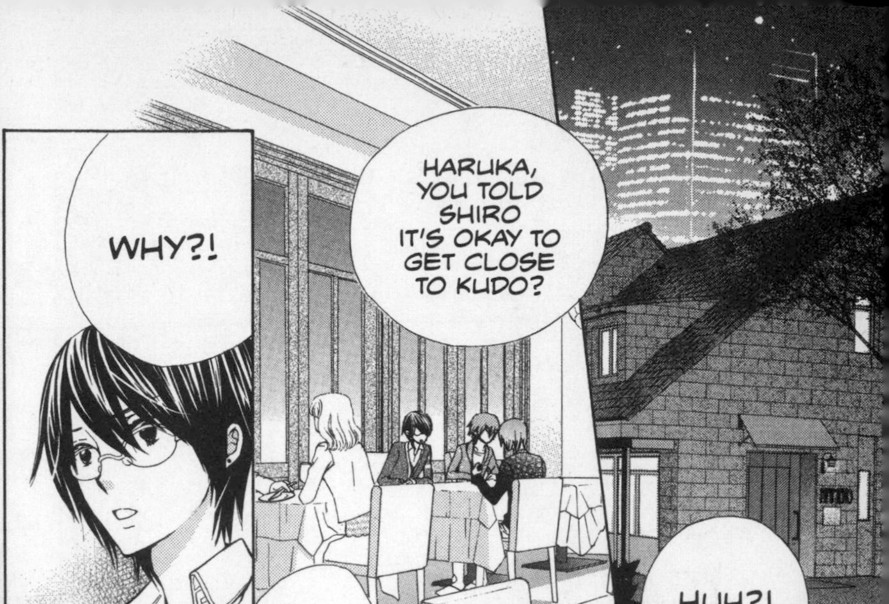
HARUKA, YOU TOLD SHIRO IT'S OKAY TO GET CLOSE TO KUDO?
HUH?!
YES.
WHY?!
IT'S A TEST...

• Mini Cup Noodles •

I always have cup soup or mini cup noodles on hand in case I get hungry, especially at night while working on a manuscript. I don't want to get fat, so I control myself, but when I notice the smell of someone else eating, the next thing I know, I'm pouring hot water for my own! Late-nite cup noodles!

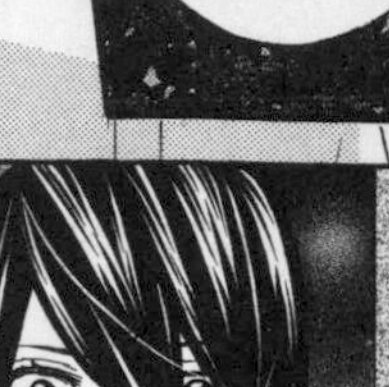

{ Deeeeeelicious!!!!!! }

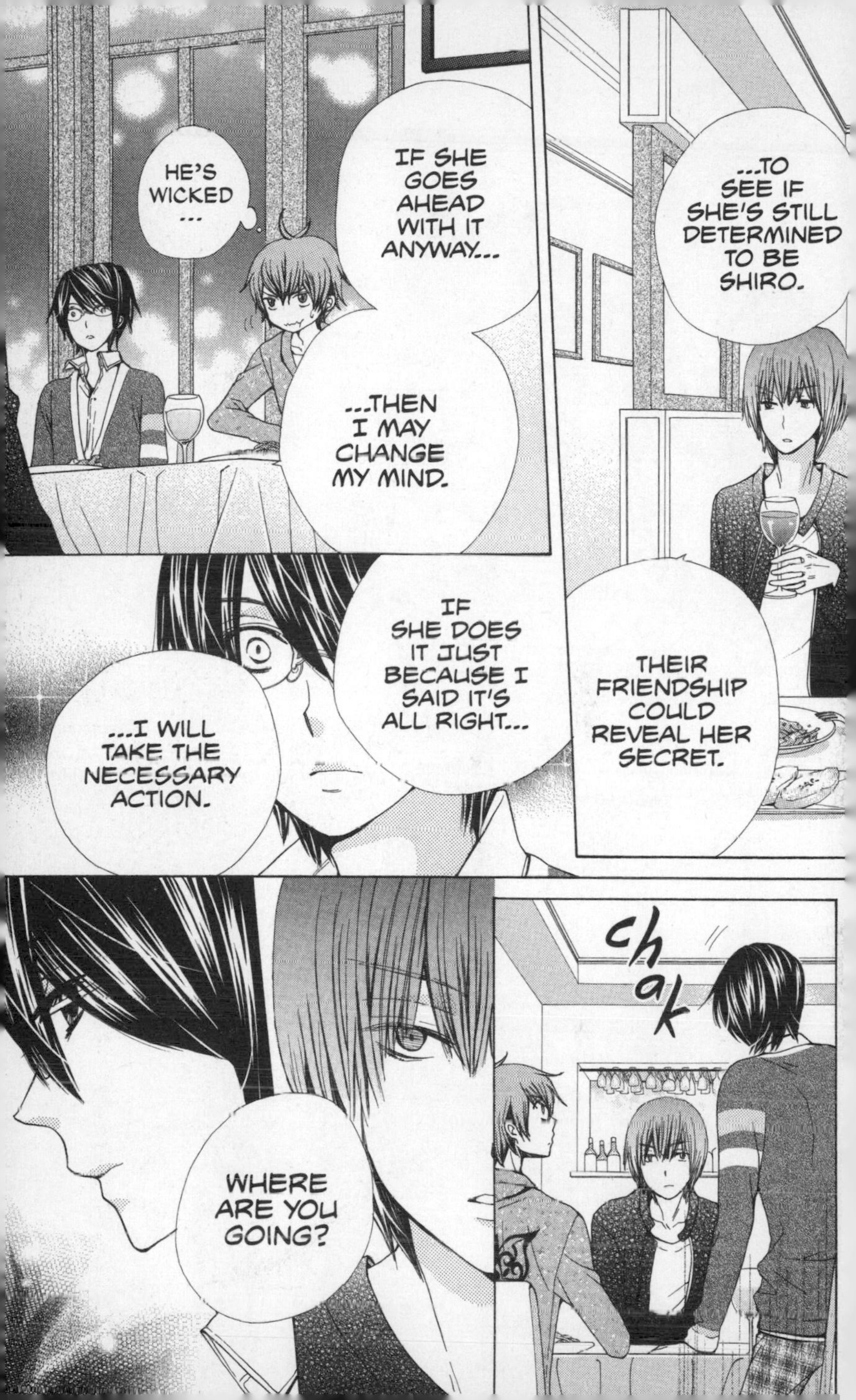
...TO SEE IF SHE'S STILL DETERMINED TO BE SHIRO.
IF SHE GOES AHEAD WITH IT ANYWAY...
...THEN I MAY CHANGE MY MIND.
HE'S WICKED...
THEIR FRIENDSHIP COULD REVEAL HER SECRET.
IF SHE DOES IT JUST BECAUSE I SAID IT'S ALL RIGHT...
...I WILL TAKE THE NECESSARY ACTION.
CHAK
WHERE ARE YOU GOING?

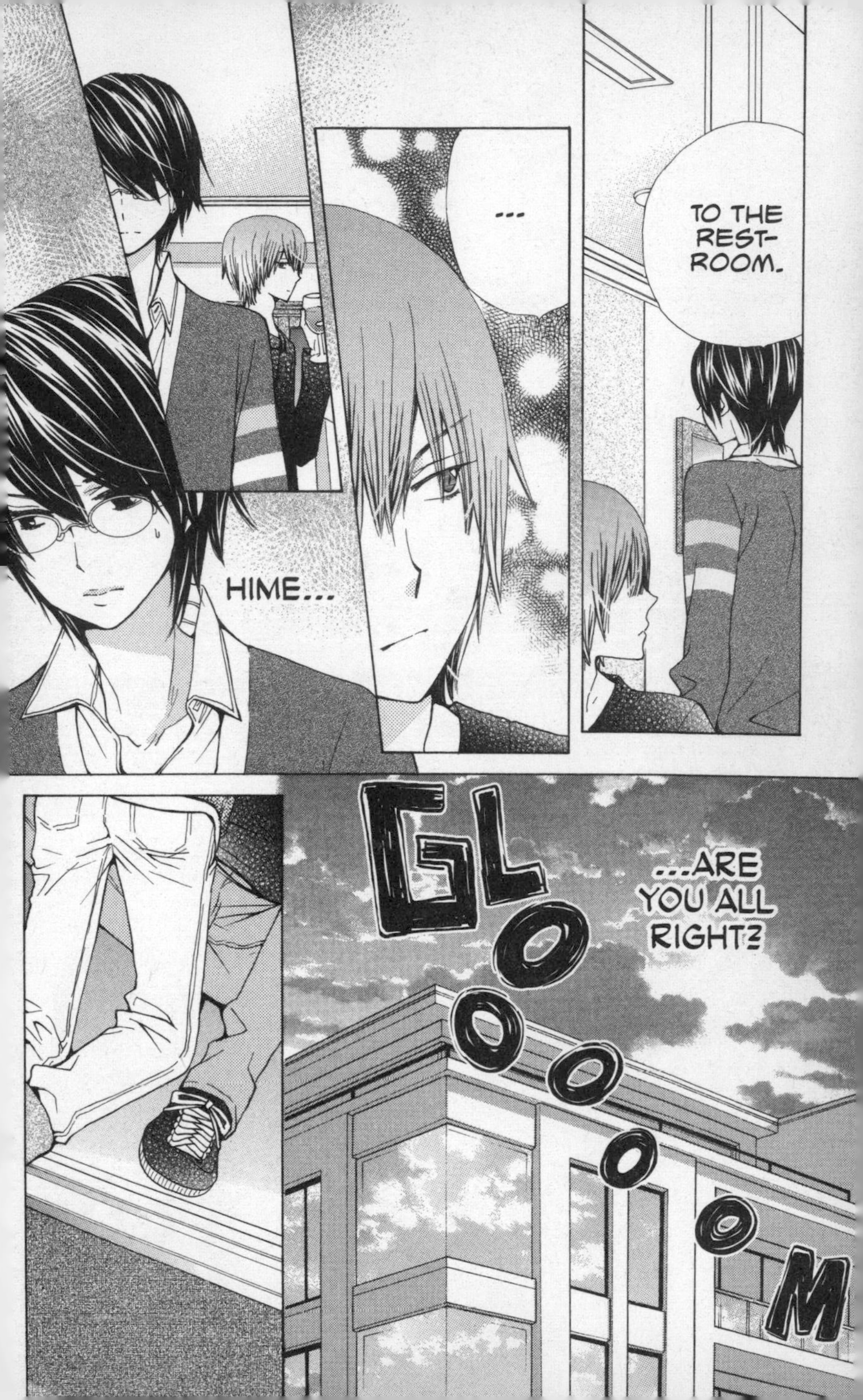
TO THE REST-ROOM.
...
HIME...
...ARE YOU ALL RIGHT?
GLOOOOOM

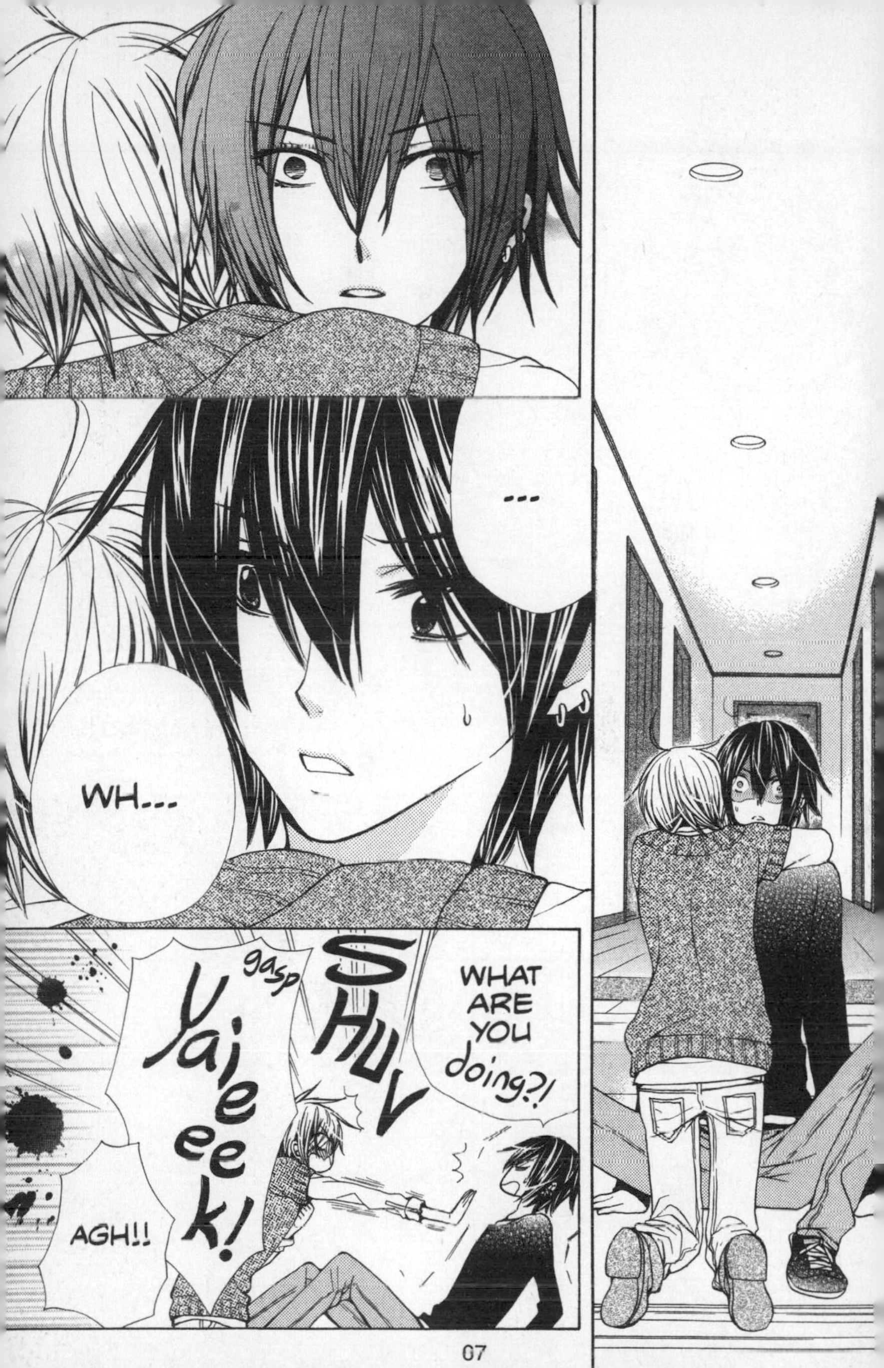
...
WH...
WHAT ARE YOU doing?!
SHUV
gasp
Yaieeeek!
AGH!!

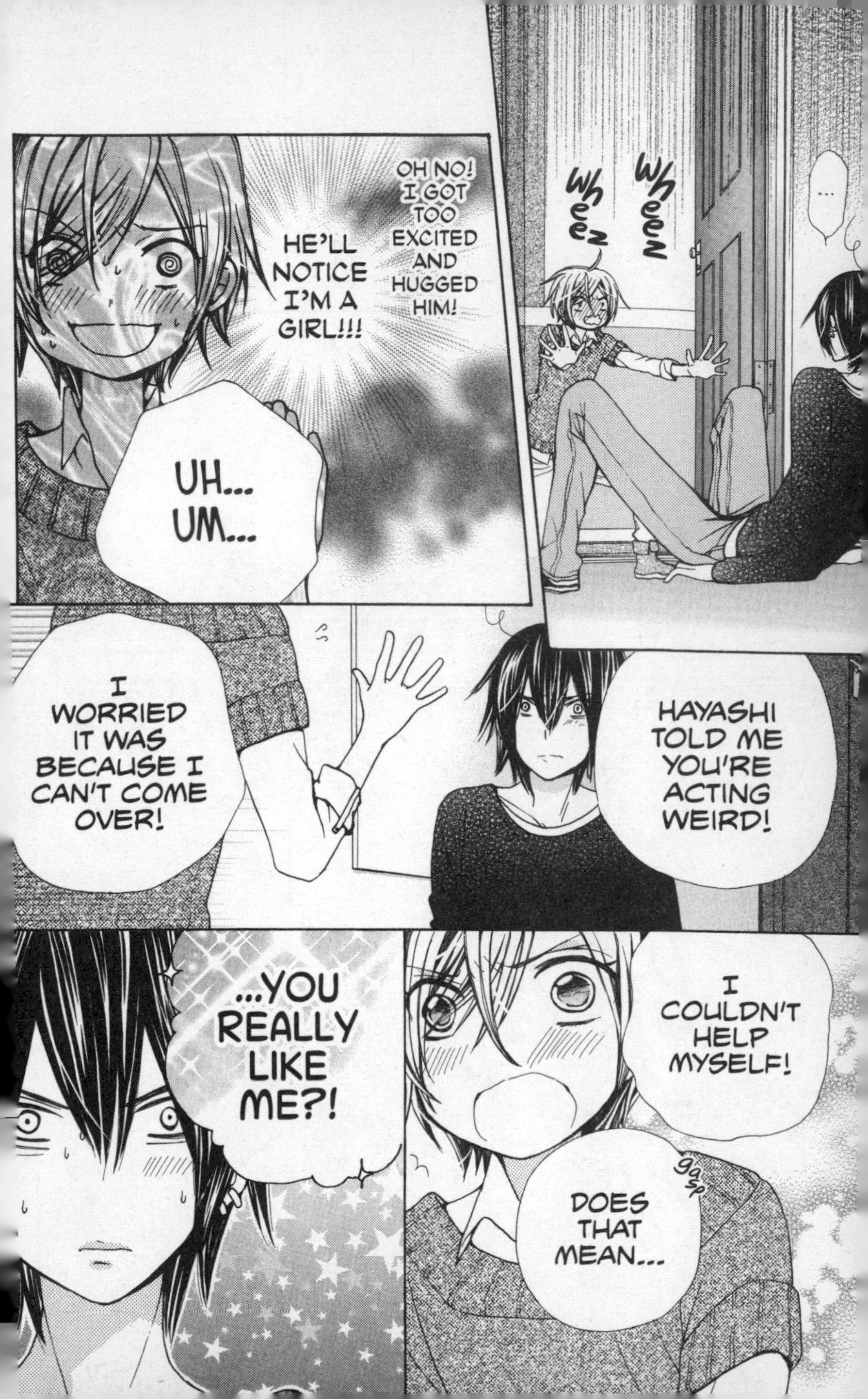
wheeez
wheez
...
OH NO! I GOT TOO EXCITED AND HUGGED HIM!
HE'LL NOTICE I'M A GIRL!!!
UH... UM...
HAYASHI TOLD ME YOU'RE ACTING WEIRD!
I WORRIED IT WAS BECAUSE I CAN'T COME OVER!
I COULDN'T HELP MYSELF!
gasp
DOES THAT MEAN...
...YOU REALLY LIKE ME?!

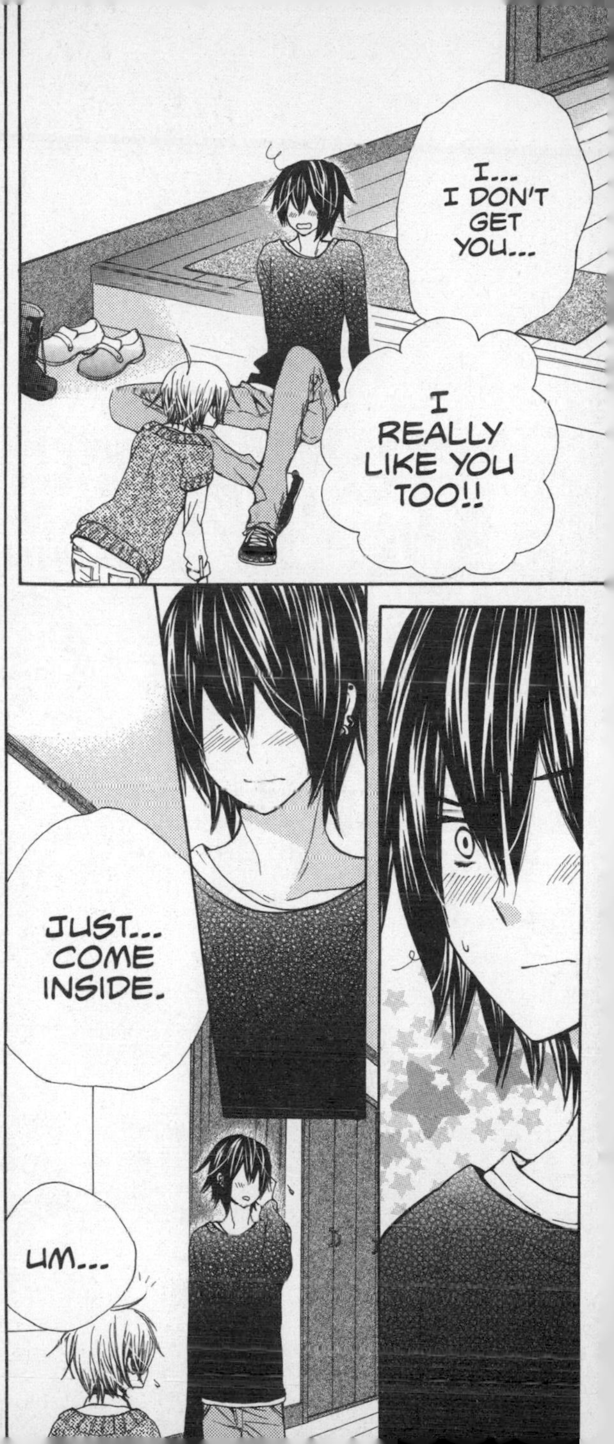
I... I DON'T GET YOU...
I REALLY LIKE YOU TOO!!
JUST... COME INSIDE.
UM...

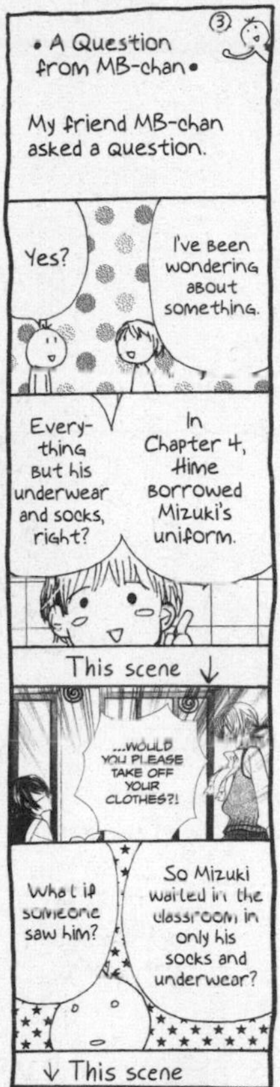
3
• A Question from MB-chan •
My friend MB-chan asked a question.
I've been wondering about something.
Yes?
In Chapter 4, Hime borrowed Mizuki's uniform.
Everything but his underwear and socks, right?
This scene ↓
...WOULD YOU PLEASE TAKE OFF YOUR CLOTHES?!
So Mizuki waited in the classroom in only his socks and underwear?
What if someone saw him?
↓ This scene
Some girl... heh heh...
...stripped me down.
Pulling back the camera...
She stripped me! ♡
What a nut!
Undies only!!
whish
I hadn't really thought about it...

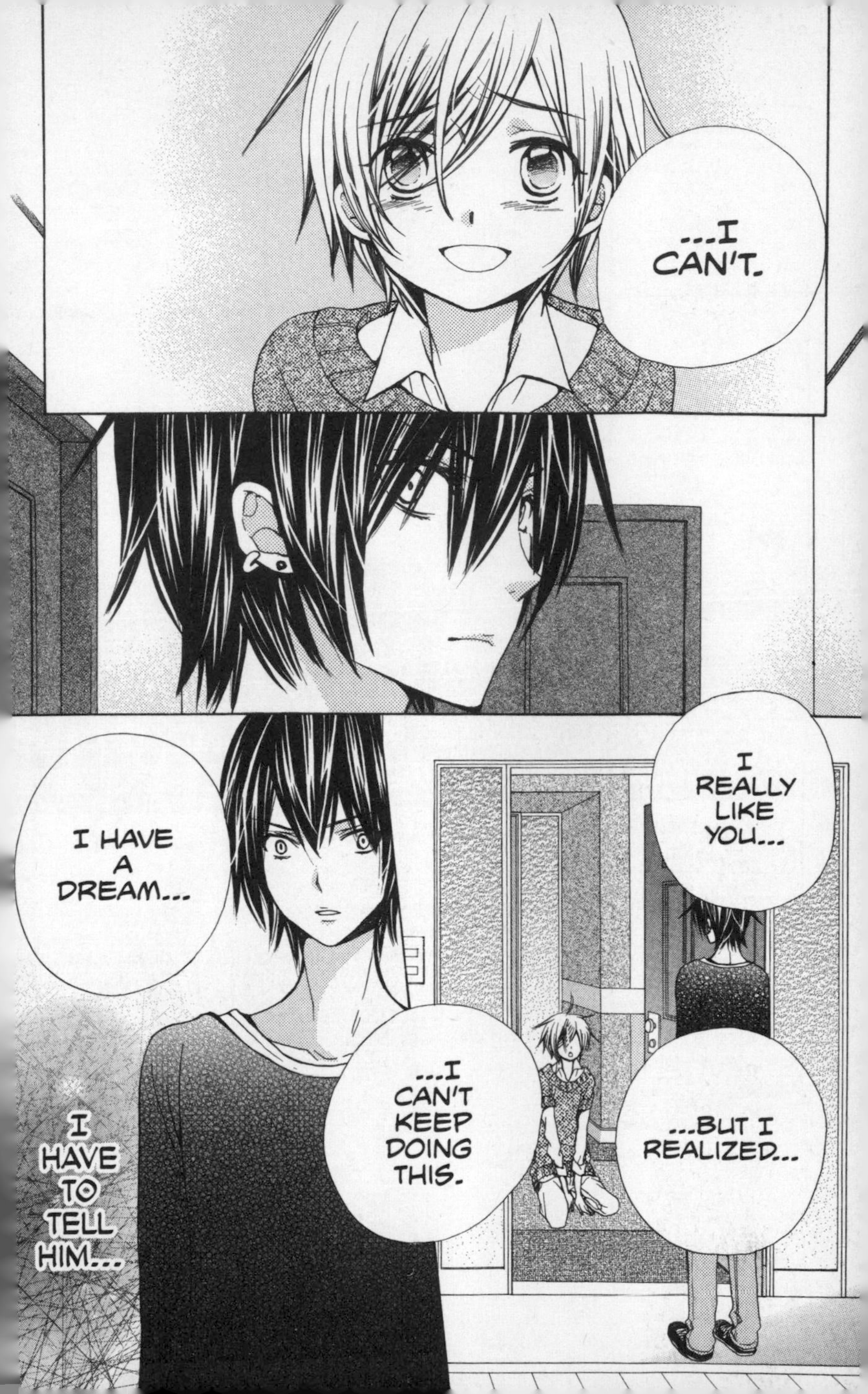
...I CAN'T.
I REALLY LIKE YOU...
...BUT I REALIZED...
I HAVE A DREAM...
...I CAN'T KEEP DOING THIS.
I HAVE TO TELL HIM...

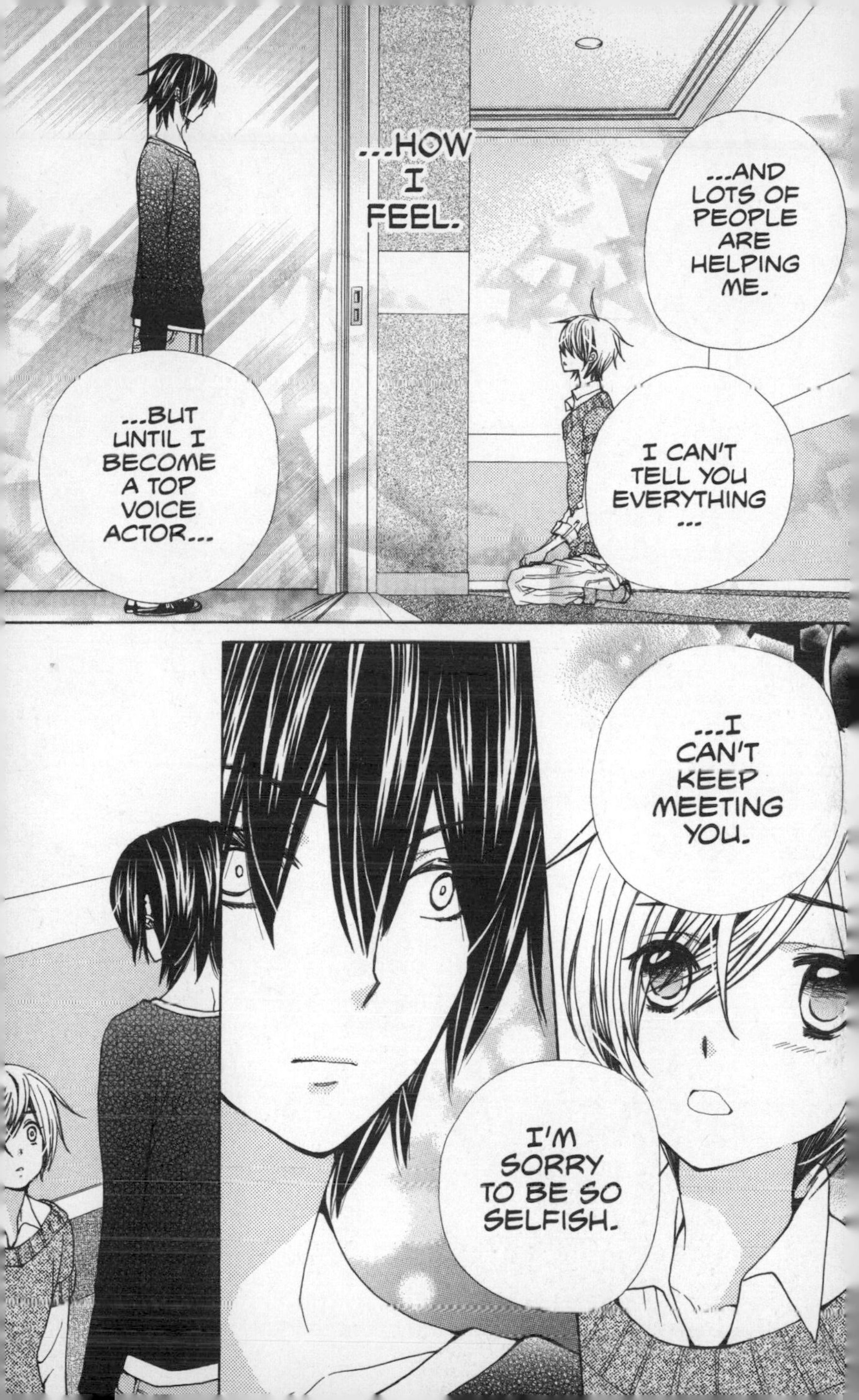
...AND LOTS OF PEOPLE ARE HELPING ME.
I CAN'T TELL YOU EVERYTHING...
...HOW I FEEL.
...BUT UNTIL I BECOME A TOP VOICE ACTOR...
...I CAN'T KEEP MEETING YOU.
I'M SORRY TO BE SO SELFISH.

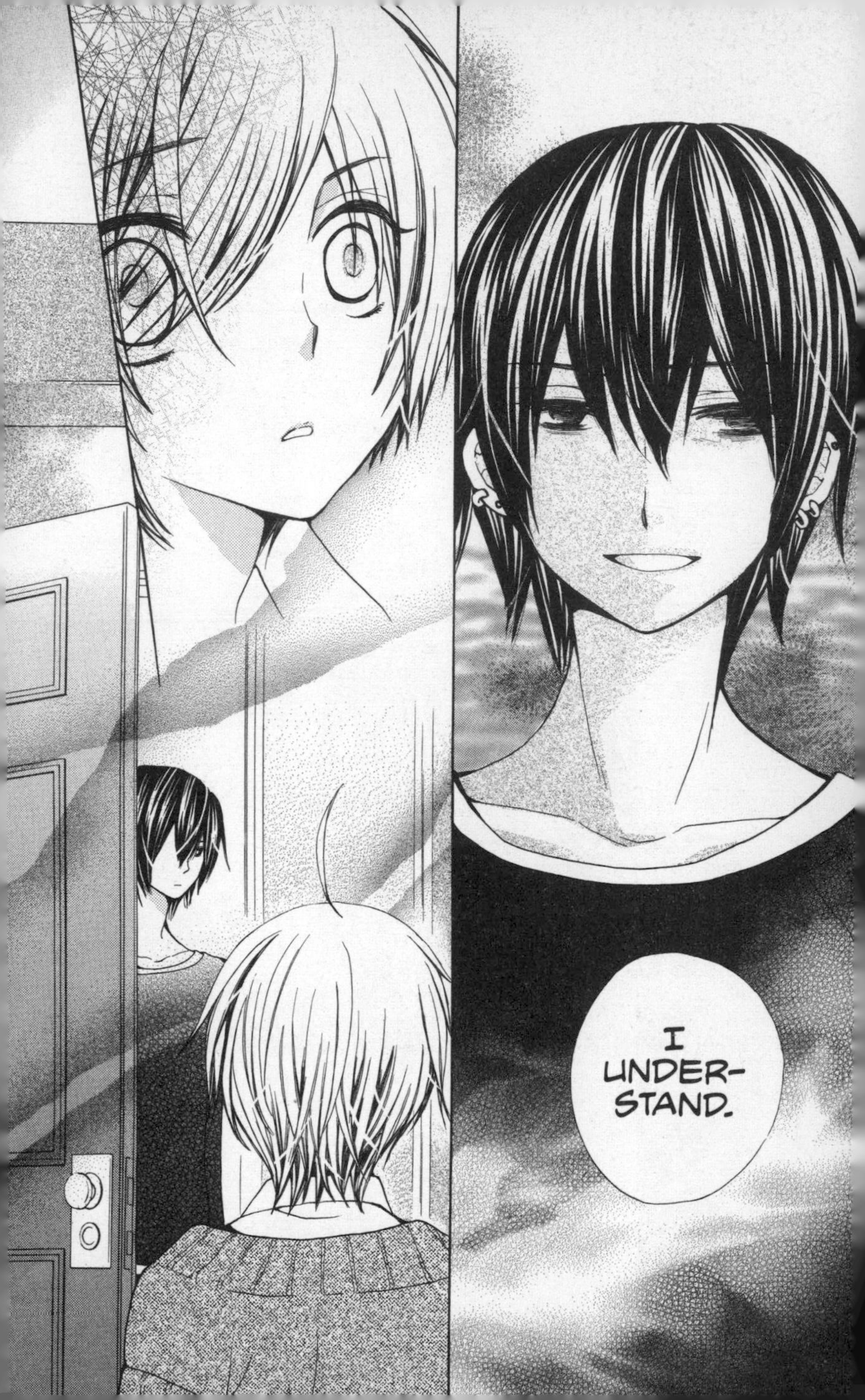
I UNDER-STAND.

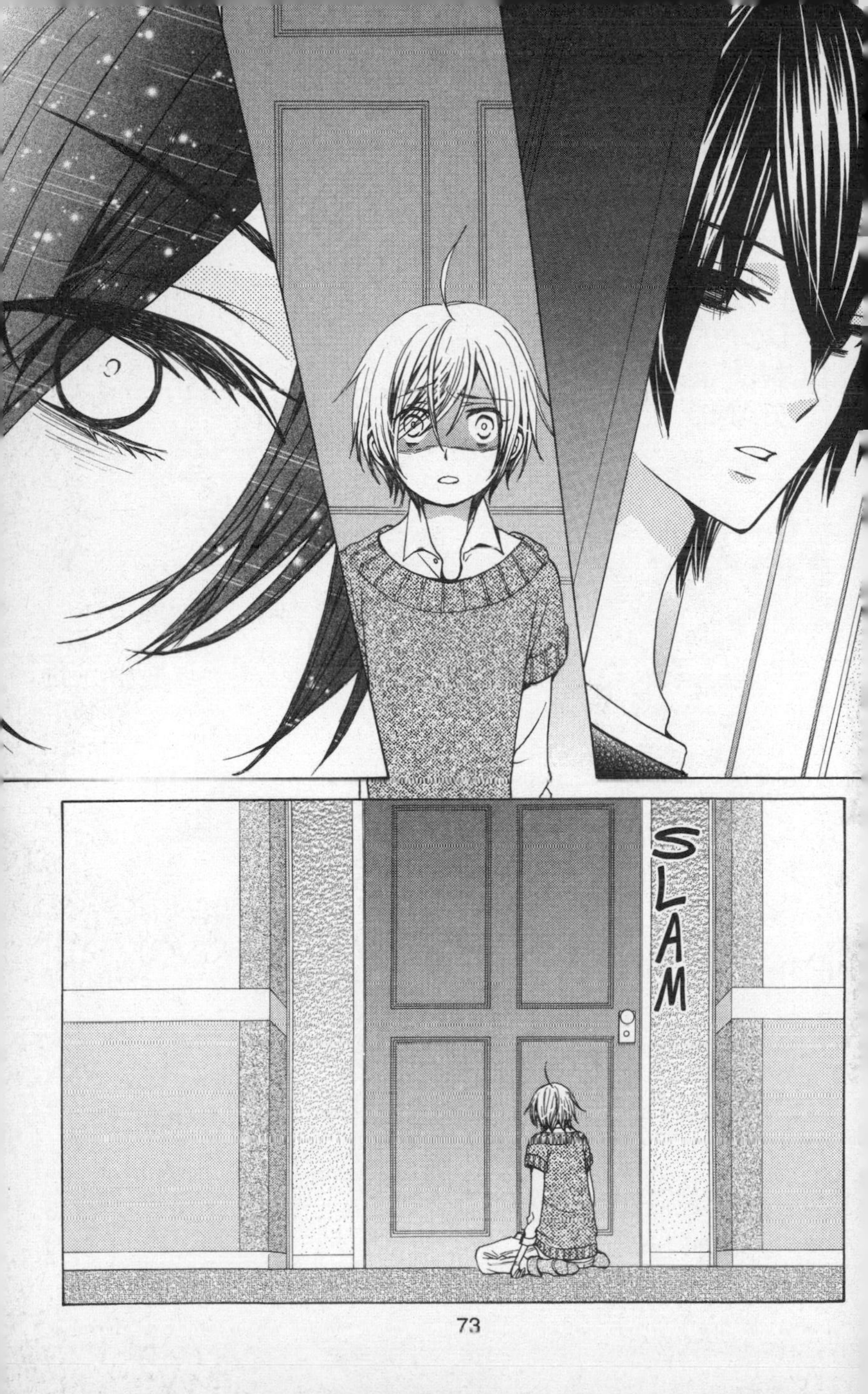
SLAM

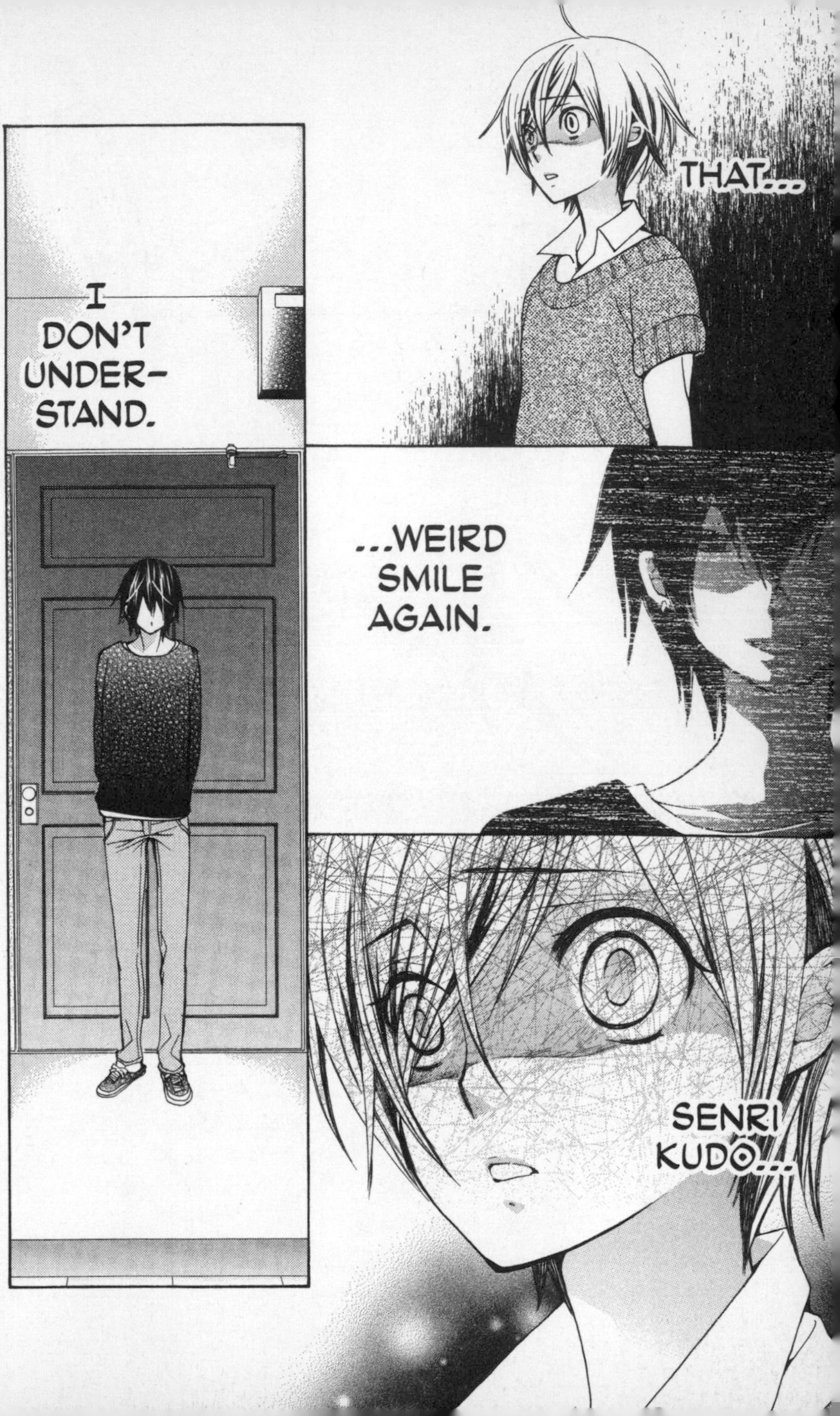
THAT...
...WEIRD SMILE AGAIN.
SENRI KUDŌ...
I DON'T UNDER-STAND.

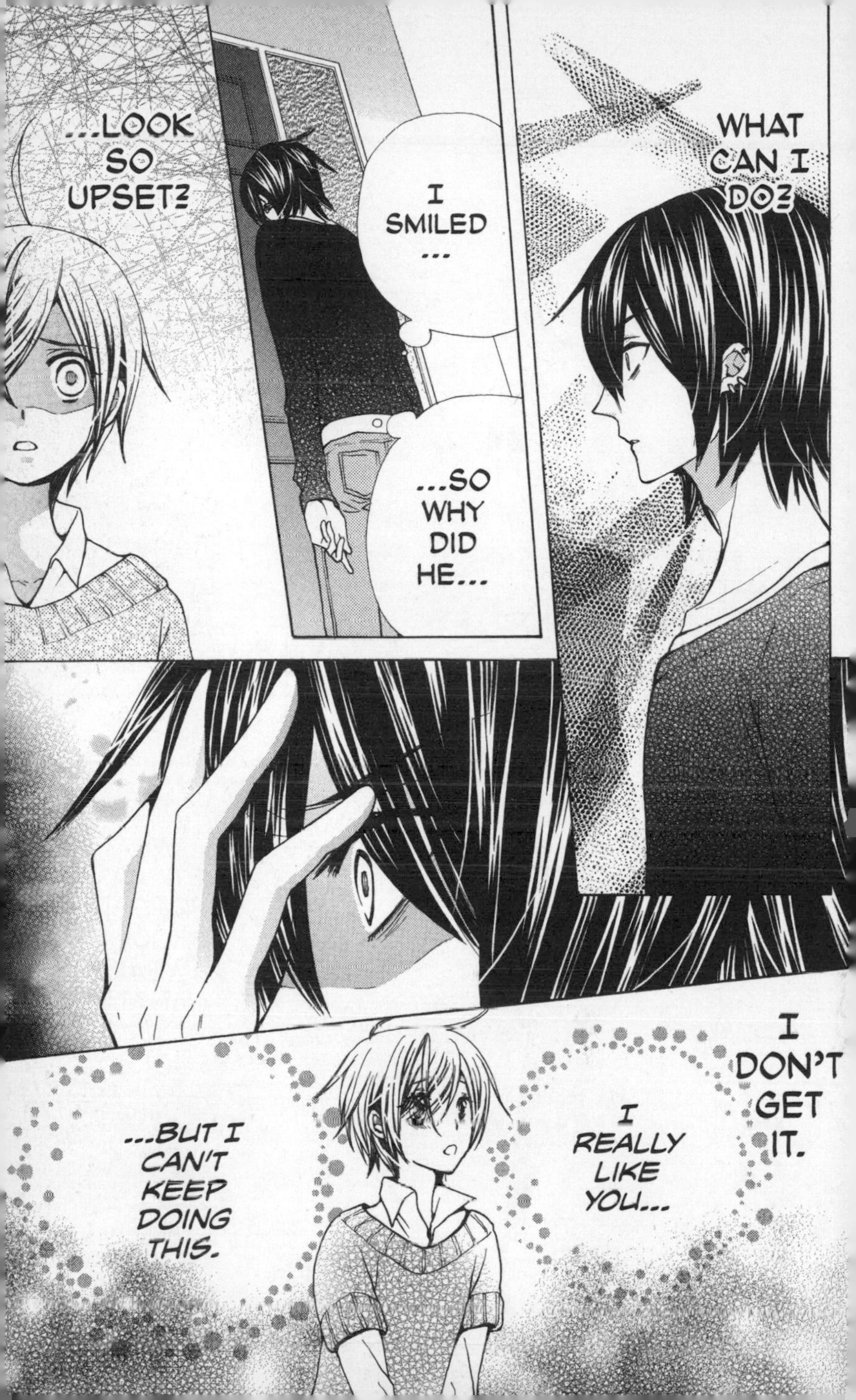
WHAT CAN I DO?
I SMILED ...
...SO WHY DID HE...
...LOOK SO UPSET?
I DON'T GET IT.
I REALLY LIKE YOU...
...BUT I CAN'T KEEP DOING THIS.

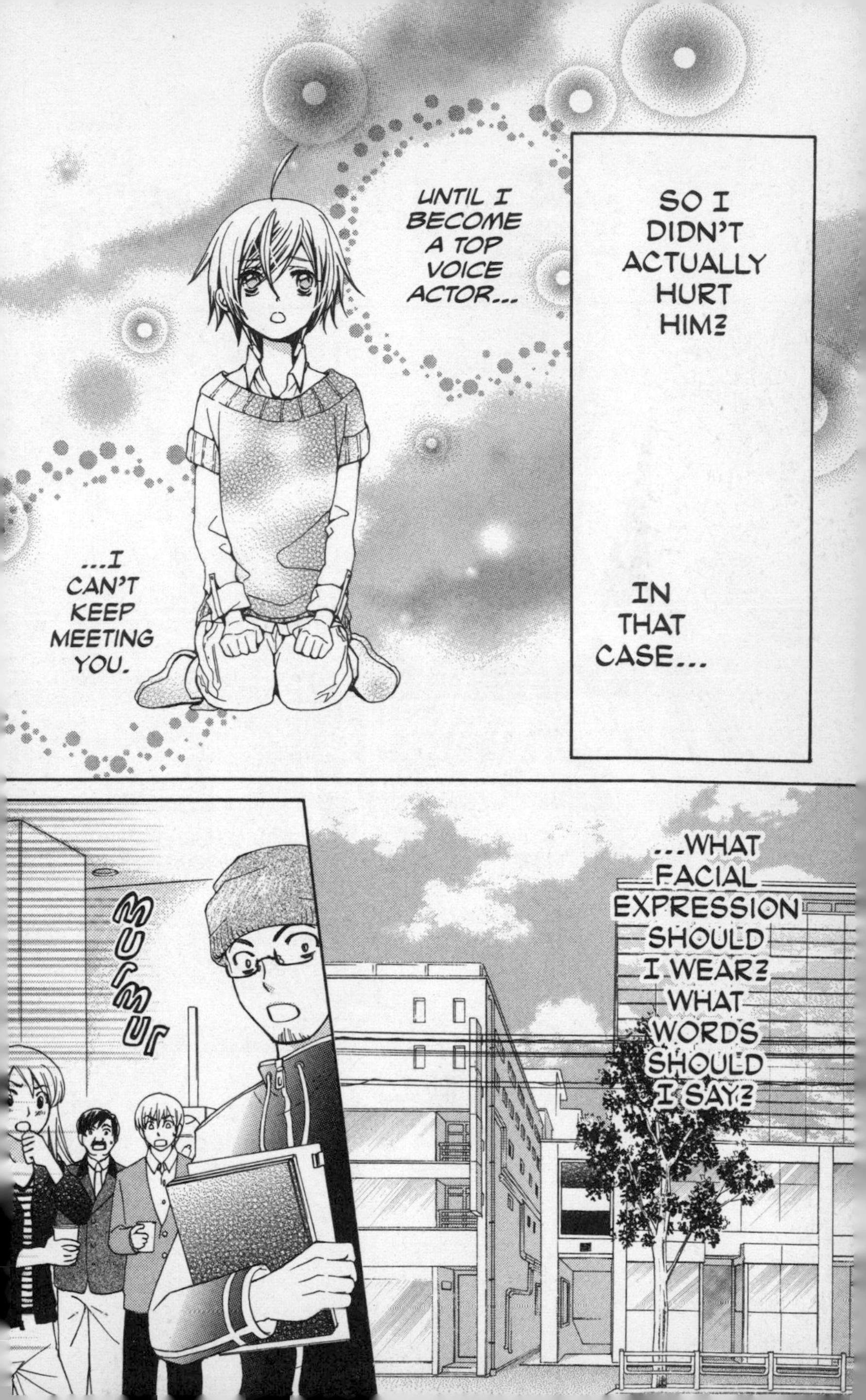
SO I DIDN'T ACTUALLY HURT HIM?
IN THAT CASE...
UNTIL I BECOME A TOP VOICE ACTOR...
...I CAN'T KEEP MEETING YOU.
...WHAT FACIAL EXPRESSION SHOULD I WEAR? WHAT WORDS SHOULD I SAY?
MURMUR

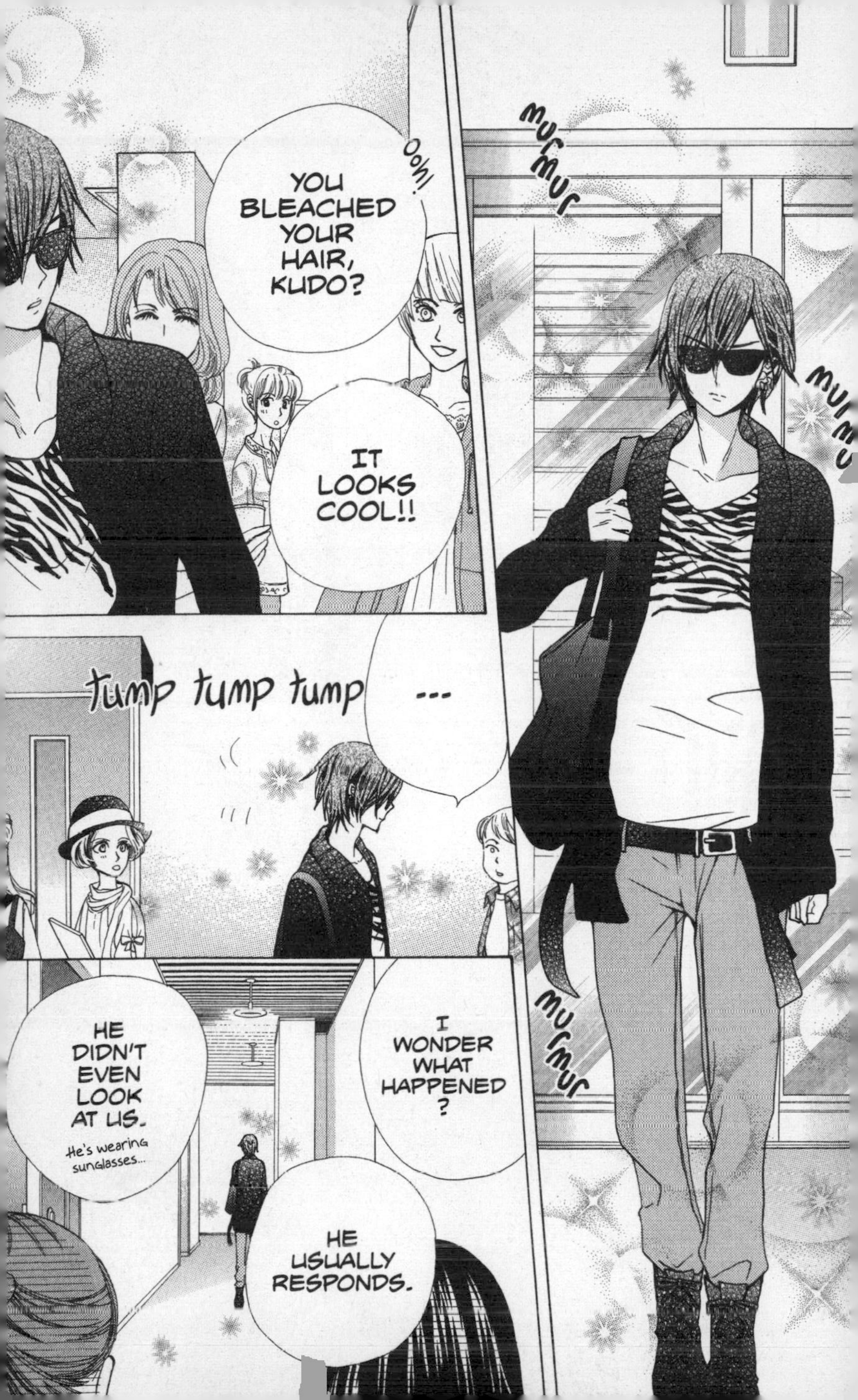
murmur
murmu
murmur
Ooh!
YOU BLEACHED YOUR HAIR, KUDO?
IT LOOKS COOL!!
tump tump tump
...
I WONDER WHAT HAPPENED?
HE DIDN'T EVEN LOOK AT US.
He's wearing sunglasses...
HE USUALLY RESPONDS.

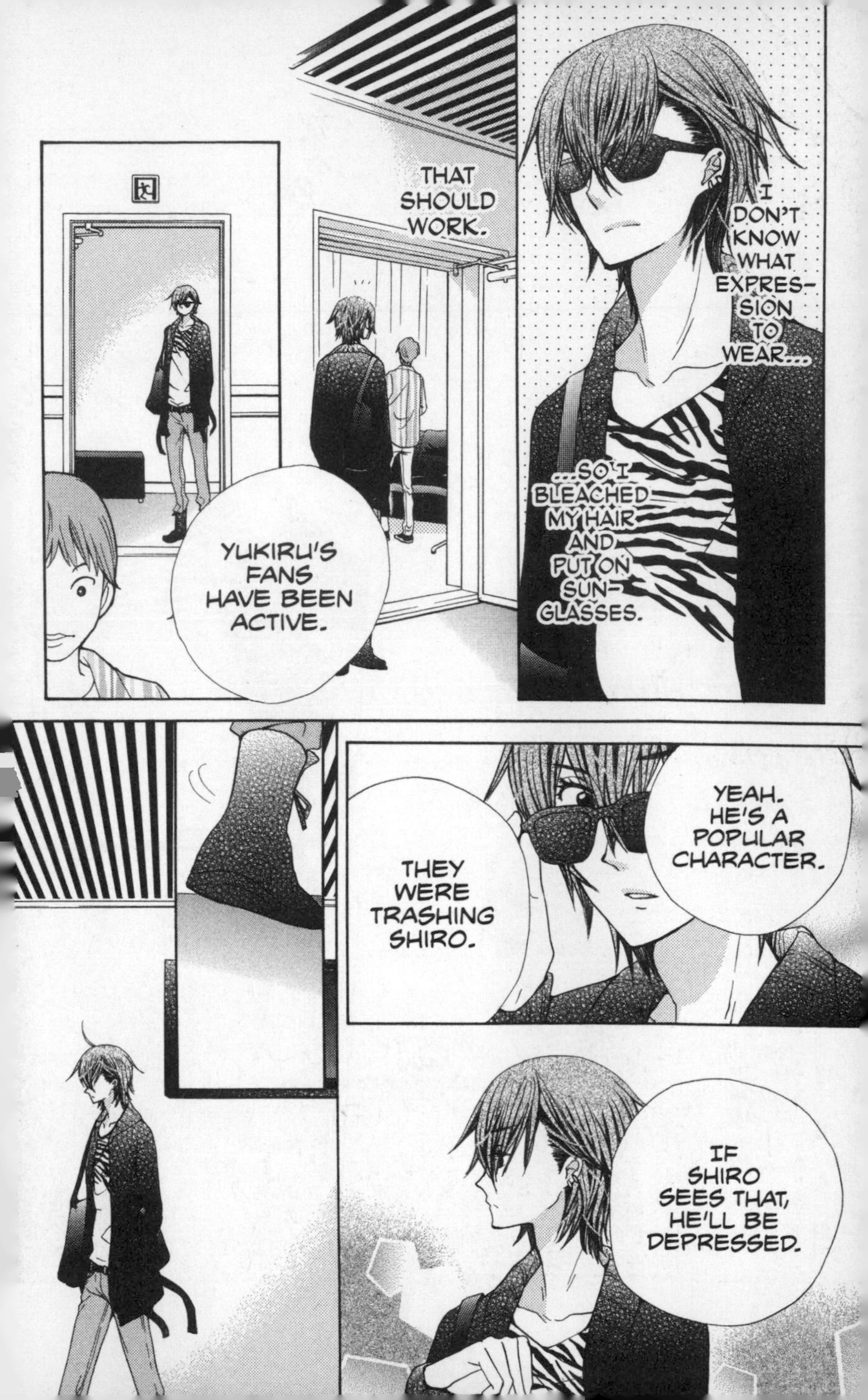
I DON'T KNOW WHAT EXPRES-SION TO WEAR...
...SO I BLEACHED MY HAIR AND PUT ON SUN-GLASSES.
THAT SHOULD WORK.
YUKIRU'S FANS HAVE BEEN ACTIVE.
YEAH. HE'S A POPULAR CHARACTER.
THEY WERE TRASHING SHIRO.
IF SHIRO SEES THAT, HE'LL BE DEPRESSED.

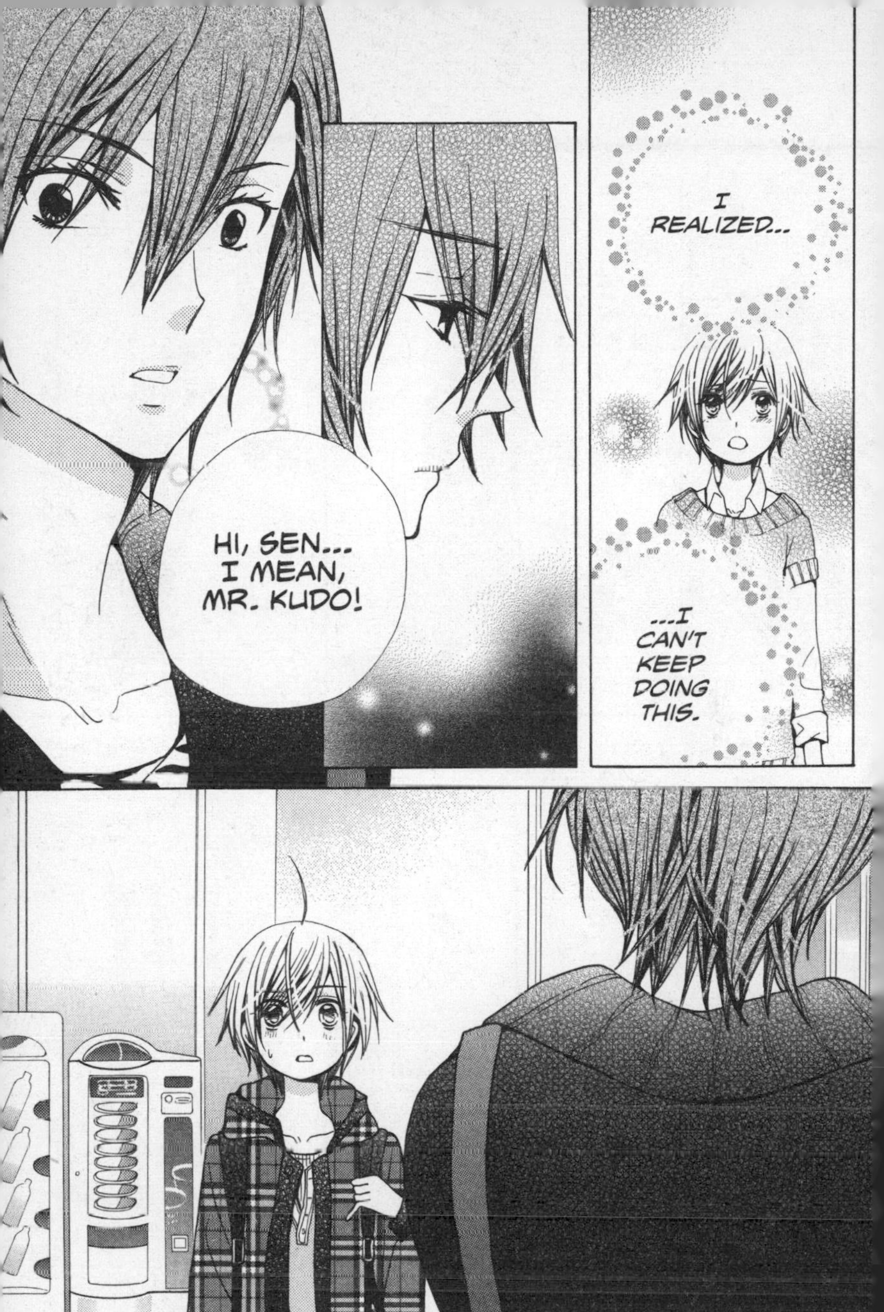
I REALIZED...
...I CAN'T KEEP DOING THIS.
HI, SEN... I MEAN, MR. KUDO!

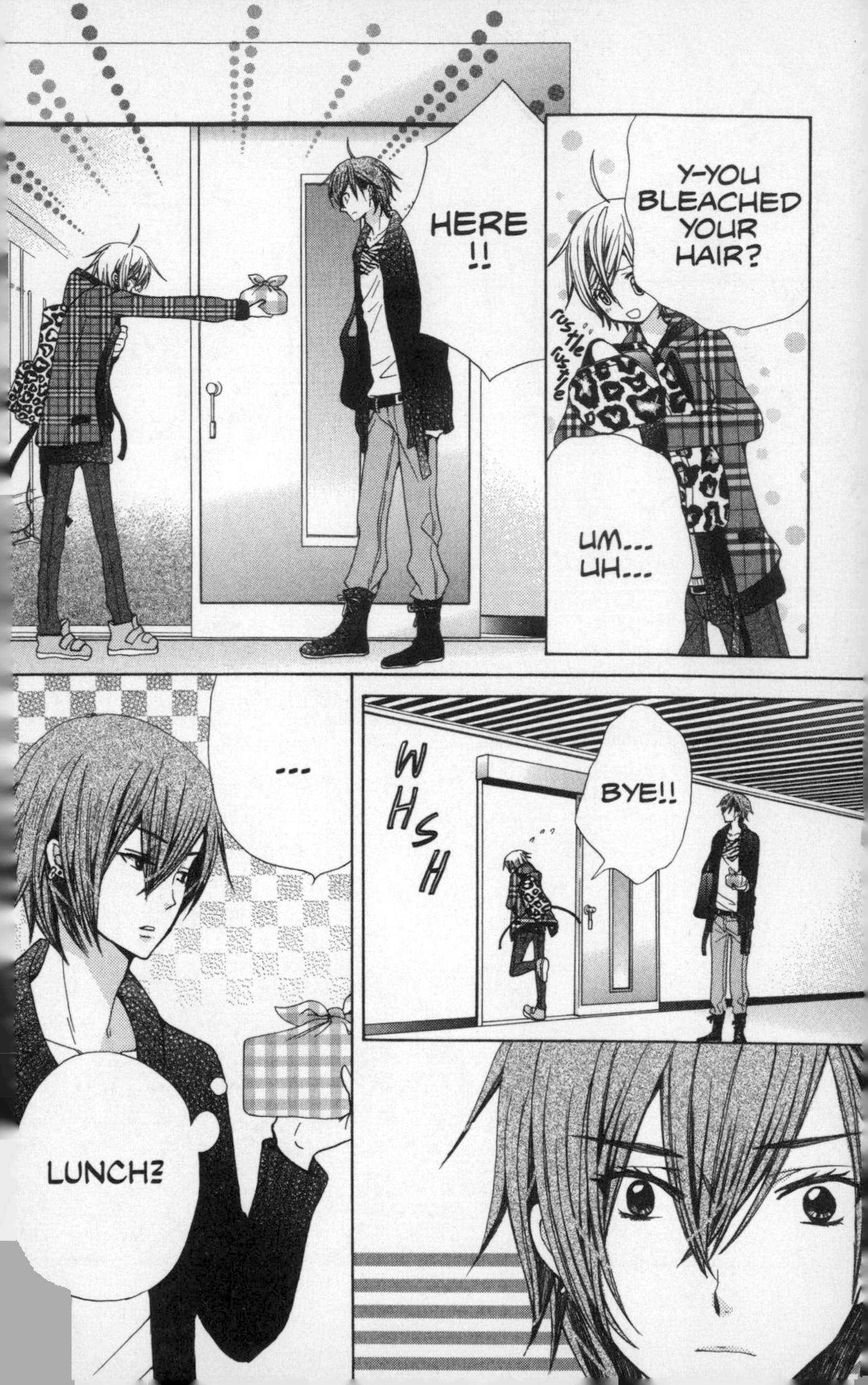
Y-YOU BLEACHED YOUR HAIR?
rustle rustle
UM... UH...
HERE !!
BYE!!
WHSH
...
LUNCH?

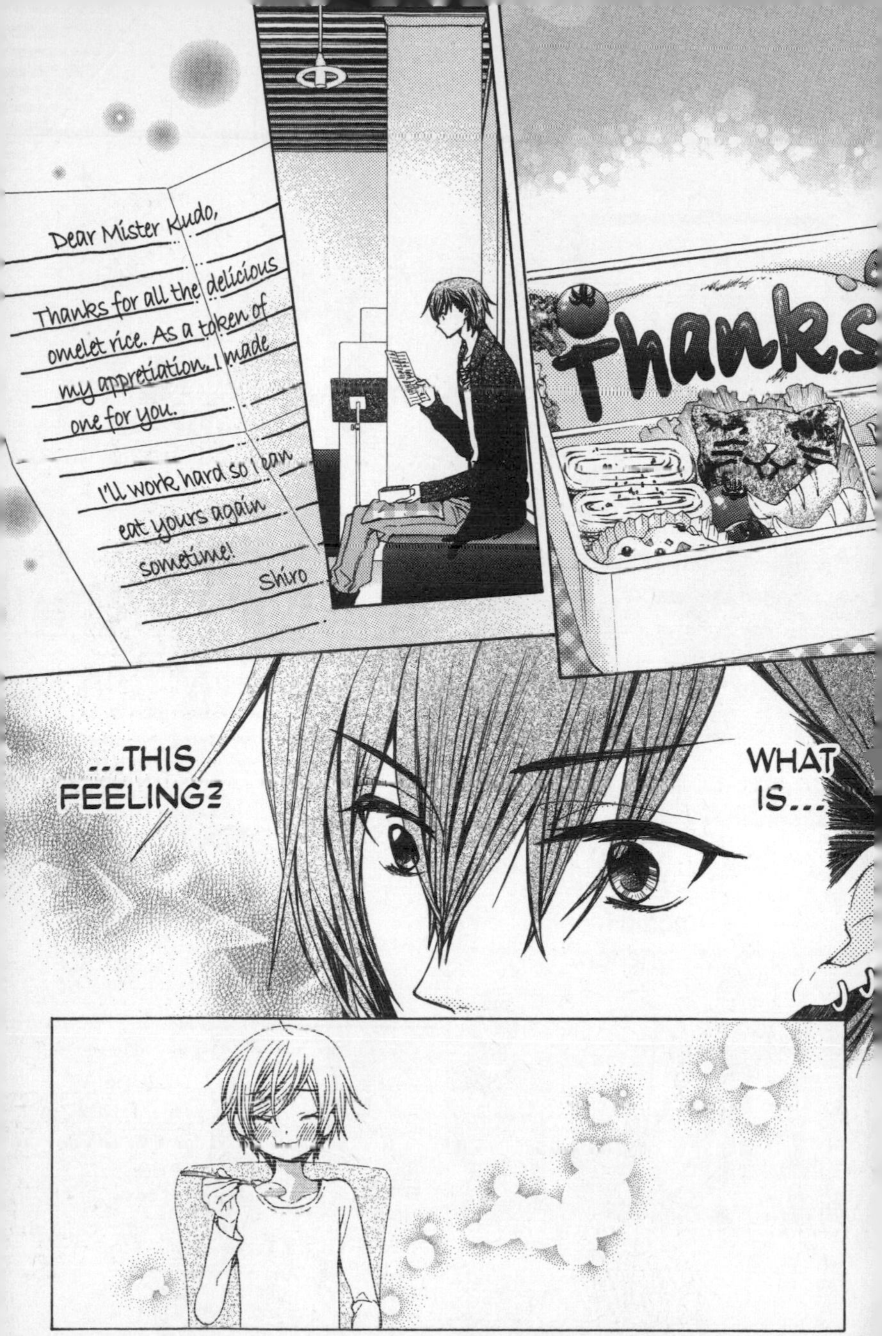
Thanks
Dear Mister Kudo,
Thanks for all the delicious omelet rice. As a token of my appretiation, I made one for you.
I'll work hard so I can eat yours again sometime!
Shiro
WHAT IS...
...THIS FEELING?

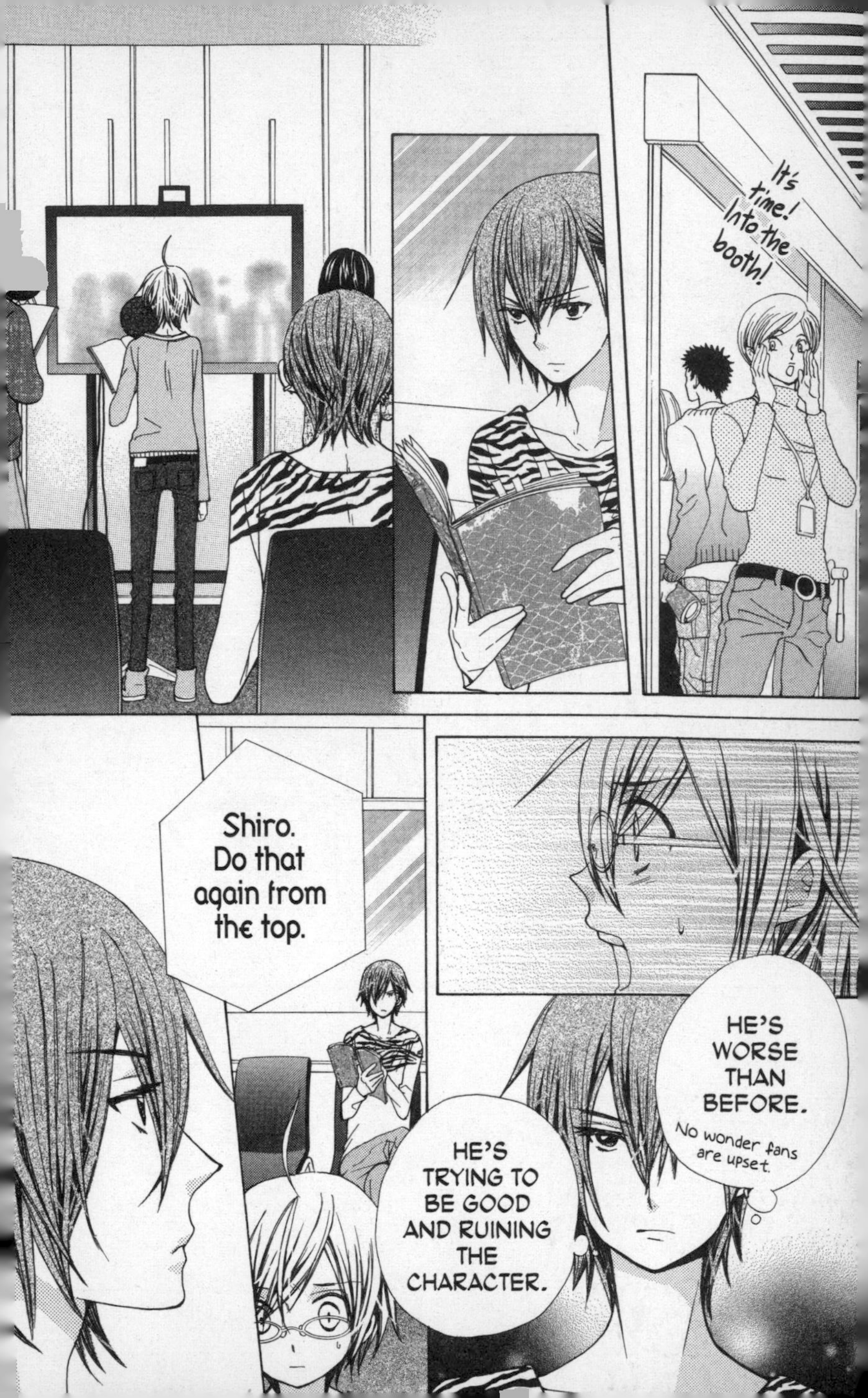
It's time! Into the booth!
Shiro. Do that again from the top.
HE'S WORSE THAN BEFORE.
No wonder fans are upset.
HE'S TRYING TO BE GOOD AND RUINING THE CHARACTER.

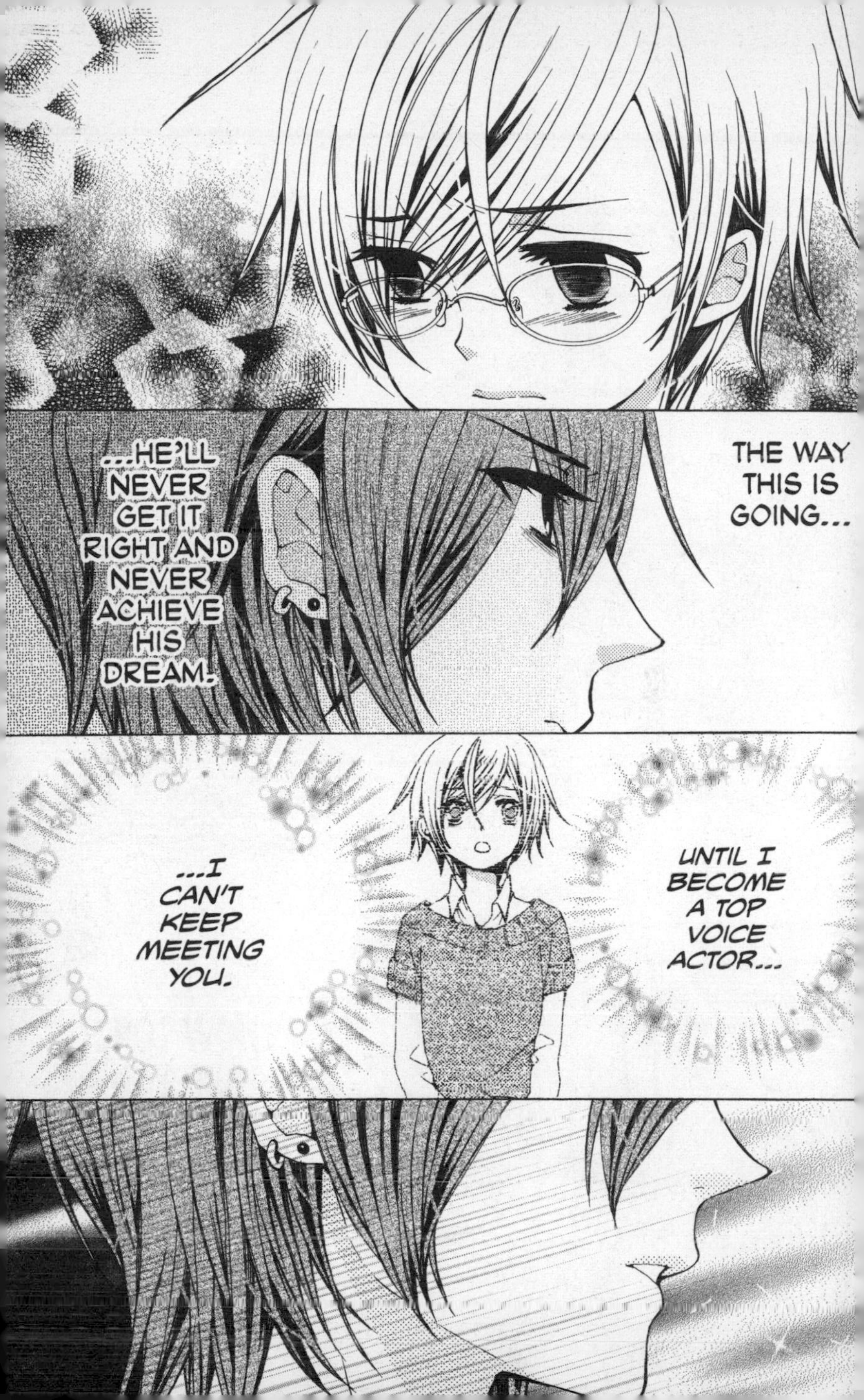
THE WAY THIS IS GOING...
...HE'LL NEVER GET IT RIGHT AND NEVER ACHIEVE HIS DREAM.
UNTIL I BECOME A TOP VOICE ACTOR...
...I CAN'T KEEP MEETING YOU.

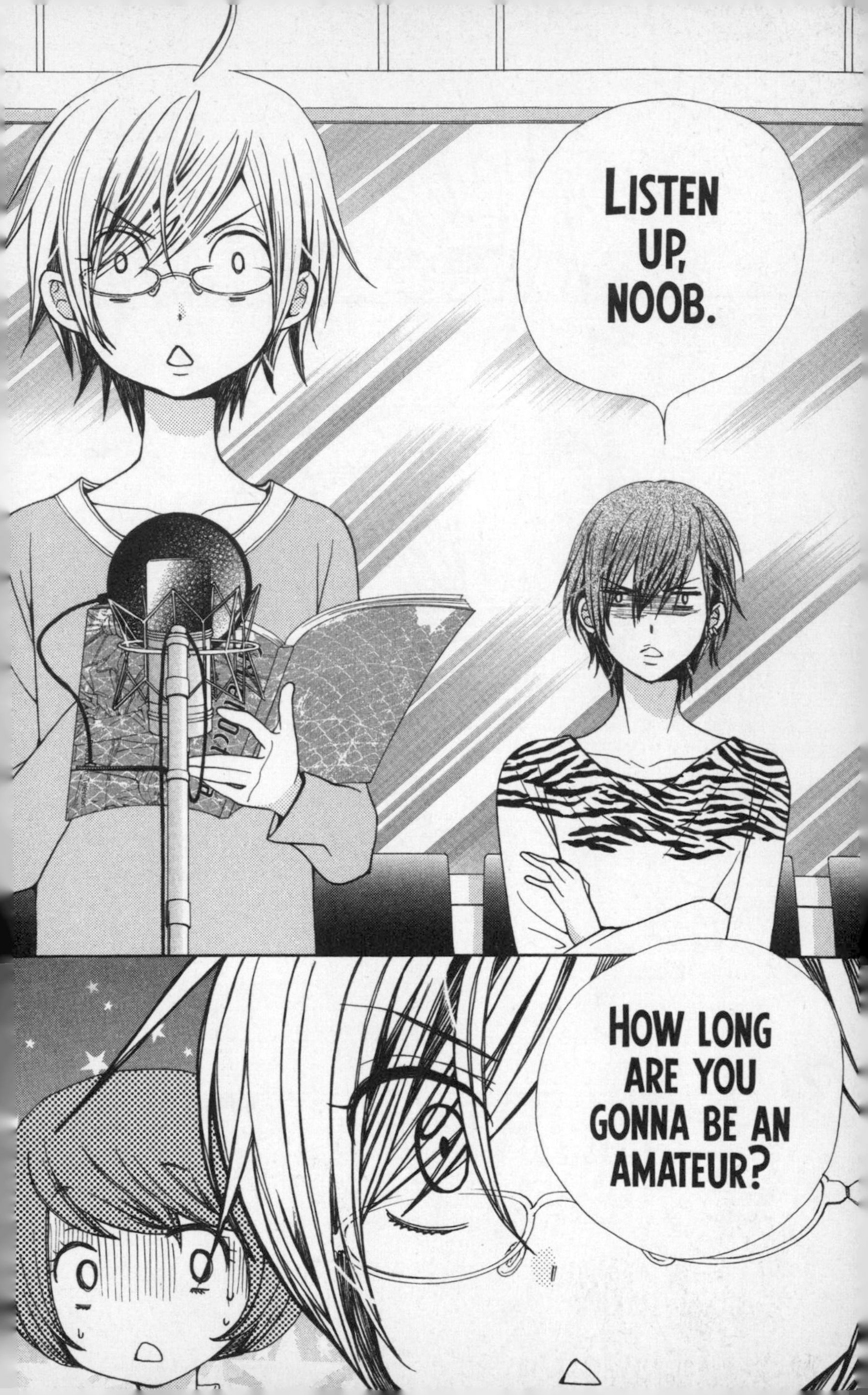
LISTEN UP, NOOB.
HOW LONG ARE YOU GONNA BE AN AMATEUR?

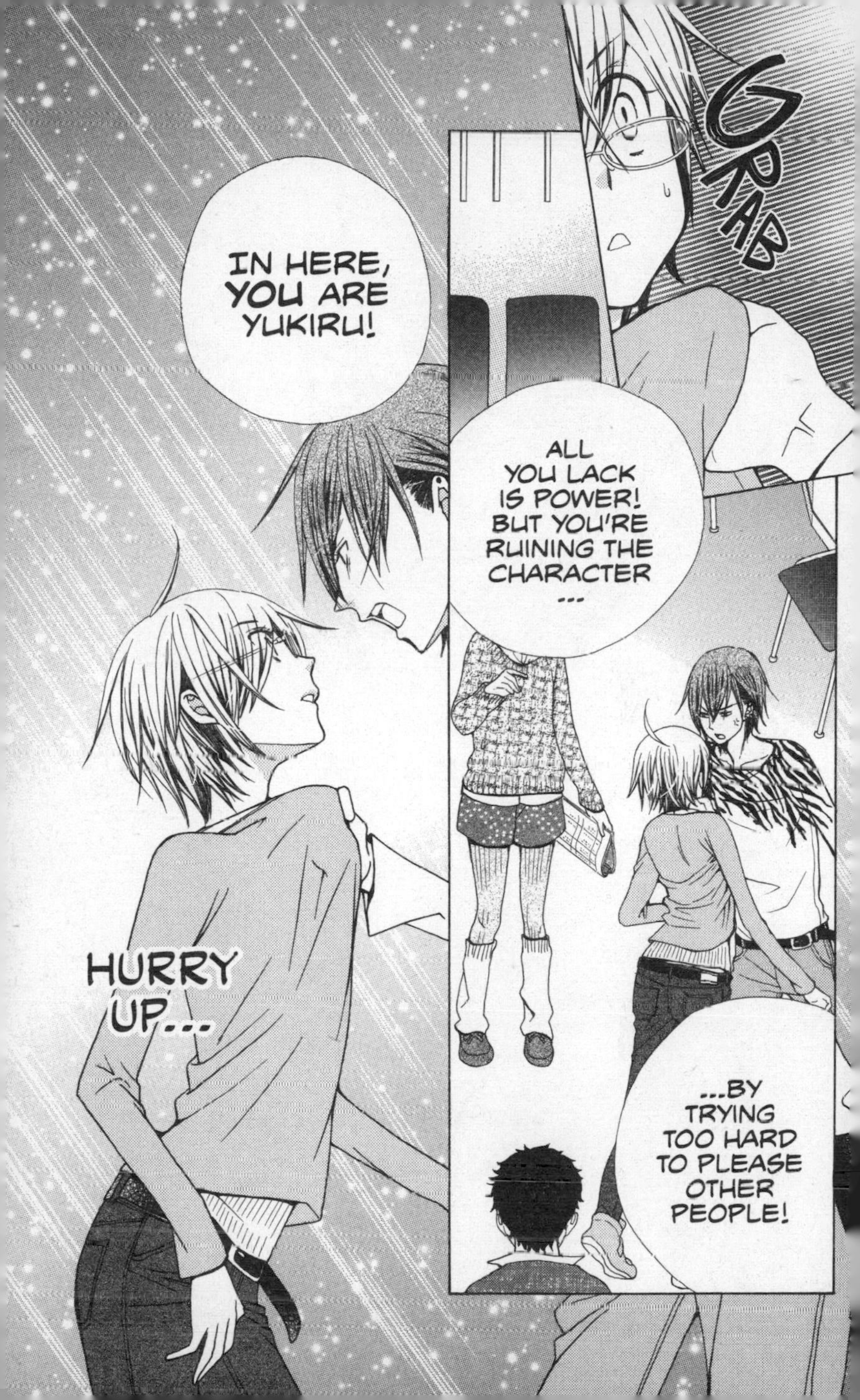
GRAB
ALL YOU LACK IS POWER! BUT YOU'RE RUINING THE CHARACTER ...
...BY TRYING TOO HARD TO PLEASE OTHER PEOPLE!
IN HERE, YOU ARE YUKIRU!
HURRY UP...

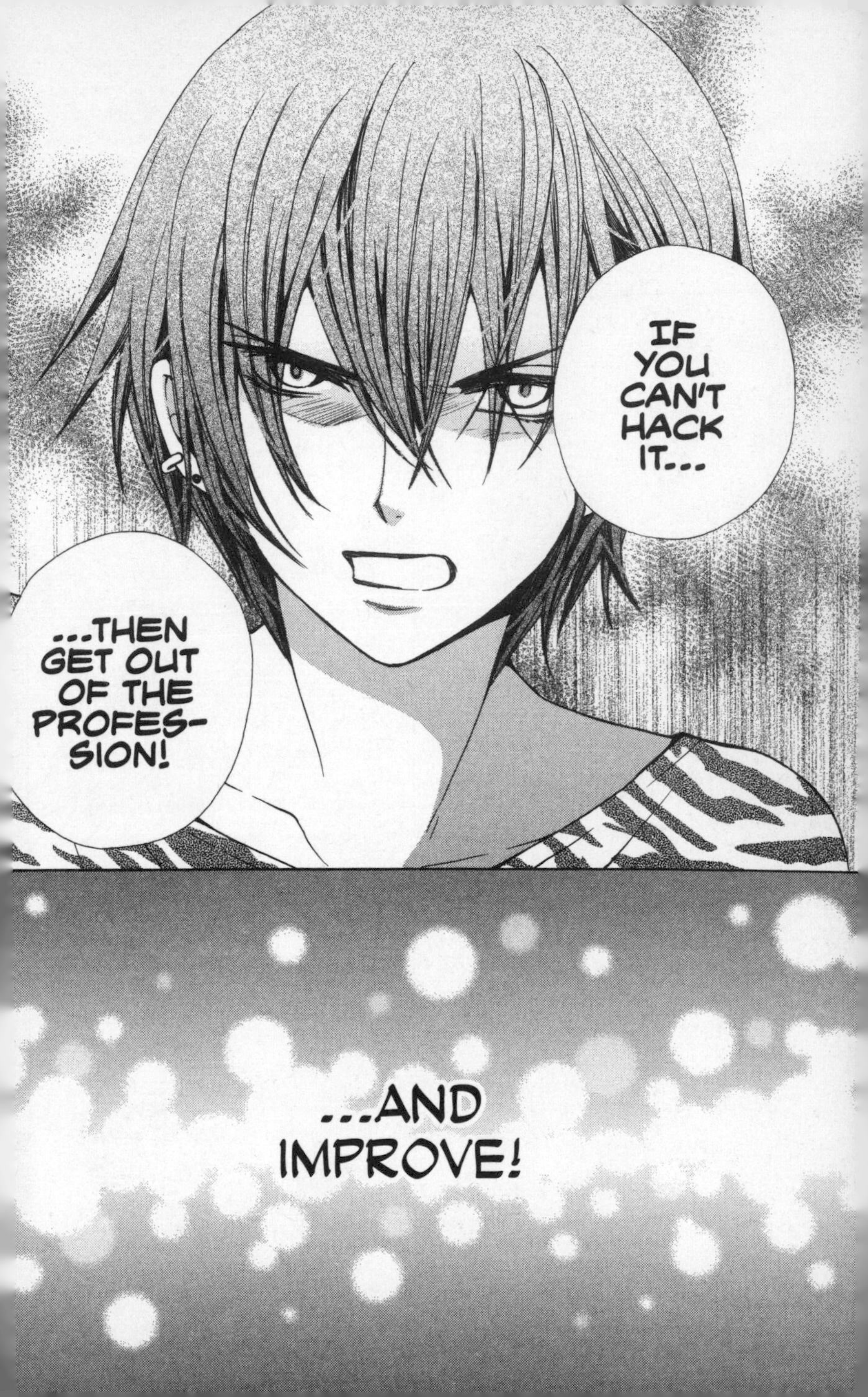
IF YOU CAN'T HACK IT...
...THEN GET OUT OF THE PROFES-SION!
...AND IMPROVE!

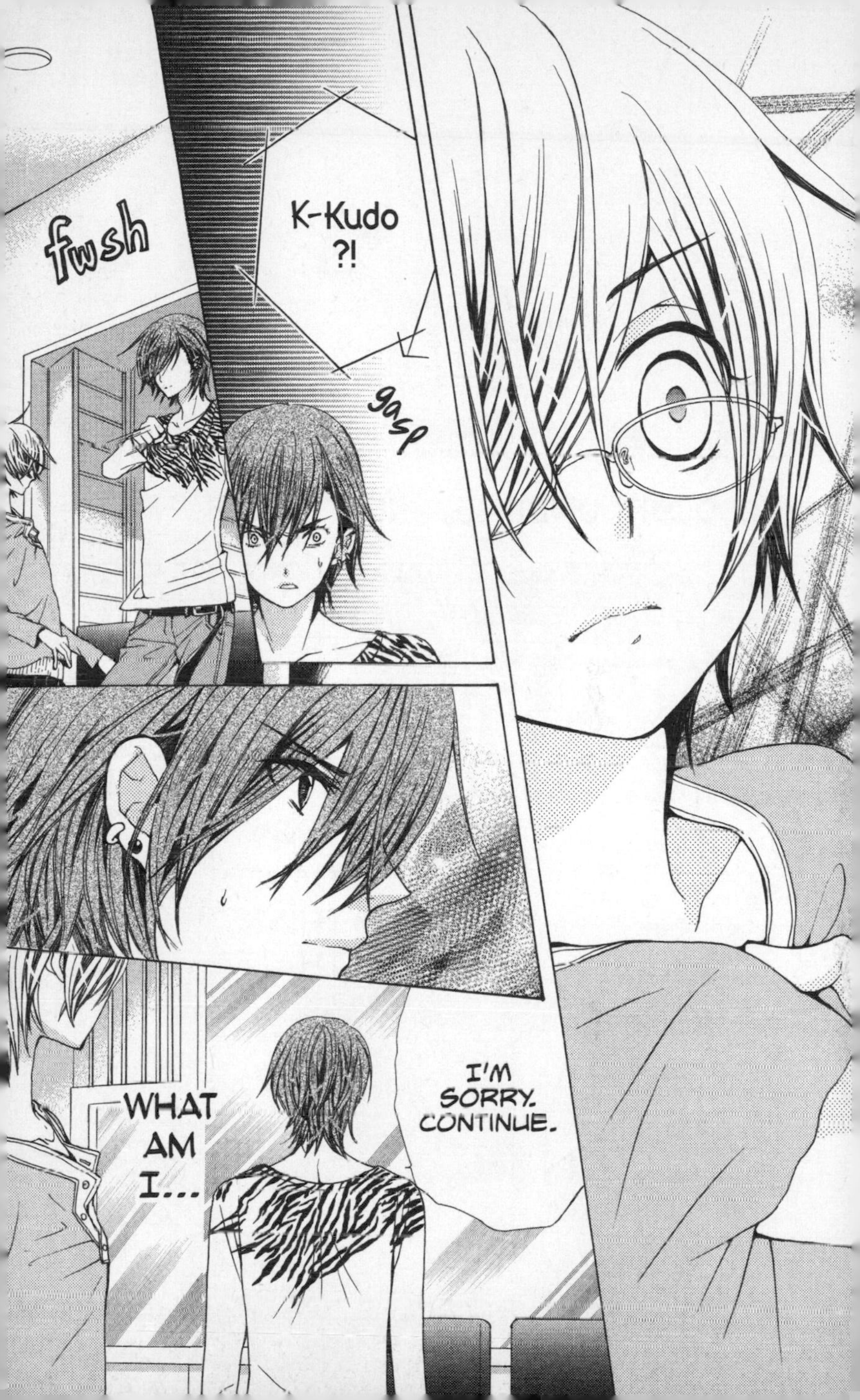
K-Kudo ?!
fwsh
gasp
I'M SORRY. CONTINUE.
WHAT AM I...

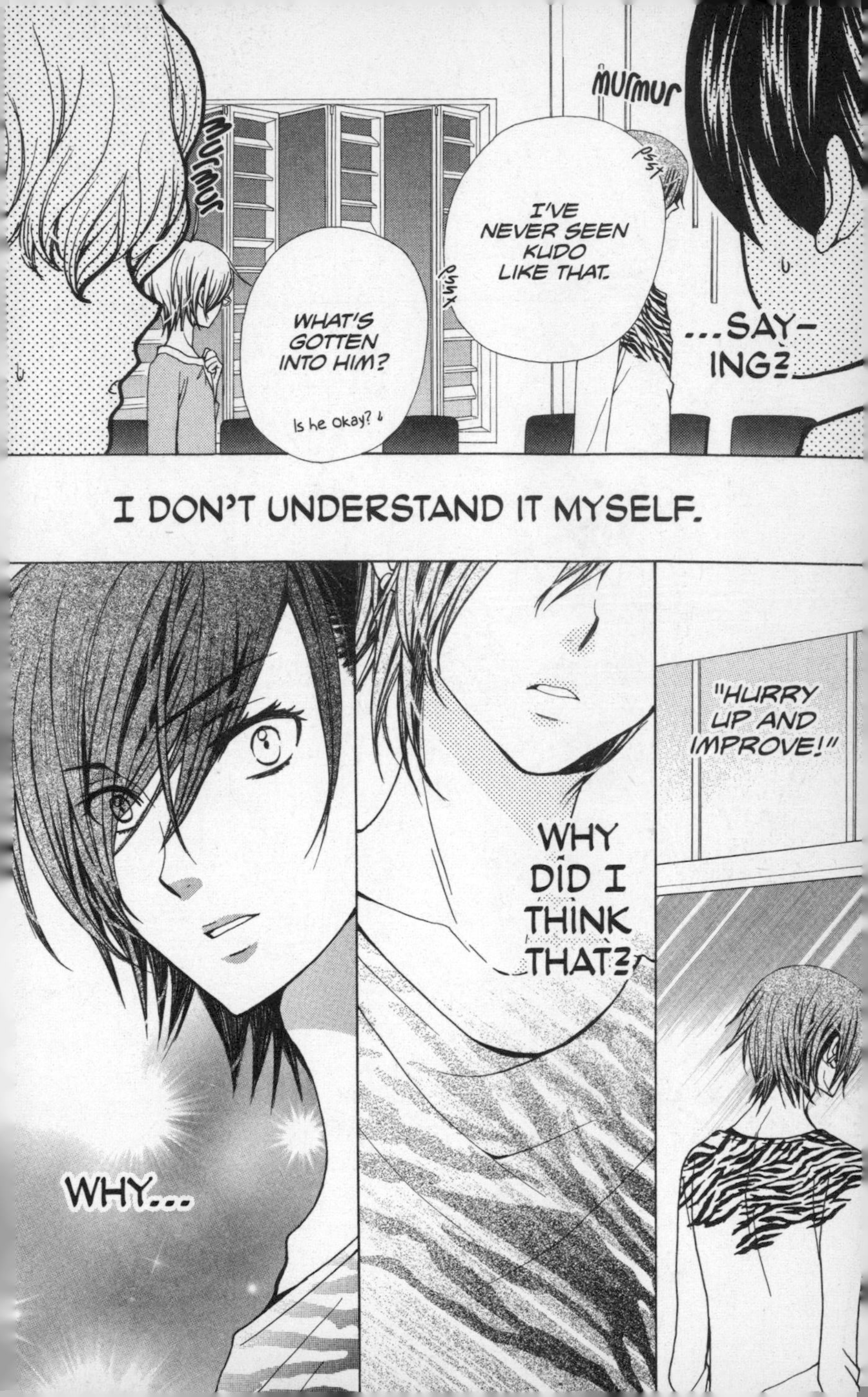
MURMUR
...SAY-ING?
PSST
I'VE NEVER SEEN KUDO LIKE THAT.
PSST
WHAT'S GOTTEN INTO HIM?
Is he okay?
MURMUR
I DON'T UNDERSTAND IT MYSELF.
"HURRY UP AND IMPROVE!"
WHY DID I THINK THAT?
WHY...

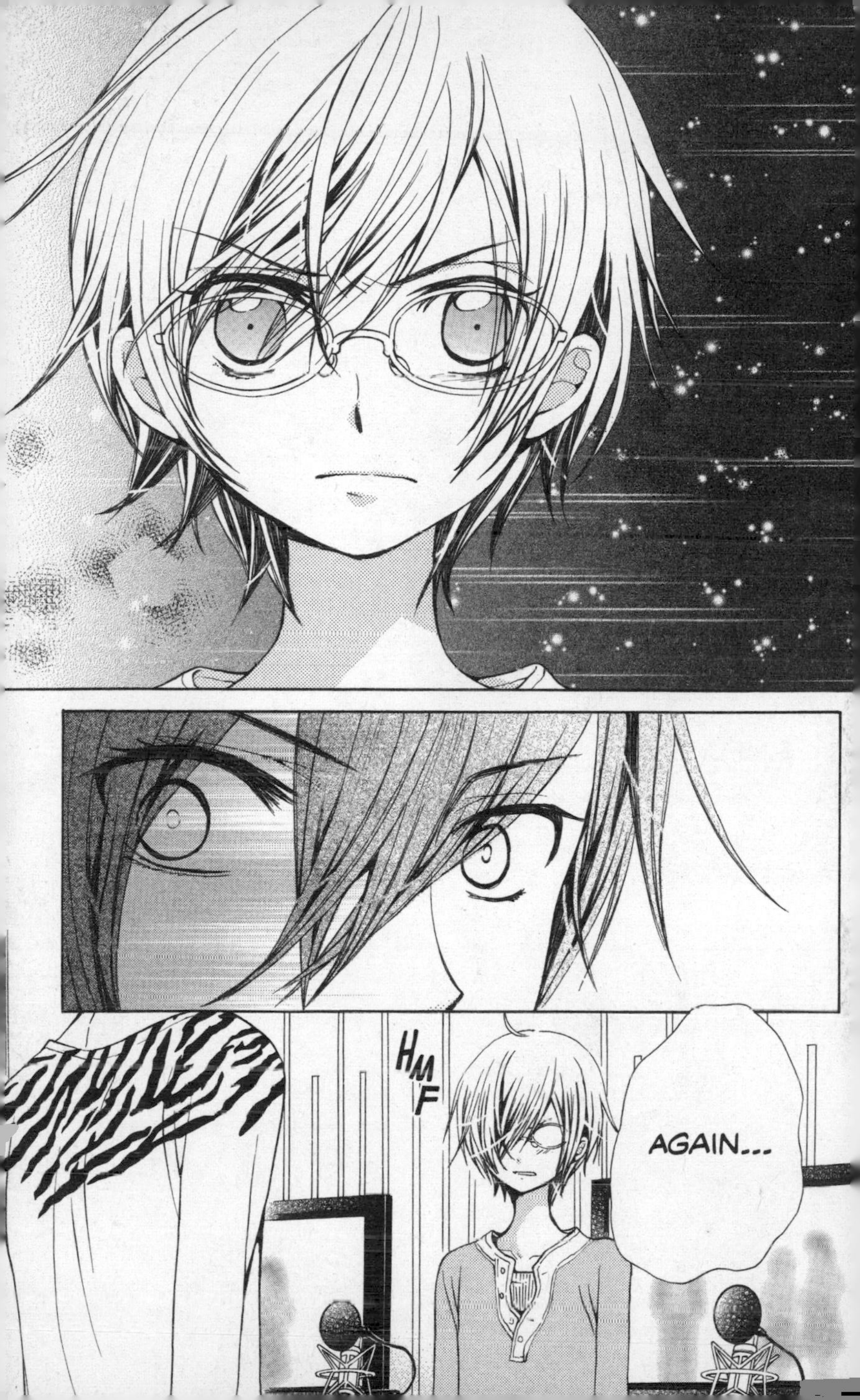
AGAIN...
HMF

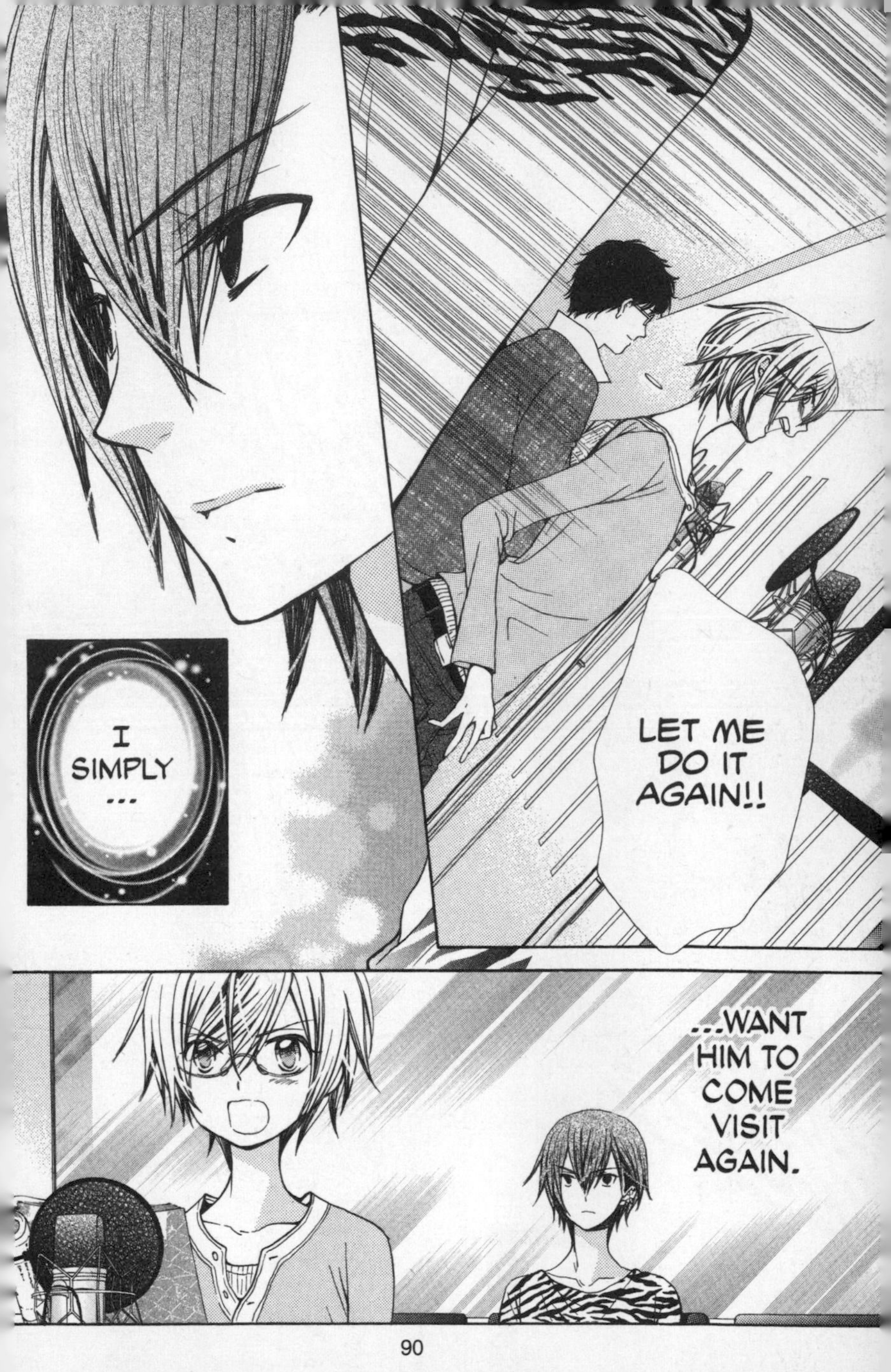
LET ME DO IT AGAIN!!
I SIMPLY ...
...WANT HIM TO COME VISIT AGAIN.

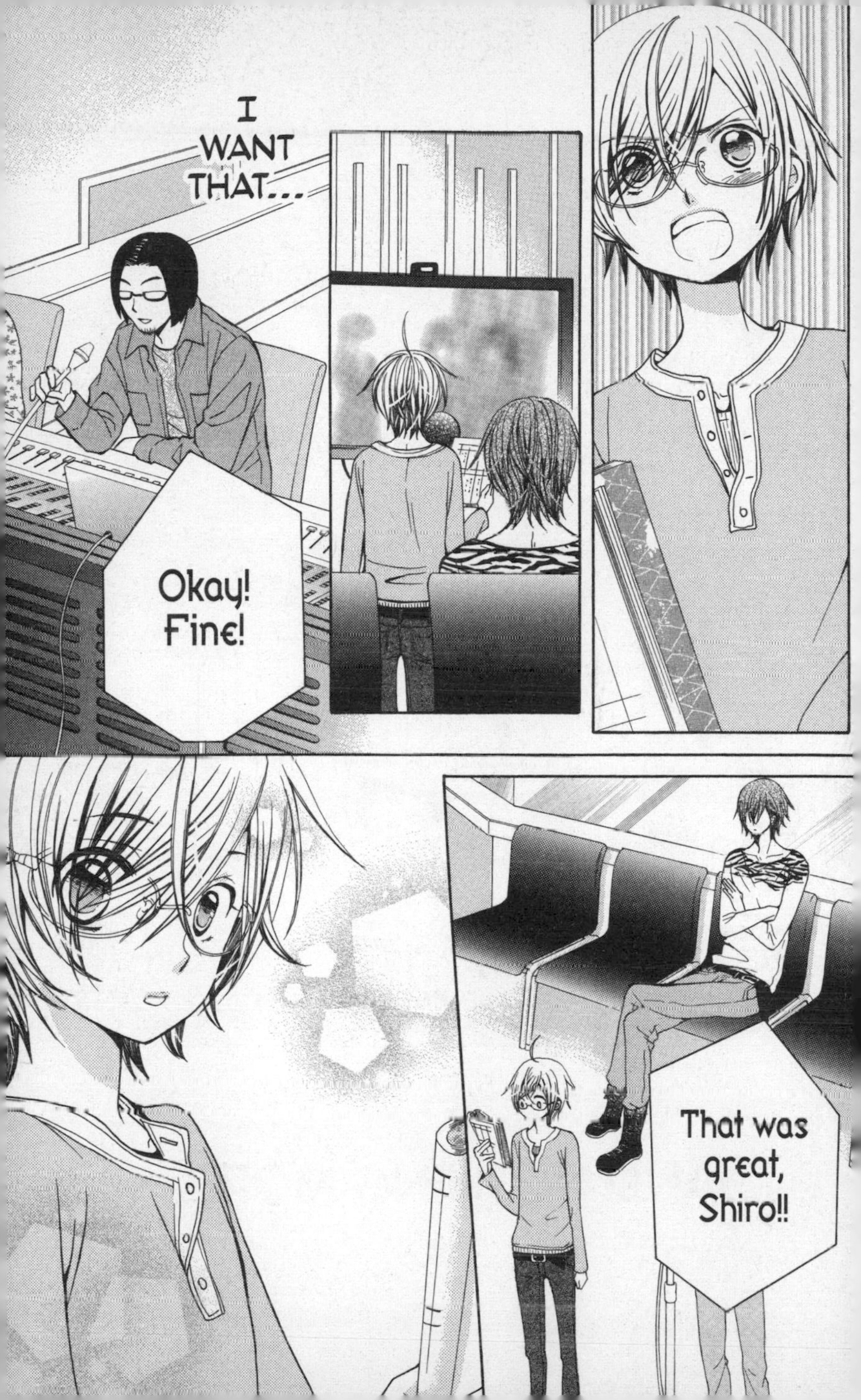
I WANT THAT...
Okay! Fine!
That was great, Shiro!!

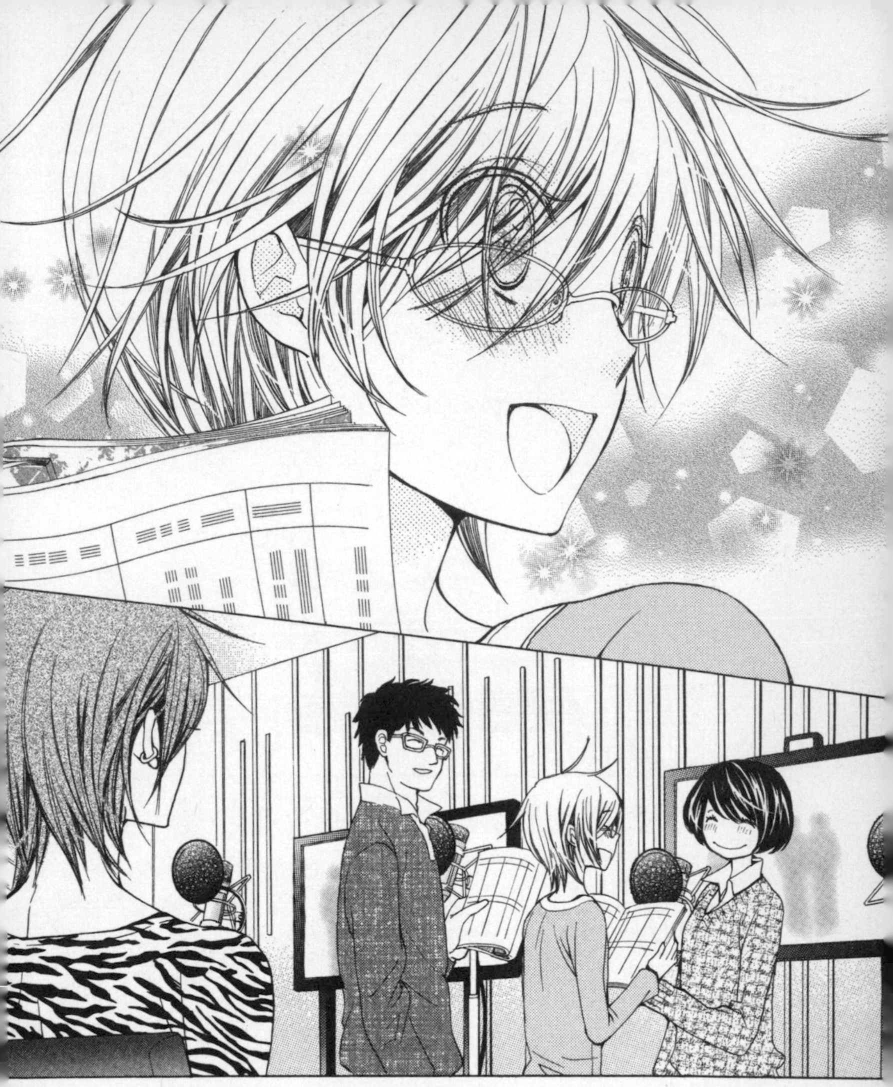

...AND NOTHING MORE.

Chapter 56

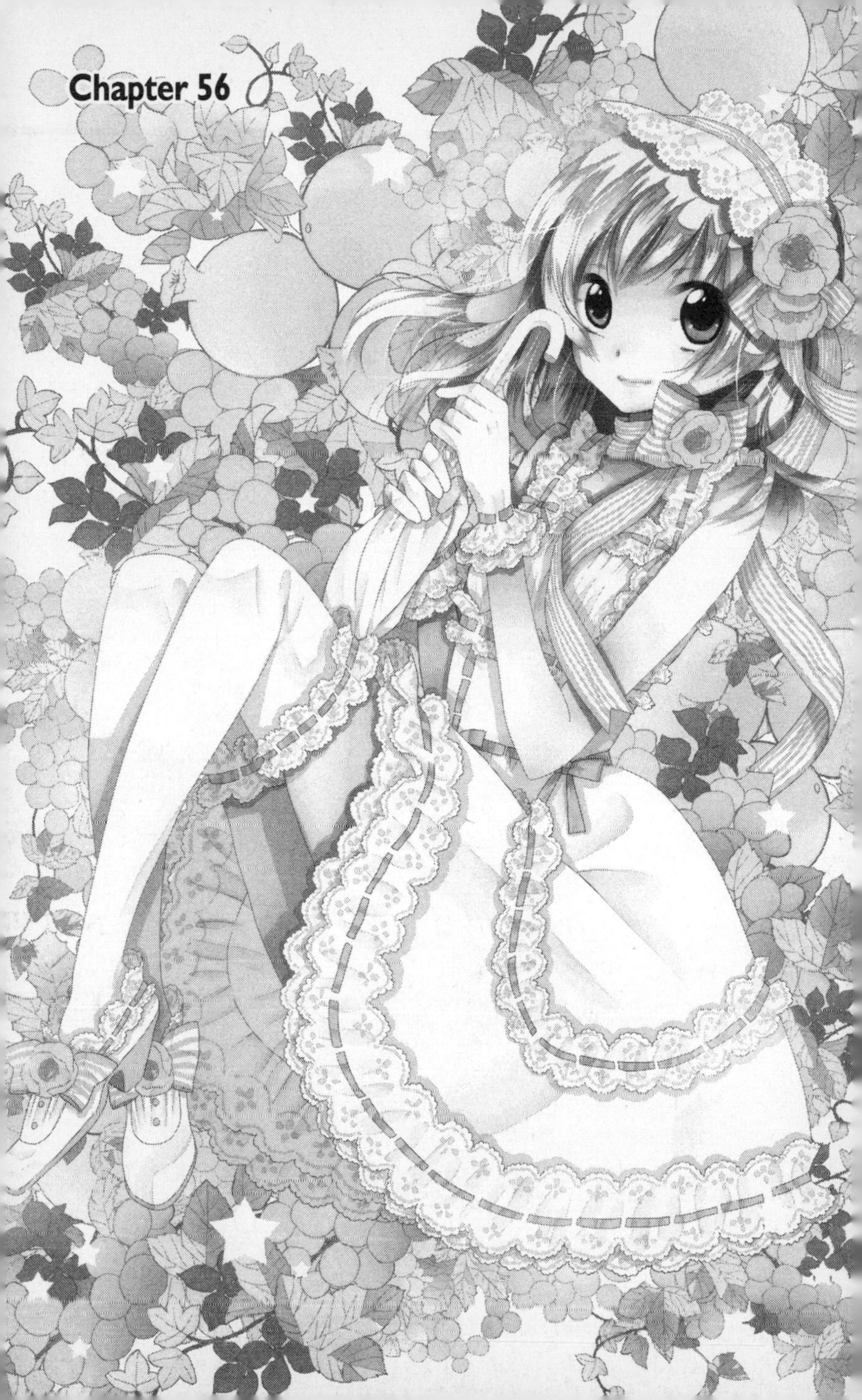

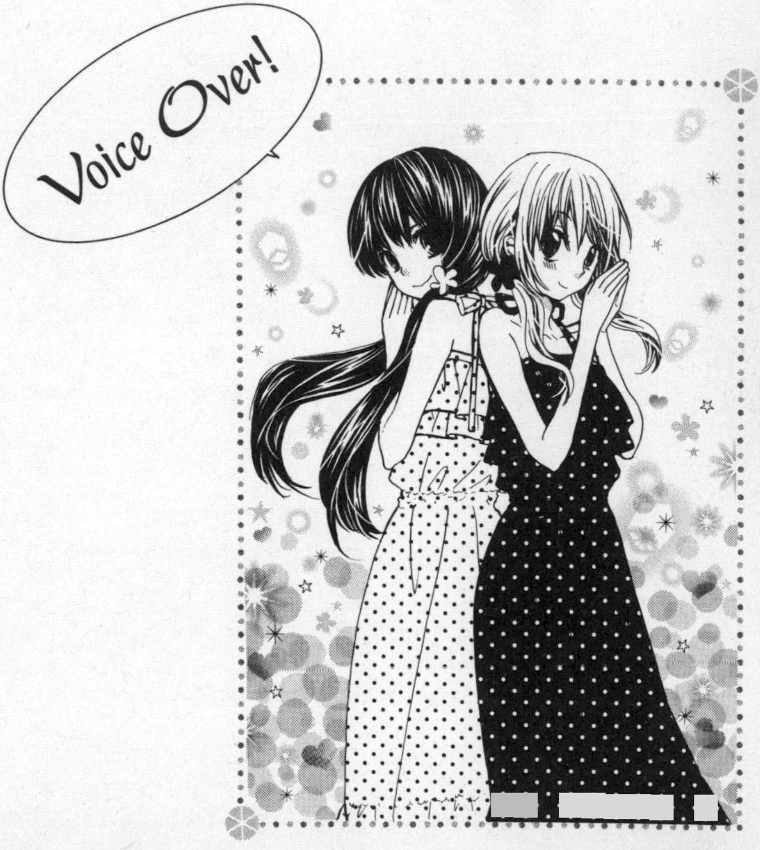
Voice Over!

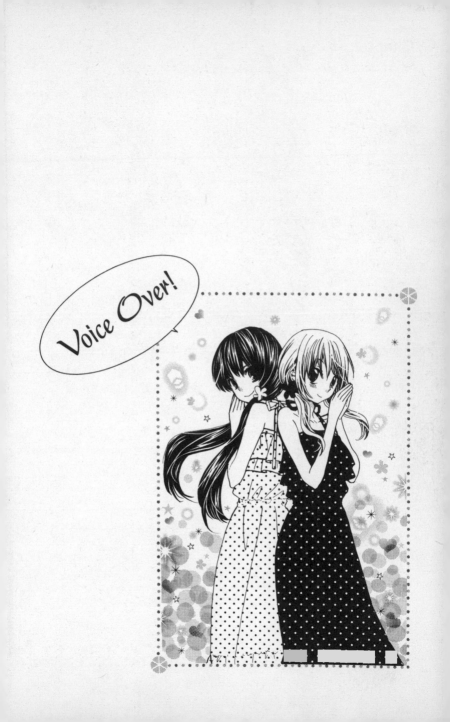

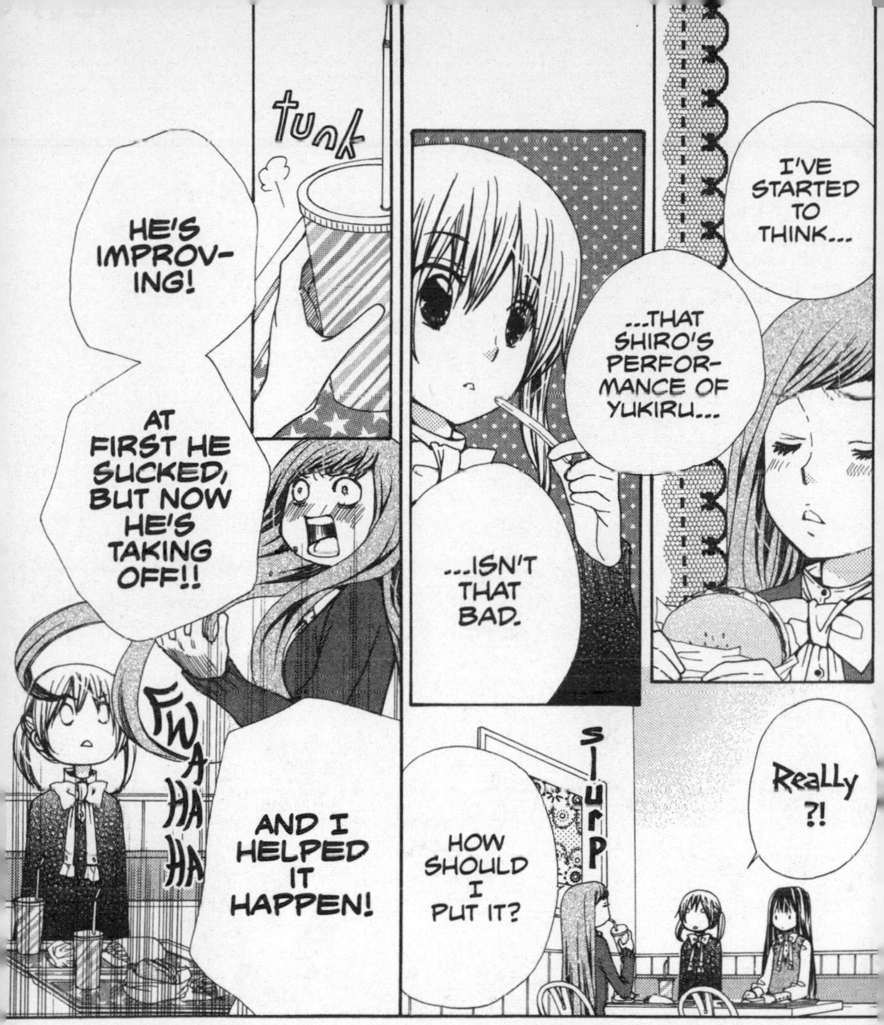
I'VE STARTED TO THINK...
...THAT SHIRO'S PERFORMANCE OF YUKIRU...
...ISN'T THAT BAD.
Really?!
SLURP
HOW SHOULD I PUT IT?
tunk
HE'S IMPROVING!
AT FIRST HE SUCKED, BUT NOW HE'S TAKING OFF!!
FWAHAHAHA
AND I HELPED IT HAPPEN!

• Fireworks •

Once each year in the summer, we all set off fireworks during work. I say in the summer, but it's often in October. When we do, we're all smiles. We smile so much it's scary. We'll do it again this year. It's a blast!

D

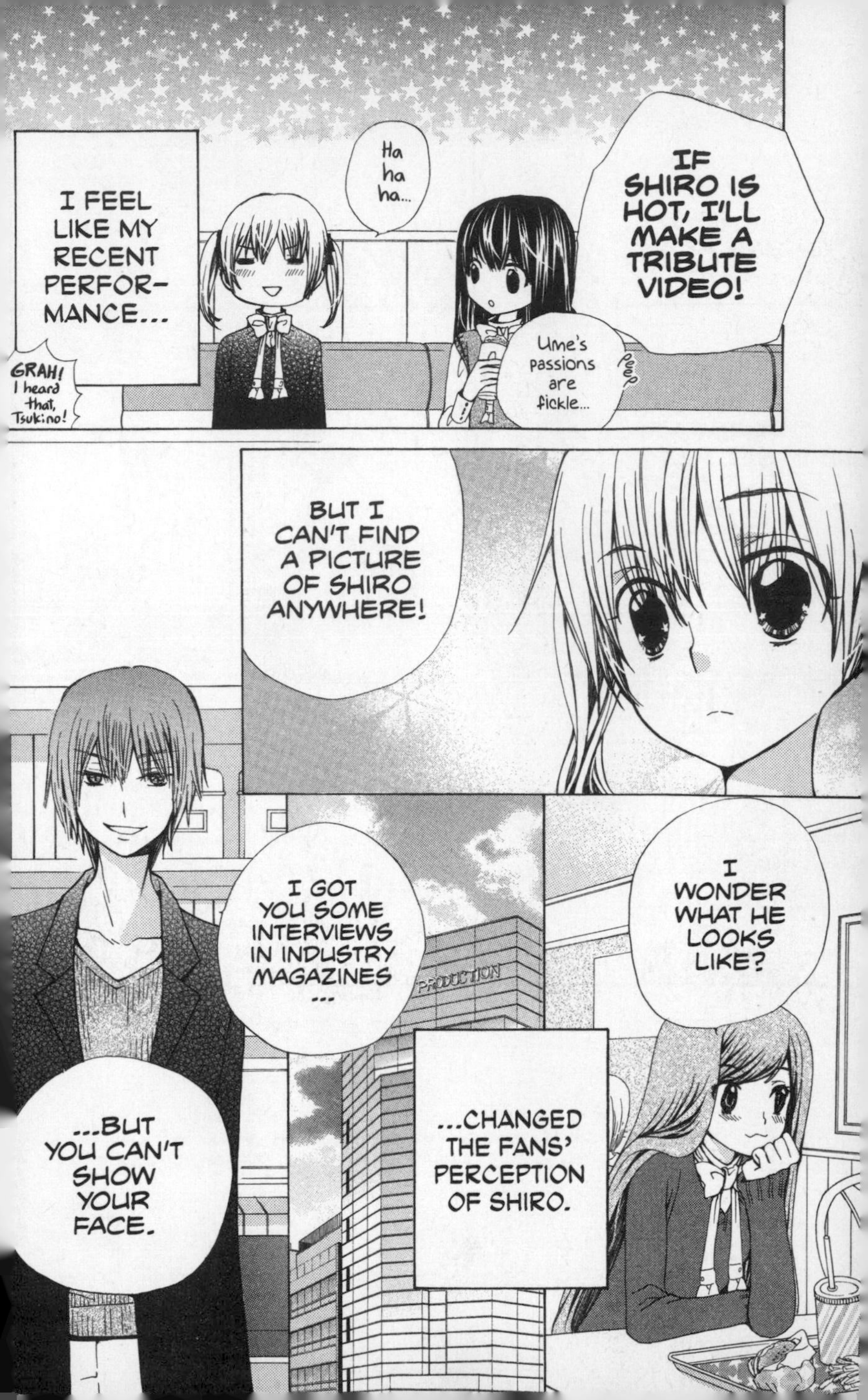
IF SHIRO IS HOT, I'LL MAKE A TRIBUTE VIDEO!
Ha ha ha...
Ume's passions are fickle...
peep
I FEEL LIKE MY RECENT PERFORMANCE...
GRAH! I heard that, Tsukino!
BUT I CAN'T FIND A PICTURE OF SHIRO ANYWHERE!
I WONDER WHAT HE LOOKS LIKE?
...CHANGED THE FANS' PERCEPTION OF SHIRO.
PRODUCTION
I GOT YOU SOME INTERVIEWS IN INDUSTRY MAGAZINES...
...BUT YOU CAN'T SHOW YOUR FACE.

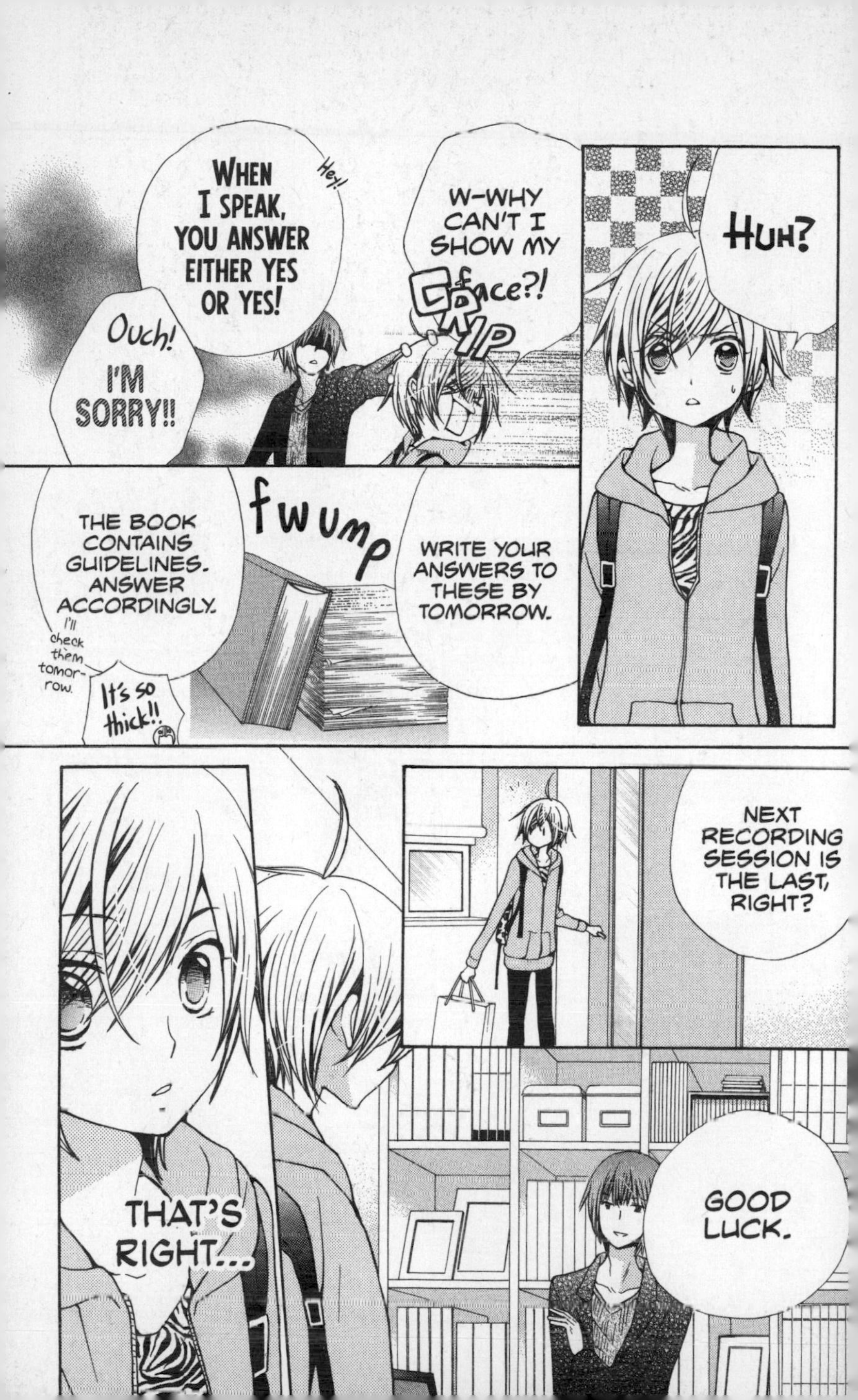
HUH?
W-WHY CAN'T I SHOW MY face?!
GRIP
Hey!
WHEN I SPEAK, YOU ANSWER EITHER YES OR YES!
Ouch! I'M SORRY!!
WRITE YOUR ANSWERS TO THESE BY TOMORROW.
fwump
THE BOOK CONTAINS GUIDELINES. ANSWER ACCORDINGLY.
I'll check them tomor-row.
It's so thick!!
NEXT RECORDING SESSION IS THE LAST, RIGHT?
GOOD LUCK.
THAT'S RIGHT...

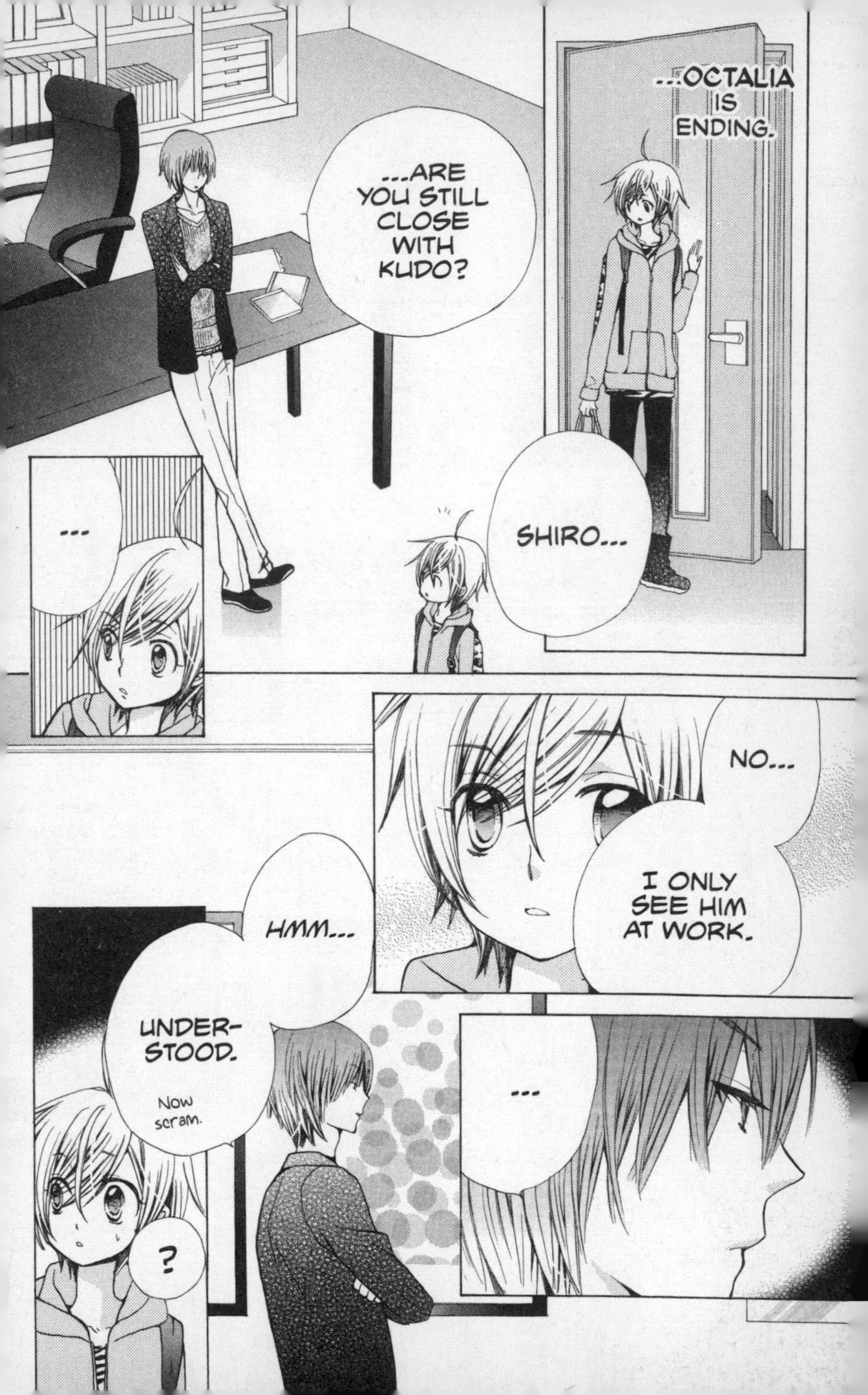
...OCTALIA IS ENDING.
...ARE YOU STILL CLOSE WITH KUDO?
SHIRO...
...
NO...
I ONLY SEE HIM AT WORK.
HMM...
...
UNDER-STOOD.
Now scram.
?

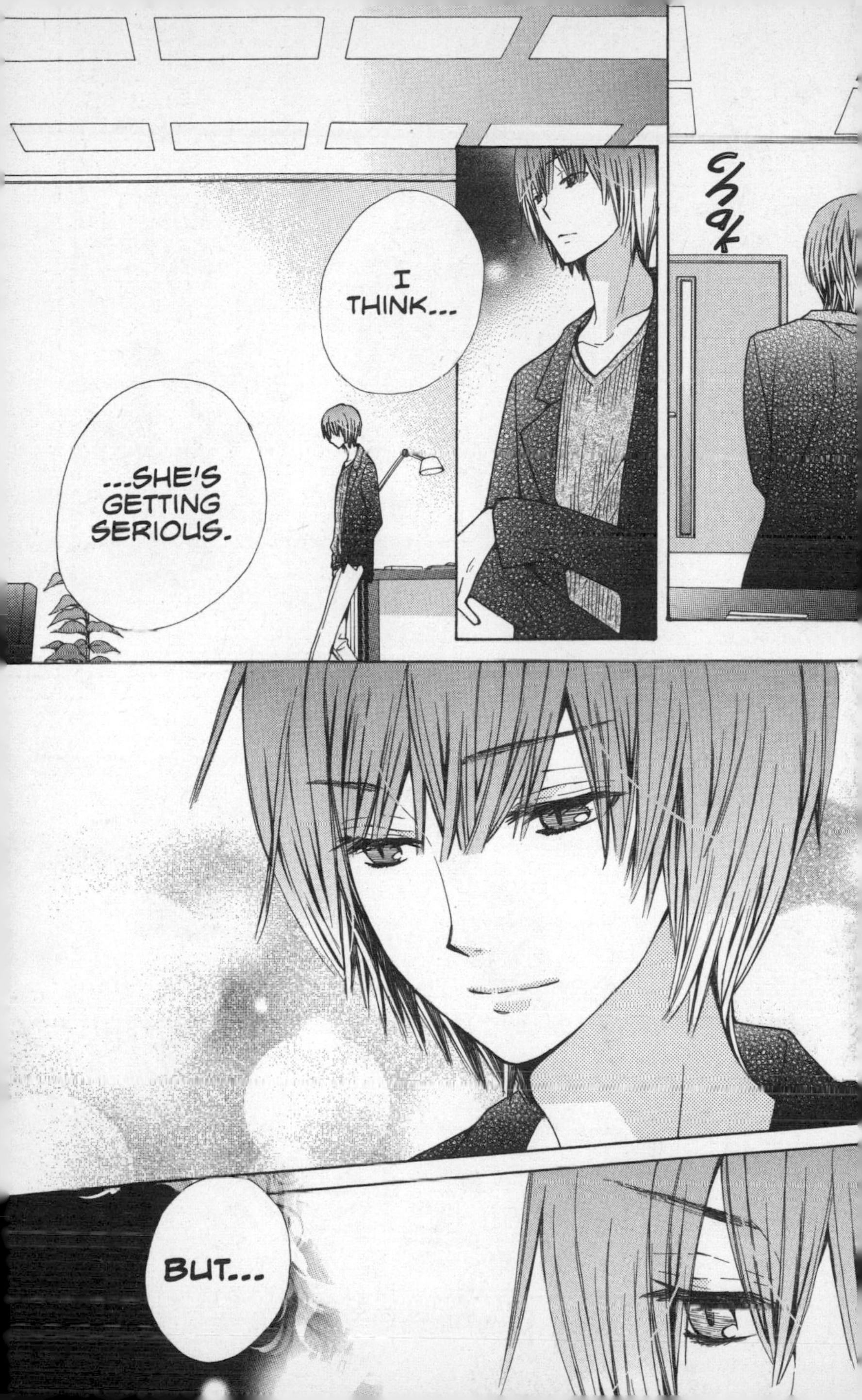
CHAK
I THINK...
...SHE'S GETTING SERIOUS.
BUT...

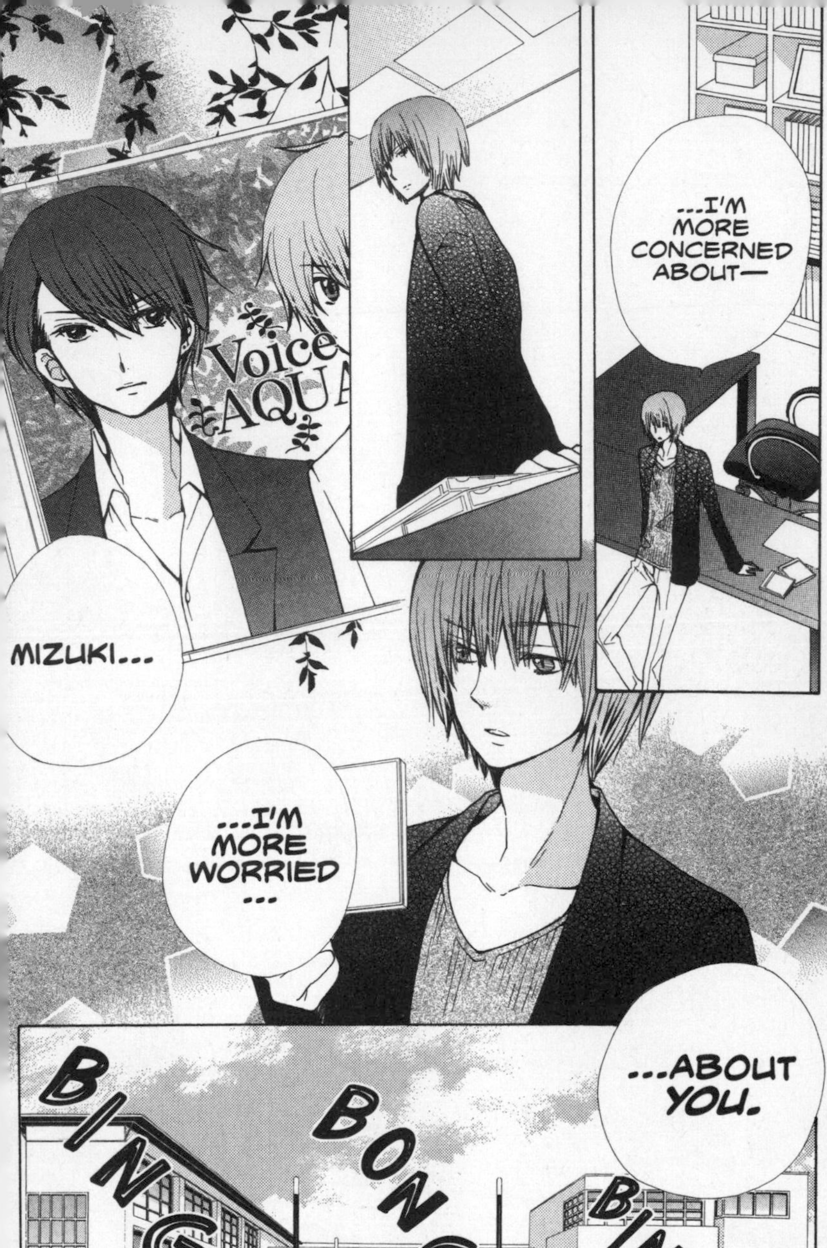
...I'M MORE CONCERNED ABOUT—
MIZUKI...
...I'M MORE WORRIED ...
...ABOUT YOU.
BING
BONG
BING

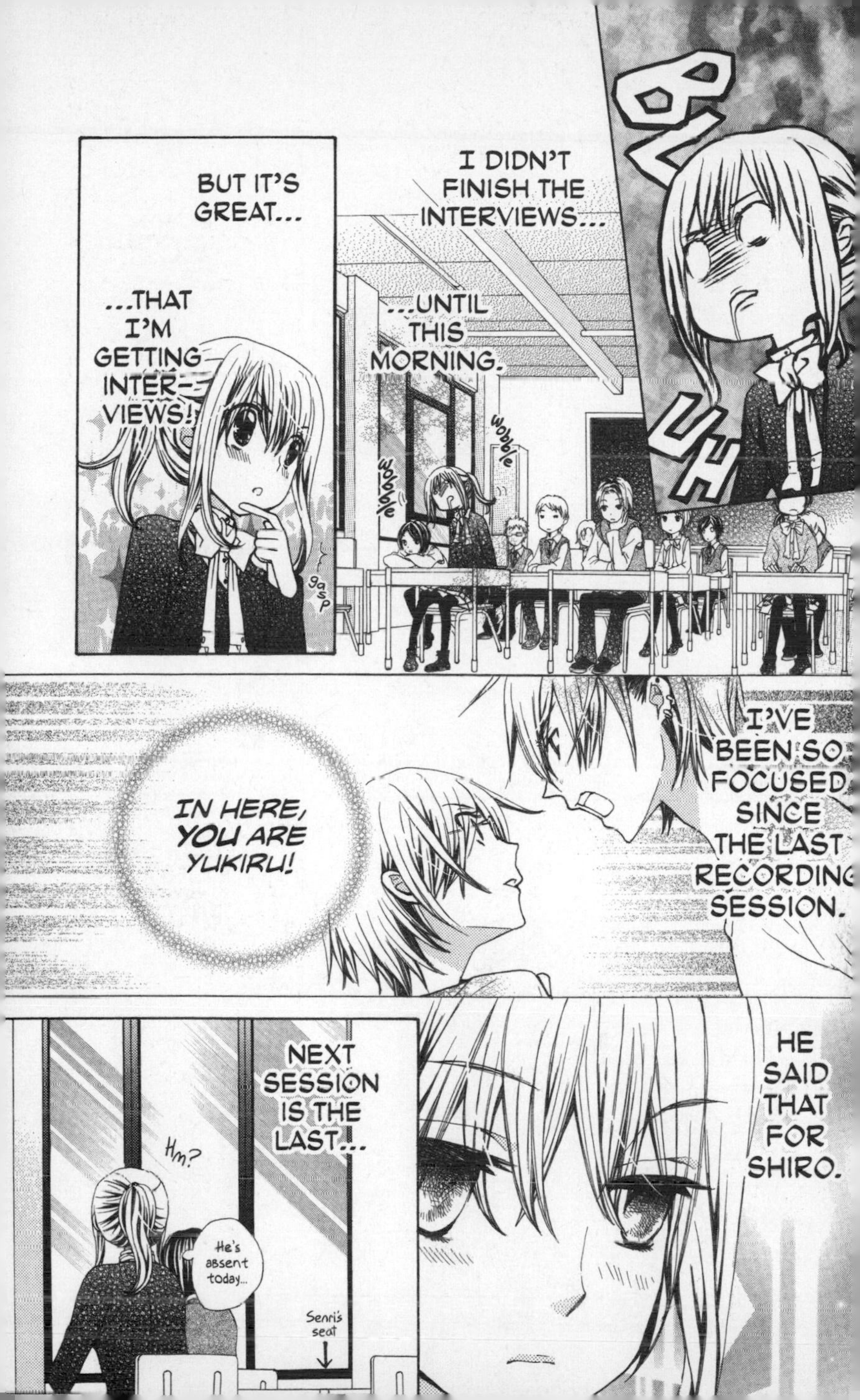
BLUH
I DIDN'T FINISH THE INTERVIEWS...
...UNTIL THIS MORNING.
wobble
wobble
BUT IT'S GREAT...
...THAT I'M GETTING INTERVIEWS!
gasp
I'VE BEEN SO FOCUSED SINCE THE LAST RECORDING SESSION.
IN HERE, YOU ARE YUKIRU!
HE SAID THAT FOR SHIRO.
NEXT SESSION IS THE LAST...
Hm?
He's absent today...
Senri's seat

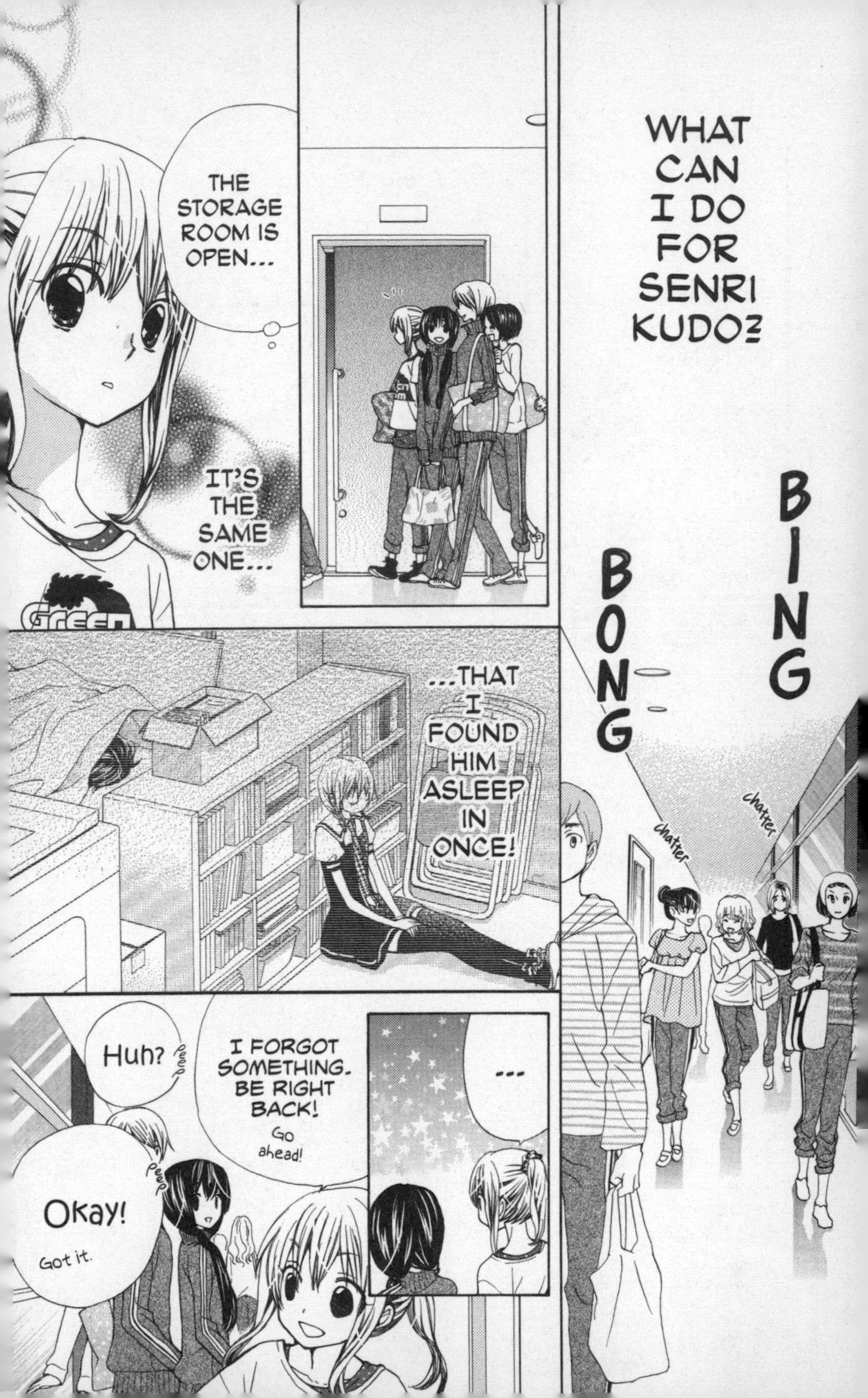
WHAT CAN I DO FOR SENRI KUDO?
BING
BONG
chatter
chatter
THE STORAGE ROOM IS OPEN...
IT'S THE SAME ONE...
...THAT I FOUND HIM ASLEEP IN ONCE!
...
I FORGOT SOMETHING. BE RIGHT BACK!
Go ahead!
Huh?
peer
Okay!
Got it.
peer

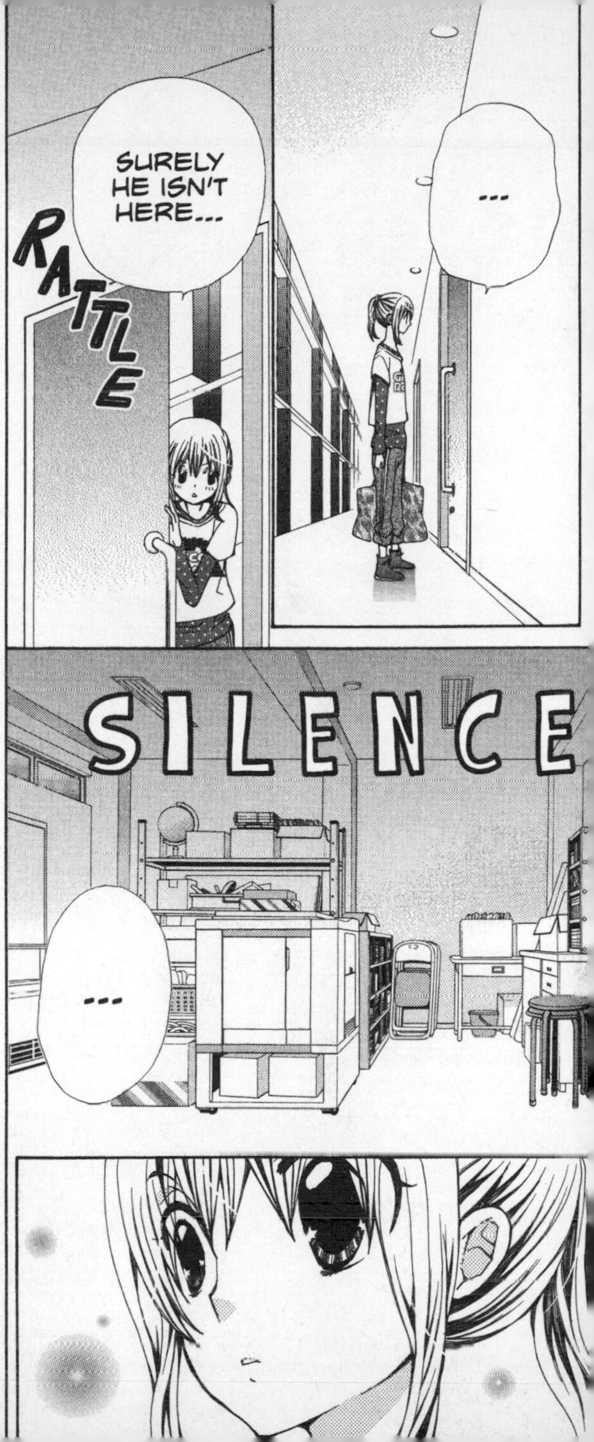
...
SURELY HE ISN'T HERE...
RATTLE
SILENCE
...

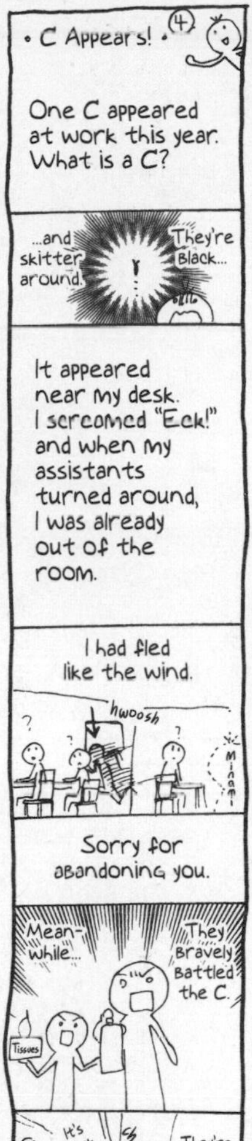
• C Appears! • 4
One C appeared at work this year. What is a C?
They're Black...
...and skitter around.
It appeared near my desk. I screamed "Eek!" and when my assistants turned around, I was already out of the room.
I had fled like the wind.
hwoosh
Minami
Sorry for abandoning you.
They Bravely Battled the C.
Meanwhile...
Tissues
They're so cool! ♡
chatter
It's weak in the light!
chatter
The final spotlight of its life! ☆
huff
huff
...I listened from the stairs. Sorry.

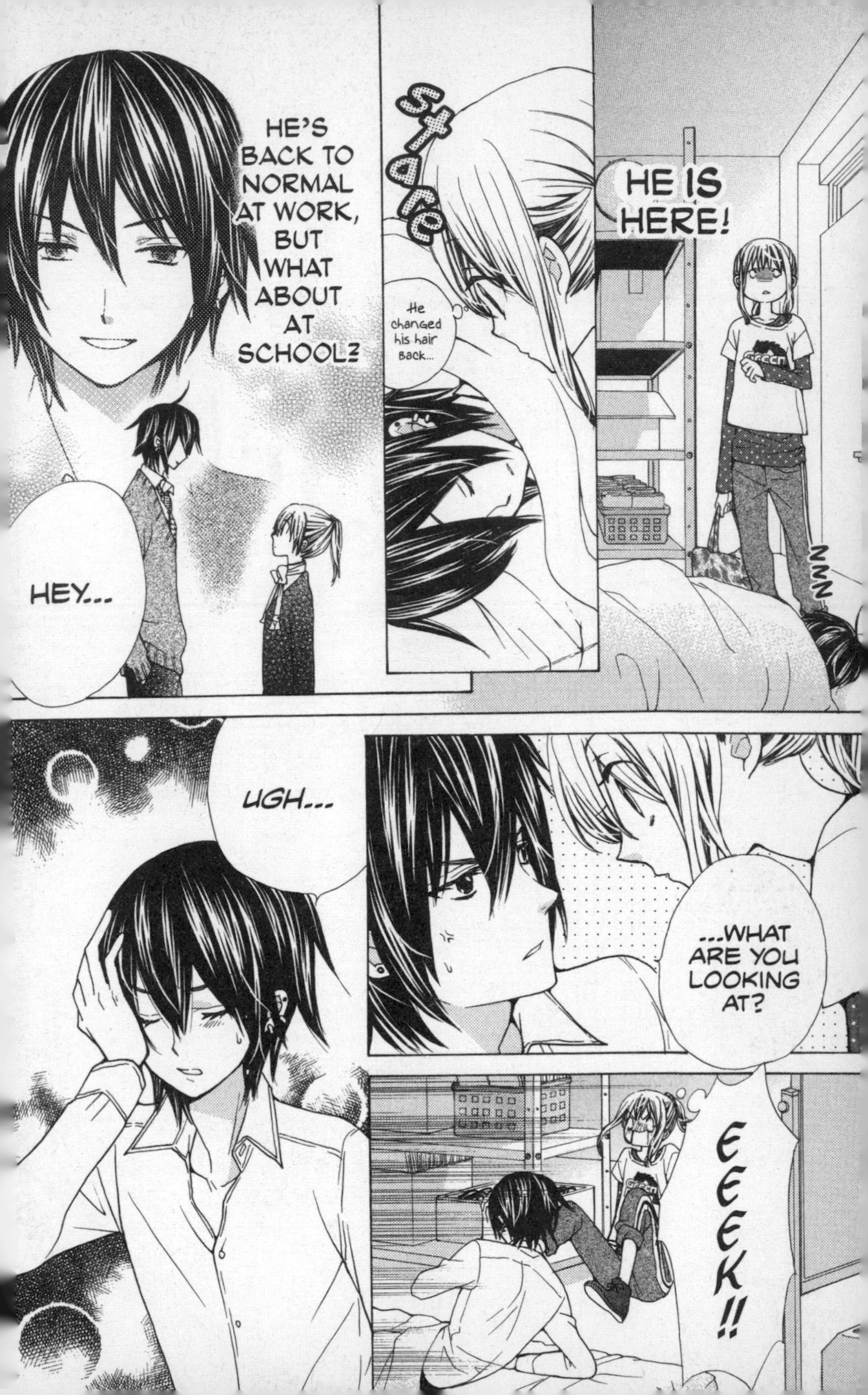
HE IS HERE!
ZZZ
Stare
He changed his hair back...
HE'S BACK TO NORMAL AT WORK, BUT WHAT ABOUT AT SCHOOL?
HEY...
...WHAT ARE YOU LOOKING AT?
EEEK!!
UGH...

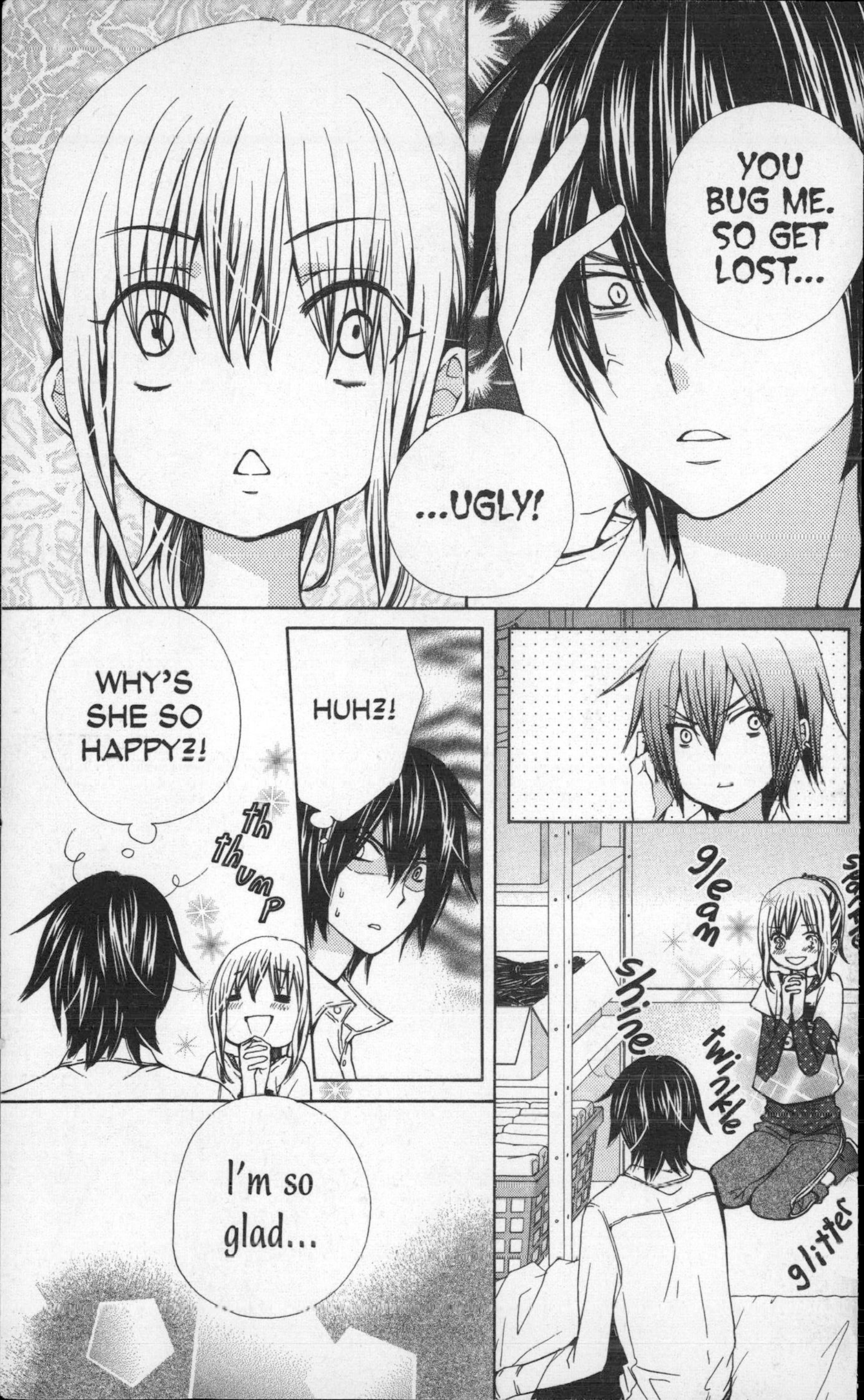
YOU BUG ME. SO GET LOST...
...UGLY!
gleam
shine
twinkle
glitter
HUH?!
WHY'S SHE SO HAPPY?!
th thump
I'm so glad...

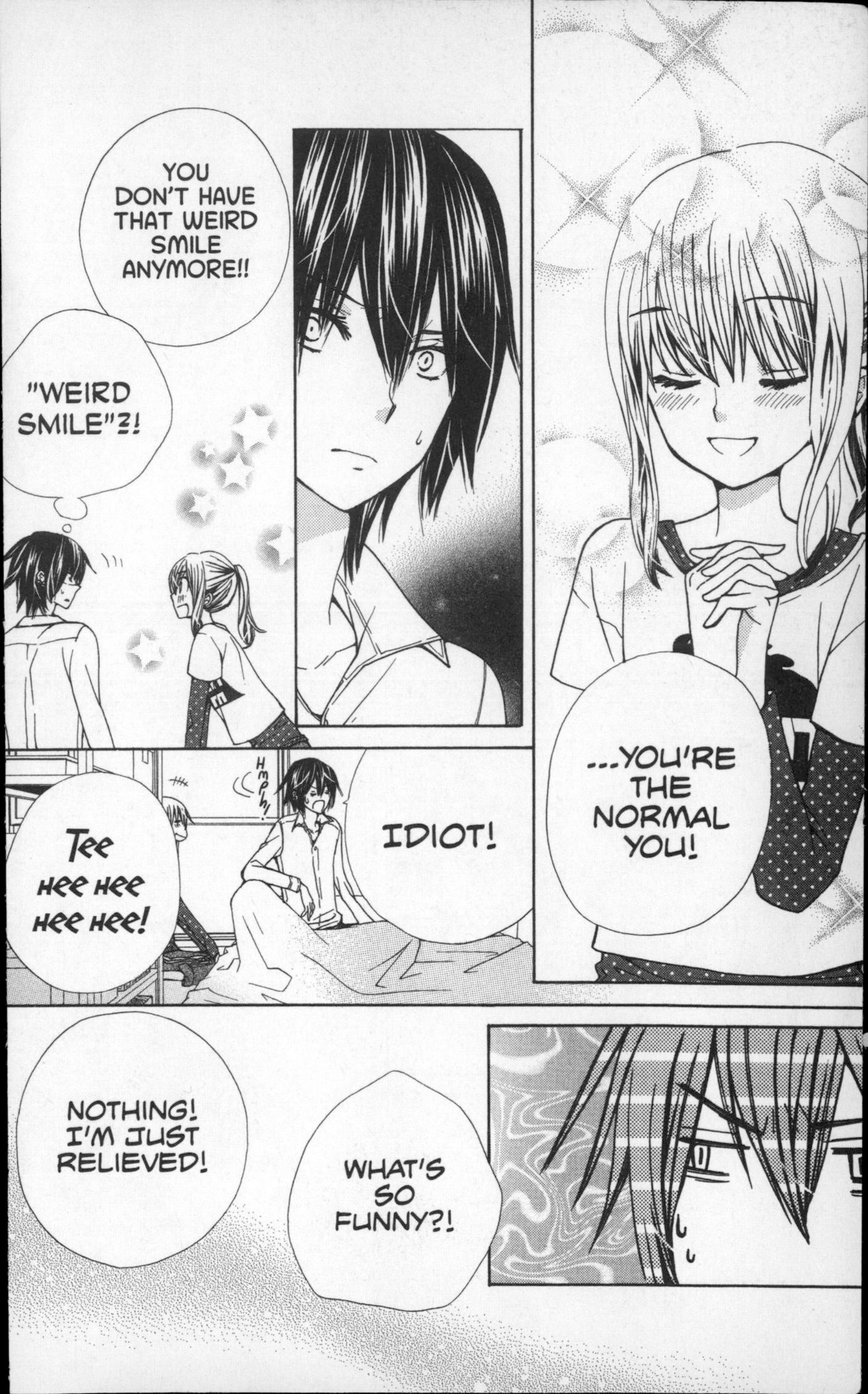
...YOU'RE THE NORMAL YOU!
YOU DON'T HAVE THAT WEIRD SMILE ANYMORE!!
"WEIRD SMILE"?!
HMPH!
IDIOT!
Tee hee hee hee hee!
WHAT'S SO FUNNY?!
NOTHING! I'M JUST RELIEVED!

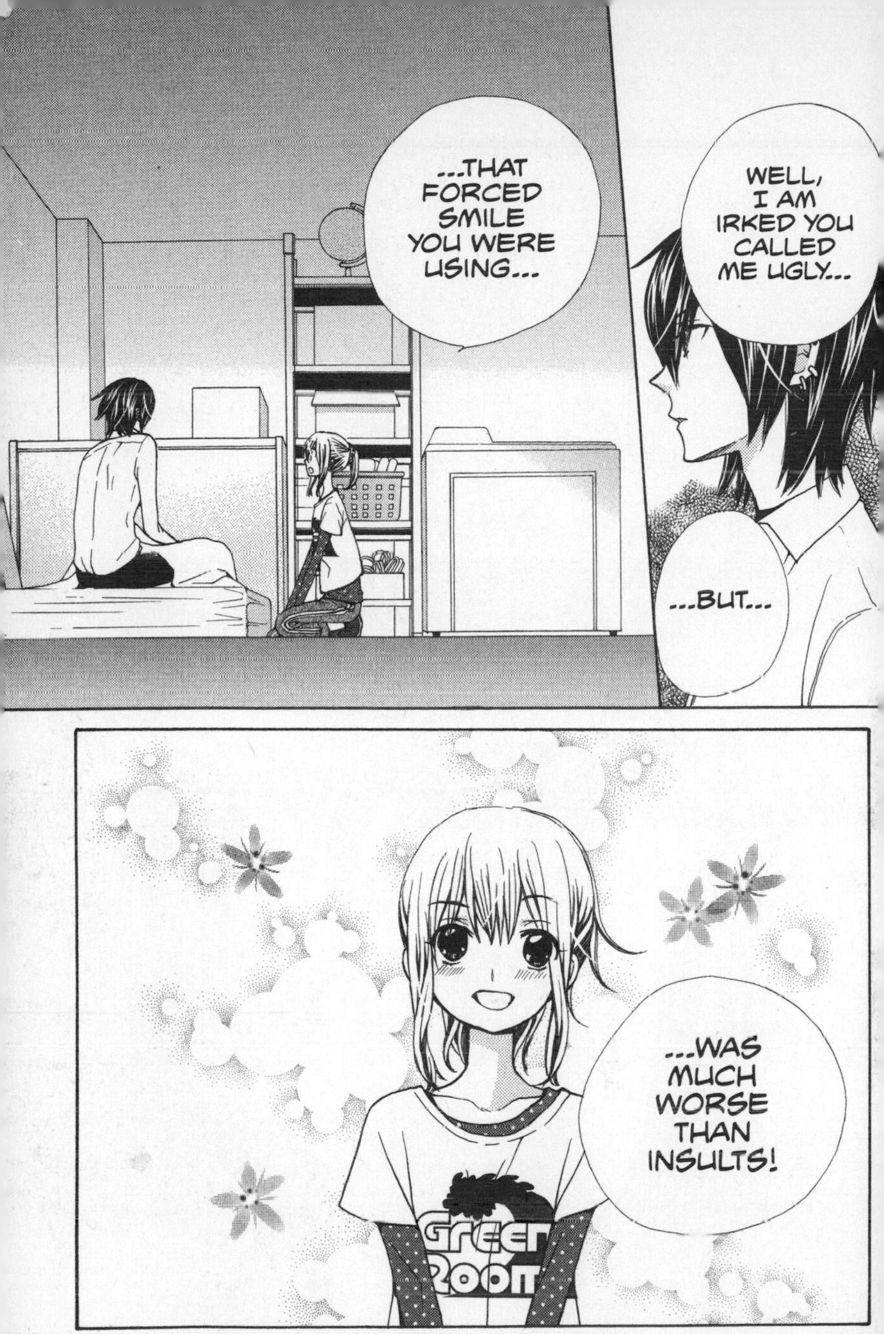
WELL, I AM IRKED YOU CALLED ME UGLY...
...BUT...
...THAT FORCED SMILE YOU WERE USING...
...WAS MUCH WORSE THAN INSULTS!
Green Room

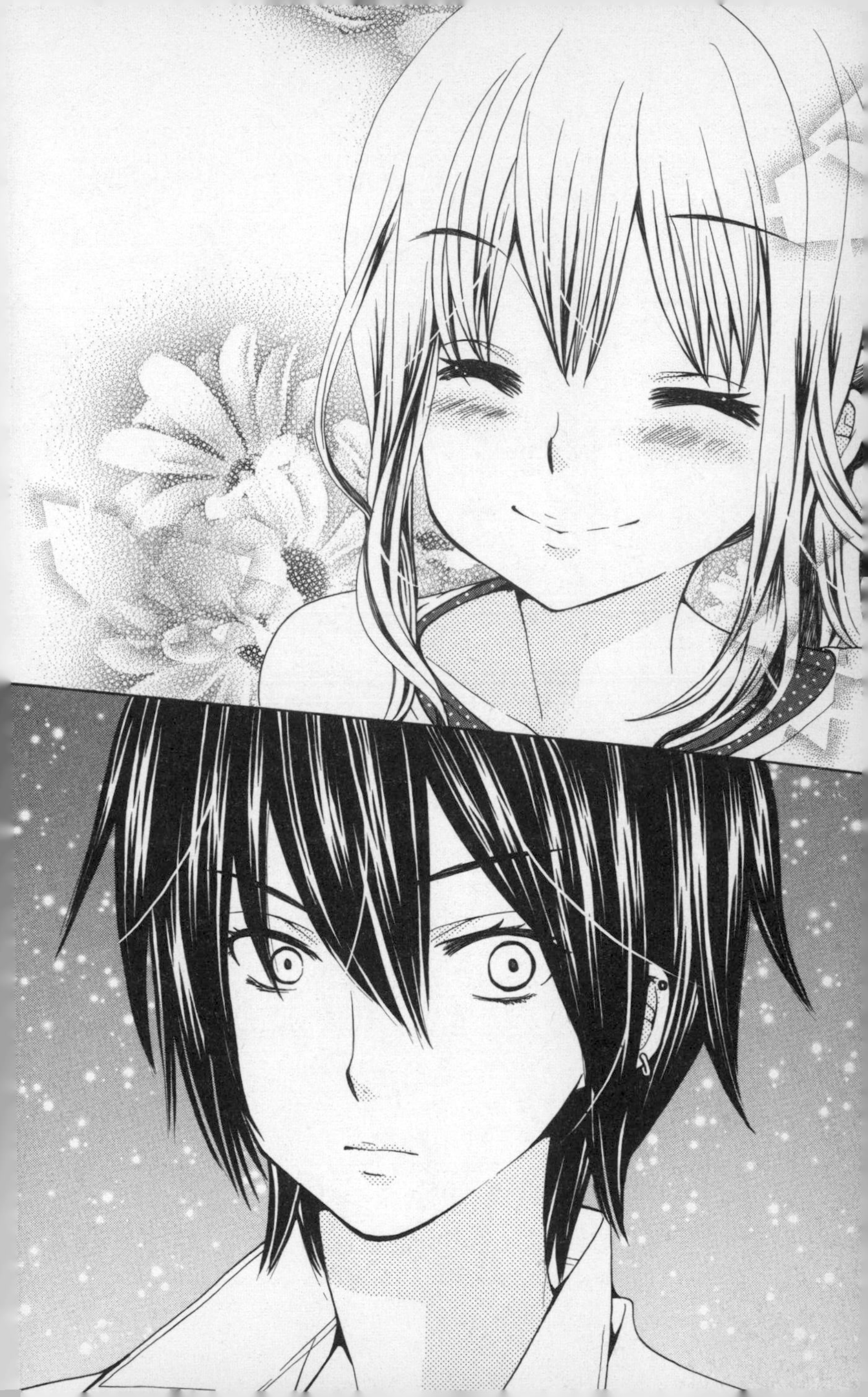

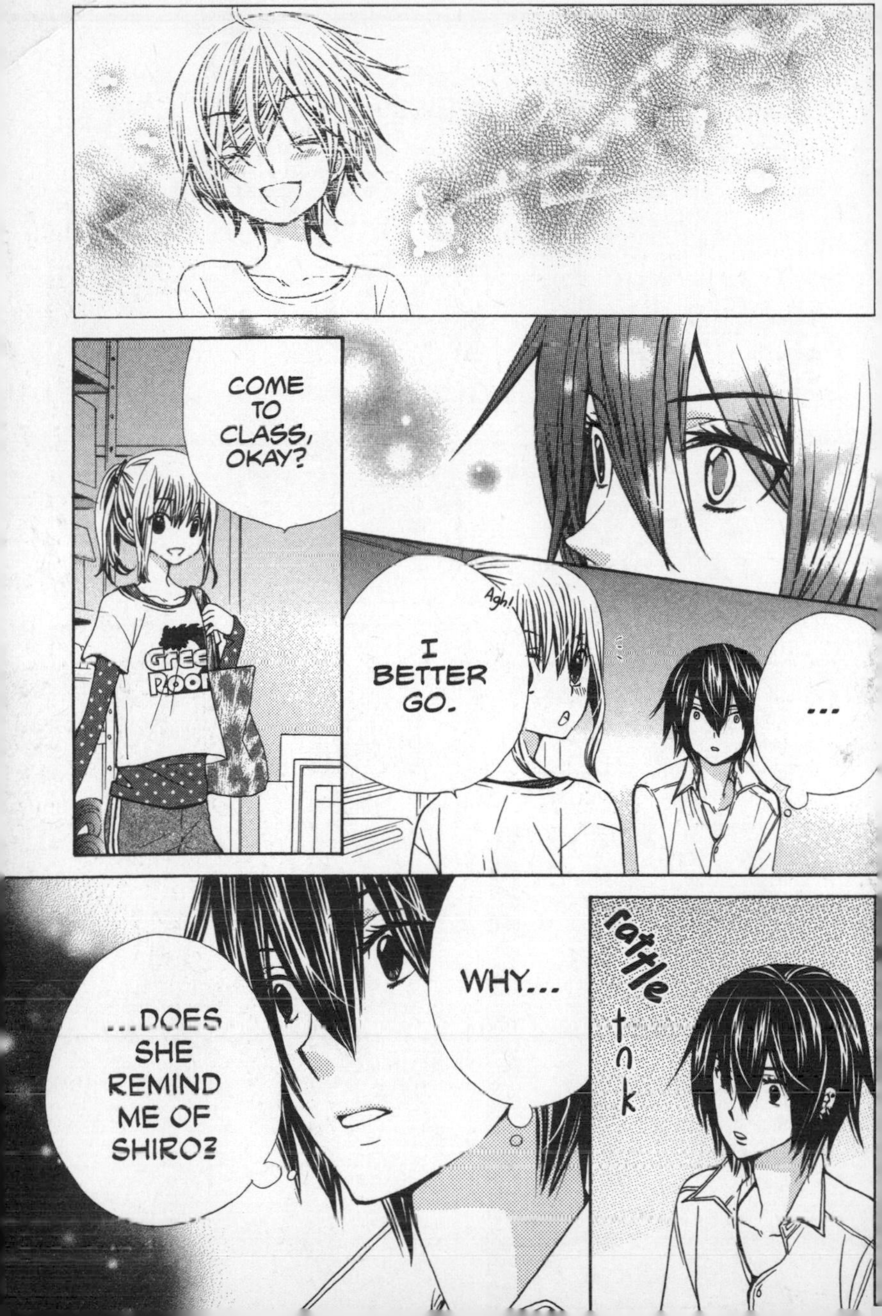
...
Agh!
I BETTER GO.
COME TO CLASS, OKAY?
rattle
tnk
WHY...
...DOES SHE REMIND ME OF SHIRO?

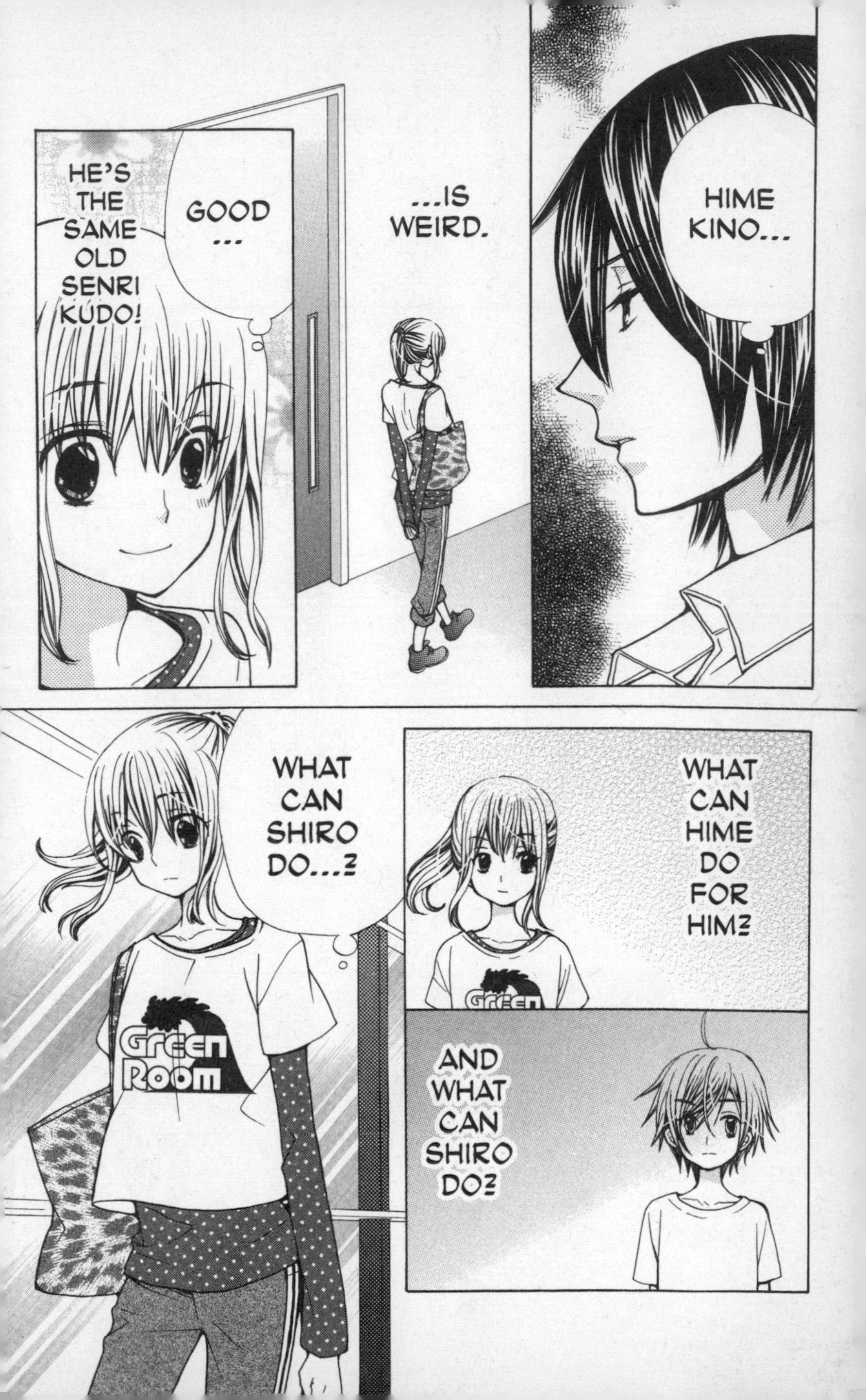
HIME KINO...
...IS WEIRD.
GOOD...
HE'S THE SAME OLD SENRI KŪDO!
WHAT CAN HIME DO FOR HIM?
AND WHAT CAN SHIRO DO?
WHAT CAN SHIRO DO...?
Green Room

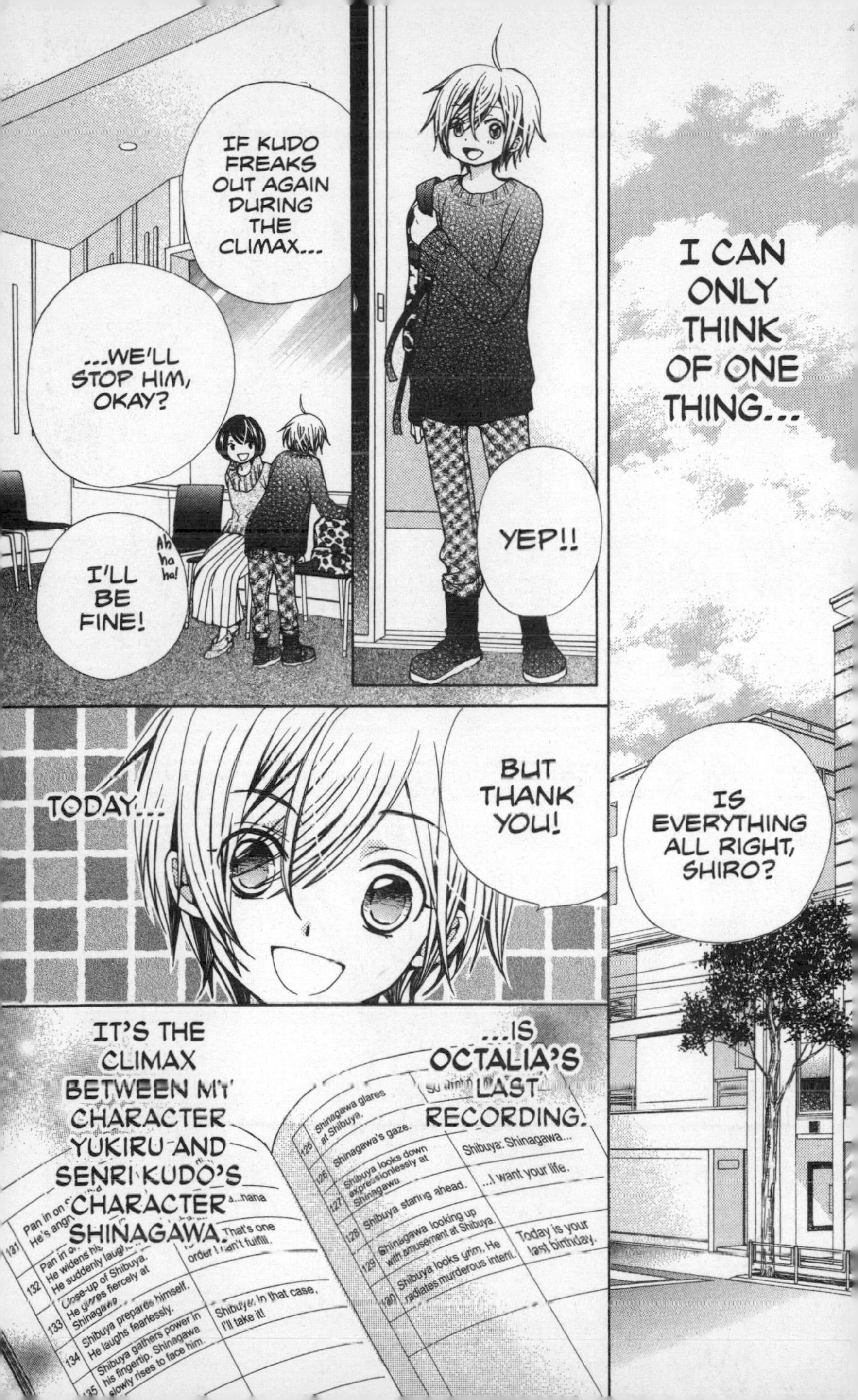
I CAN ONLY THINK OF ONE THING...
IS EVERYTHING ALL RIGHT, SHIRO?
YEP!!
IF KUDO FREAKS OUT AGAIN DURING THE CLIMAX...
...WE'LL STOP HIM, OKAY?
Ah ha ha!
I'LL BE FINE!
BUT THANK YOU!
TODAY...
...IS OCTALIA'S LAST RECORDING.
IT'S THE CLIMAX BETWEEN MY CHARACTER YUKIRU AND SENRI KUDO'S CHARACTER SHINAGAWA.
Shinagawa glares at Shibuya.
Shinagawa's gaze.
Shibuya: Shinagawa...
...I want your life.
Shinagawa looking up with amusement at Shibuya.
Today is your last birthday.
Shibuya looks grim. He radiates murderous intent.
That's one order I can't fulfill.
Shibuya prepares himself. He laughs fearlessly.
Shibuya: In that case, I'll take it!
Shibuya gathers power in his fingertip. Shinagawa slowly rises to face him.

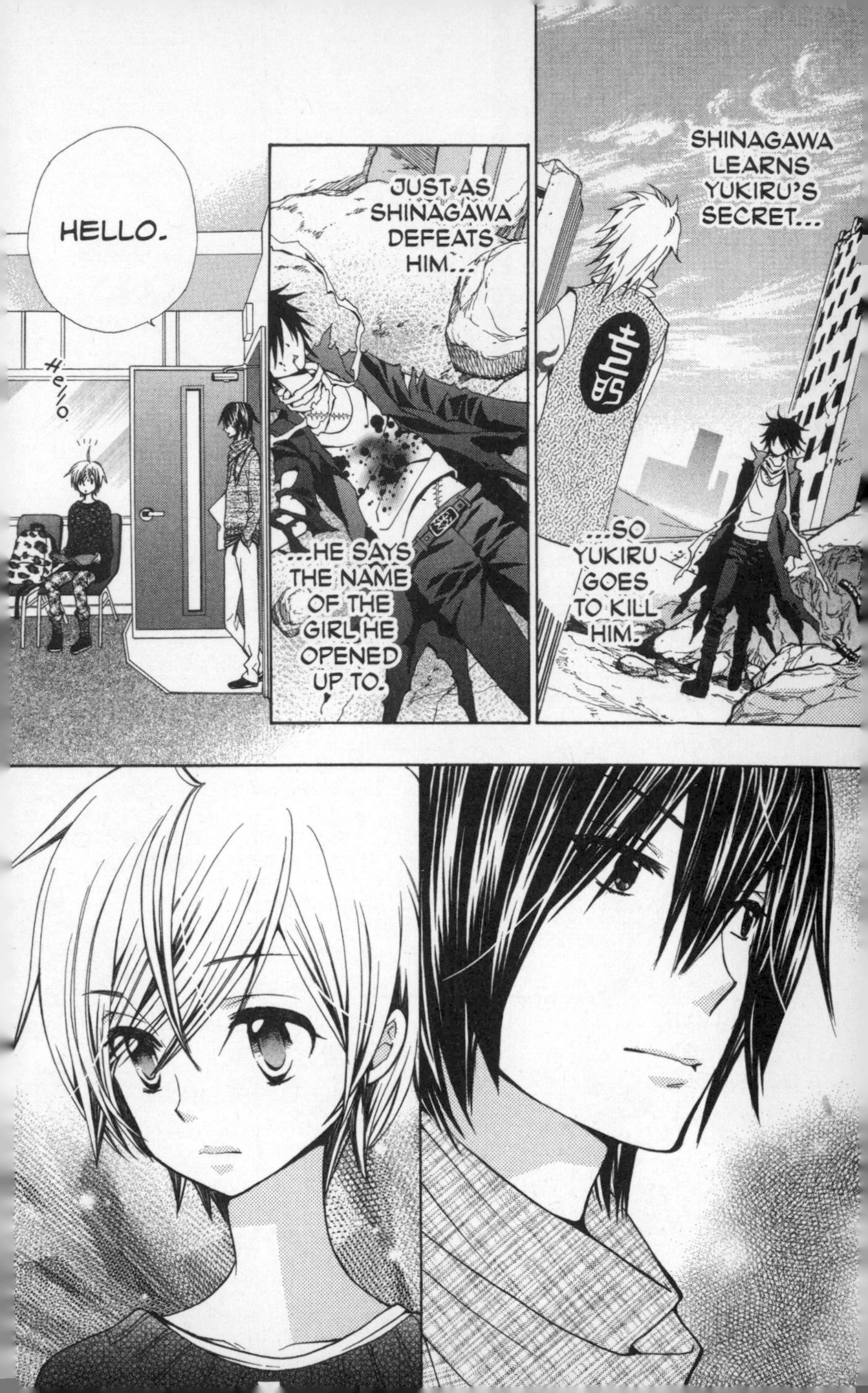
SHINAGAWA LEARNS YUKIRU'S SECRET...
...SO YUKIRU GOES TO KILL HIM.
JUST AS SHINAGAWA DEFEATS HIM...
...HE SAYS THE NAME OF THE GIRL HE OPENED UP TO.
HELLO.
Hello.

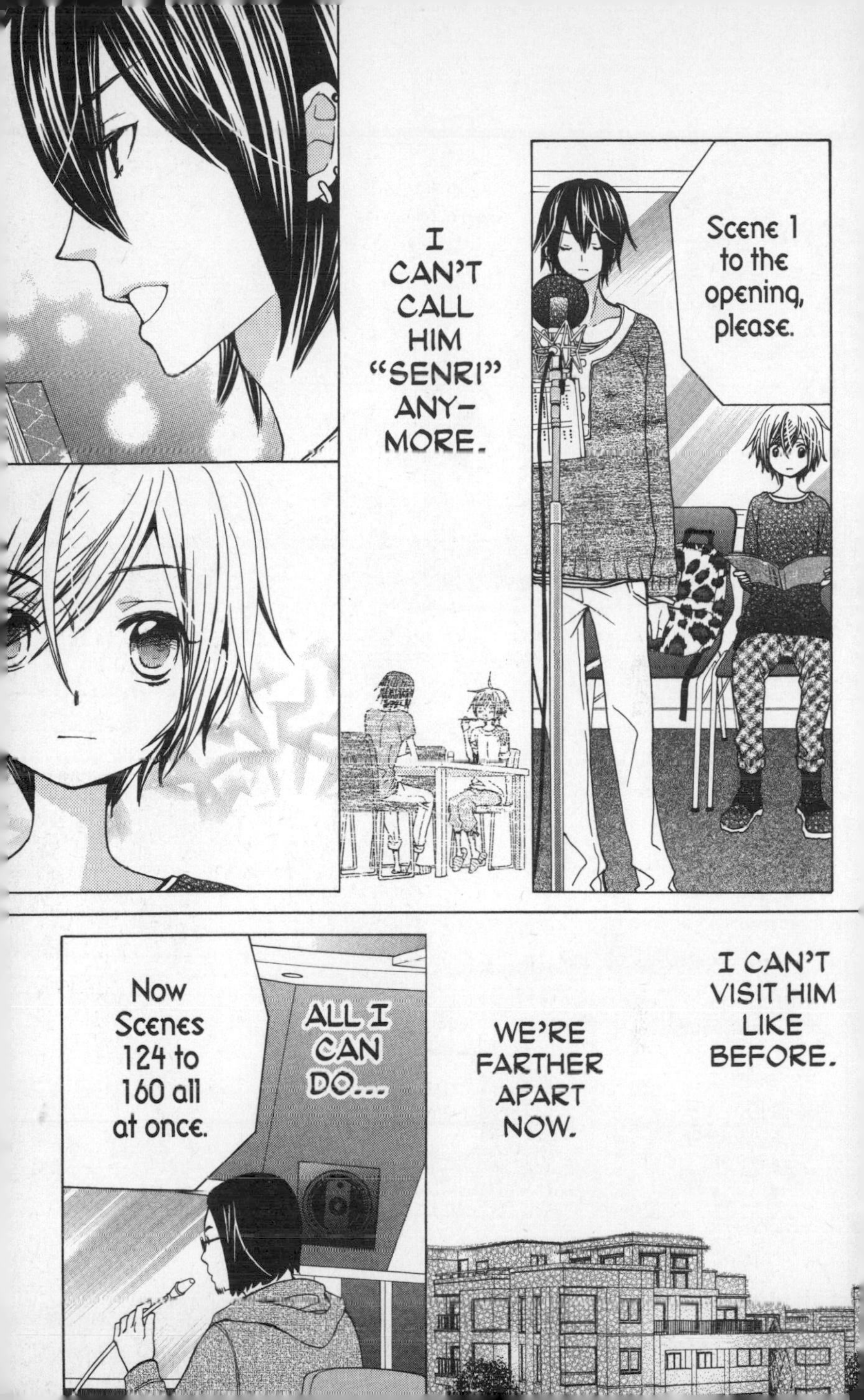
Scene 1 to the opening, please.
I CAN'T CALL HIM "SENRI" ANYMORE.
I CAN'T VISIT HIM LIKE BEFORE.
WE'RE FARTHER APART NOW.
ALL I CAN DO...
Now Scenes 124 to 160 all at once.

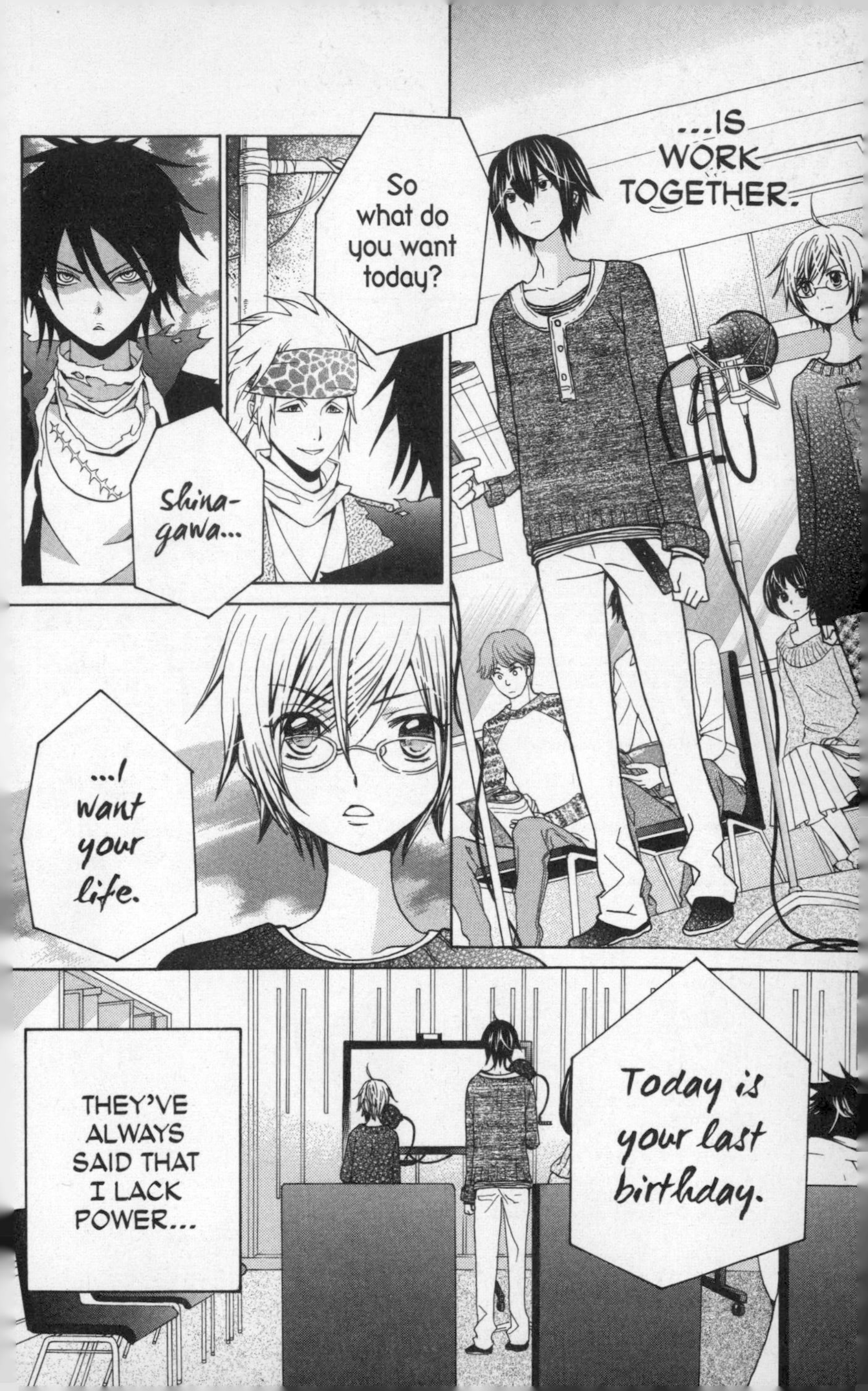
...IS WORK TOGETHER.
So what do you want today?
Shina-gawa...
...I want your life.
Today is your last birthday.
THEY'VE ALWAYS SAID THAT I LACK POWER...

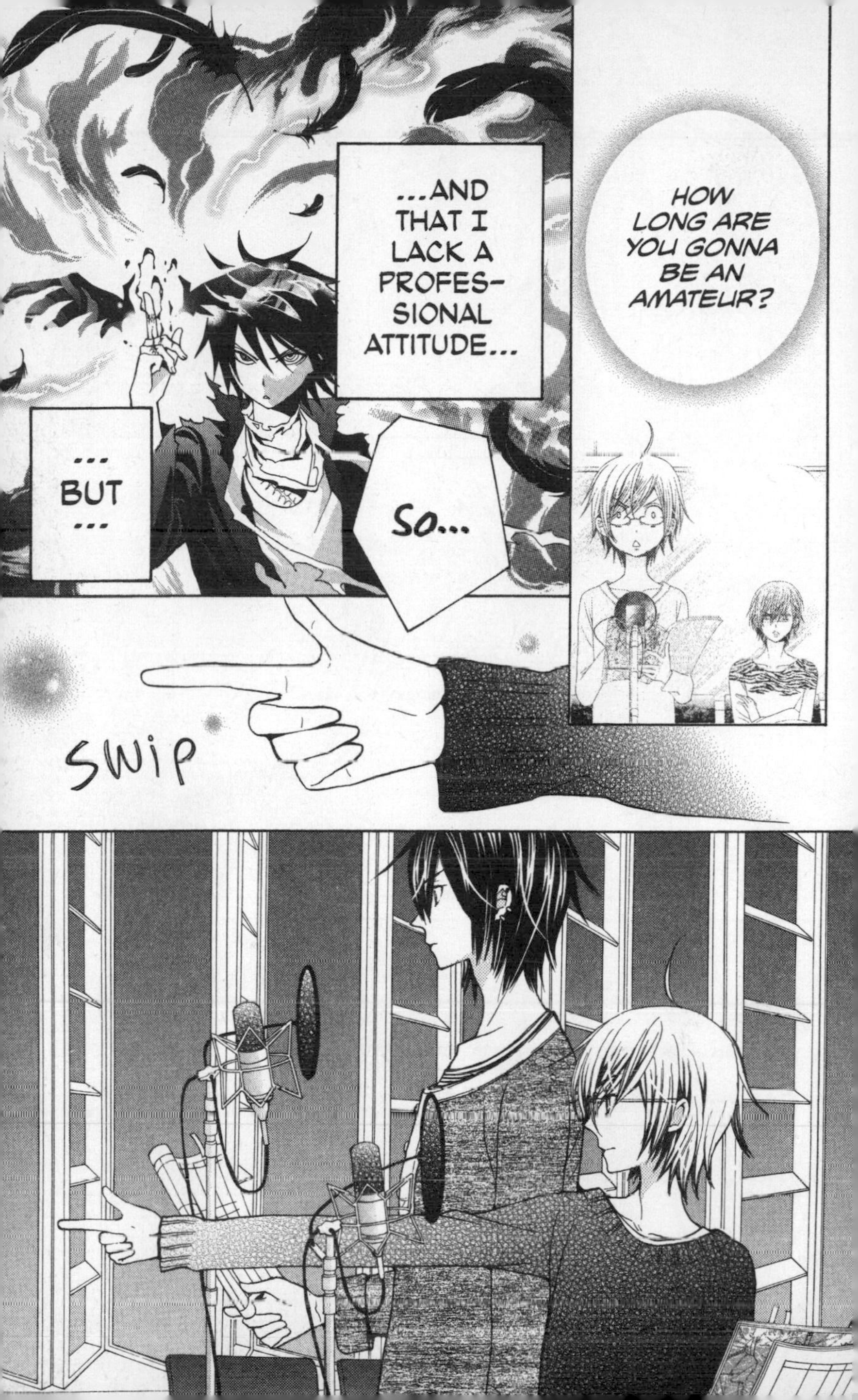
HOW LONG ARE YOU GONNA BE AN AMATEUR?
...AND THAT I LACK A PROFES-SIONAL ATTITUDE...
...BUT...
SO...
SWIP

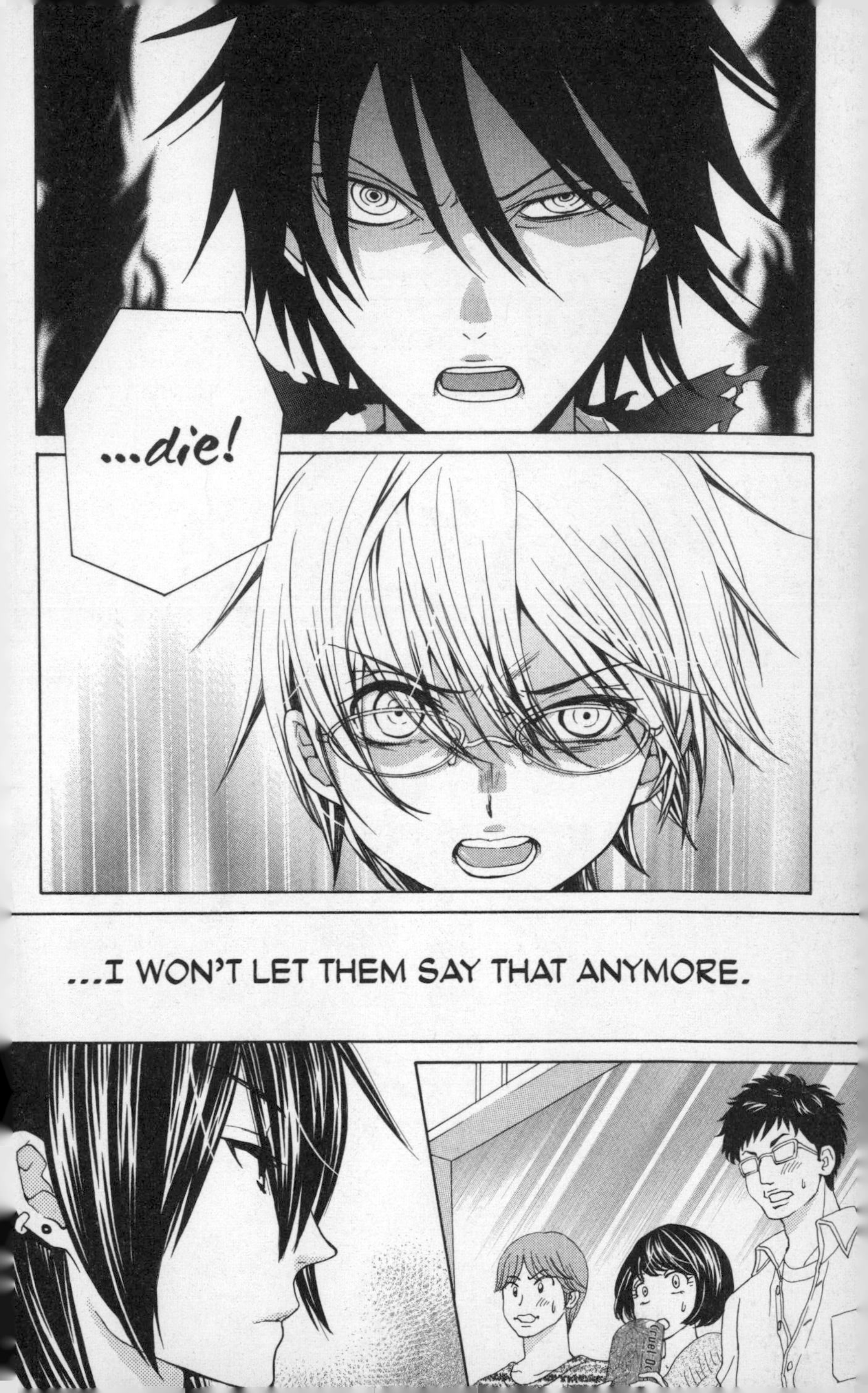
...die!
...I WON'T LET THEM SAY THAT ANYMORE.

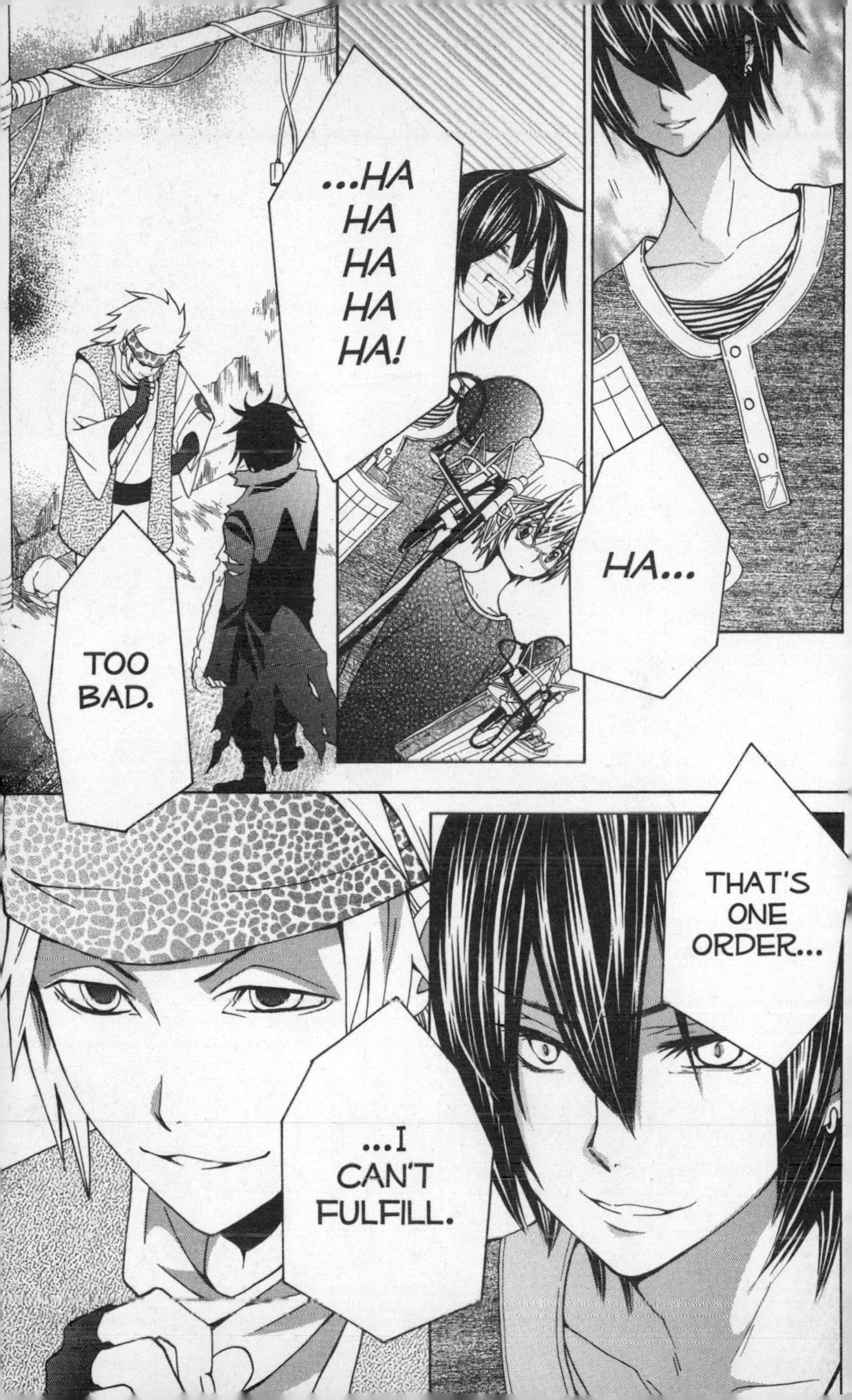
HA...
...HA HA HA HA HA!
TOO BAD.
THAT'S ONE ORDER...
...I CAN'T FULFILL.

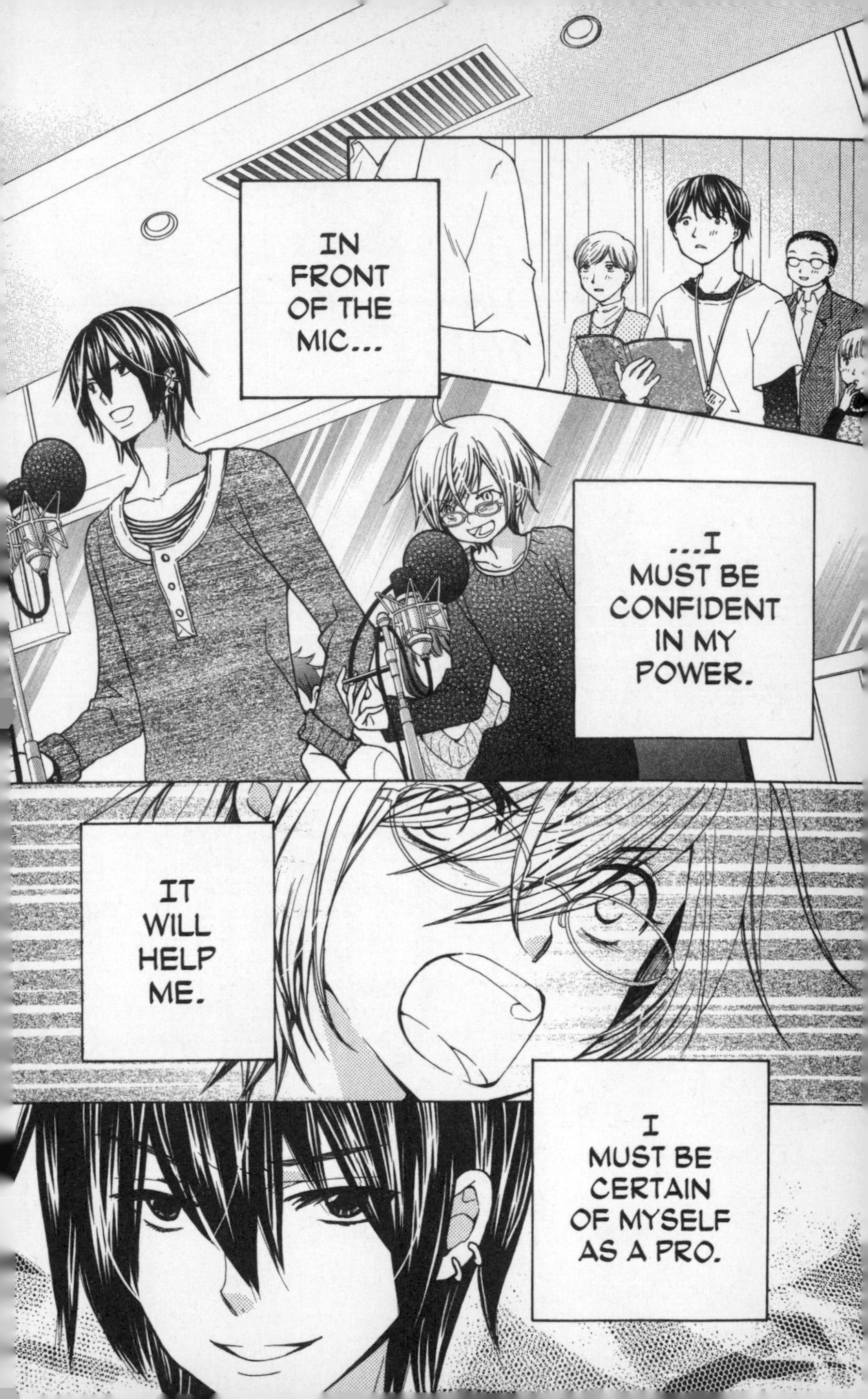
IN FRONT OF THE MIC...
...I MUST BE CONFIDENT IN MY POWER.
IT WILL HELP ME.
I MUST BE CERTAIN OF MYSELF AS A PRO.

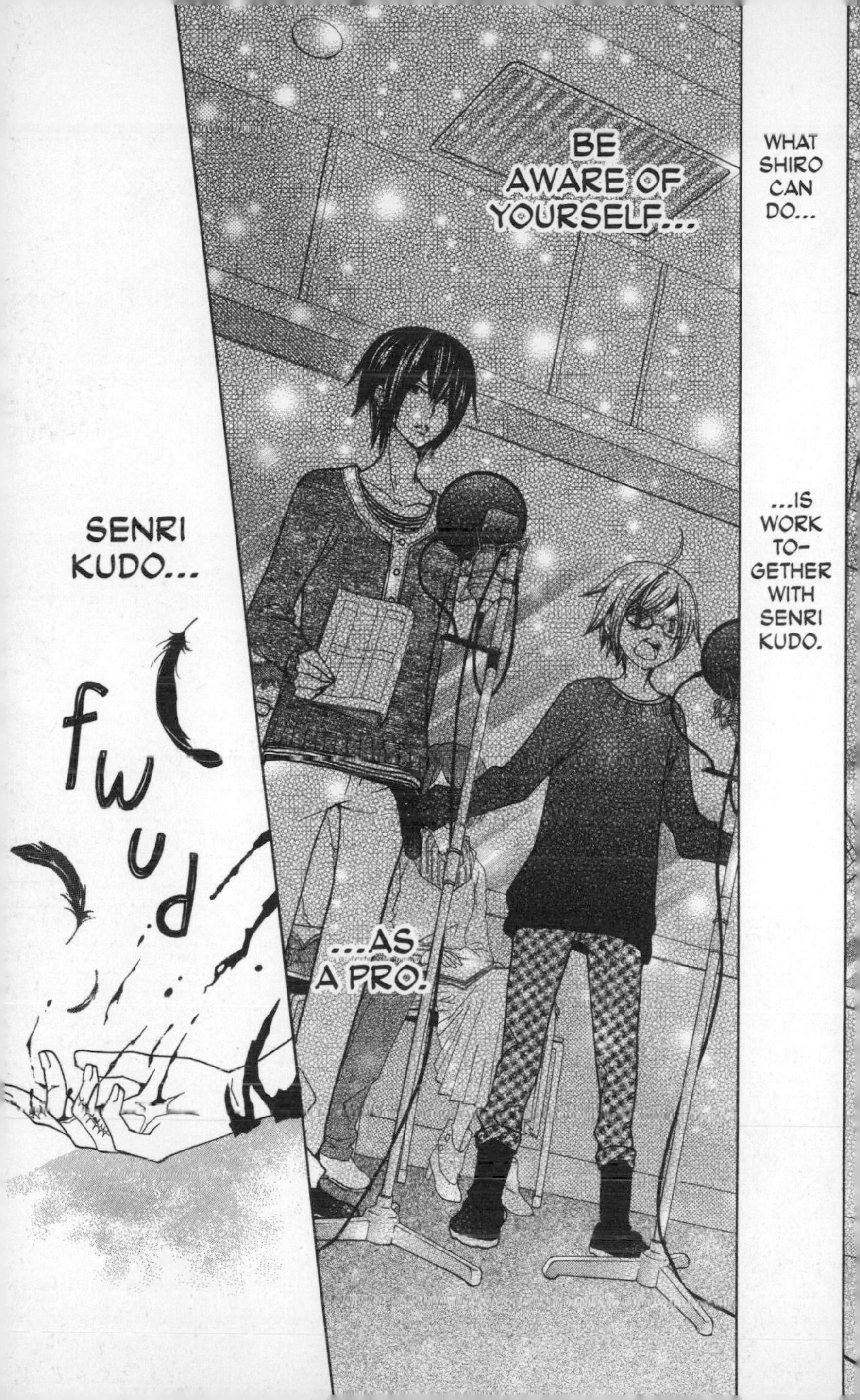
WHAT SHIRO CAN DO...
...IS WORK TO-GETHER WITH SENRI KUDO.
BE AWARE OF YOURSELF...
...AS A PRO.
SENRI KUDO...
fwud

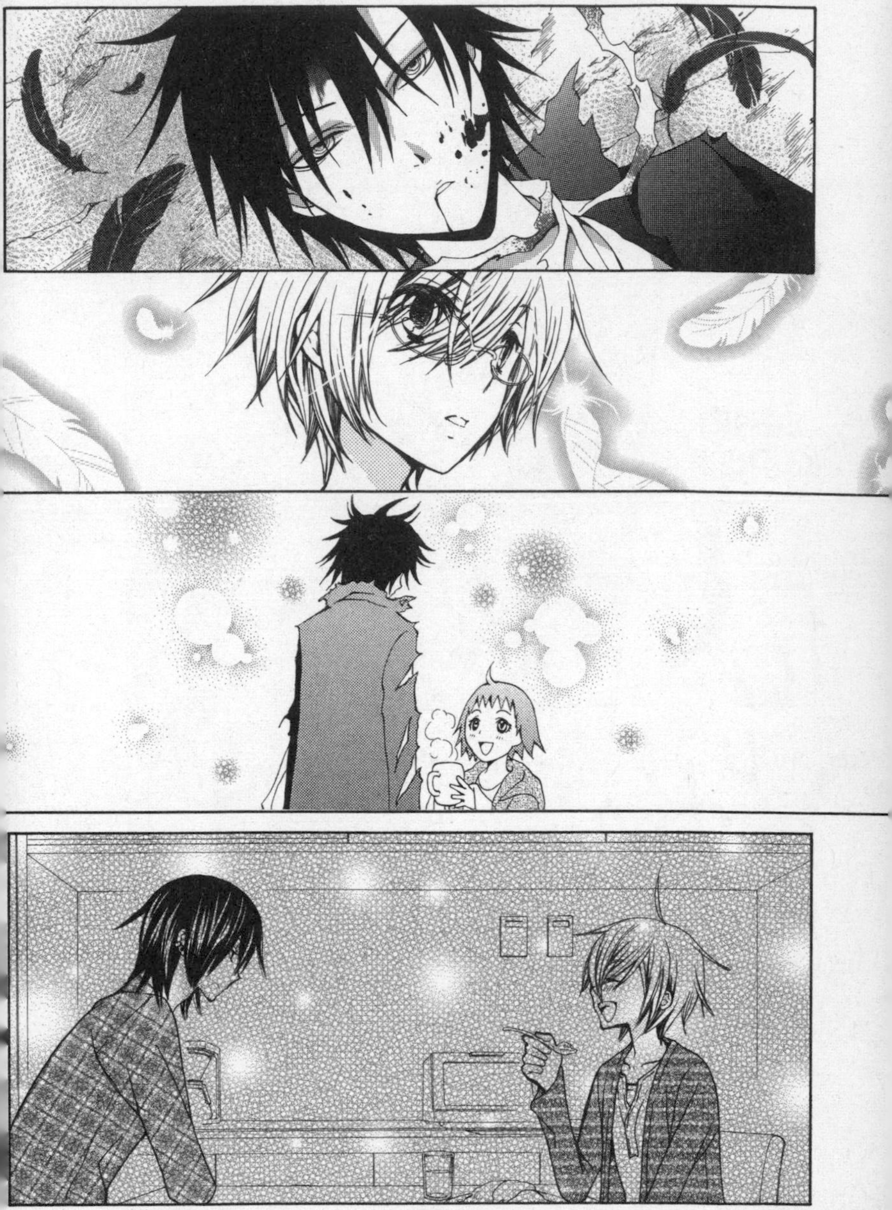

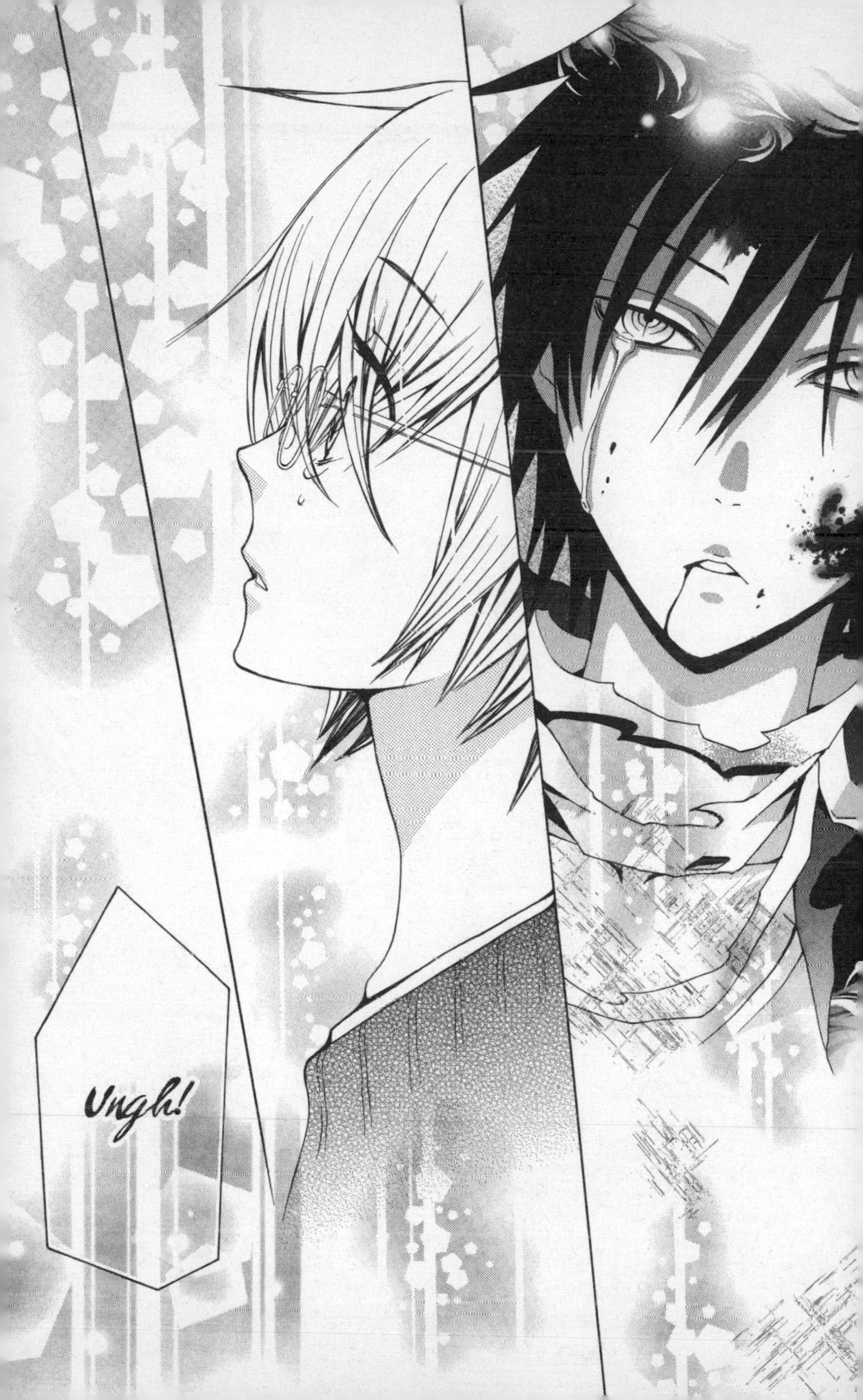
Ungh!

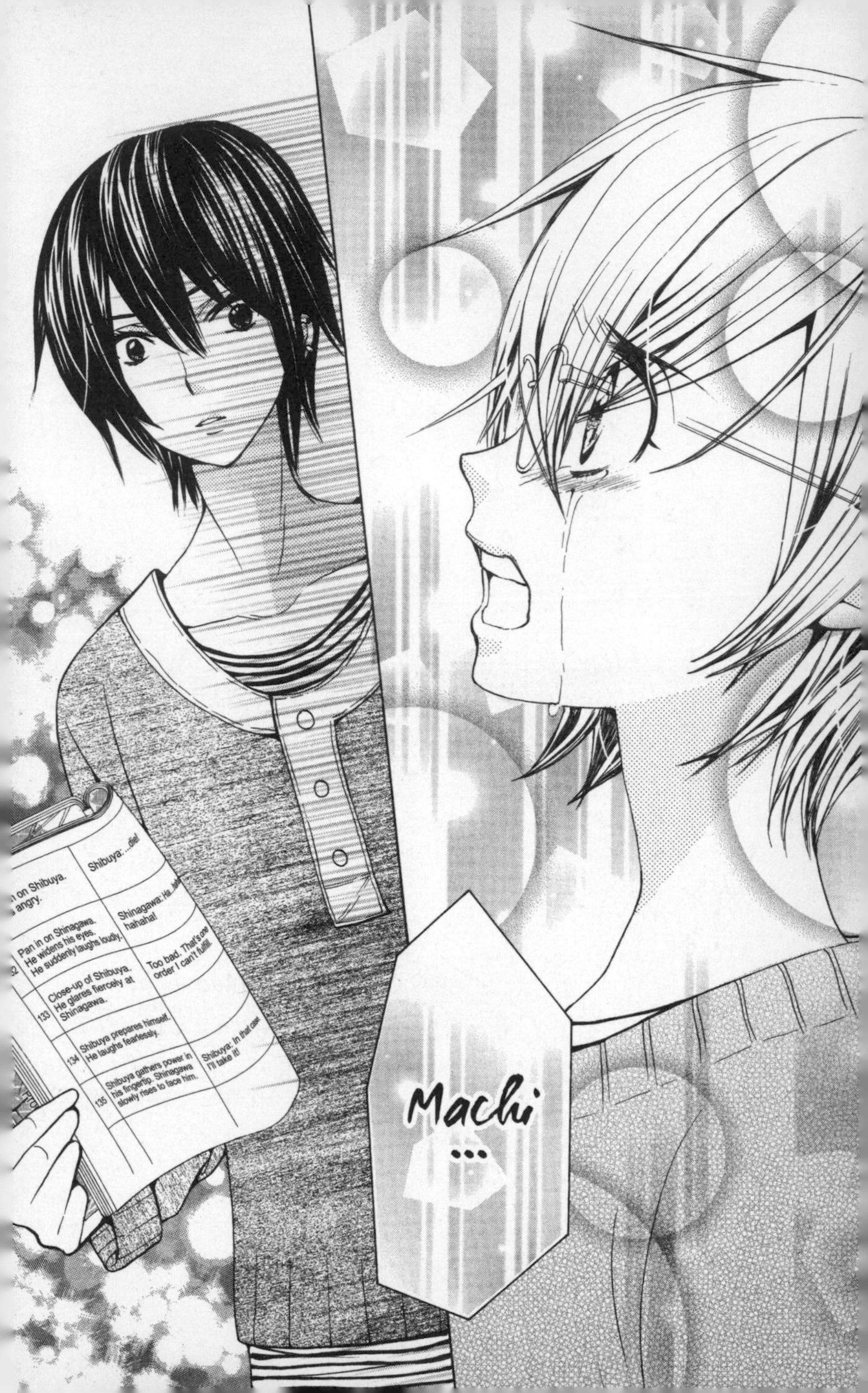
Machi ...
Shibuya: ...die!
Pan in on Shinagawa. He widens his eyes. He suddenly laughs loudly.
hahaha!
Too bad. That's one order I can't fulfill.
133
Close-up of Shibuya. He glares fiercely at Shinagawa.
134
Shibuya prepares himself. He laughs fearlessly.
135
Shibuya gathers power in his fingertip. Shinagawa slowly rises to face him.
I'll take it!

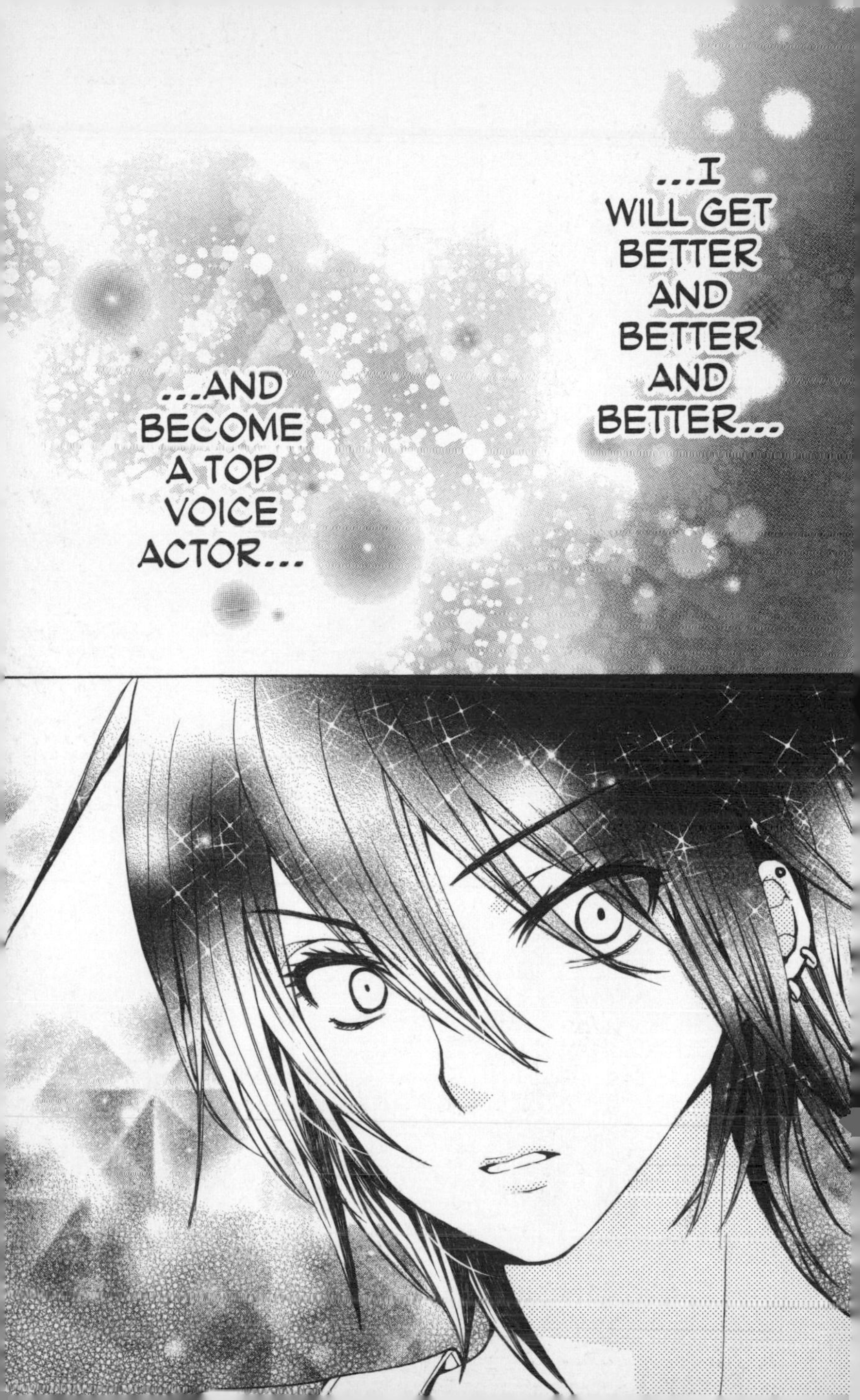
...I WILL GET BETTER AND BETTER AND BETTER...
...AND BECOME A TOP VOICE ACTOR...

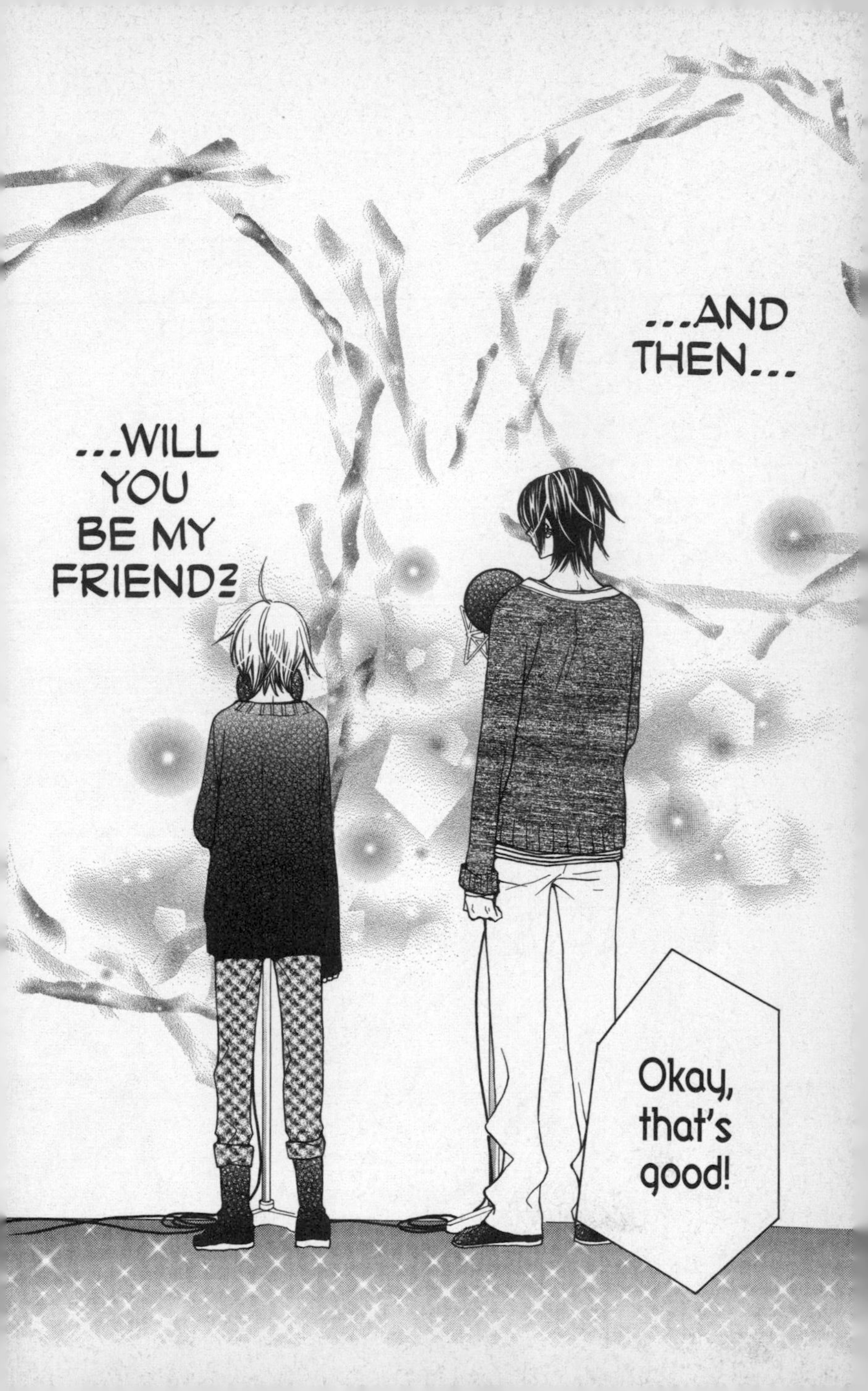
...AND THEN...
...WILL YOU BE MY FRIEND?
Okay, that's good!

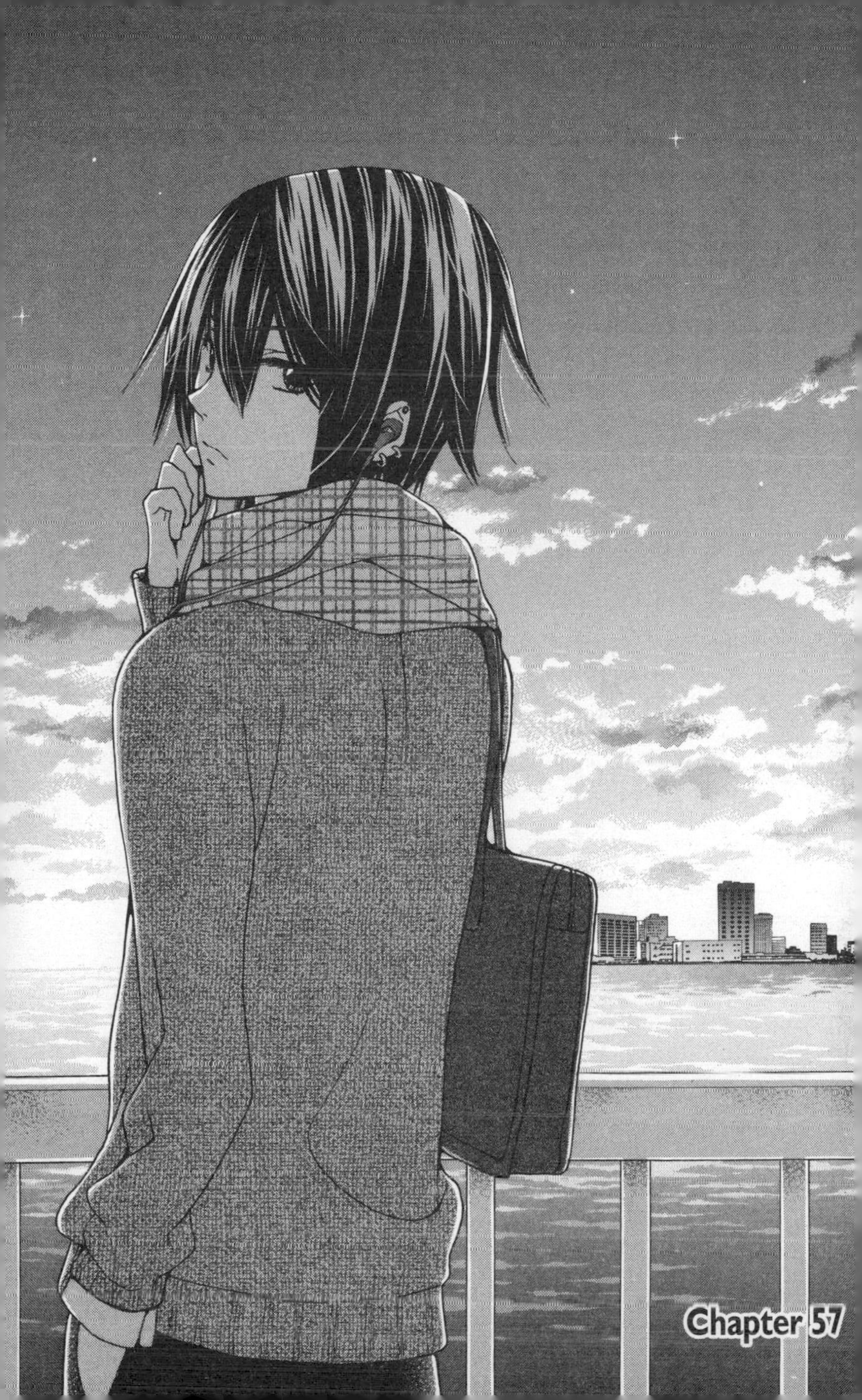
Chapter 57

...OR WHO I AM.

I FEEL LIKE I BARELY KNOW WHERE I'VE BEEN...

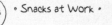

• Snacks at Work •

These days when I go to the department store, I put in an order to have them deliver a particular dessert that keeps well.

Our hearts cry out "a present from Santa!" and we eat them together. They're pretty tasty!

Ⓔ

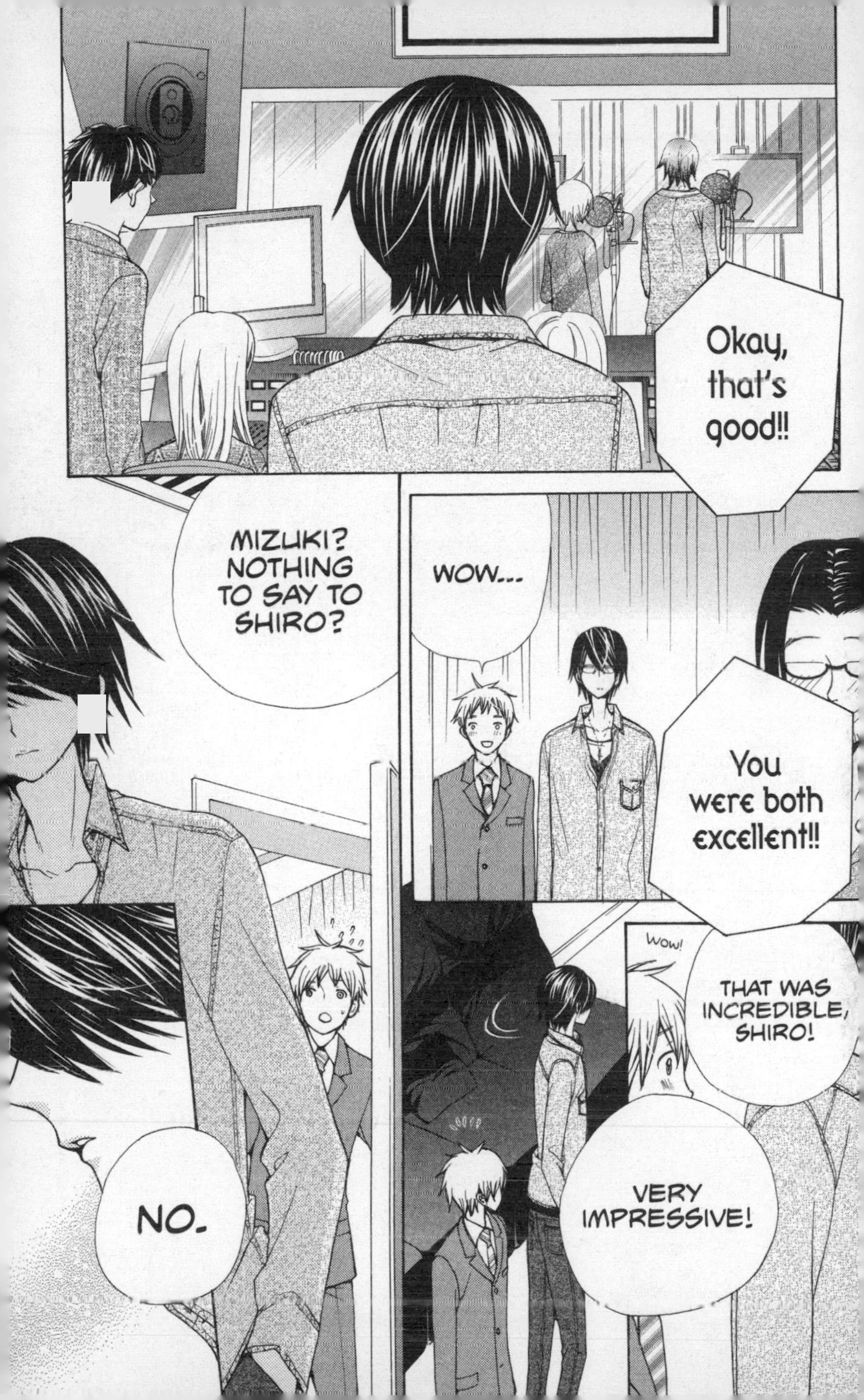
Okay, that's good!!
You were both excellent!!
WOW...
MIZUKI? NOTHING TO SAY TO SHIRO?
Wow!
THAT WAS INCREDIBLE, SHIRO!
VERY IMPRESSIVE!
NO.

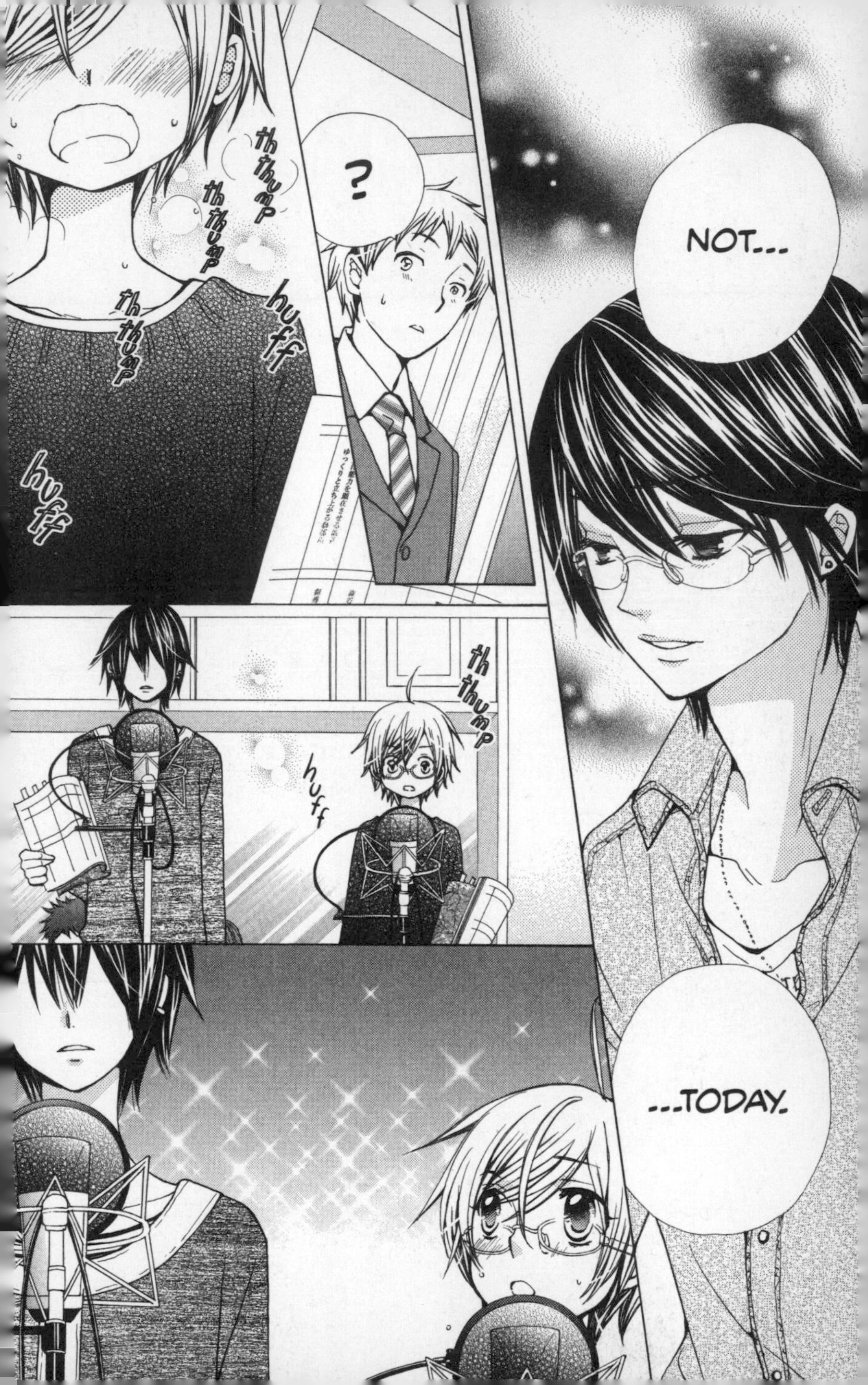
NOT...
...TODAY.
?
th thump
th thump
th thump
huff
huff
th thump
huff

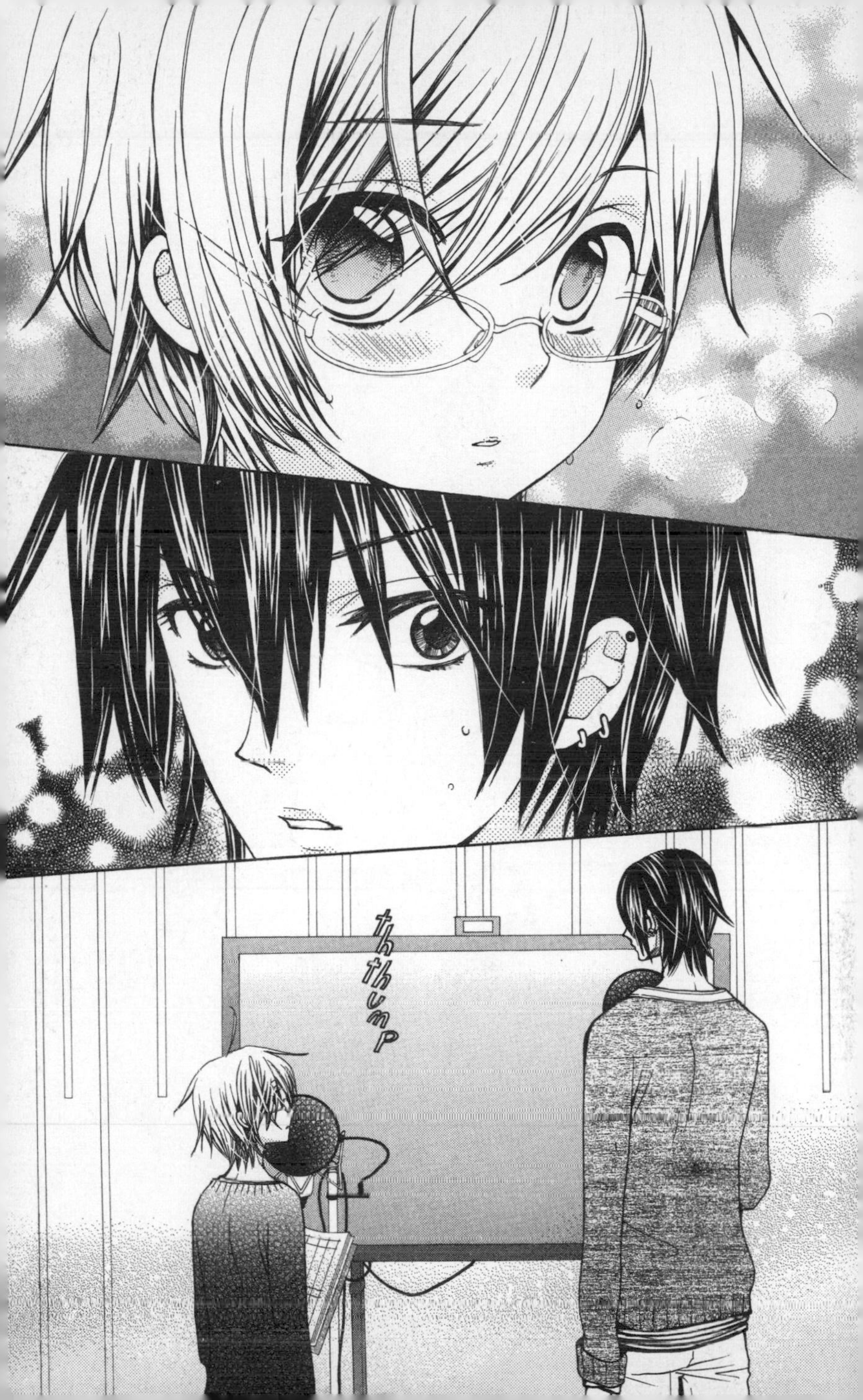
th thump

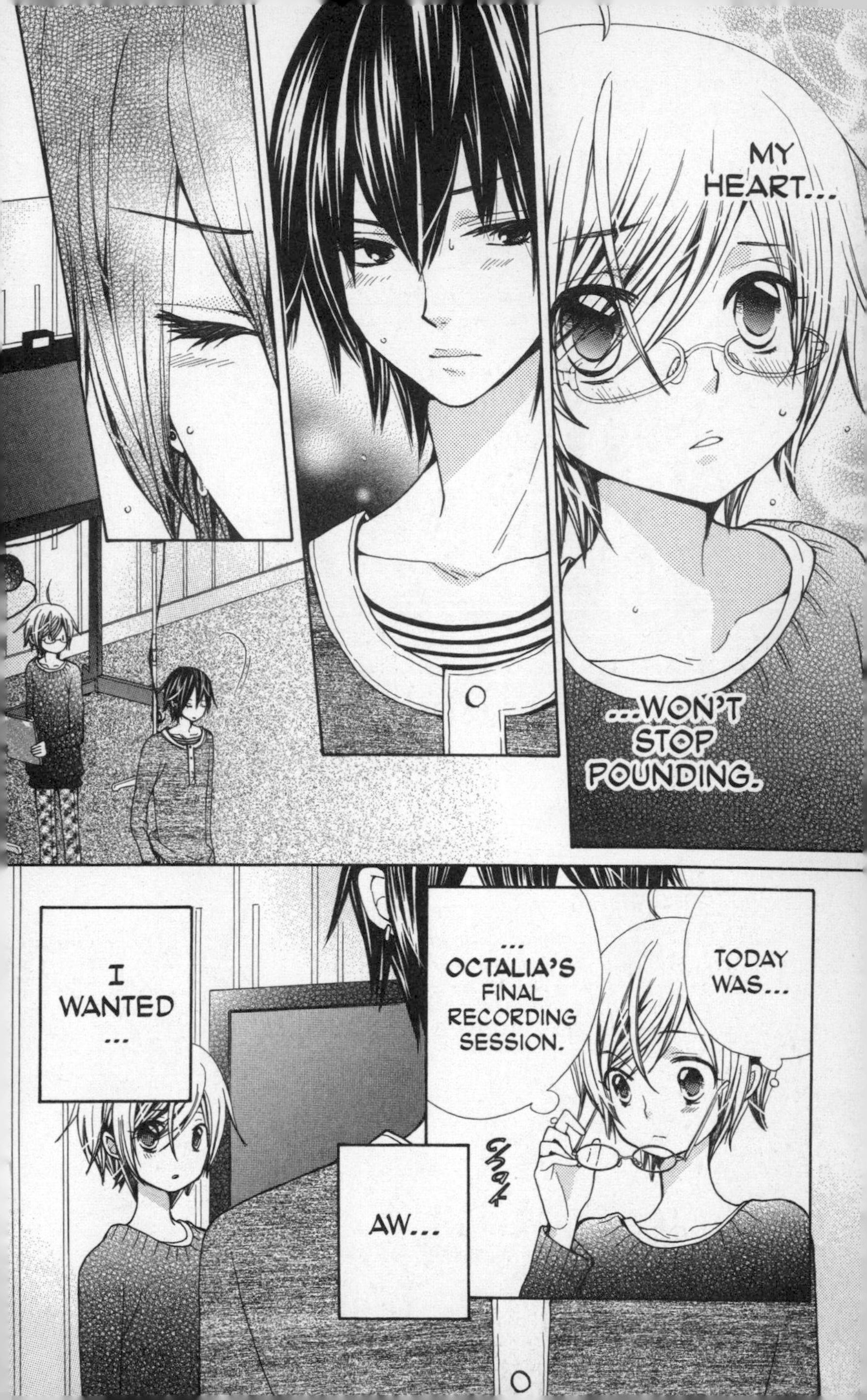
MY HEART...
...WON'T STOP POUNDING.
TODAY WAS...
...OCTALIA'S FINAL RECORDING SESSION.
AW...
I WANTED ...

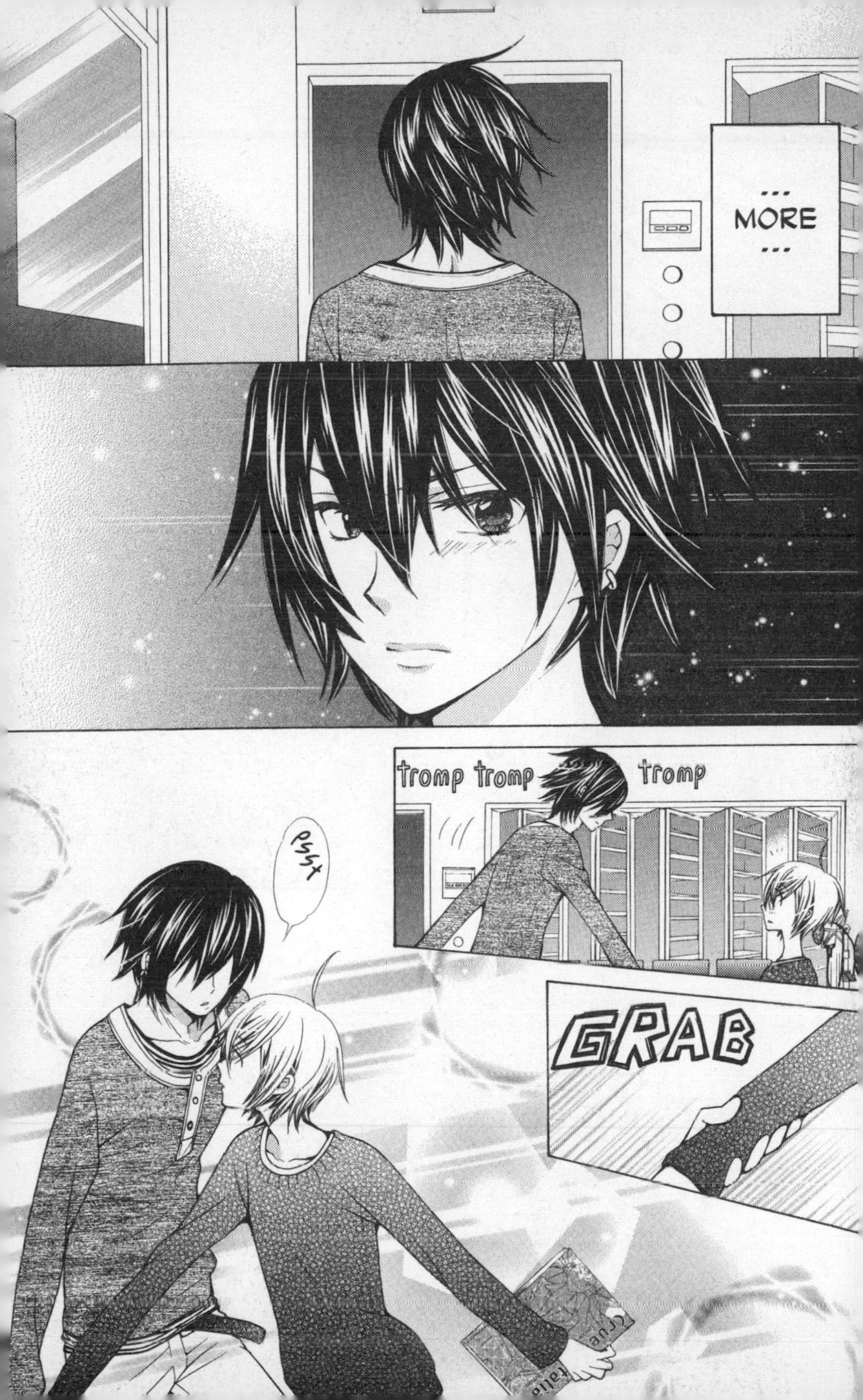
... MORE ...
tromp tromp tromp
GRAB
psst

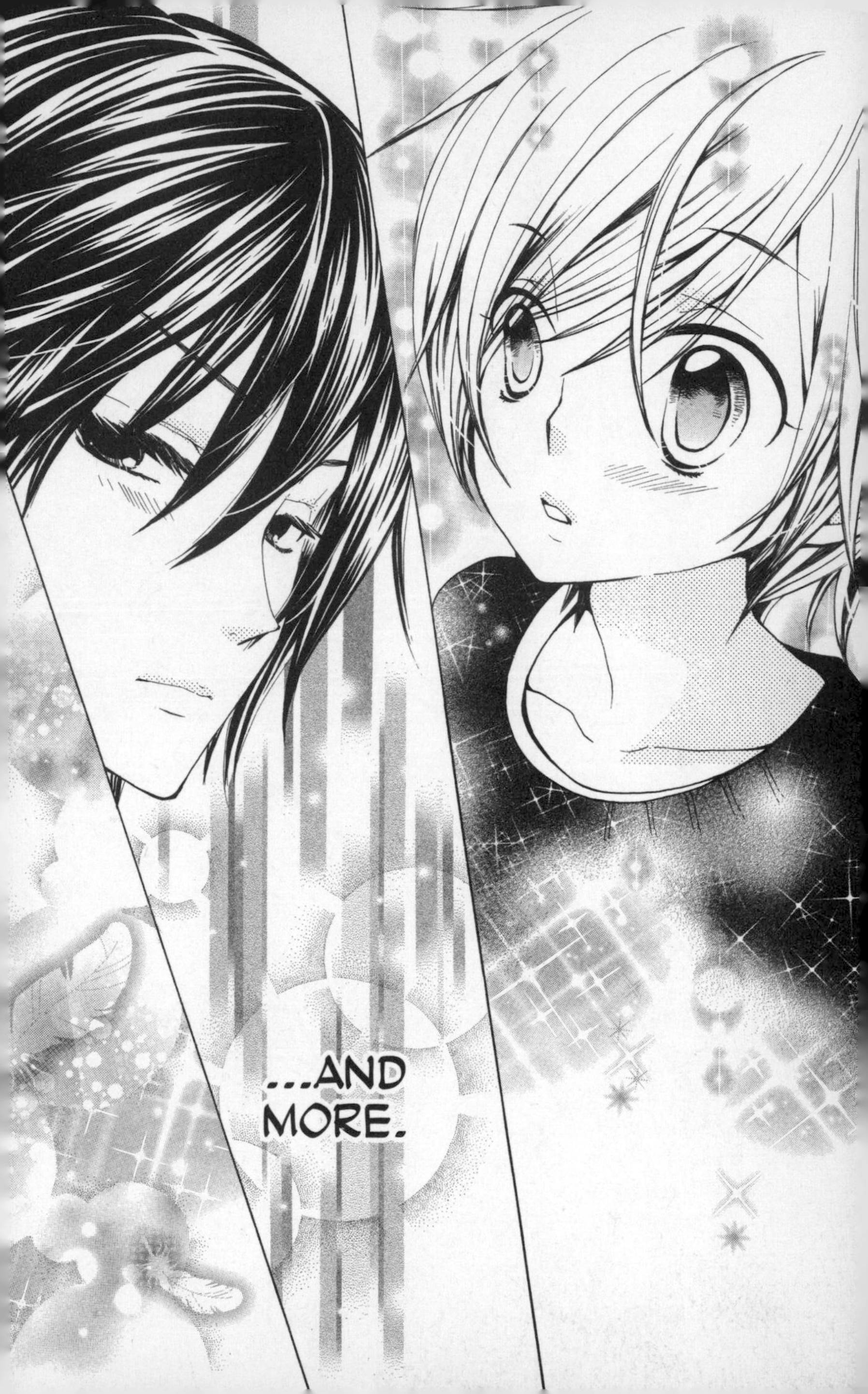
...AND MORE.

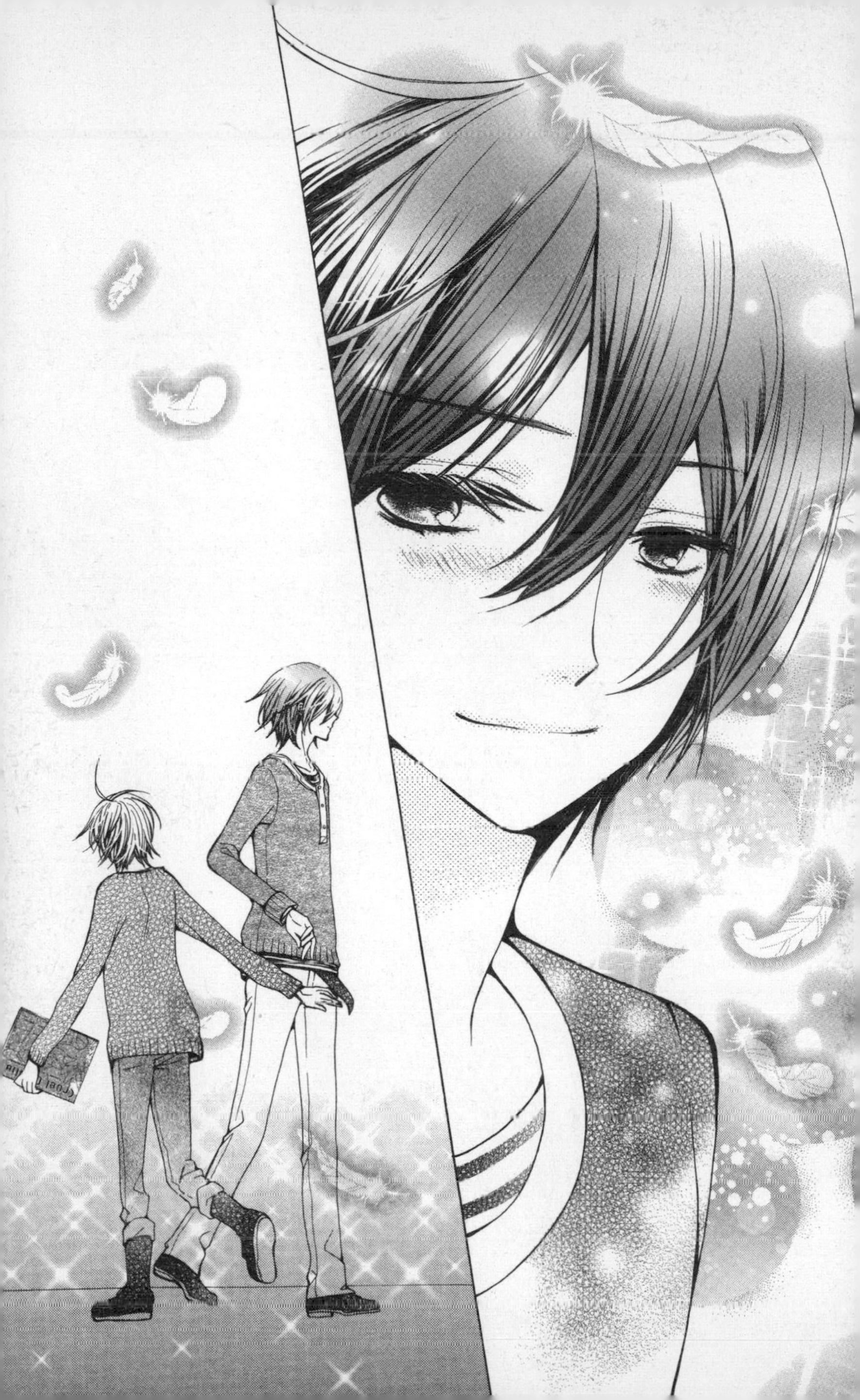

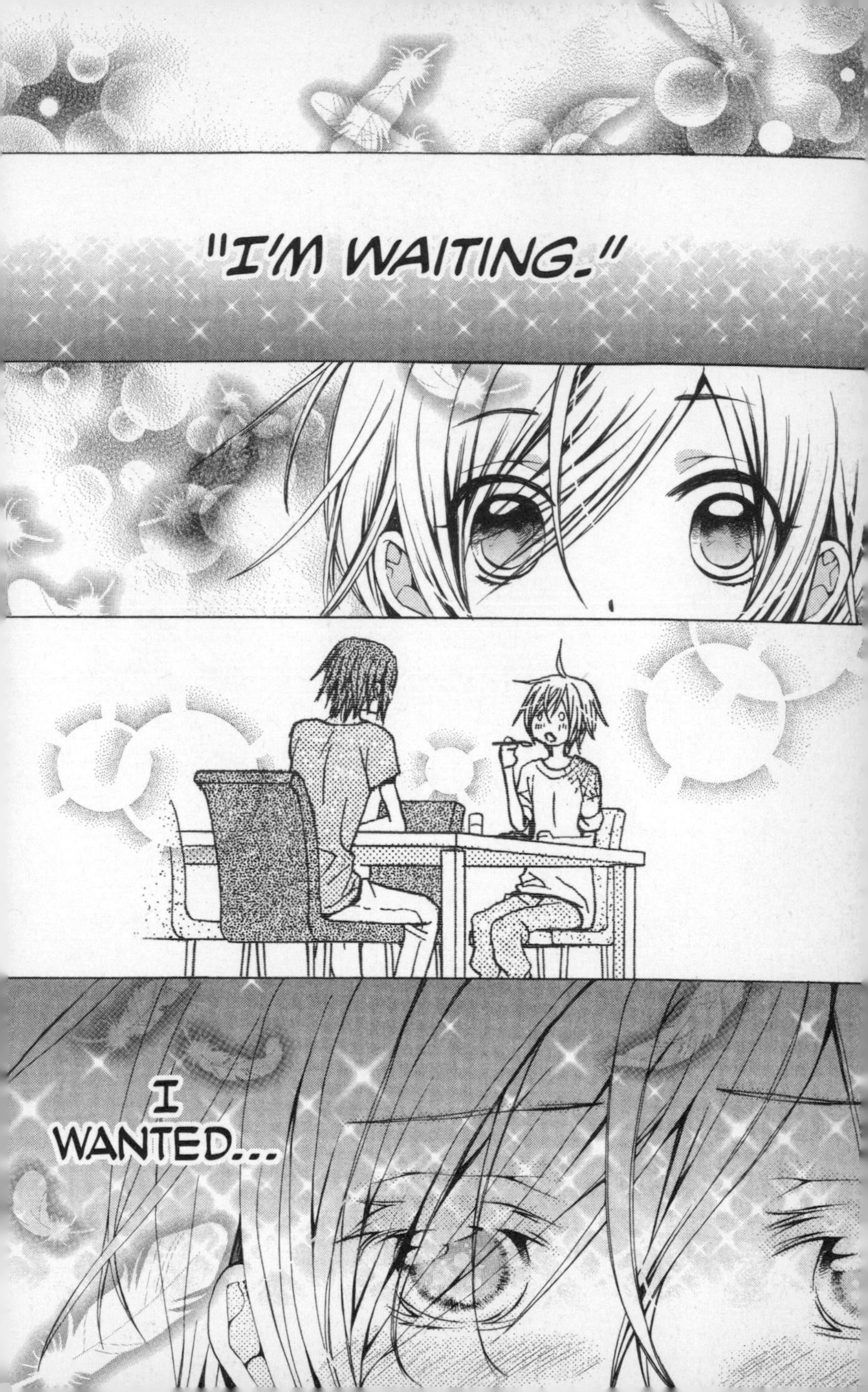
"I'M WAITING."
I WANTED...

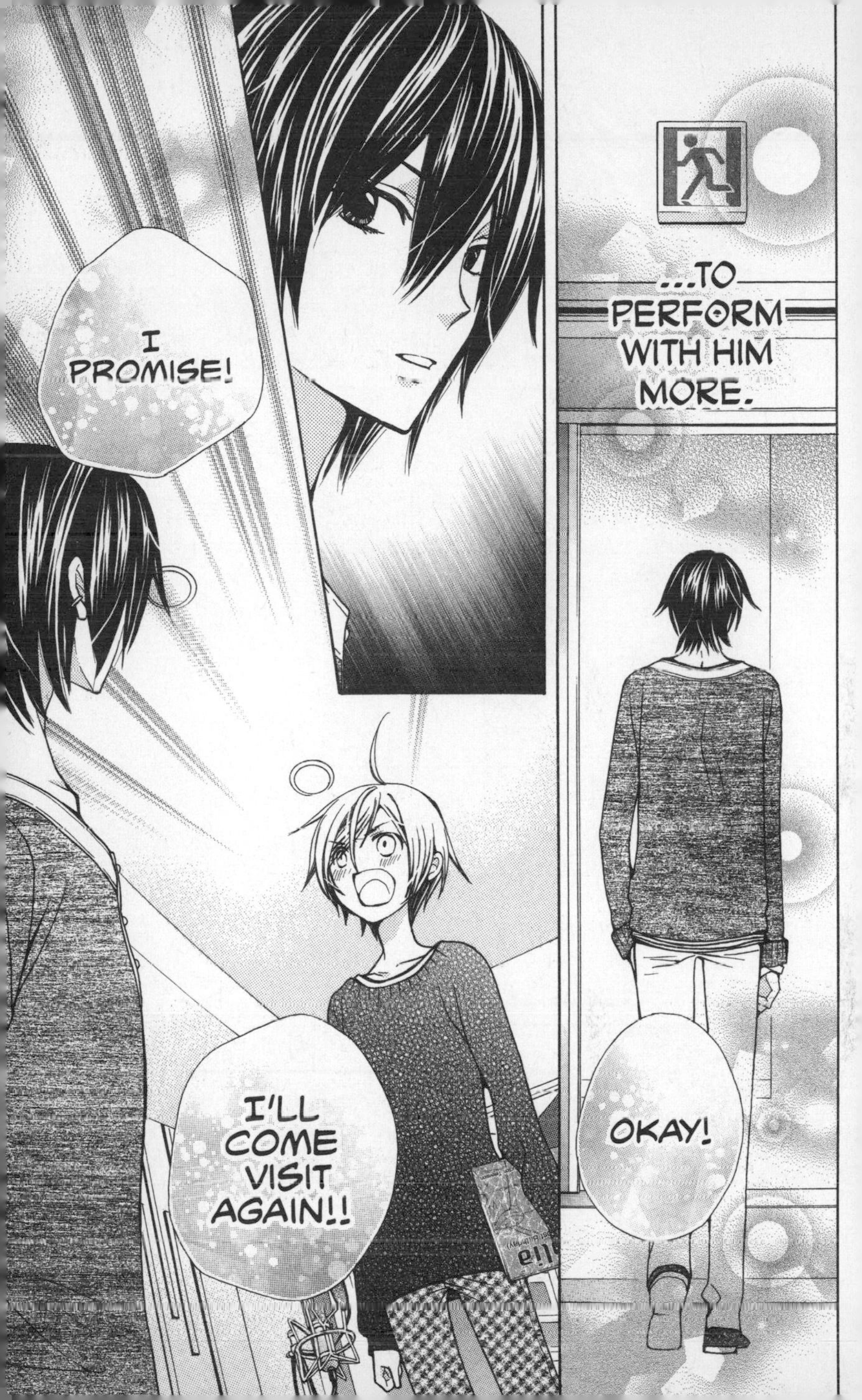
...TO PERFORM WITH HIM MORE.
OKAY!
I PROMISE!
I'LL COME VISIT AGAIN!!

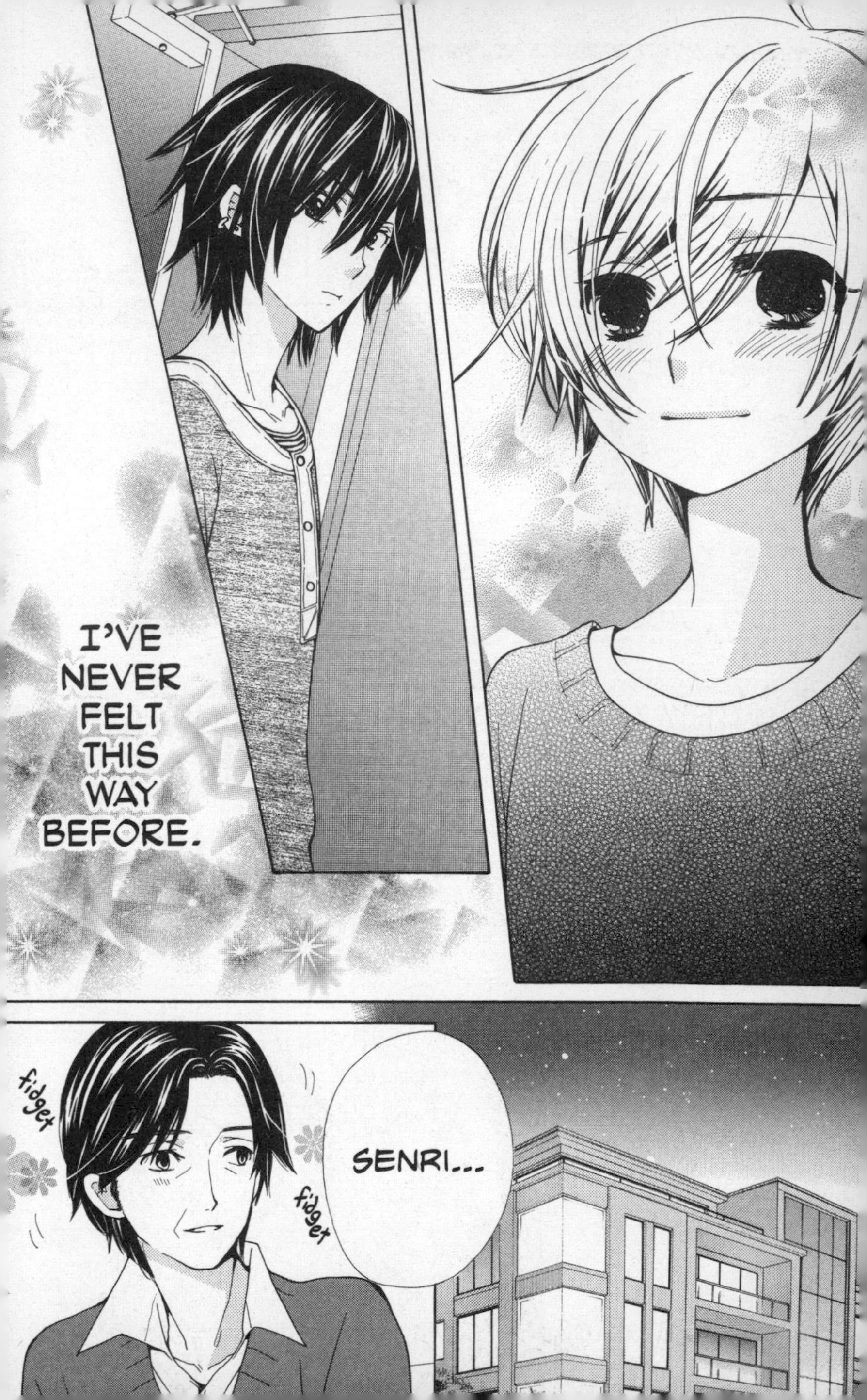
I'VE NEVER FELT THIS WAY BEFORE.
SENRI...
fidget
fidget

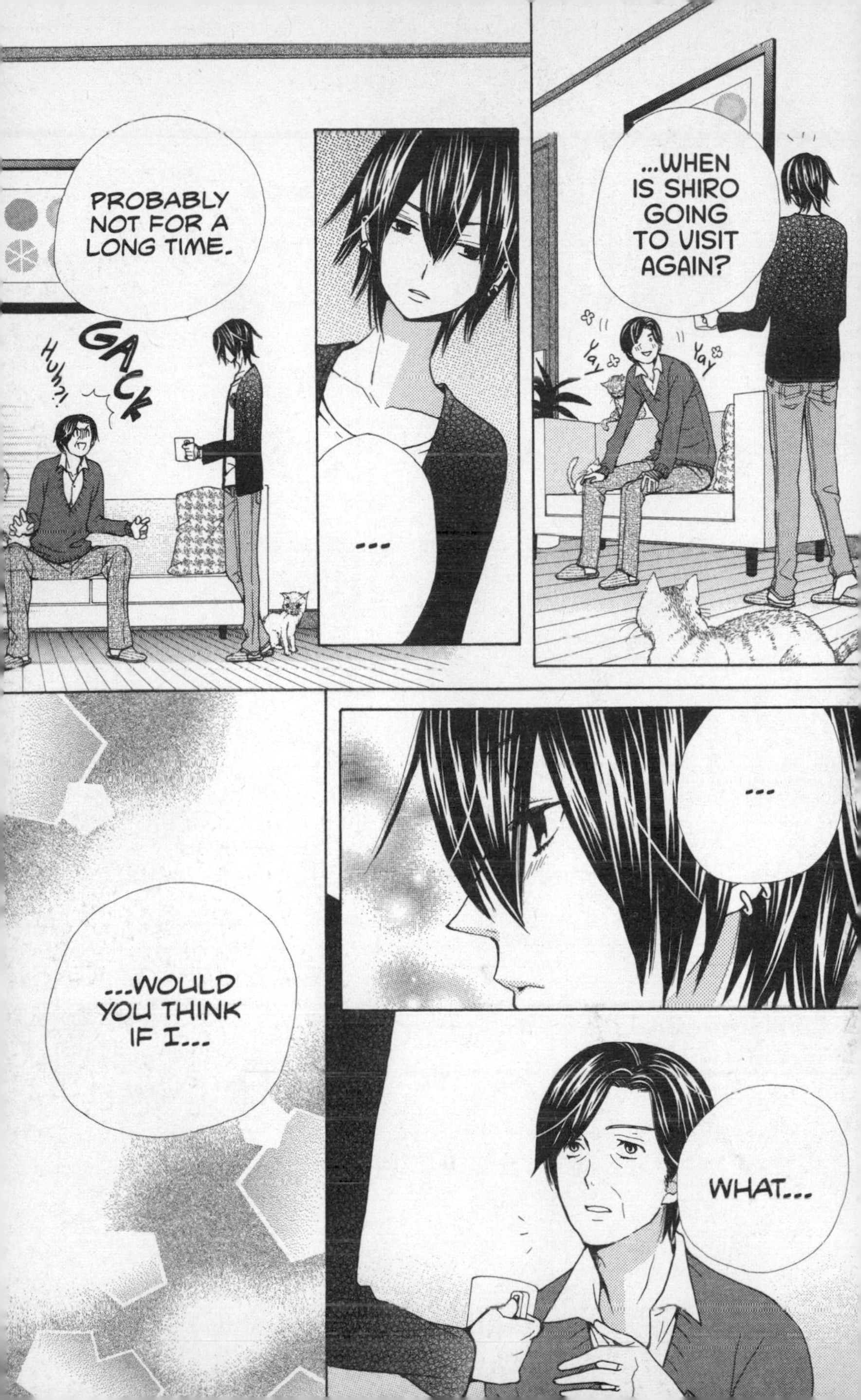
...WHEN IS SHIRO GOING TO VISIT AGAIN?
Yay
Yay
...
PROBABLY NOT FOR A LONG TIME.
GACK
Huh?!
...
WHAT...
...WOULD YOU THINK IF I...

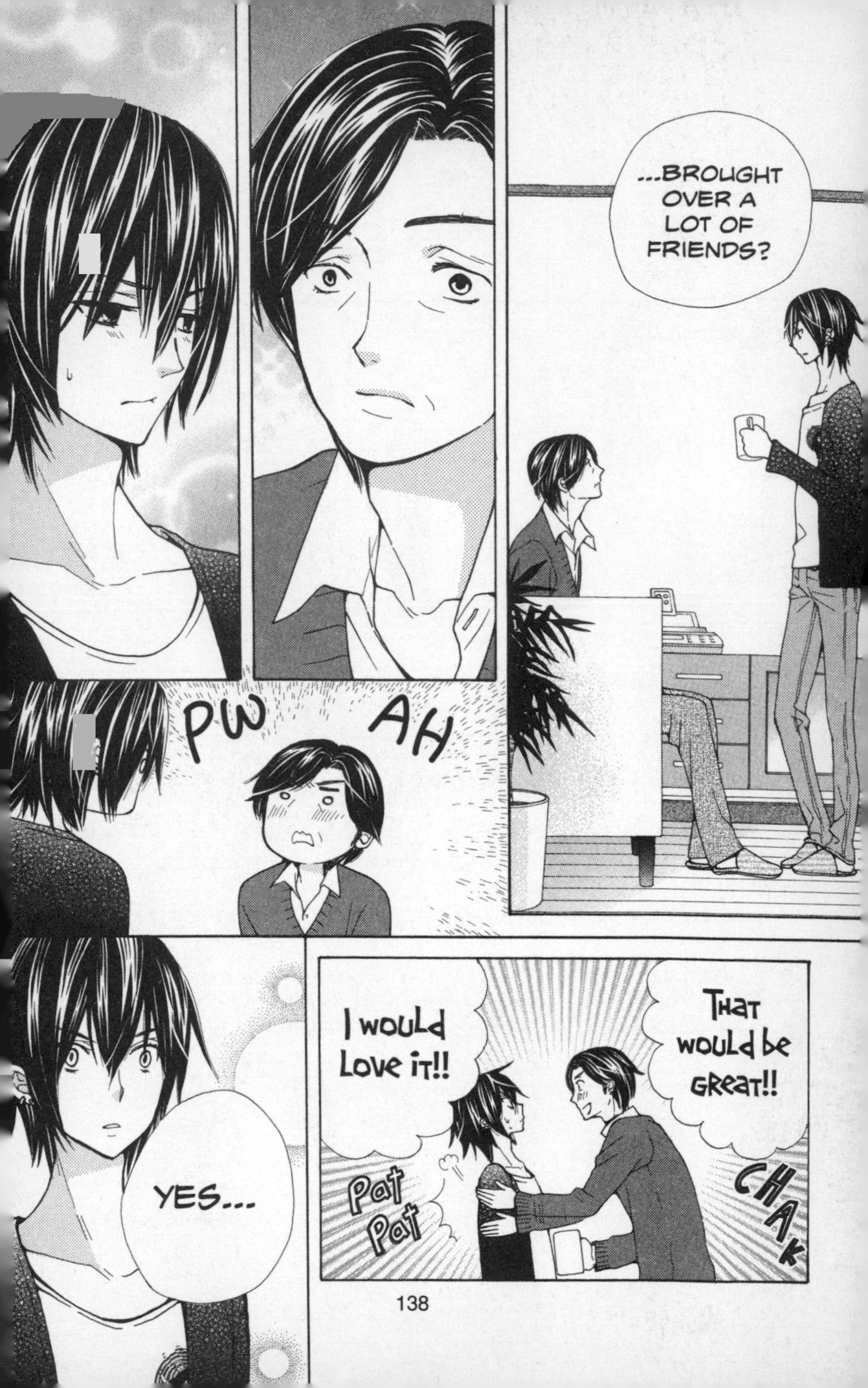
...BROUGHT OVER A LOT OF FRIENDS?
PW AH
That would be great!!
CHAK
I would Love it!!
Pat Pat
YES...

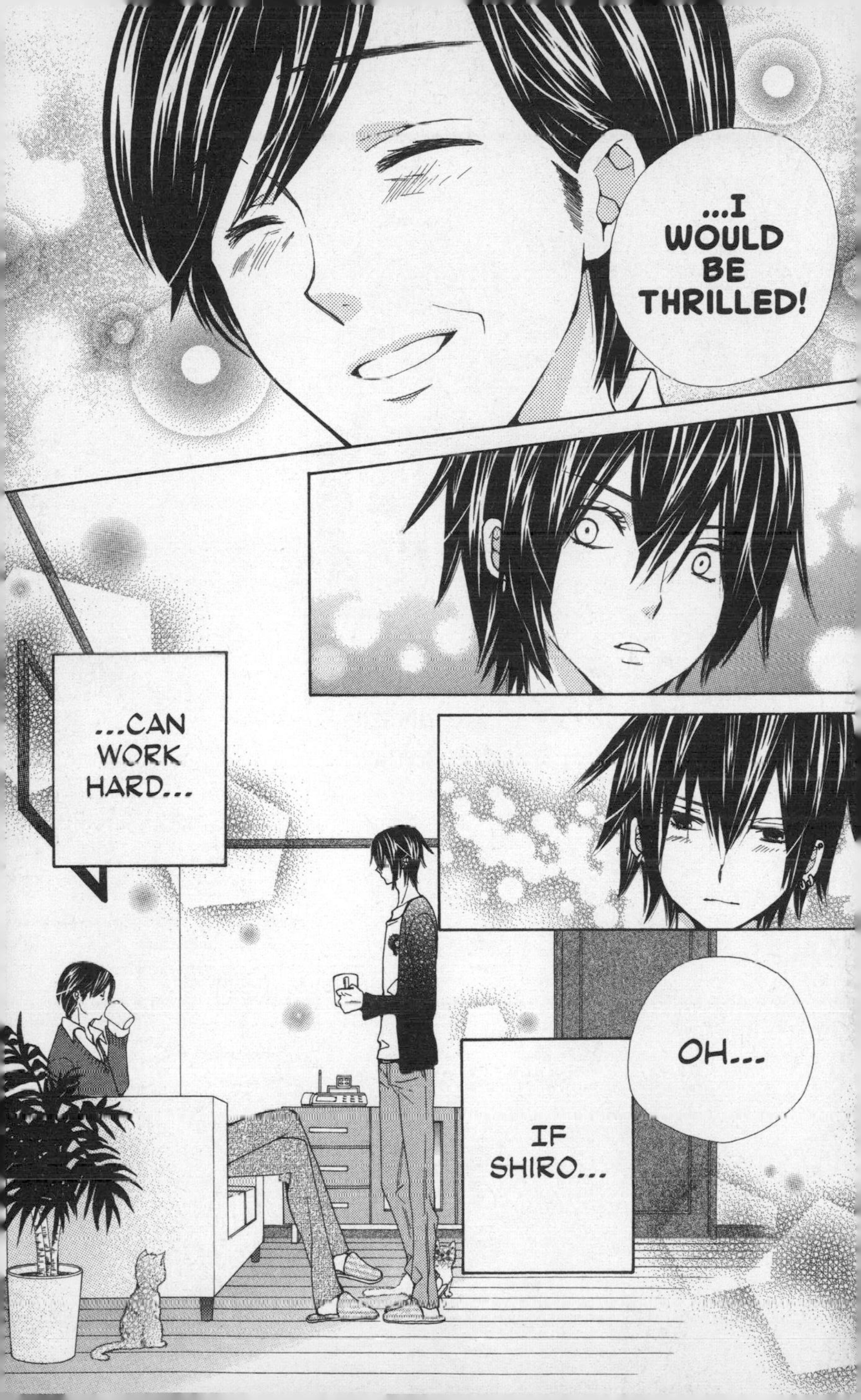
...I WOULD BE THRILLED!
OH...
IF SHIRO...
...CAN WORK HARD...

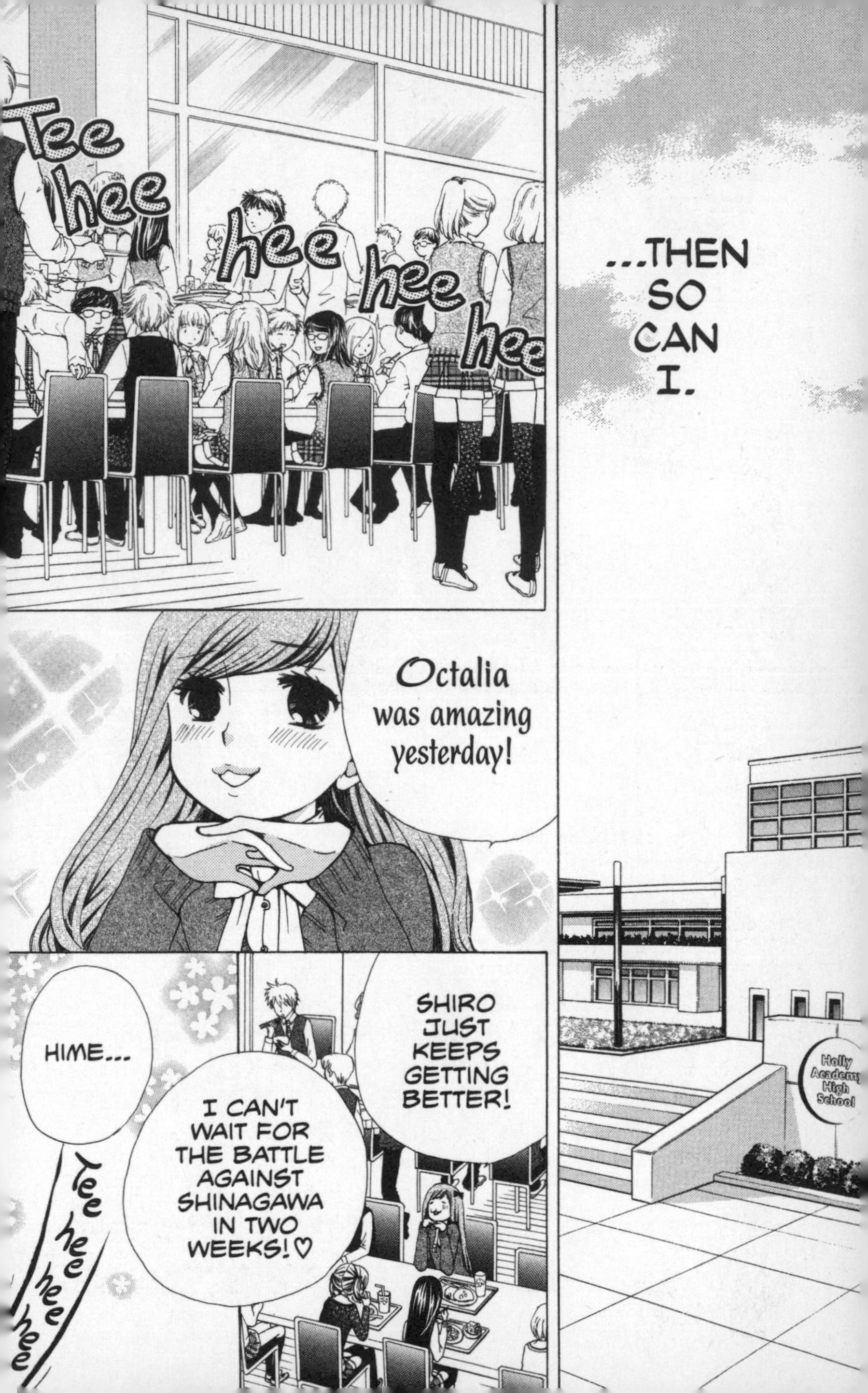
...THEN SO CAN I.
Holly Academy High School
Tee hee hee hee hee
Octalia was amazing yesterday!
SHIRO JUST KEEPS GETTING BETTER!
I CAN'T WAIT FOR THE BATTLE AGAINST SHINAGAWA IN TWO WEEKS! ♡
HIME...
Tee hee hee hee hee

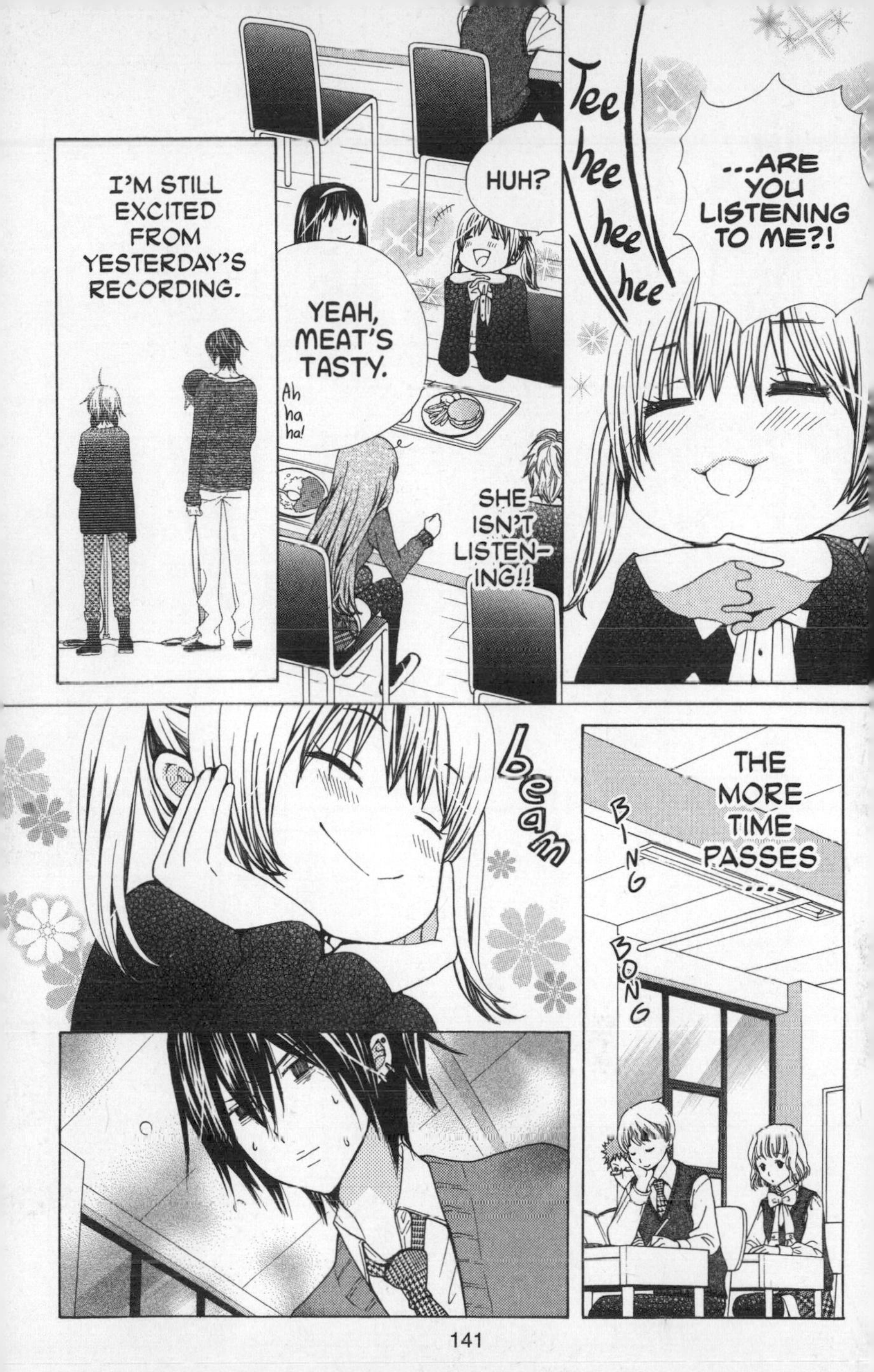
...ARE YOU LISTENING TO ME?!
Tee hee hee hee
HUH?
YEAH, MEAT'S TASTY.
Ah ha ha!
SHE ISN'T LISTEN-ING!!
I'M STILL EXCITED FROM YESTERDAY'S RECORDING.
THE MORE TIME PASSES...
BING
BONG
beam

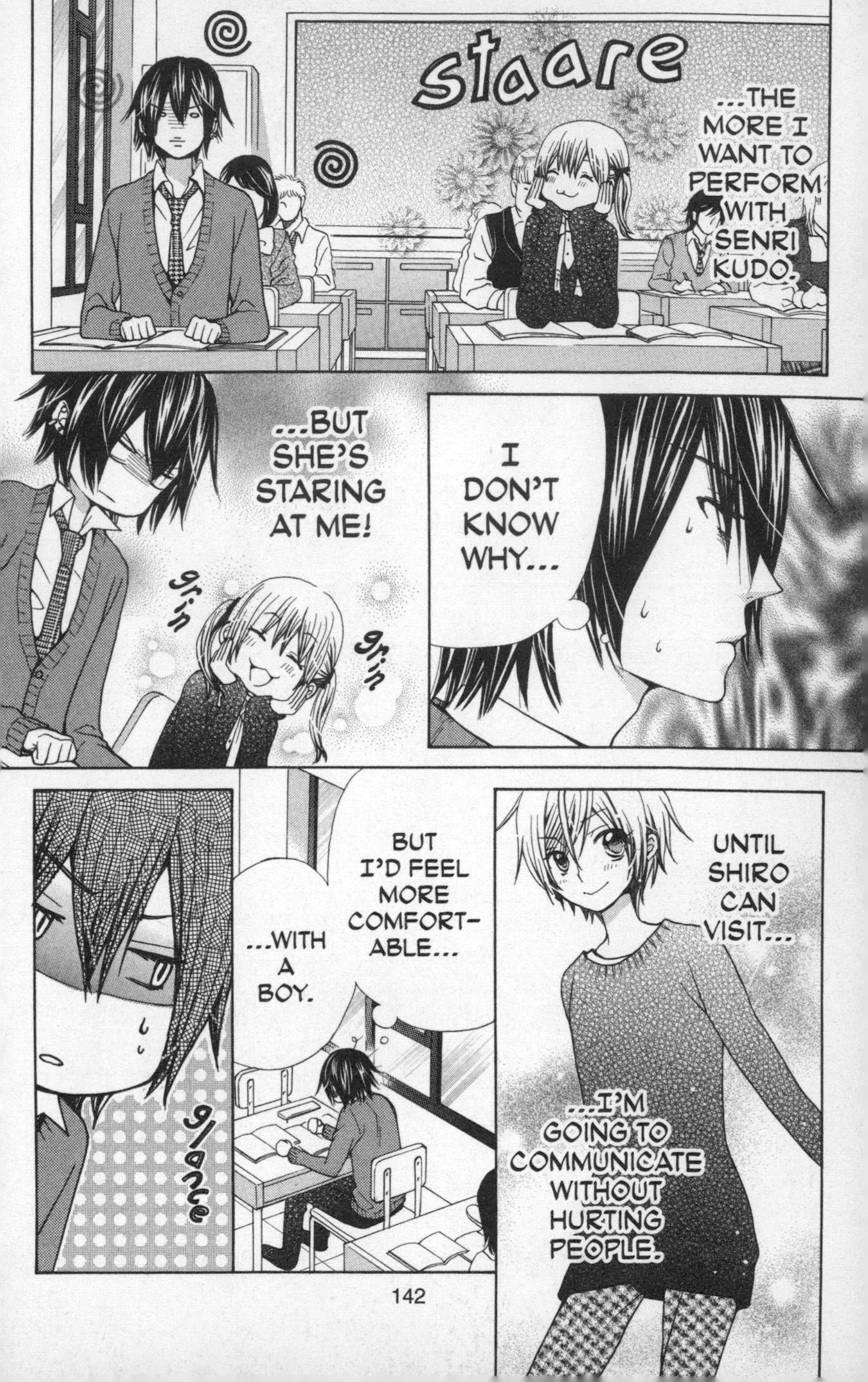
...THE MORE I WANT TO PERFORM WITH SENRI KUDO.
staare
I DON'T KNOW WHY...
...BUT SHE'S STARING AT ME!
grin
grin
UNTIL SHIRO CAN VISIT...
...I'M GOING TO COMMUNICATE WITHOUT HURTING PEOPLE.
BUT I'D FEEL MORE COMFORT-ABLE...
...WITH A BOY.
glance

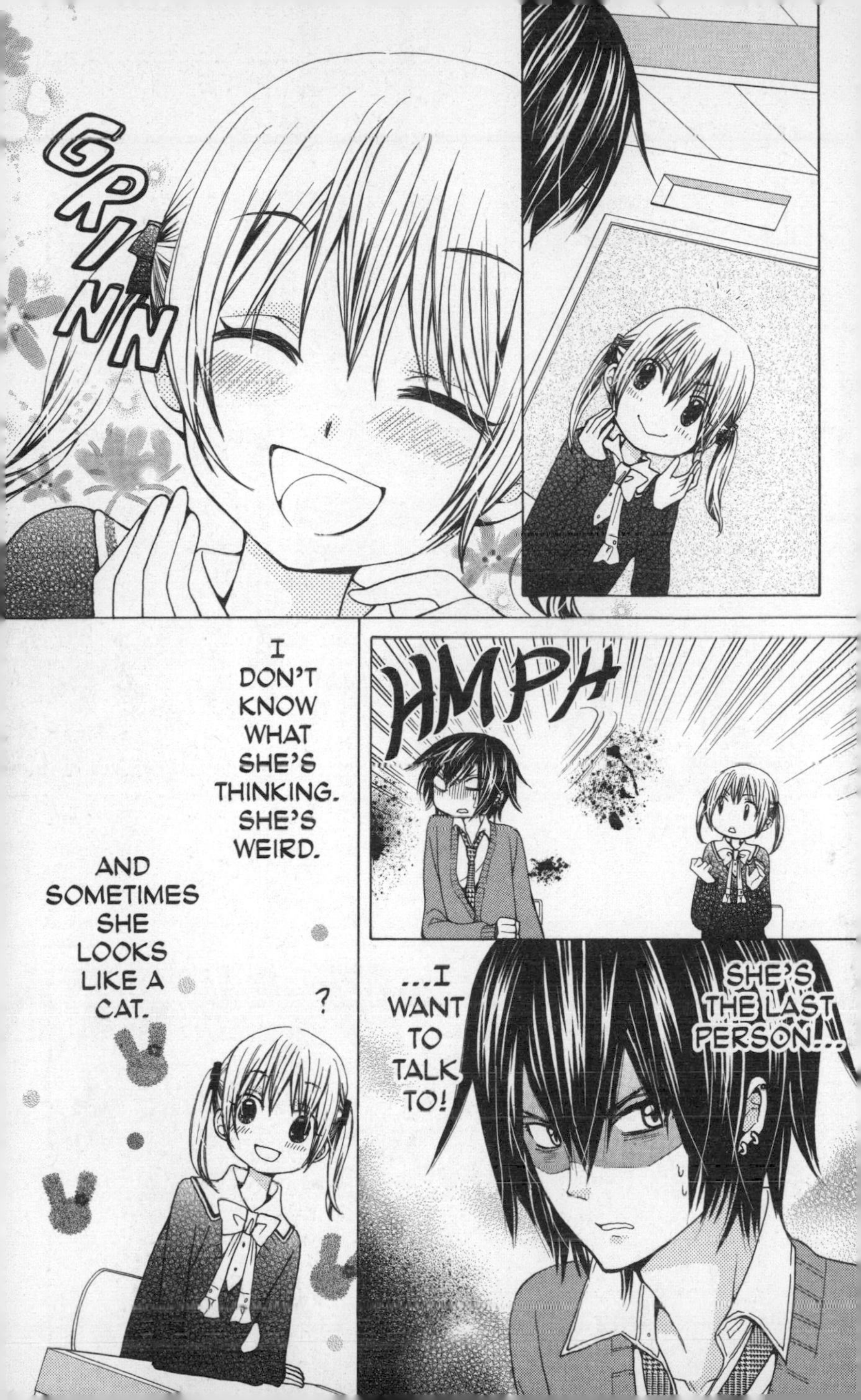
GRINN
HMPH
SHE'S THE LAST PERSON...
...I WANT TO TALK TO!
I DON'T KNOW WHAT SHE'S THINKING. SHE'S WEIRD.
AND SOMETIMES SHE LOOKS LIKE A CAT.
?

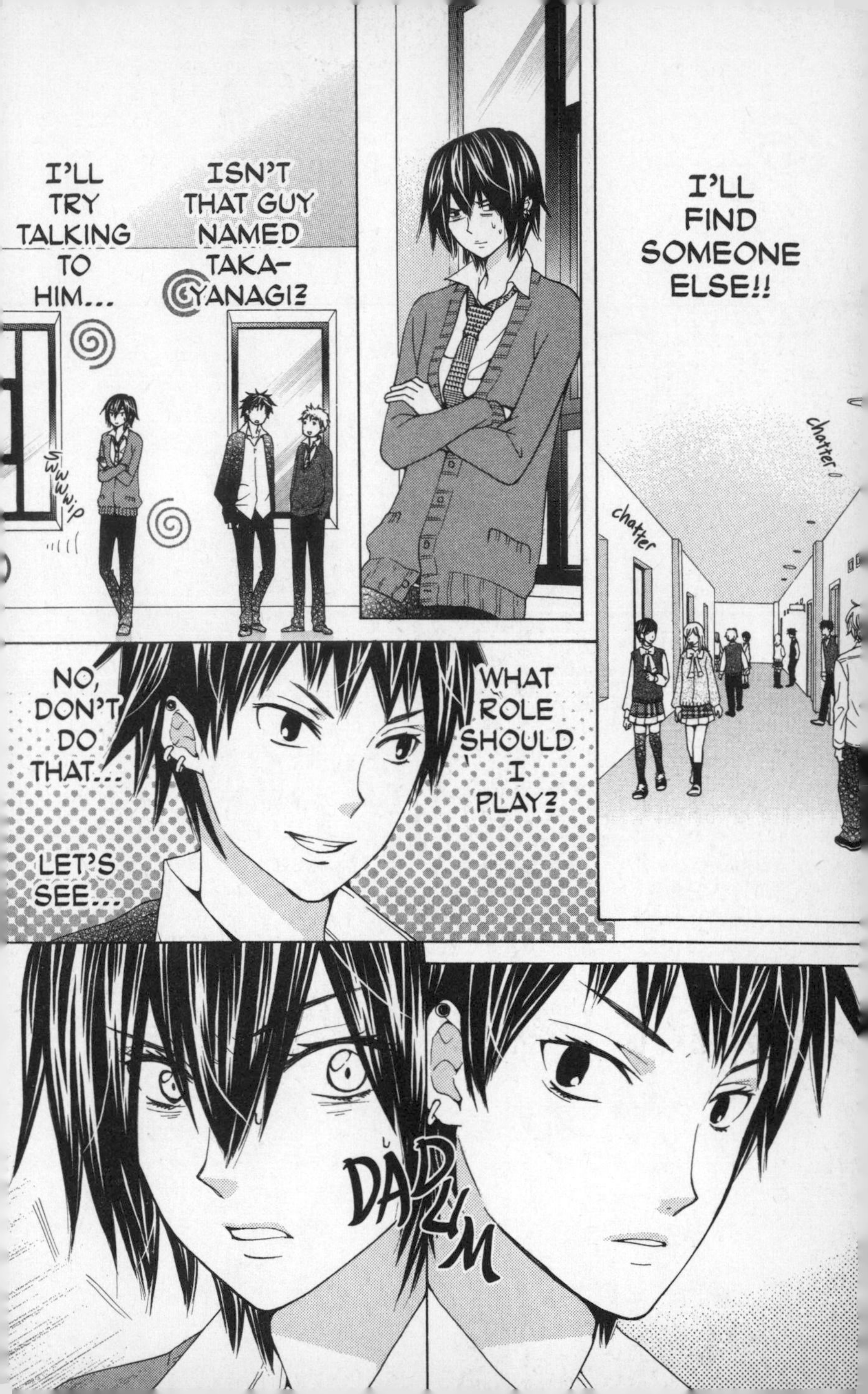

I'LL FIND SOMEONE ELSE!!
chatter
chatter
ISN'T THAT GUY NAMED TAKA-YANAGI?
I'LL TRY TALKING TO HIM...
swwwip
WHAT ROLE SHOULD I PLAY?
NO, DON'T DO THAT...
LET'S SEE...
DADUM

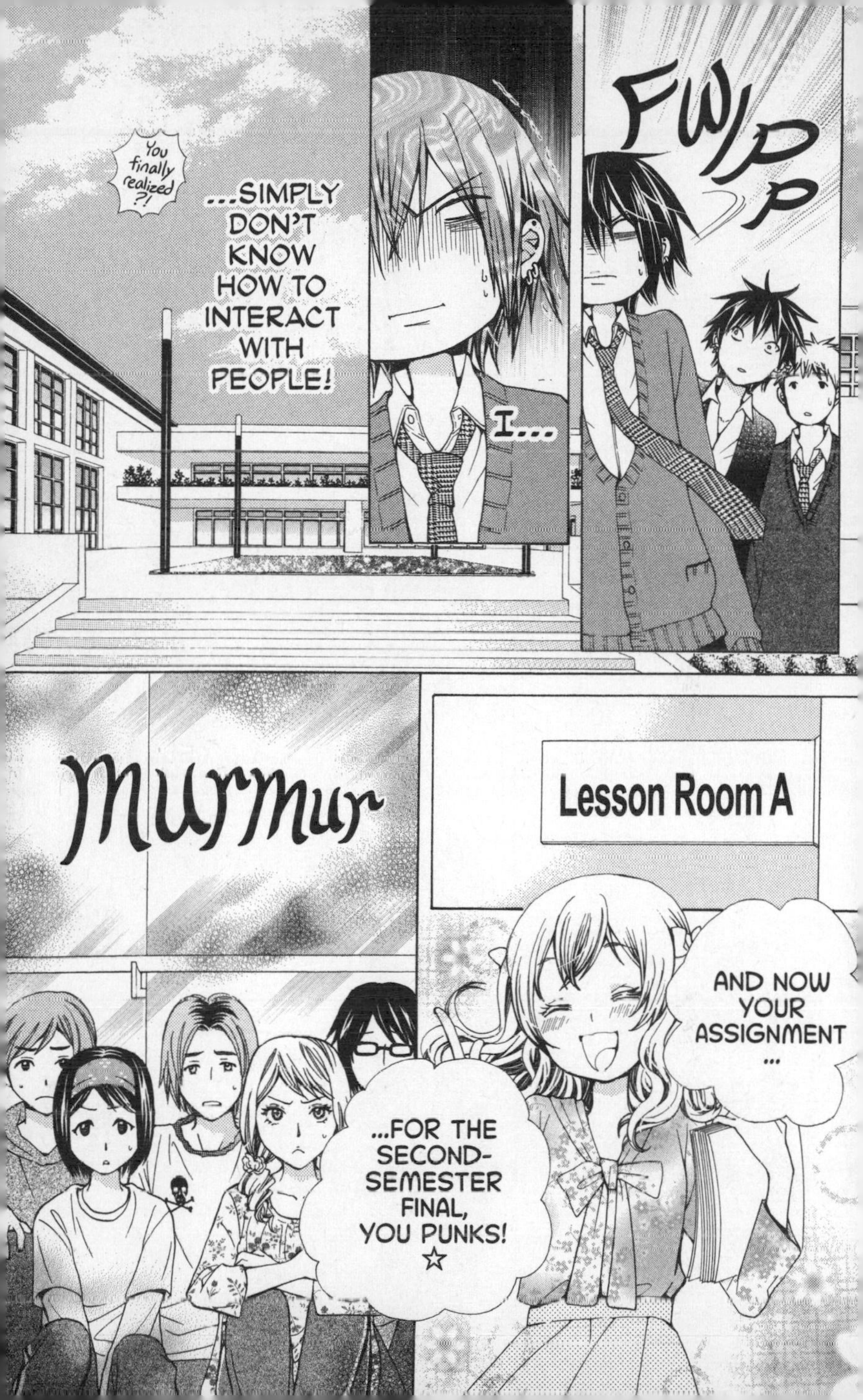
FWIP P
I...
...SIMPLY DON'T KNOW HOW TO INTERACT WITH PEOPLE!
You finally realized?!
Lesson Room A
murmur
AND NOW YOUR ASSIGNMENT ...
...FOR THE SECOND-SEMESTER FINAL, YOU PUNKS! ☆

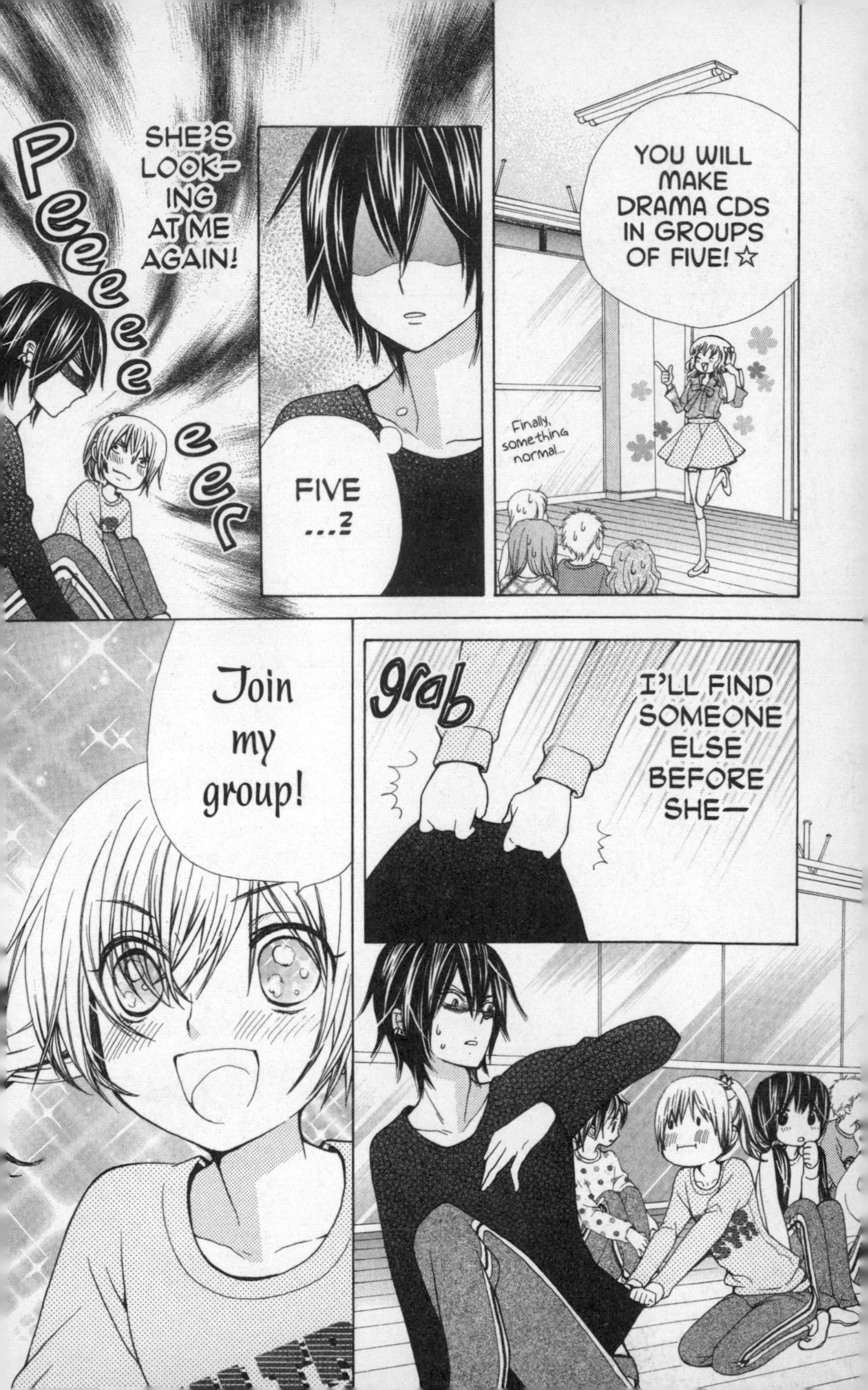
YOU WILL MAKE DRAMA CDS IN GROUPS OF FIVE! ☆
Finally, something normal...
FIVE ...?
Peeeeeeeer
SHE'S LOOK-ING AT ME AGAIN!
grab
I'LL FIND SOMEONE ELSE BEFORE SHE—
Join my group!

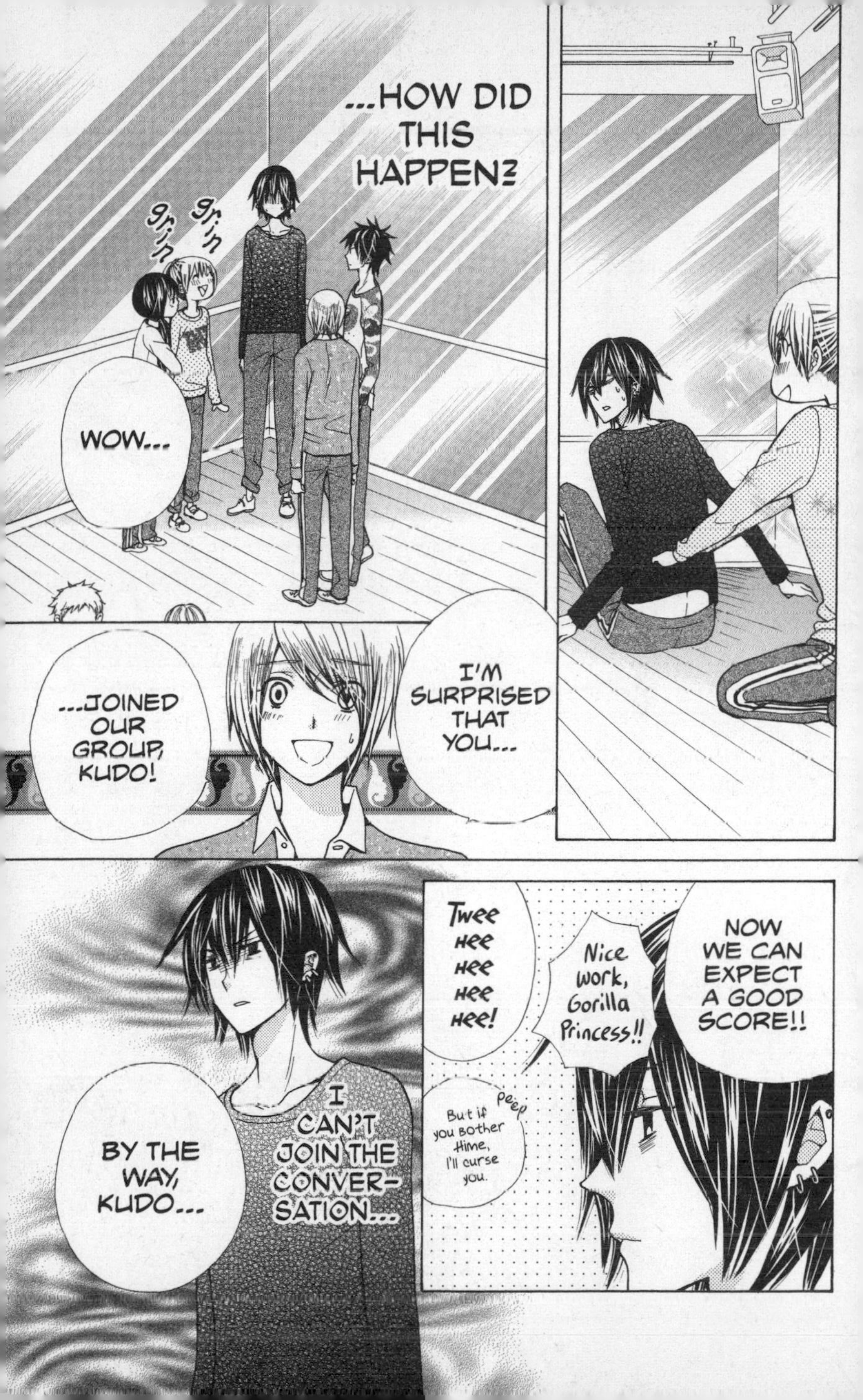
...HOW DID THIS HAPPEN?
grin
grin
WOW...
I'M SURPRISED THAT YOU...
...JOINED OUR GROUP, KUDO!
NOW WE CAN EXPECT A GOOD SCORE!!
Nice work, Gorilla Princess!!
Twee hee hee hee hee!
peep
But if you bother Hime, I'll curse you.
I CAN'T JOIN THE CONVERSATION...
BY THE WAY, KUDO...

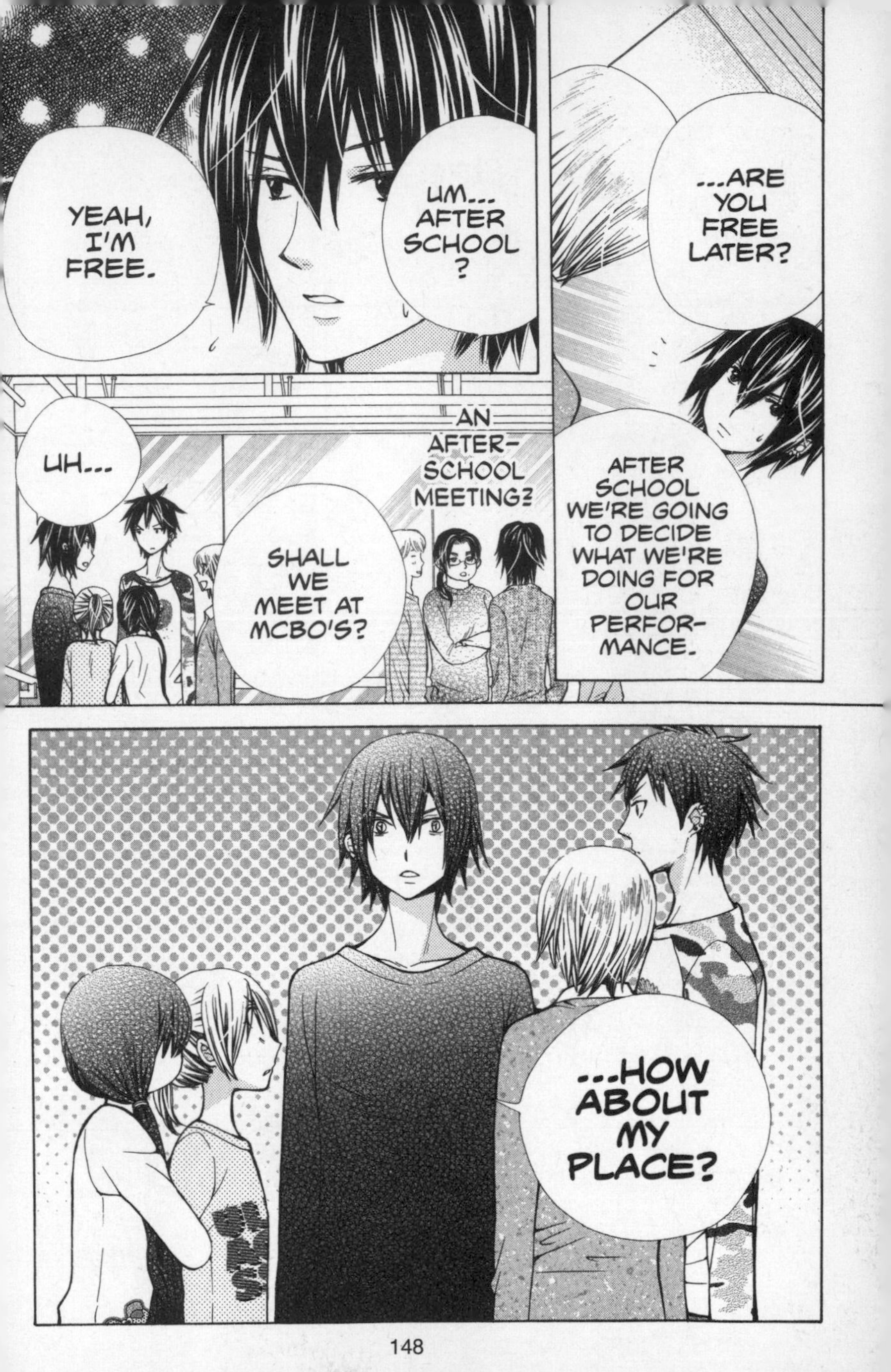
...ARE YOU FREE LATER?
UM... AFTER SCHOOL?
YEAH, I'M FREE.
AFTER SCHOOL WE'RE GOING TO DECIDE WHAT WE'RE DOING FOR OUR PERFORMANCE.
AN AFTER-SCHOOL MEETING?
SHALL WE MEET AT MCBO'S?
UH...
...HOW ABOUT MY PLACE?

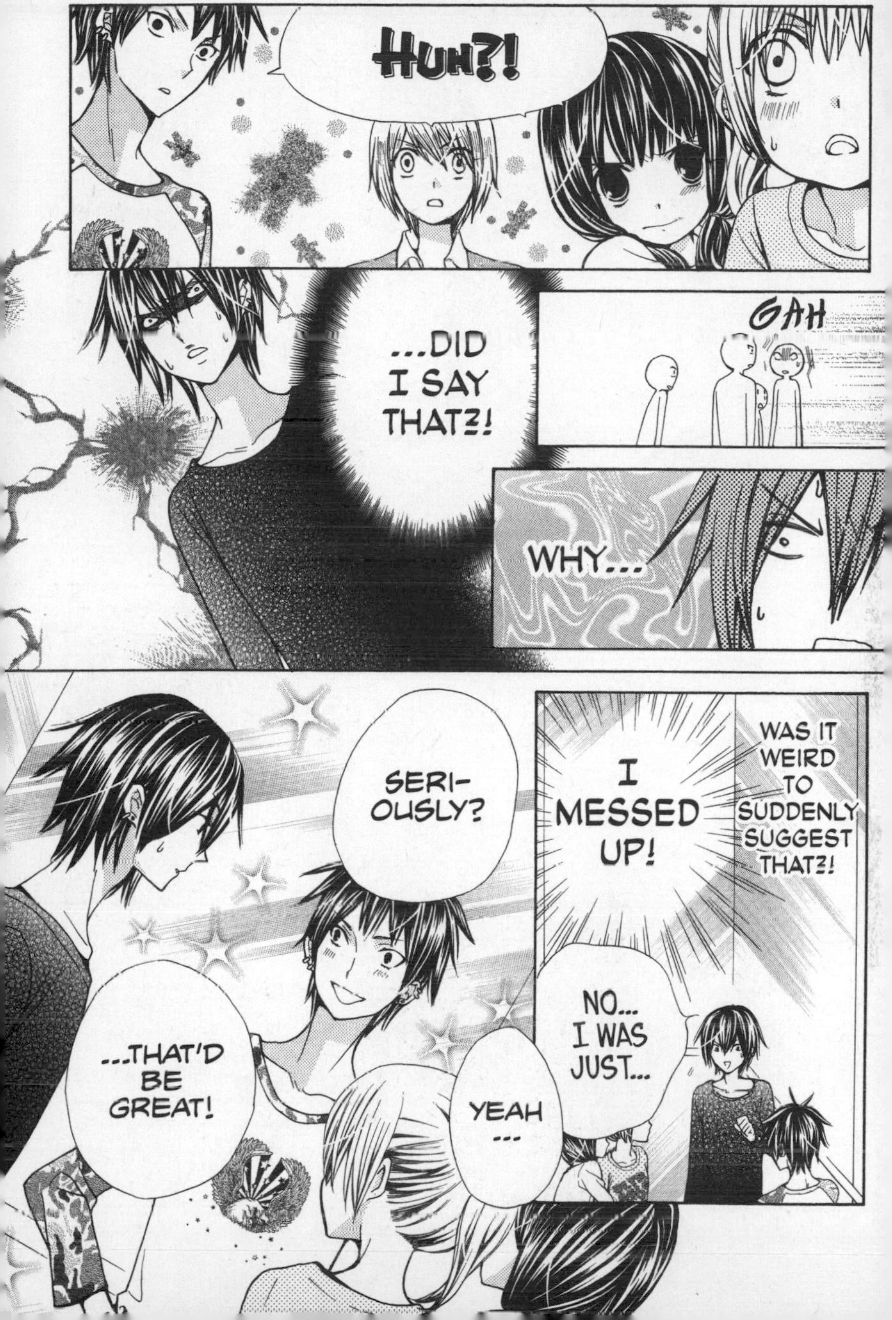
HUH?!
GAH
WHY...
...DID I SAY THAT?!
WAS IT WEIRD TO SUDDENLY SUGGEST THAT?!
I MESSED UP!
NO... I WAS JUST...
SERI-OUSLY?
YEAH ...
...THAT'D BE GREAT!

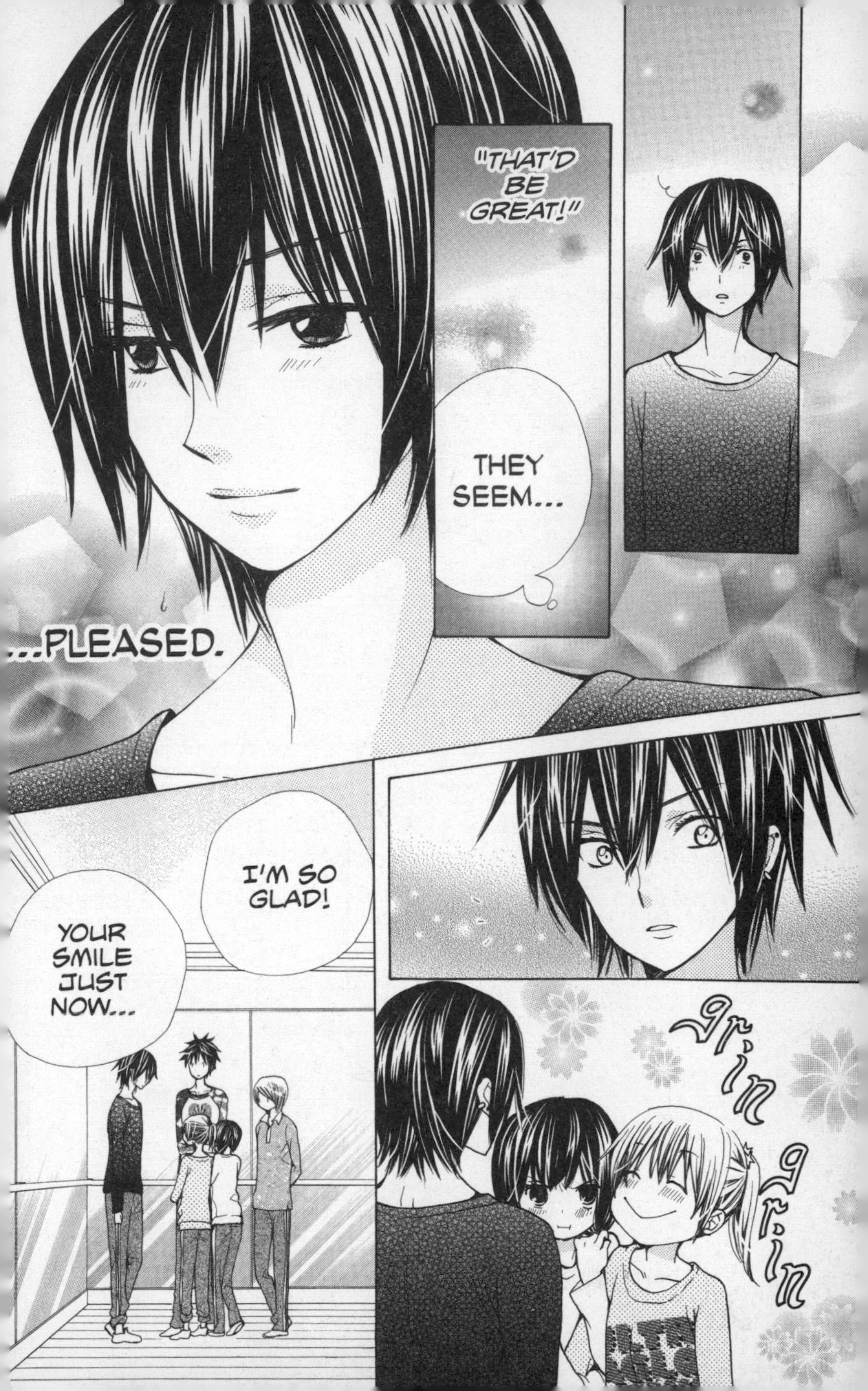
"THAT'D BE GREAT!"
THEY SEEM...
...PLEASED.
grin grin
I'M SO GLAD!
YOUR SMILE JUST NOW...

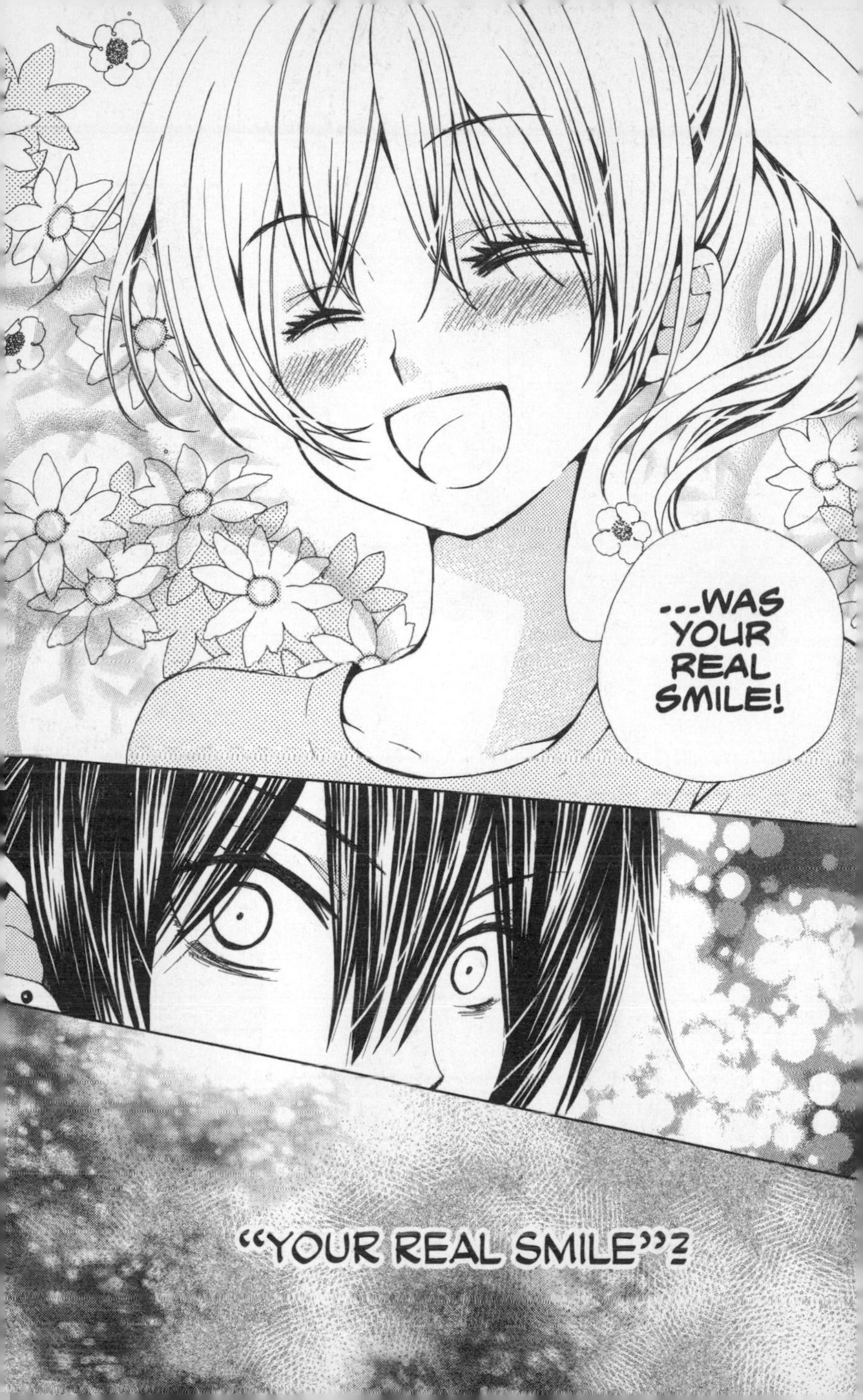
...WAS YOUR REAL SMILE!
"YOUR REAL SMILE"?

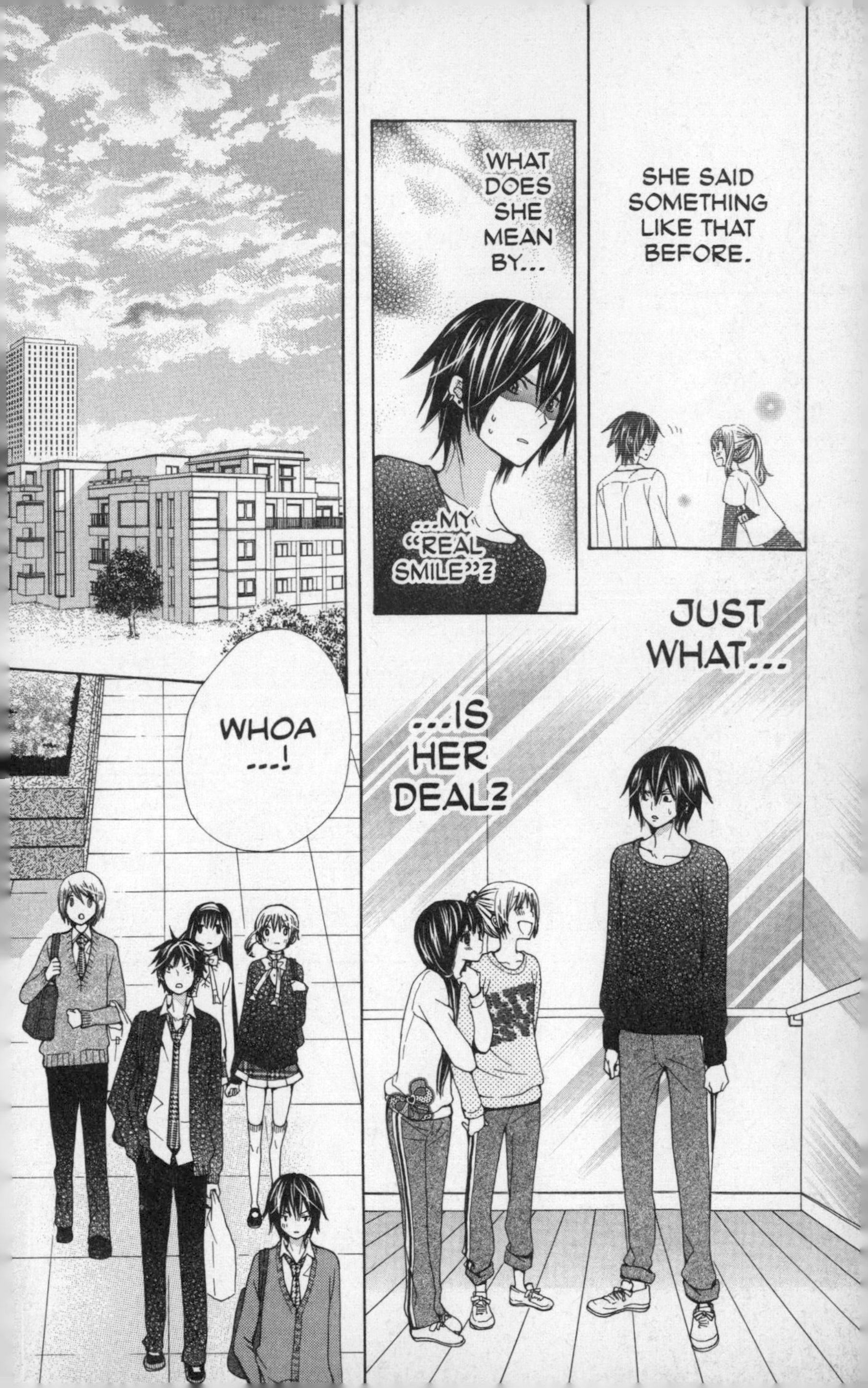
SHE SAID SOMETHING LIKE THAT BEFORE.
WHAT DOES SHE MEAN BY...
...MY "REAL SMILE"?
JUST WHAT...
...IS HER DEAL?
WHOA ...!

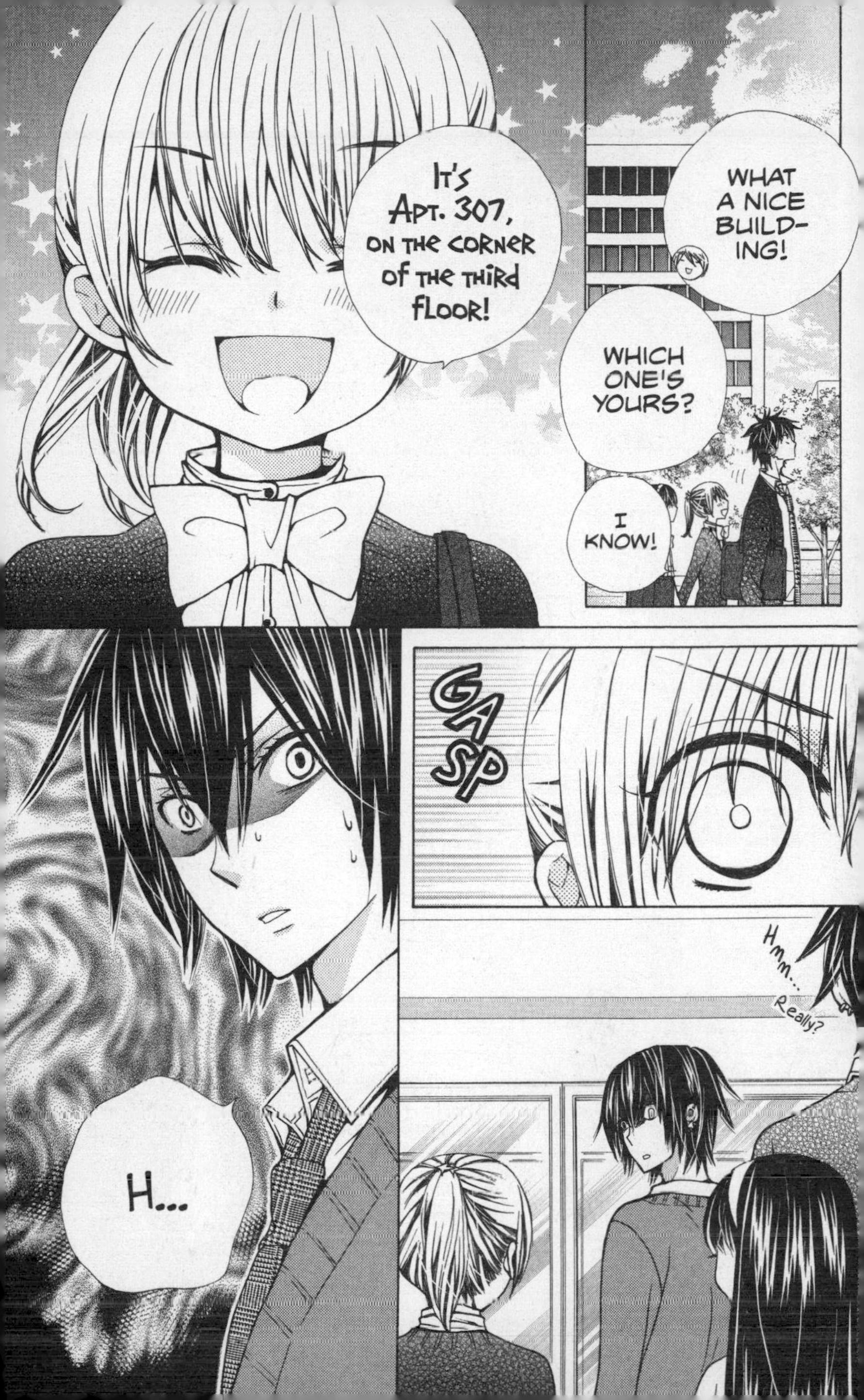
WHAT A NICE BUILD-ING!
WHICH ONE'S YOURS?
I KNOW!
It's Apt. 307, on the corner of the third floor!
GASP
Hmm... Really?
H...

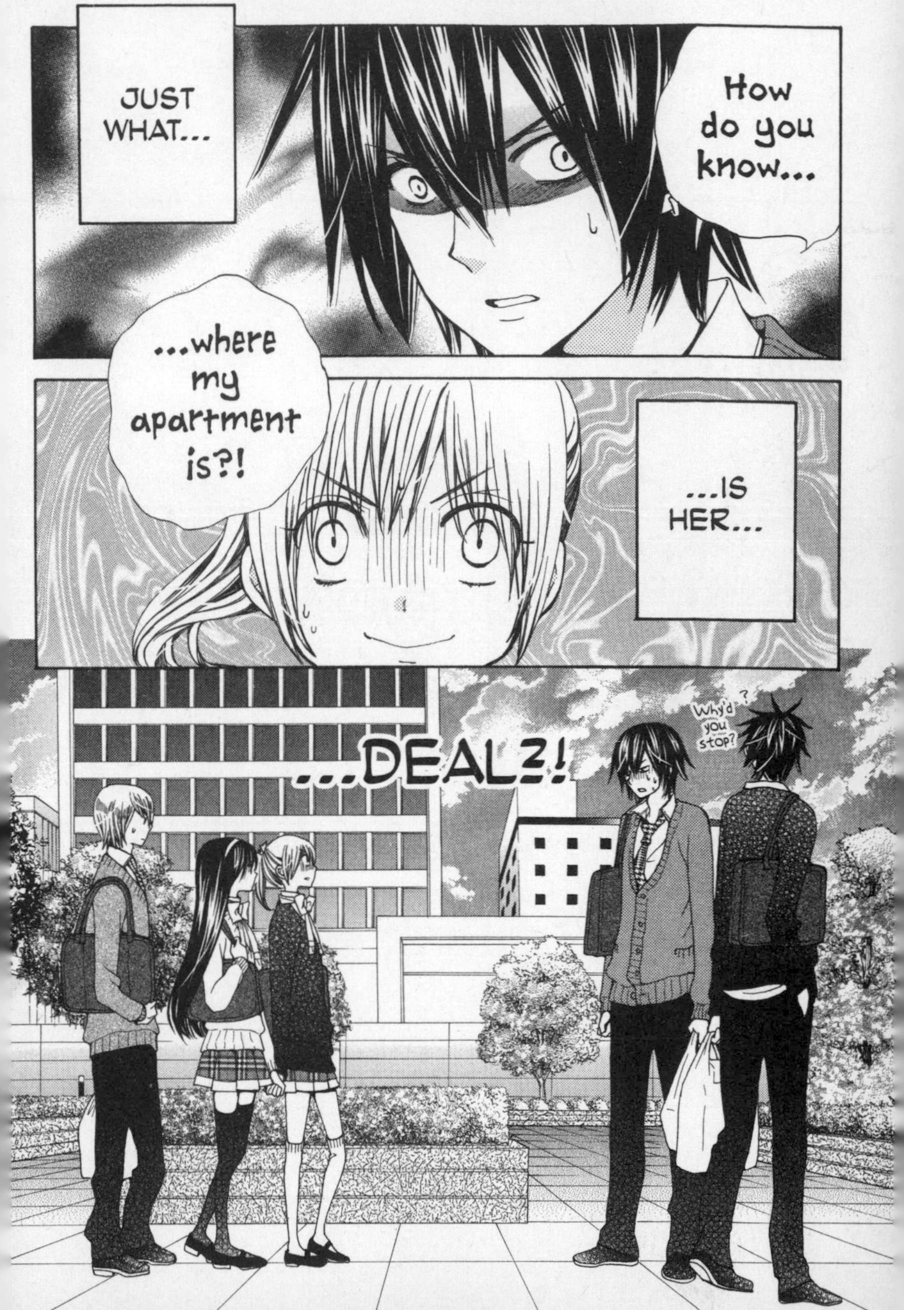
How do you know...
JUST WHAT...
...where my apartment is?!
...IS HER...
Why'd you stop?
...DEAL?!

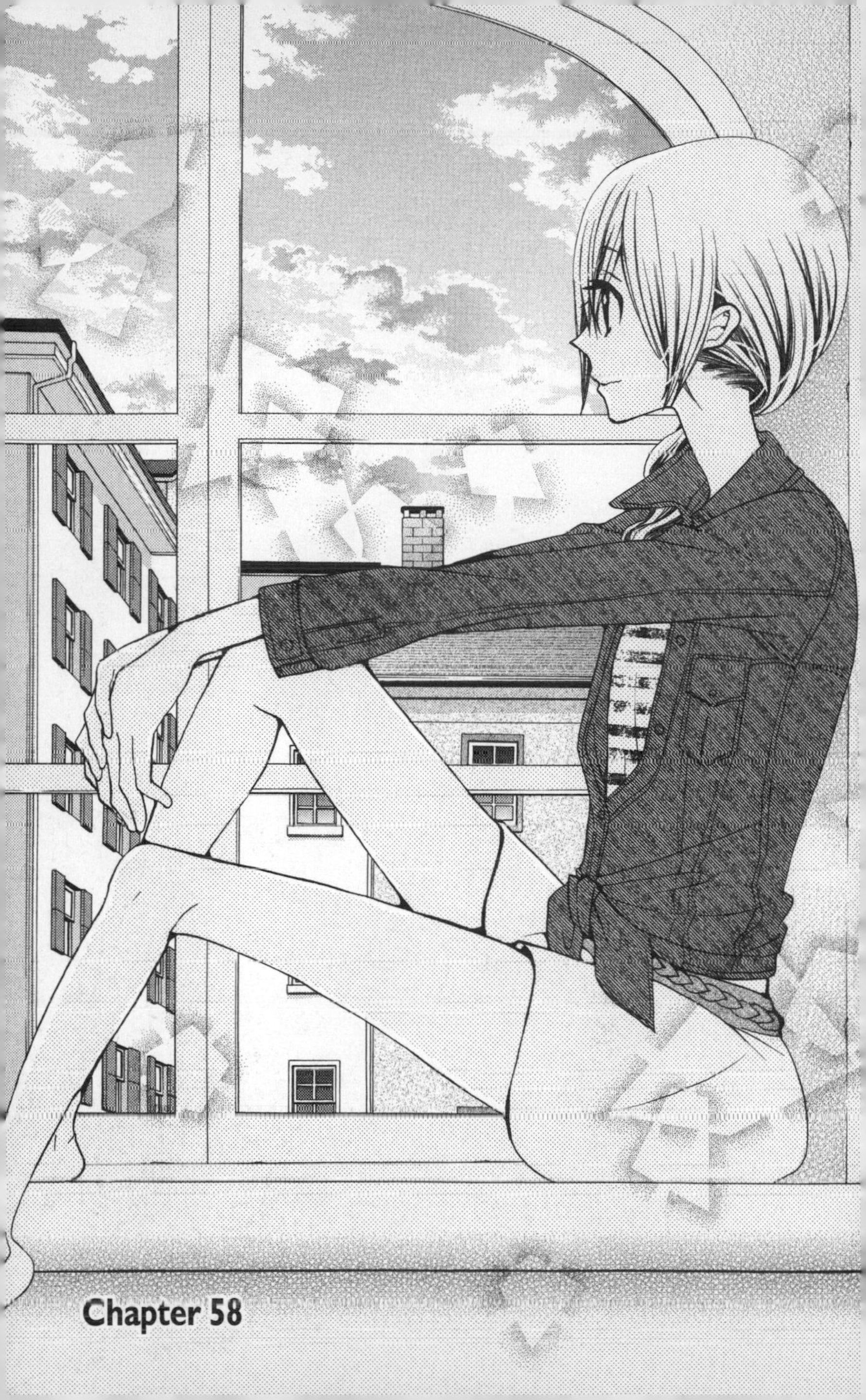

Chapter 58

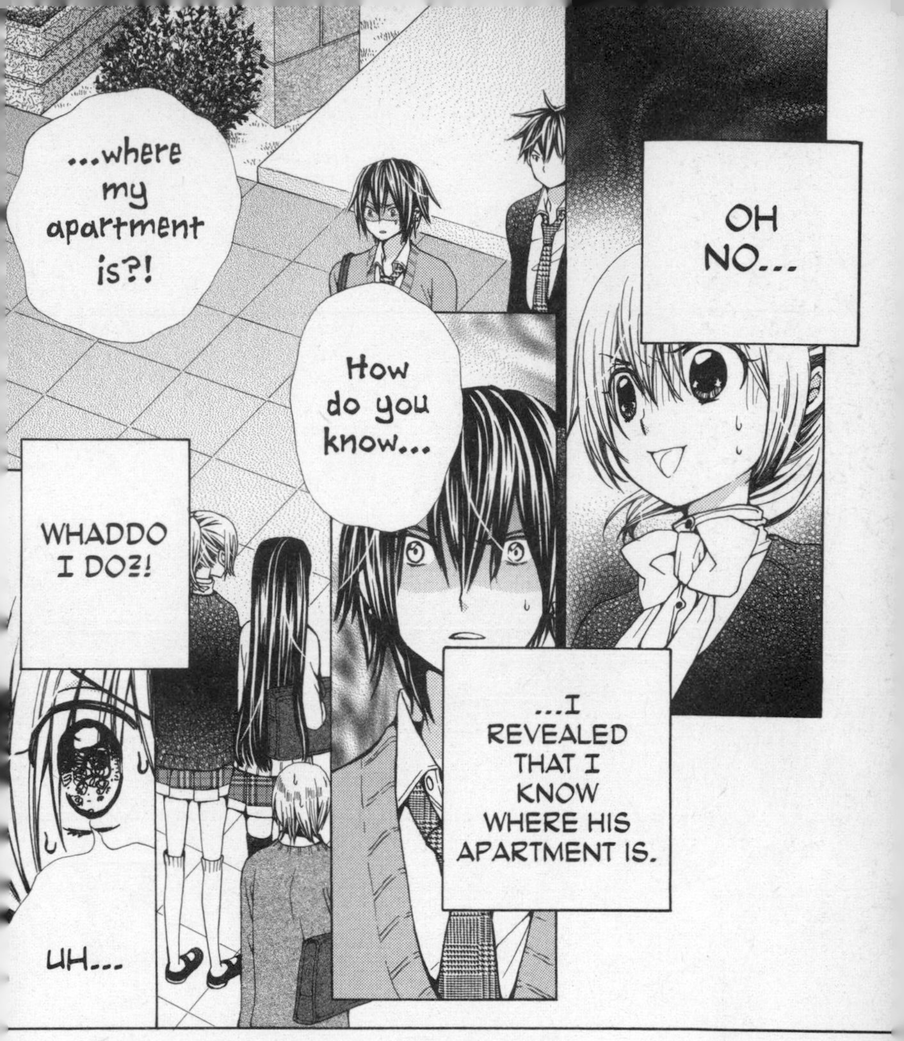
How do you know...
...where my apartment is?!
OH NO...
...I REVEALED THAT I KNOW WHERE HIS APARTMENT IS.
WHADDO I DO?!
UH...

• Various Things •

• A guest drew the bonus pages this time, so I'll use this space to say thanks!!!

• Yoko Kamio •

S-S-S-S-Sensei!! Huff huff huff huff!!! I was prepared for rejection, but when I asked you to do it, you cheerfully replied, "Okay! ★" Thank you!! You're an angel! You've taken care of and been kind to me ever since my assistant days, so I've always admired and wanted to be like you. No amount of thanks will ever be enough. You drew Senri handsome and me 2,900 times better! Thank you for the great bonus manga!!

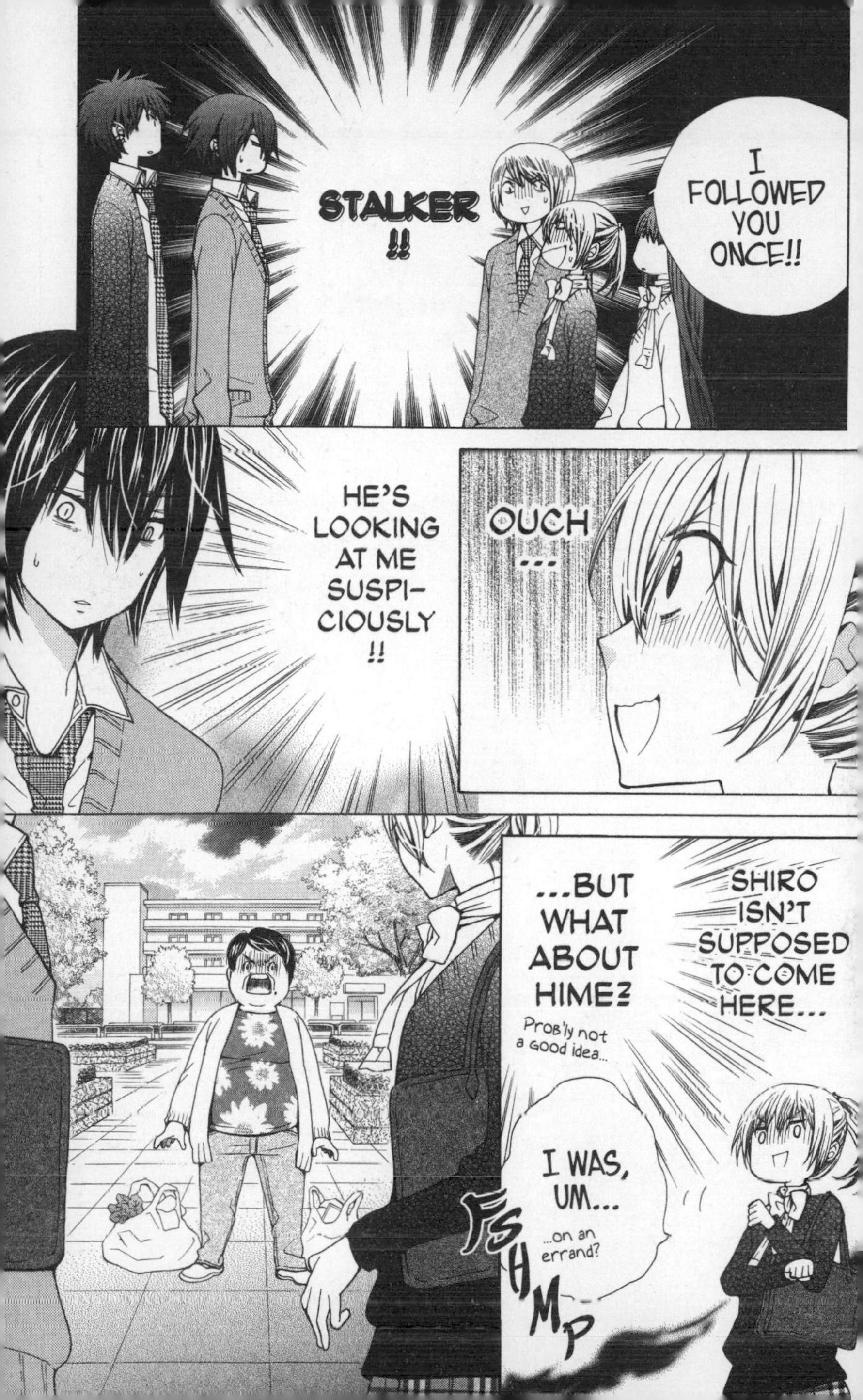
I FOLLOWED YOU ONCE!!
STALKER !!
OUCH...
HE'S LOOKING AT ME SUSPICIOUSLY!!
SHIRO ISN'T SUPPOSED TO COME HERE...
...BUT WHAT ABOUT HIME?
Prob'ly not a good idea...
I WAS, UM...
...on an errand?
FSHMP

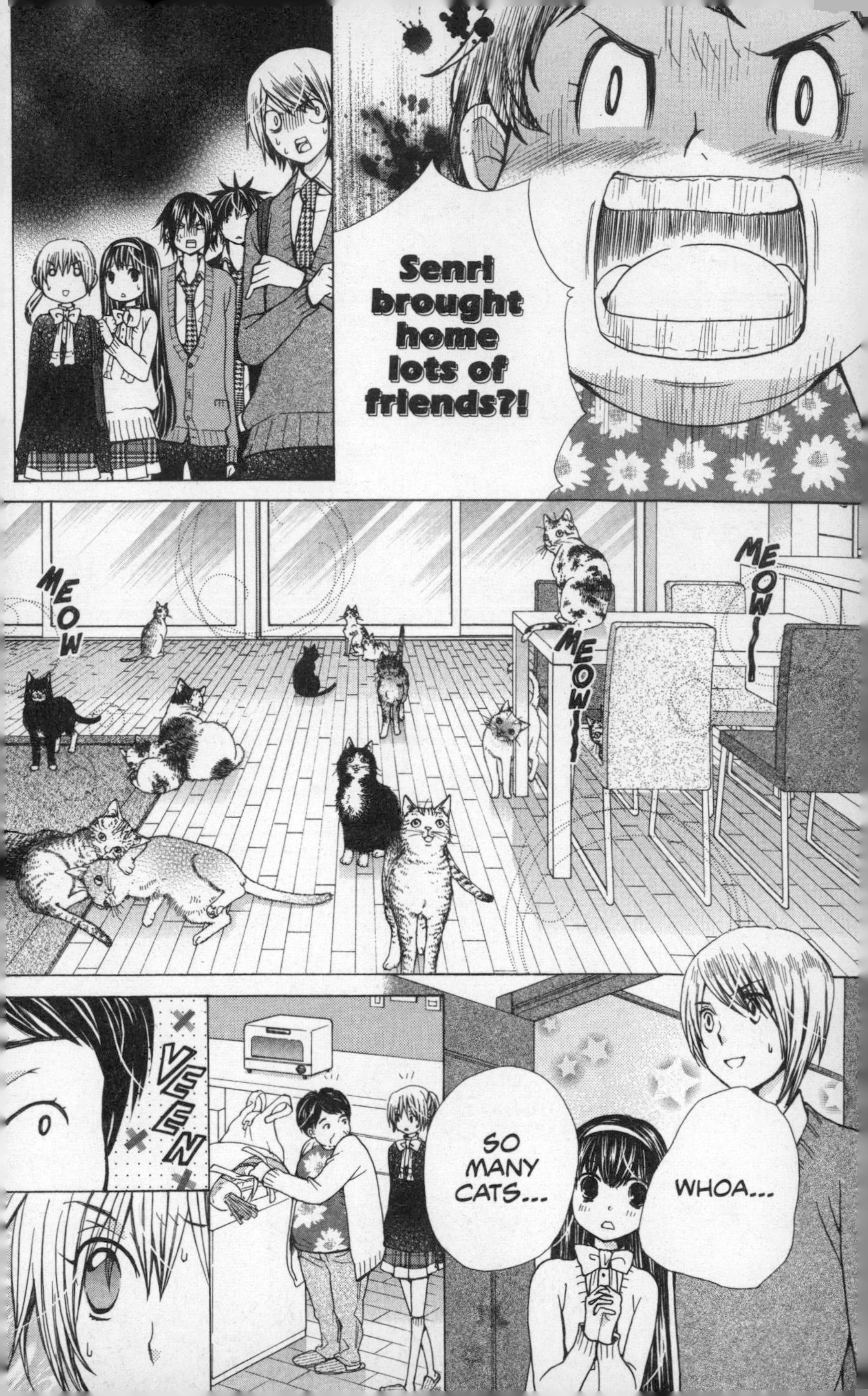
Senri brought home lots of friends?!
MEOW!
MEOW!
MEOW
WHOA...
SO MANY CATS...
VEEN

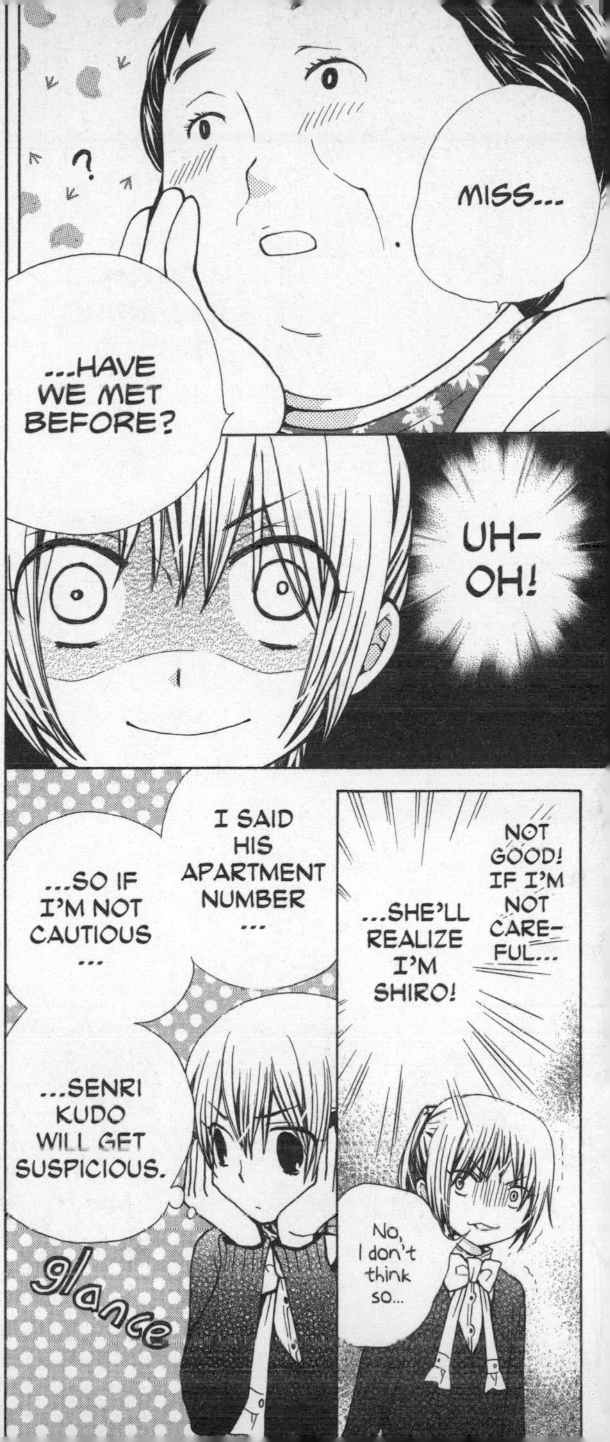
MISS...
...HAVE WE MET BEFORE?
UH-OH!
NOT GOOD! IF I'M NOT CARE-FUL...
...SHE'LL REALIZE I'M SHIRO!
No, I don't think so...
I SAID HIS APARTMENT NUMBER...
...SO IF I'M NOT CAUTIOUS...
...SENRI KUDO WILL GET SUSPICIOUS.
glance

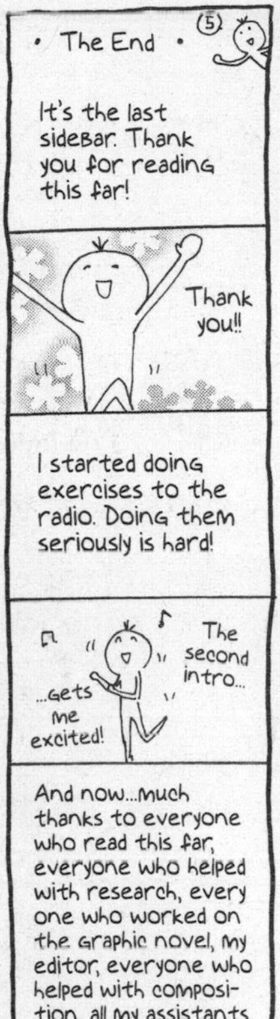
• The End • ⑤
It's the last sidebar. Thank you for reading this far!
Thank you!!
I started doing exercises to the radio. Doing them seriously is hard!
The second intro...
...gets me excited!
And now...much thanks to everyone who read this far, everyone who helped with research, every one who worked on the graphic novel, my editor, everyone who helped with composition, all my assistants, my friends and my family!!
♡ If you feel like it, lemme hear your thoughts! ♡
Maki Minami
c/o Shojo Beat
P.O. Box 77010
San Francisco, CA
94107
Maki Minami
南マキ
From the bottom...
...of my heart!

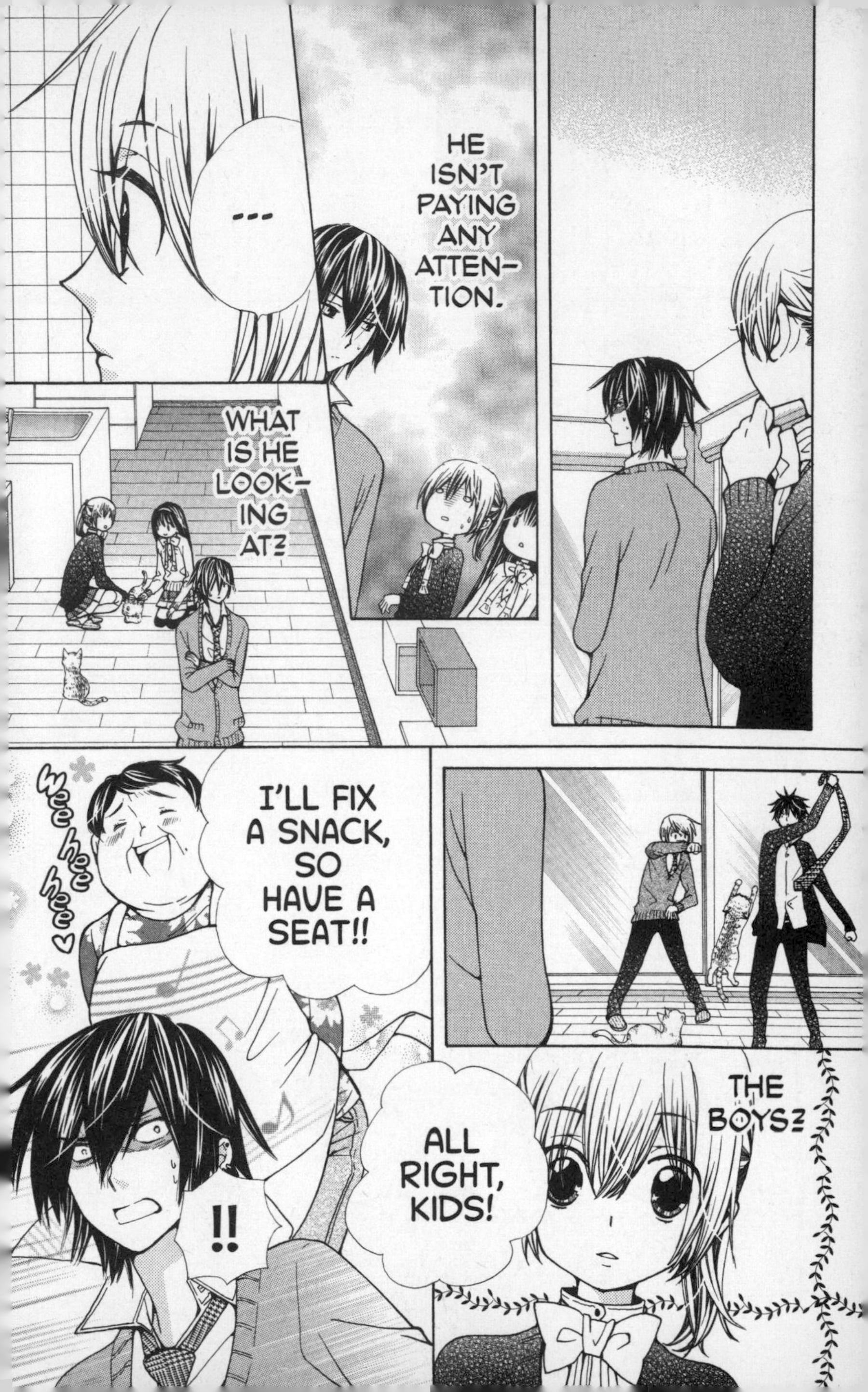
HE ISN'T PAYING ANY ATTENTION.
...
WHAT IS HE LOOKING AT?
THE BOYS?
I'LL FIX A SNACK, SO HAVE A SEAT!!
wee hee hee
ALL RIGHT, KIDS!
!!

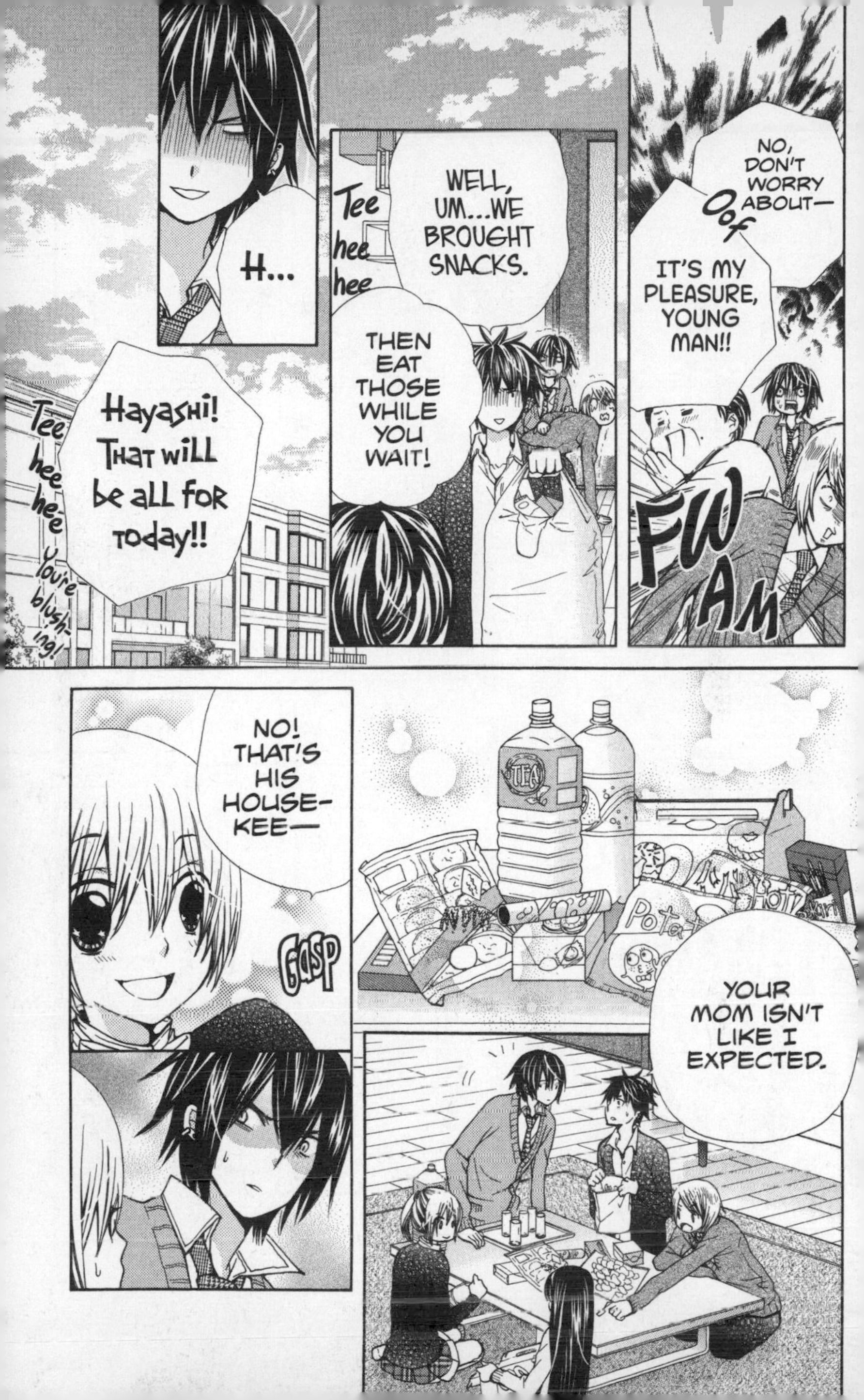
NO, DON'T WORRY ABOUT—
Oof
IT'S MY PLEASURE, YOUNG MAN!!
FWAM
WELL, UM...WE BROUGHT SNACKS.
Tee hee hee
THEN EAT THOSE WHILE YOU WAIT!
H...
Hayashi! That will be all for today!!
Tee hee hee
You're blush-ing!
TEA
YOUR MOM ISN'T LIKE I EXPECTED.
NO! THAT'S HIS HOUSE-KEE—
GASP

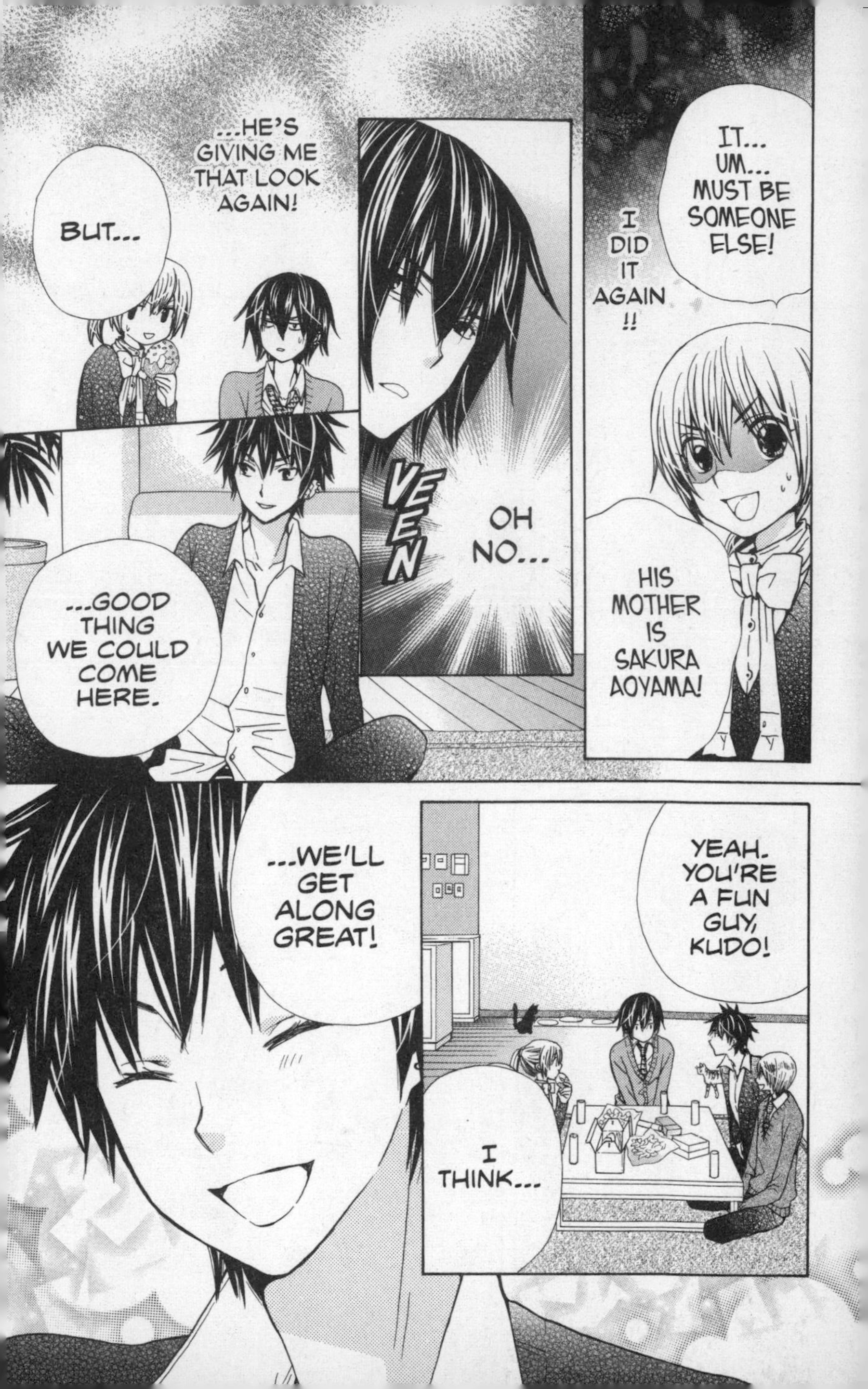
IT... UM... MUST BE SOMEONE ELSE!
I DID IT AGAIN!!
HIS MOTHER IS SAKURA AOYAMA!
VEEN
OH NO...
...HE'S GIVING ME THAT LOOK AGAIN!
BUT...
...GOOD THING WE COULD COME HERE.
YEAH. YOU'RE A FUN GUY, KUDO!
I THINK...
...WE'LL GET ALONG GREAT!

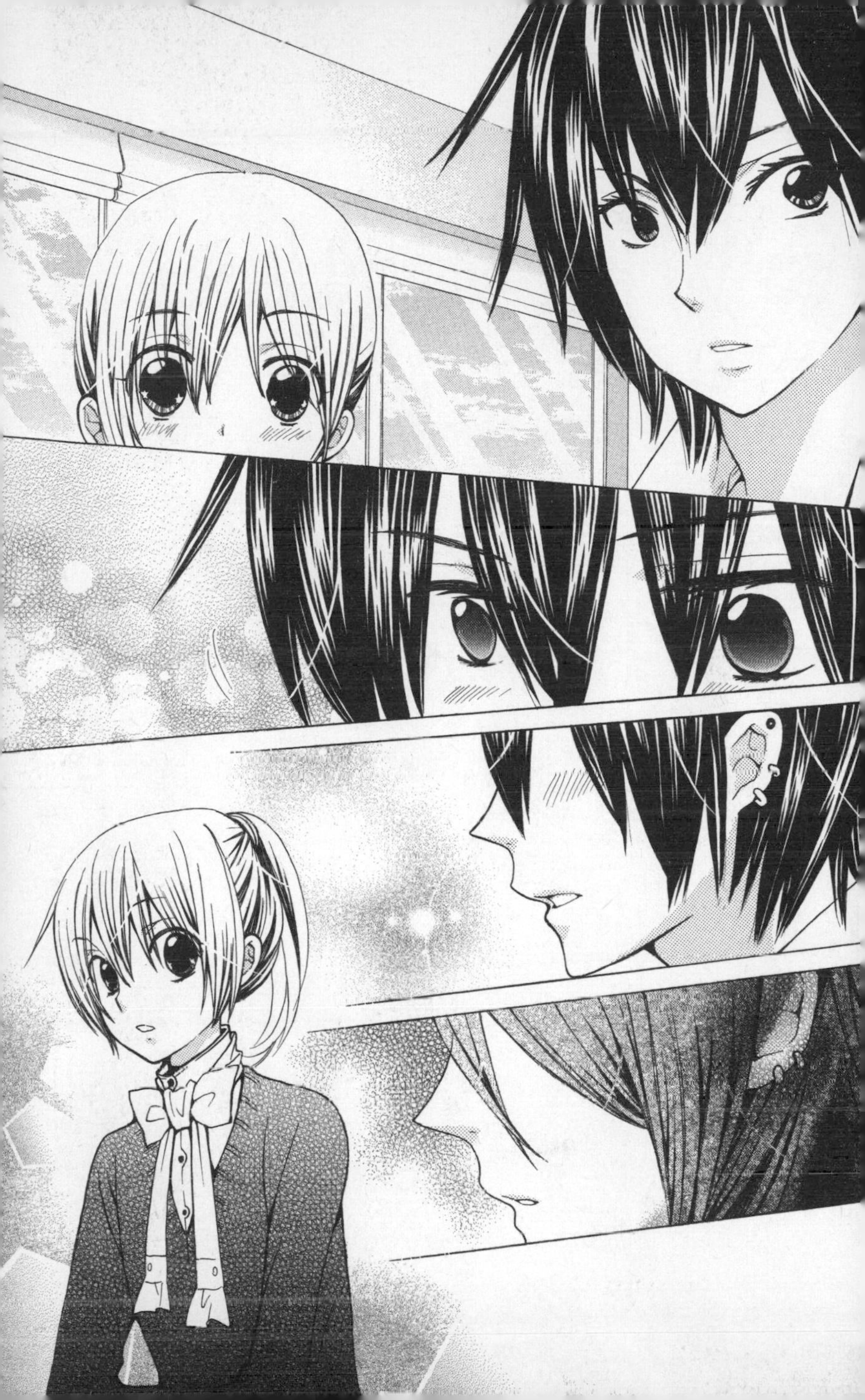

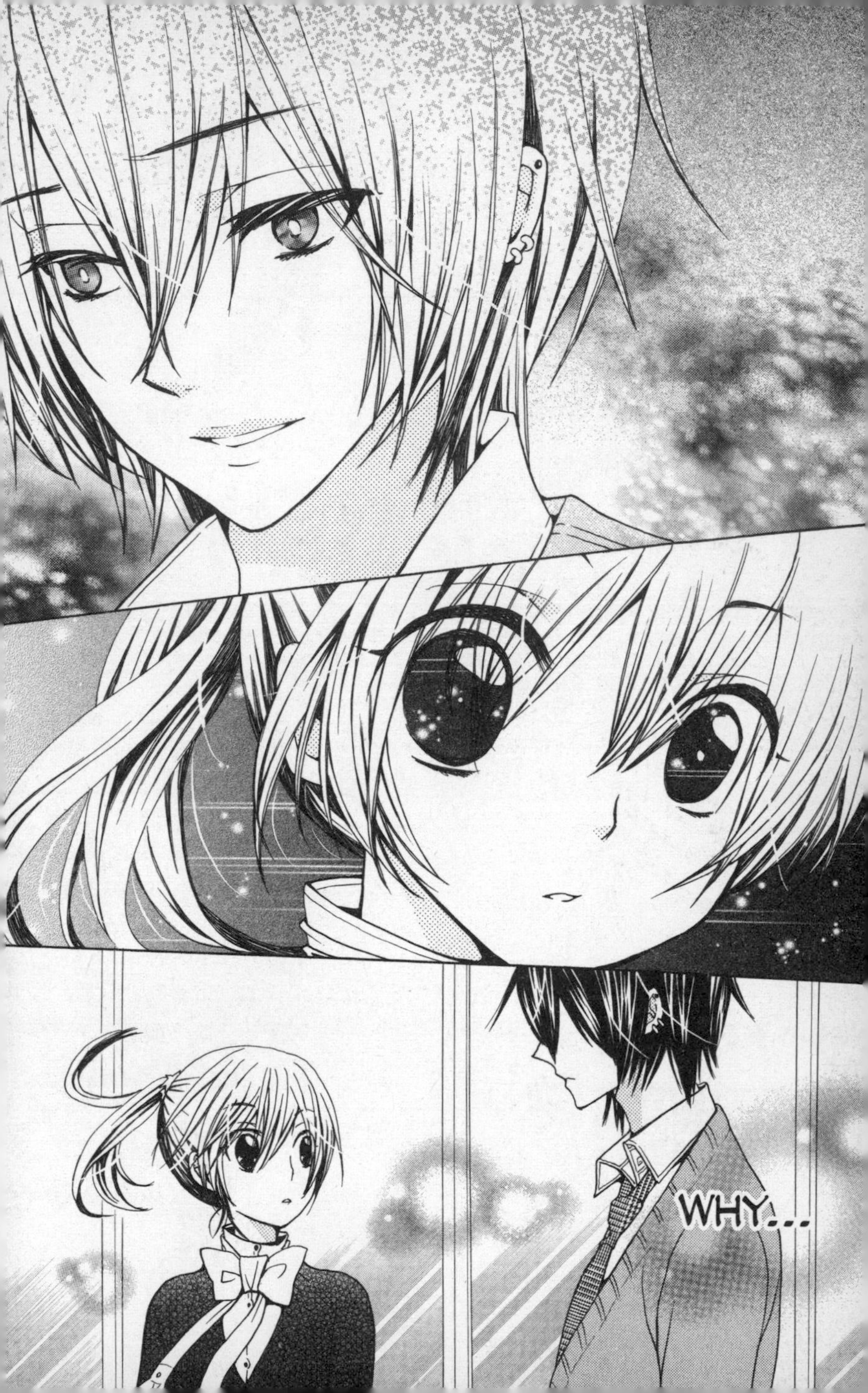
WHY...

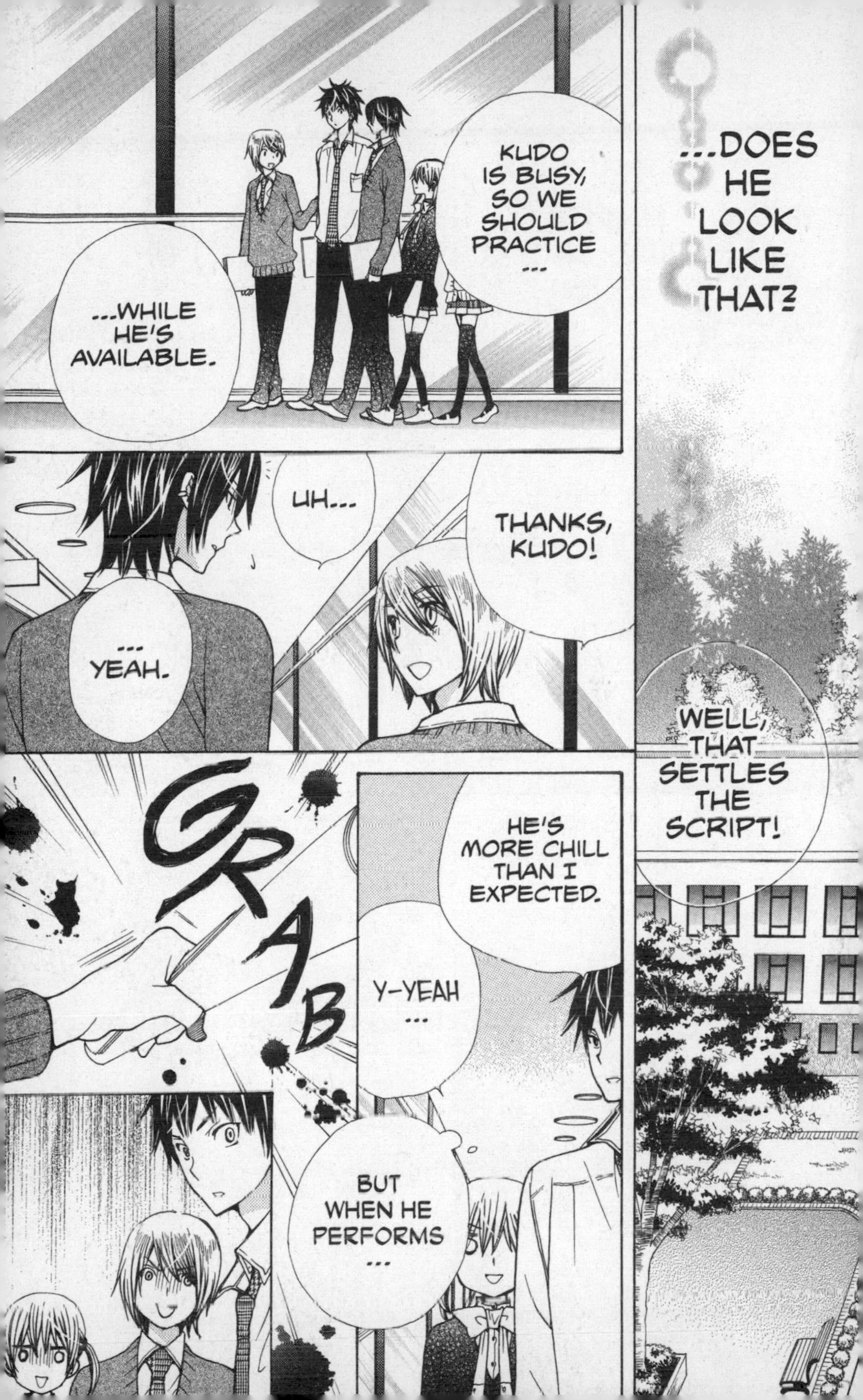
...DOES HE LOOK LIKE THAT?
WELL, THAT SETTLES THE SCRIPT!
KUDO IS BUSY, SO WE SHOULD PRACTICE...
...WHILE HE'S AVAILABLE.
THANKS, KUDO!
UH...
...YEAH.
HE'S MORE CHILL THAN I EXPECTED.
Y-YEAH...
BUT WHEN HE PERFORMS...
GRAB

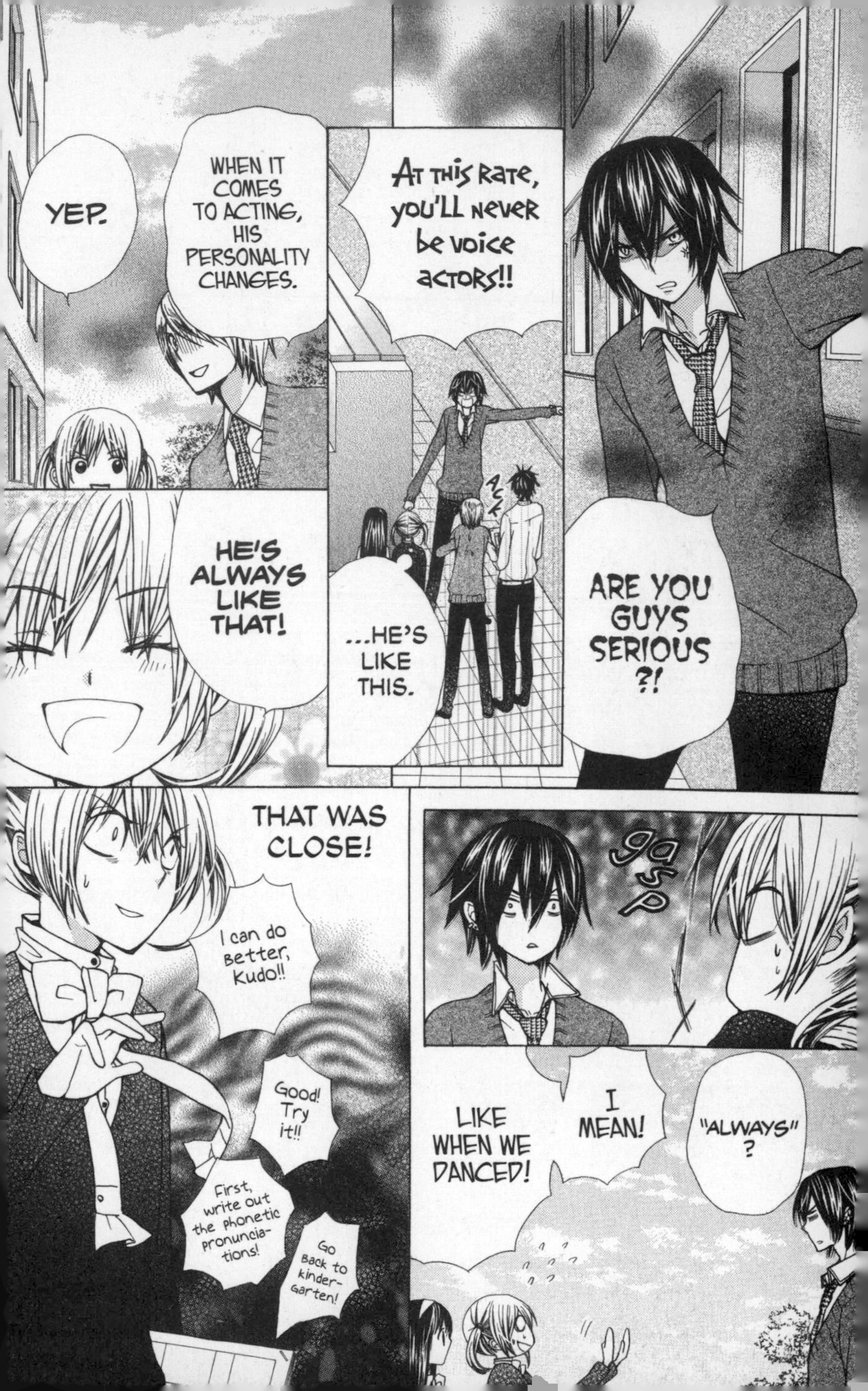
ARE YOU GUYS SERIOUS?!
At this rate, you'll never be voice actors!!
ACK
...HE'S LIKE THIS.
WHEN IT COMES TO ACTING, HIS PERSONALITY CHANGES.
YEP.
HE'S ALWAYS LIKE THAT!
gasp
"ALWAYS"?
I MEAN!
LIKE WHEN WE DANCED!
THAT WAS CLOSE!
I can do better, Kudo!!
Good! Try it!!
First, write out the phonetic pronuncia-tions!
Go back to kinder-garten!

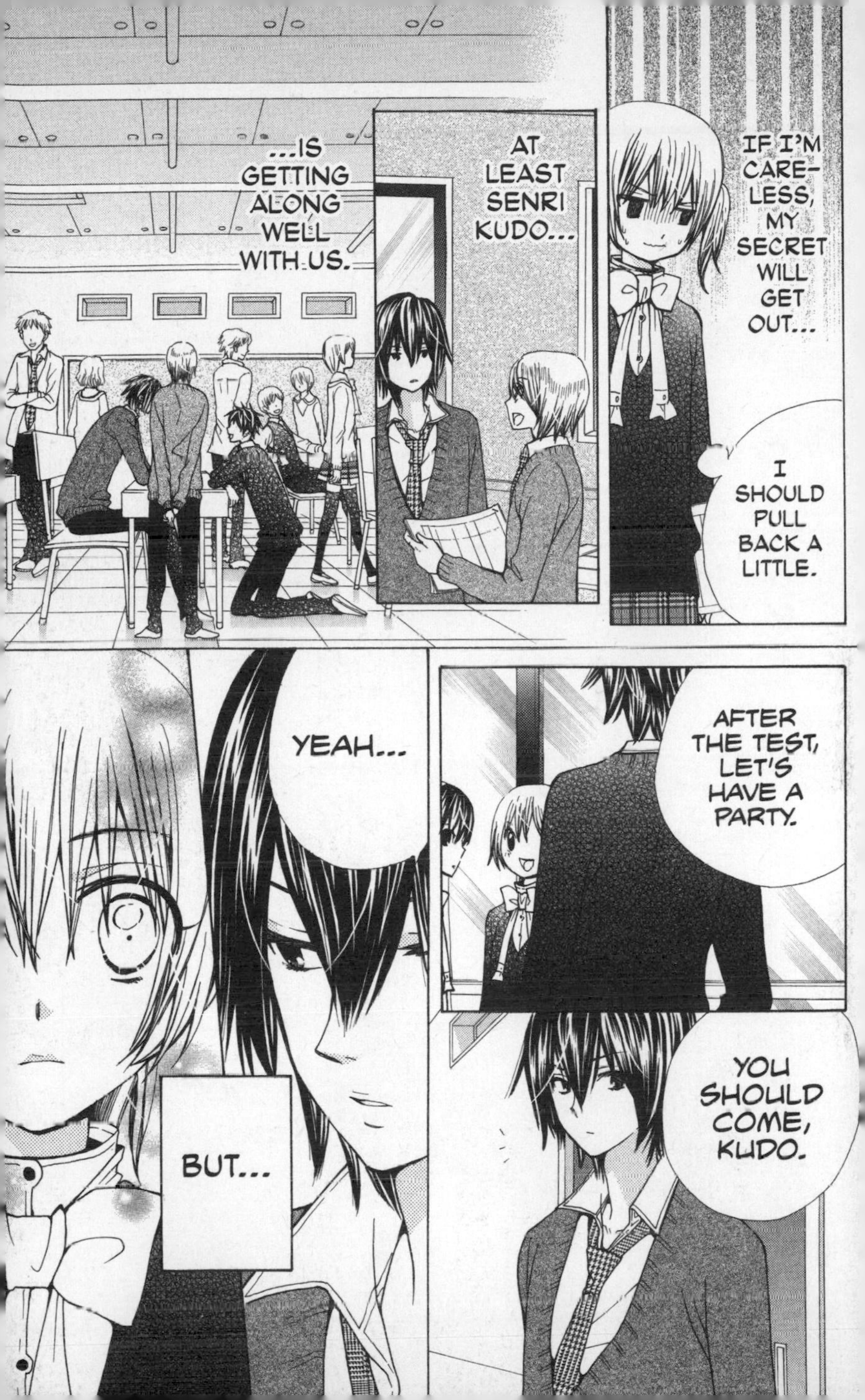
IF I'M CARELESS, MY SECRET WILL GET OUT...
I SHOULD PULL BACK A LITTLE.
AT LEAST SENRI KUDO...
...IS GETTING ALONG WELL WITH US.
AFTER THE TEST, LET'S HAVE A PARTY.
YOU SHOULD COME, KUDO.
YEAH...
BUT...

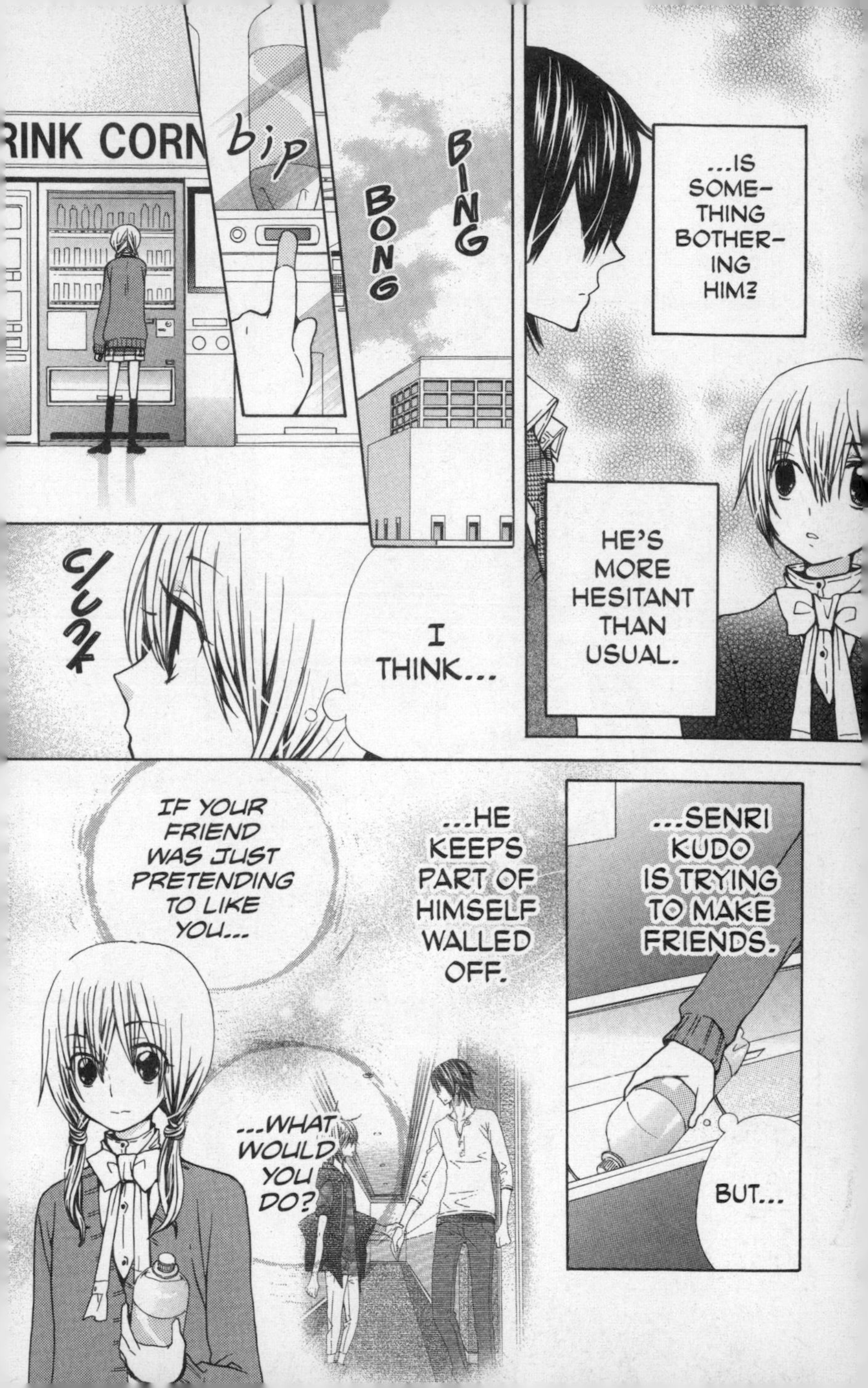
...IS SOMETHING BOTHERING HIM?
HE'S MORE HESITANT THAN USUAL.
BING
BONG
bip
RINK CORN
I THINK...
clunk
...SENRI KUDO IS TRYING TO MAKE FRIENDS.
BUT...
...HE KEEPS PART OF HIMSELF WALLED OFF.
IF YOUR FRIEND WAS JUST PRETENDING TO LIKE YOU...
...WHAT WOULD YOU DO?

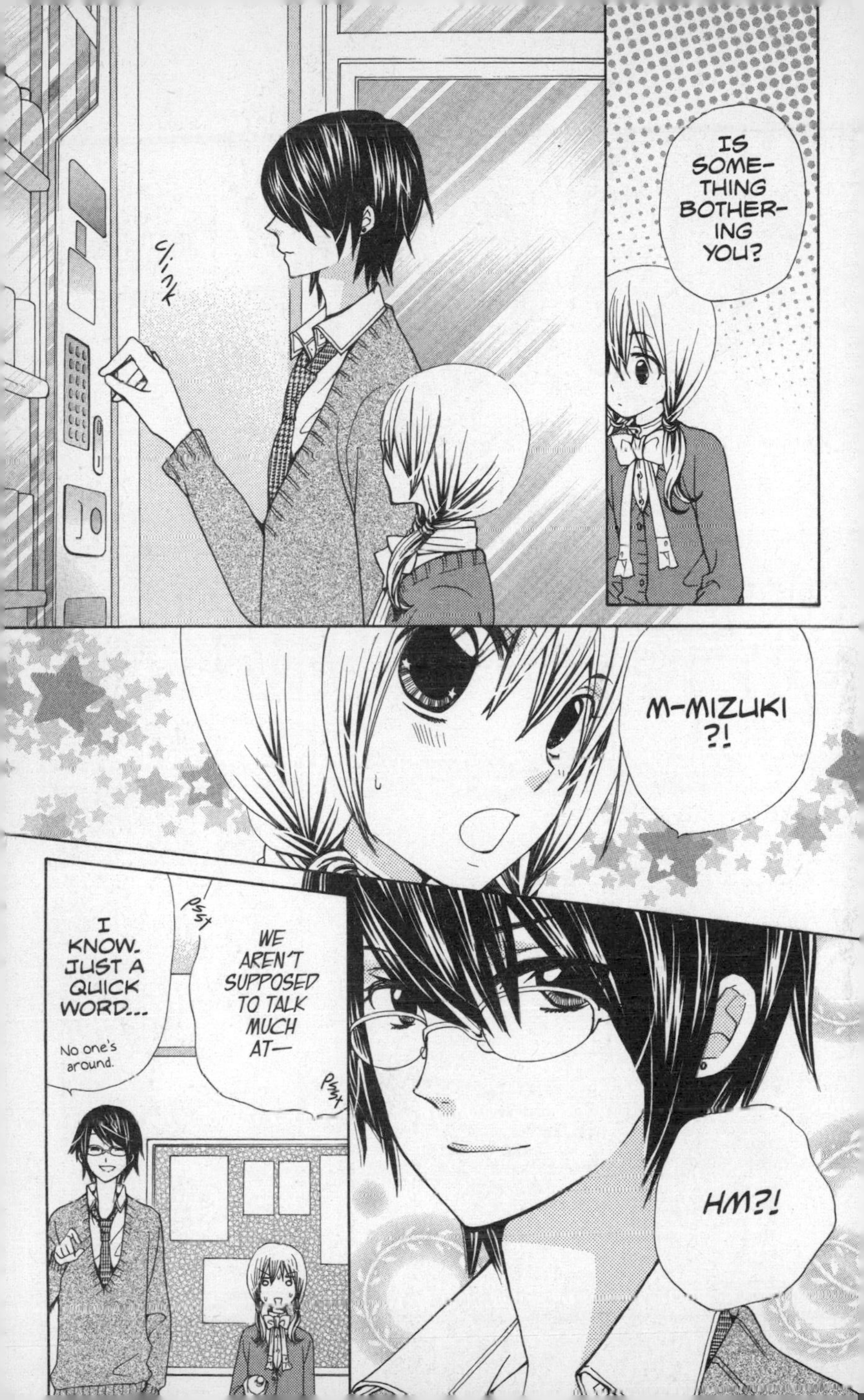
IS SOMETHING BOTHERING YOU?
clink
M-MIZUKI ?!
HM?!
Psst
WE AREN'T SUPPOSED TO TALK MUCH AT—
Psst
I KNOW. JUST A QUICK WORD...
No one's around.

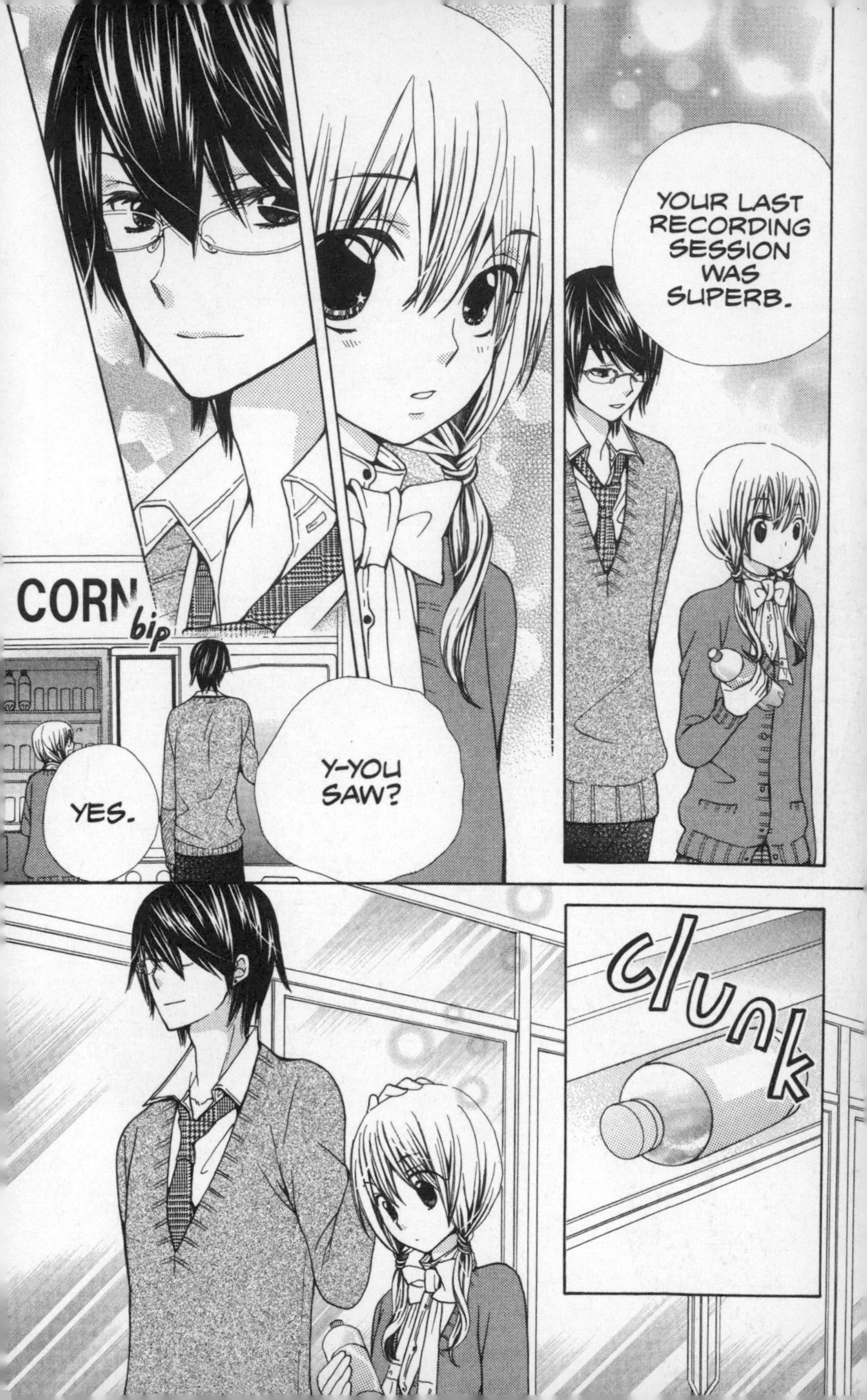
YOUR LAST RECORDING SESSION WAS SUPERB.
Y-YOU SAW?
CORN
bip
YES.
clunk

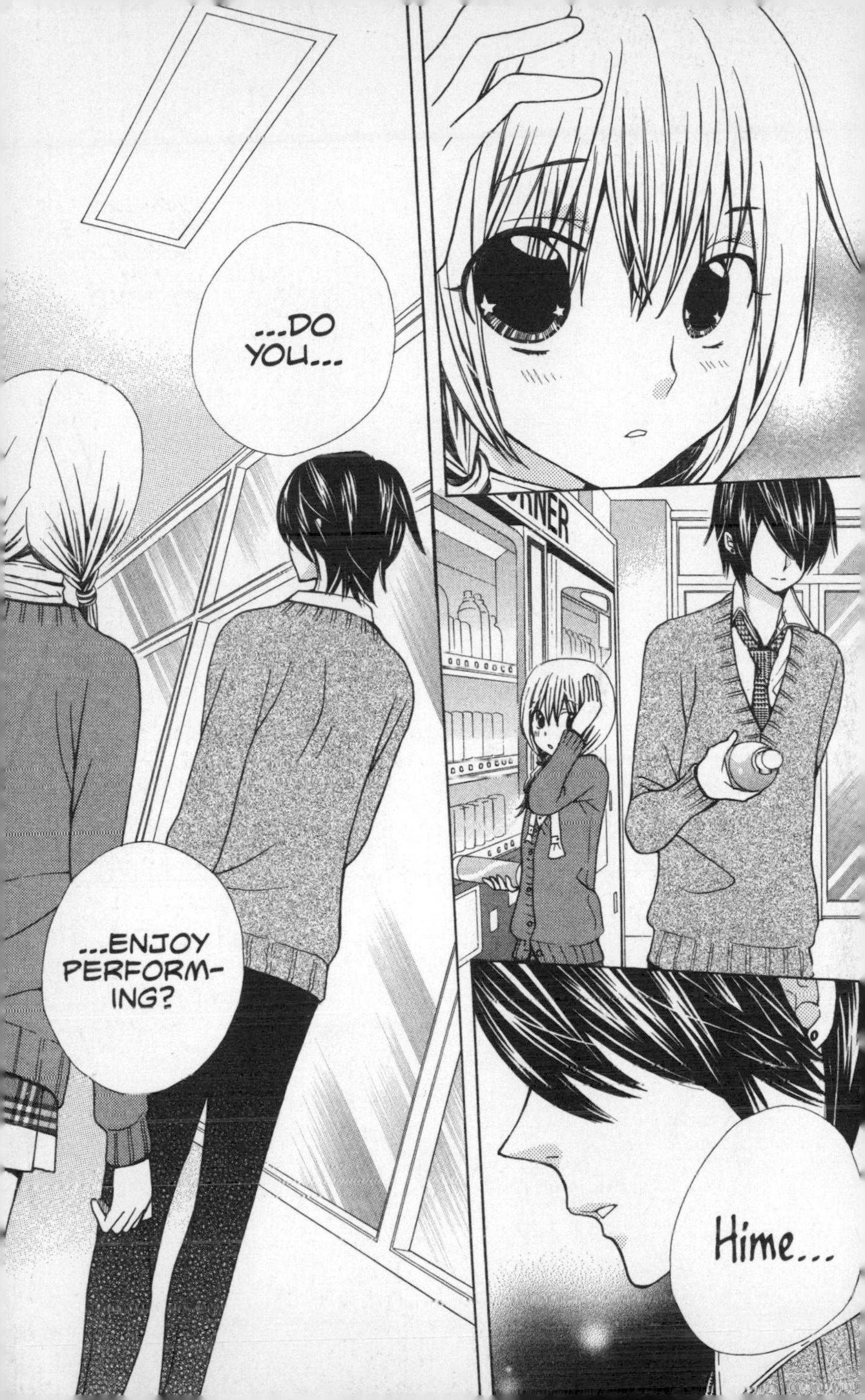
Hime...
...DO YOU...
...ENJOY PERFORMING?

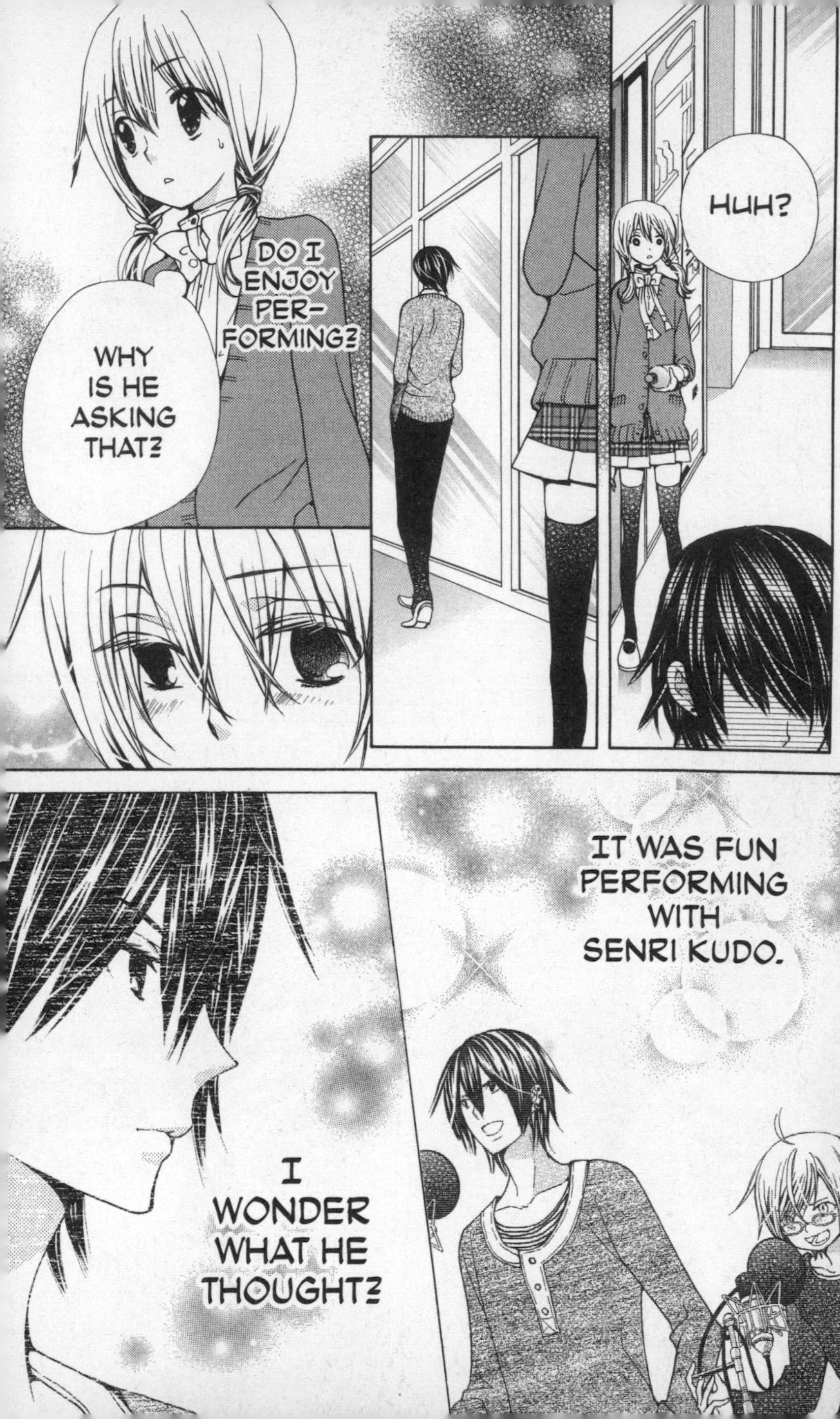
HUH?
DO I ENJOY PER-FORMING?
WHY IS HE ASKING THAT?
IT WAS FUN PERFORMING WITH SENRI KUDO.
I WONDER WHAT HE THOUGHT?

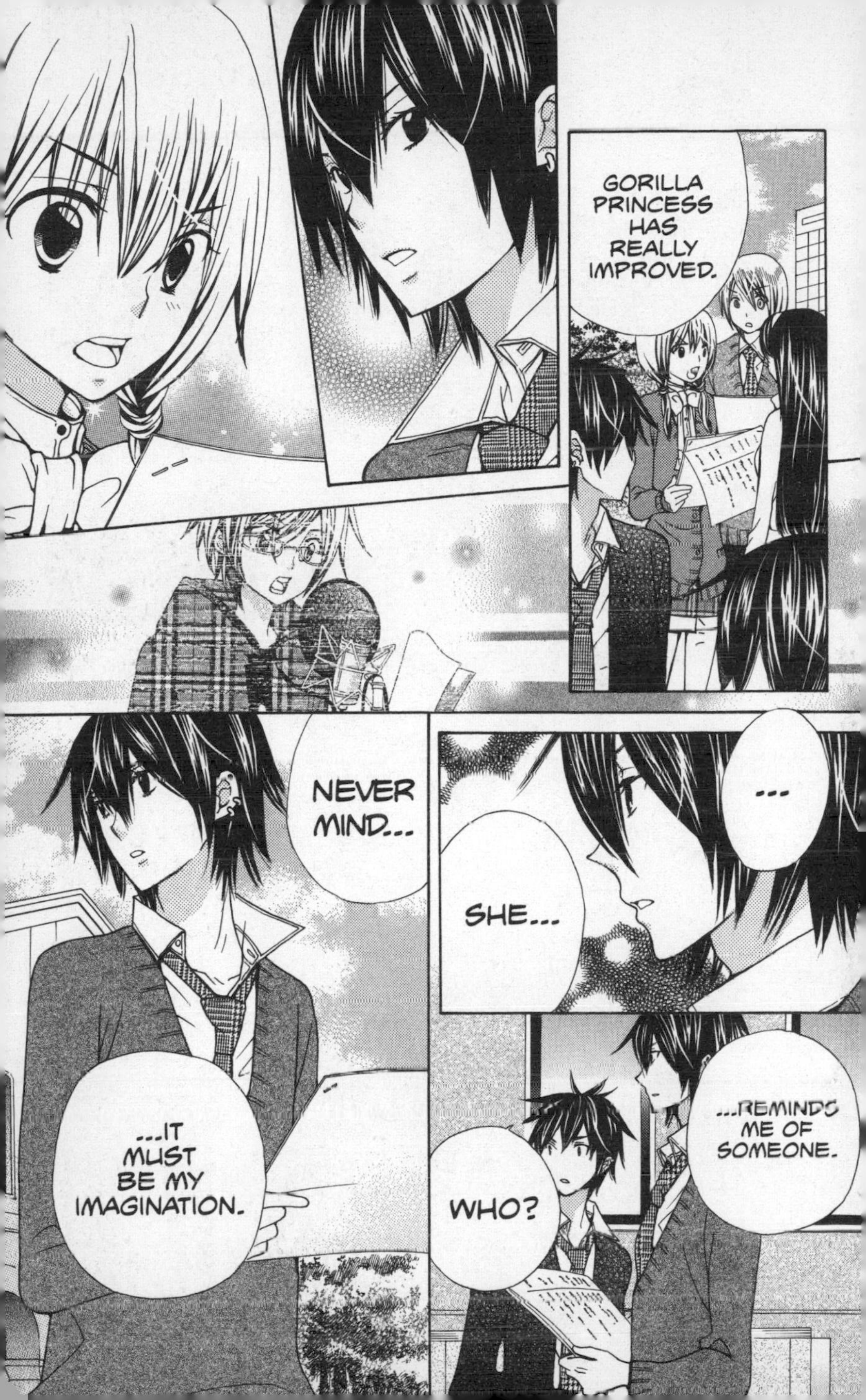
GORILLA PRINCESS HAS REALLY IMPROVED.
...
SHE...
...REMINDS ME OF SOMEONE.
WHO?
NEVER MIND...
...IT MUST BE MY IMAGINATION.

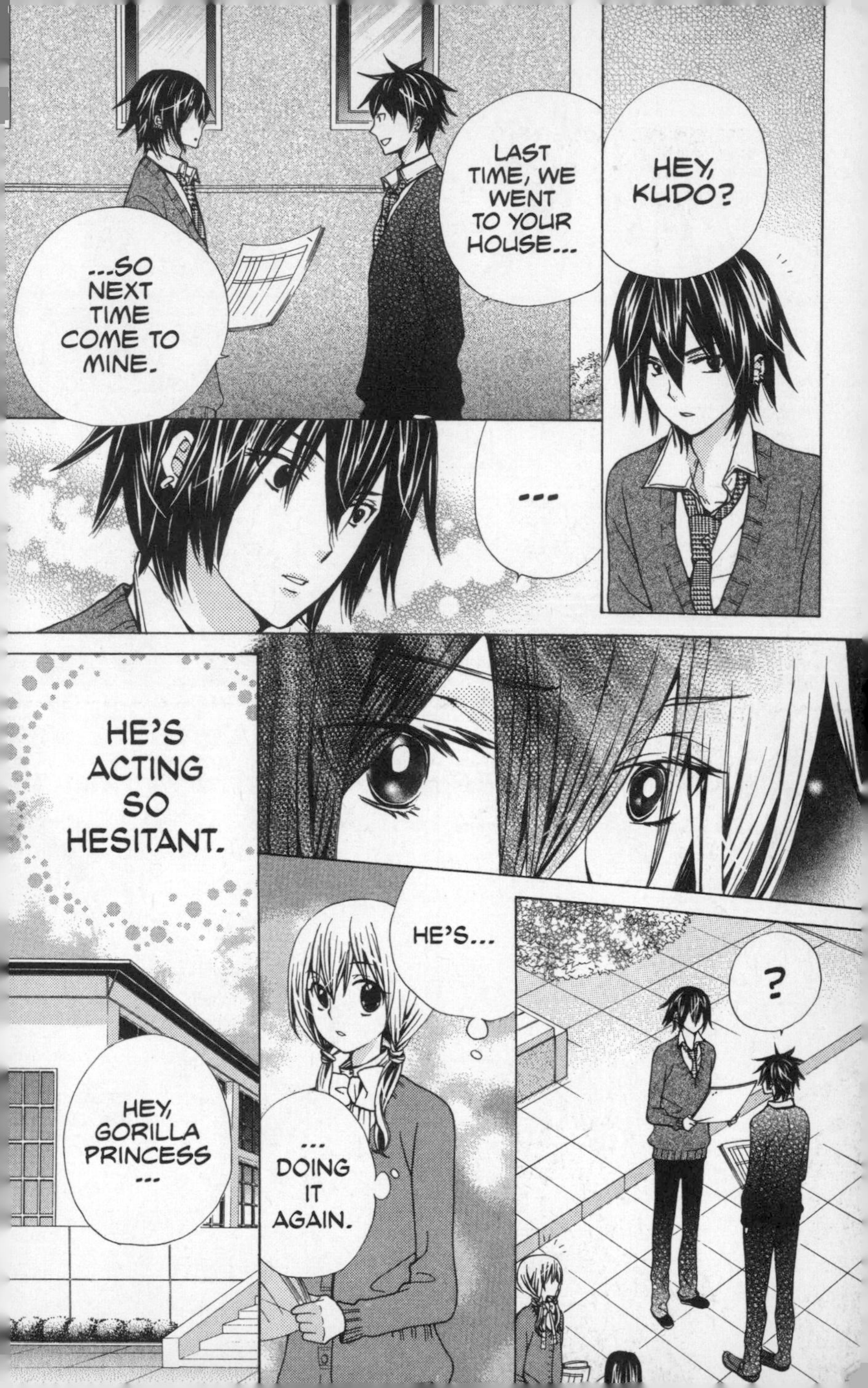
HEY, KUDO?
LAST TIME, WE WENT TO YOUR HOUSE...
...SO NEXT TIME COME TO MINE.
...
HE'S ACTING SO HESITANT.
?
HE'S...
...DOING IT AGAIN.
HEY, GORILLA PRINCESS...

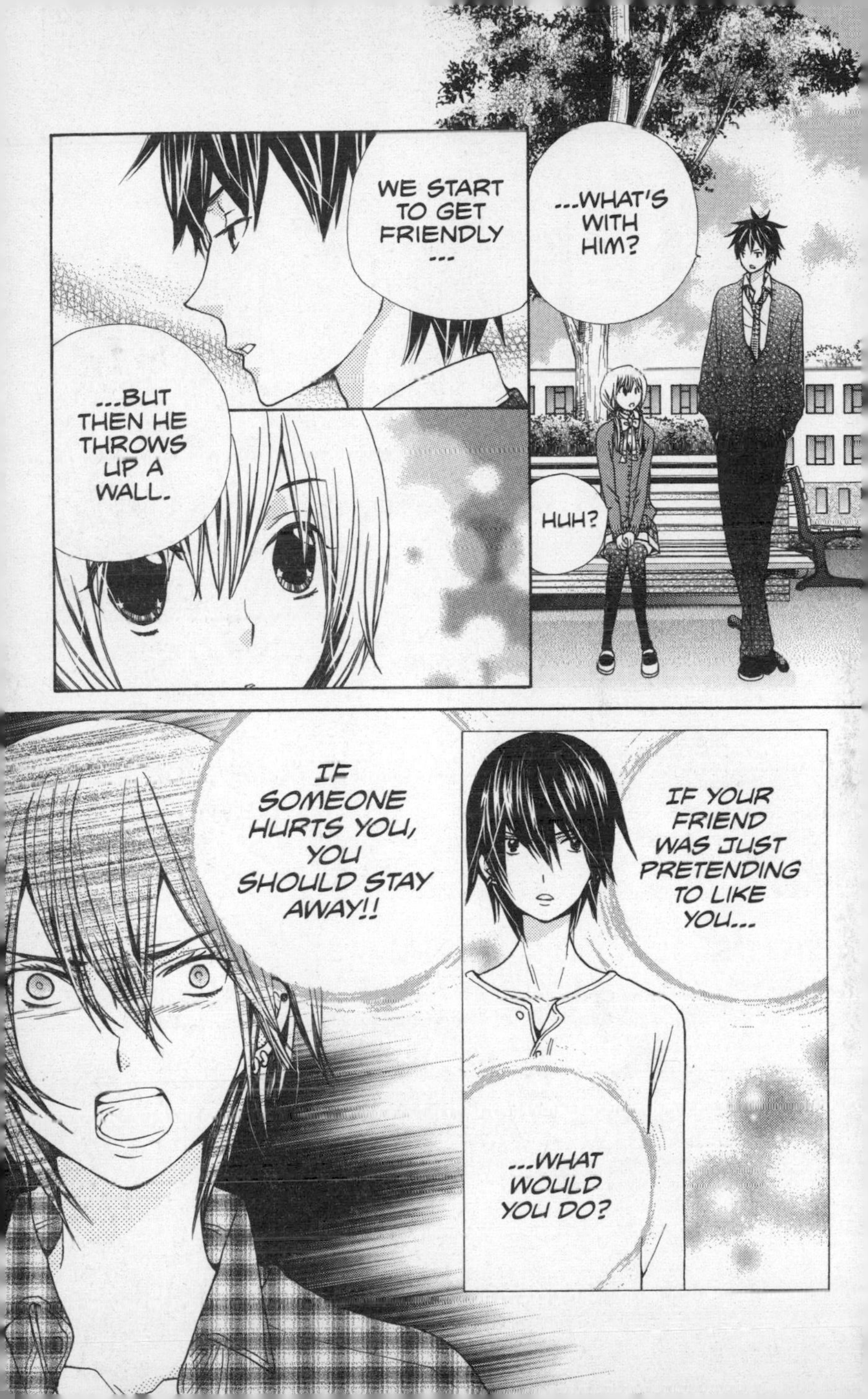
...WHAT'S WITH HIM?
HUH?
WE START TO GET FRIENDLY ...
...BUT THEN HE THROWS UP A WALL.
IF YOUR FRIEND WAS JUST PRETENDING TO LIKE YOU...
...WHAT WOULD YOU DO?
IF SOMEONE HURTS YOU, YOU SHOULD STAY AWAY!!

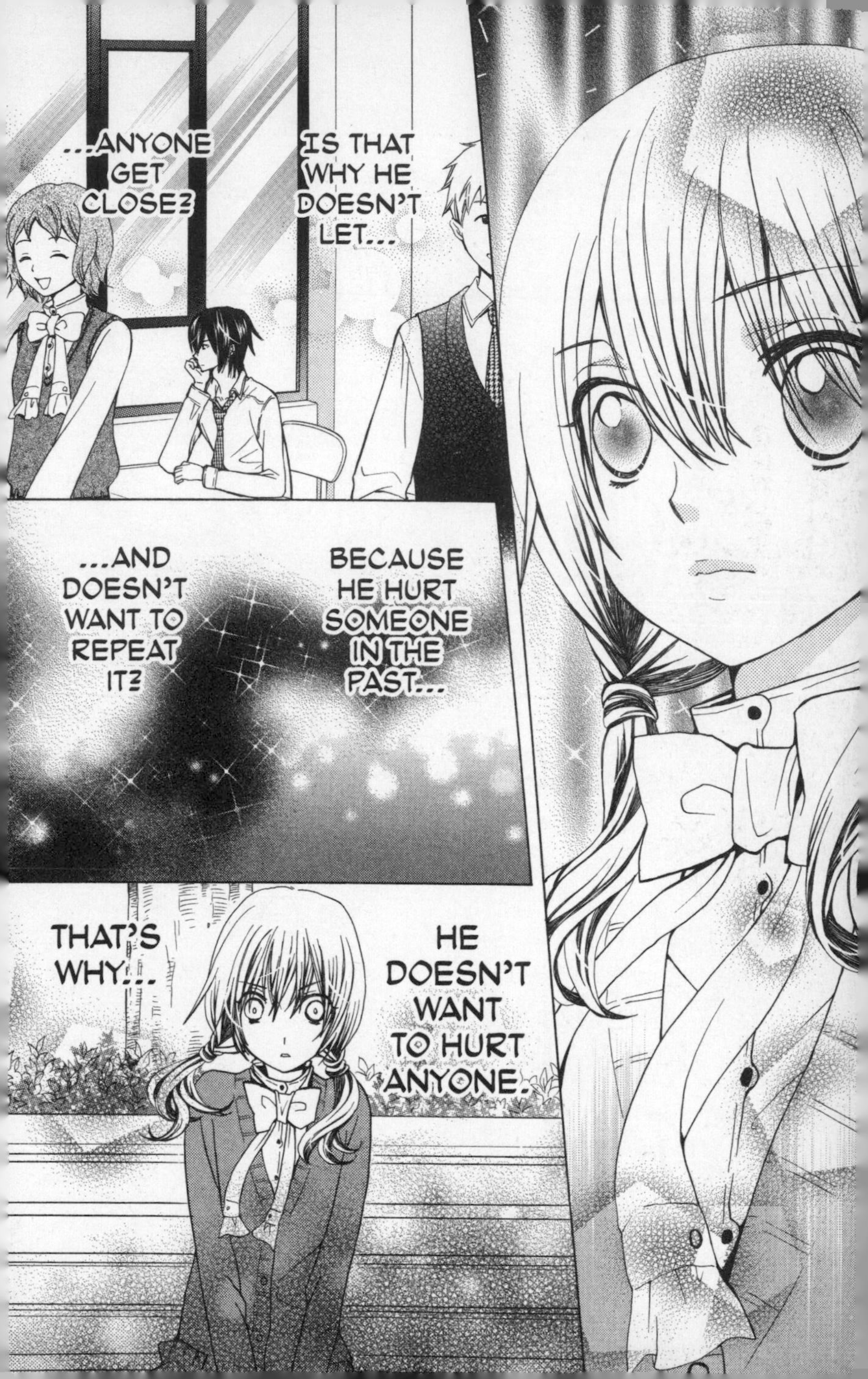
IS THAT WHY HE DOESN'T LET...
...ANYONE GET CLOSE?
BECAUSE HE HURT SOMEONE IN THE PAST...
...AND DOESN'T WANT TO REPEAT IT?
HE DOESN'T WANT TO HURT ANYONE.
THAT'S WHY...

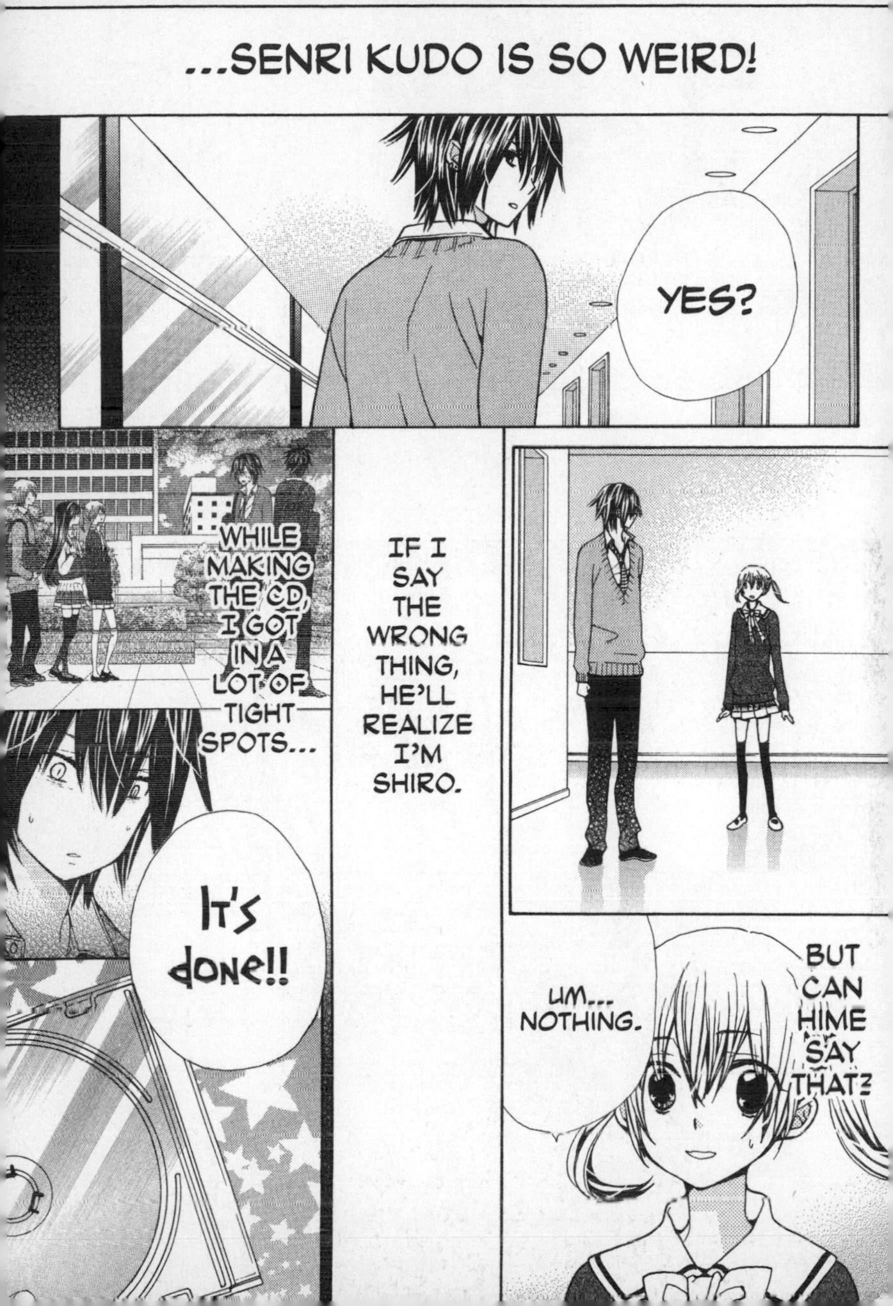
...SENRI KUDO IS SO WEIRD!
YES?
BUT CAN HIME SAY THAT?
UM... NOTHING.
IF I SAY THE WRONG THING, HE'LL REALIZE I'M SHIRO.
WHILE MAKING THE CD, I GOT IN A LOT OF TIGHT SPOTS...
It's done!!

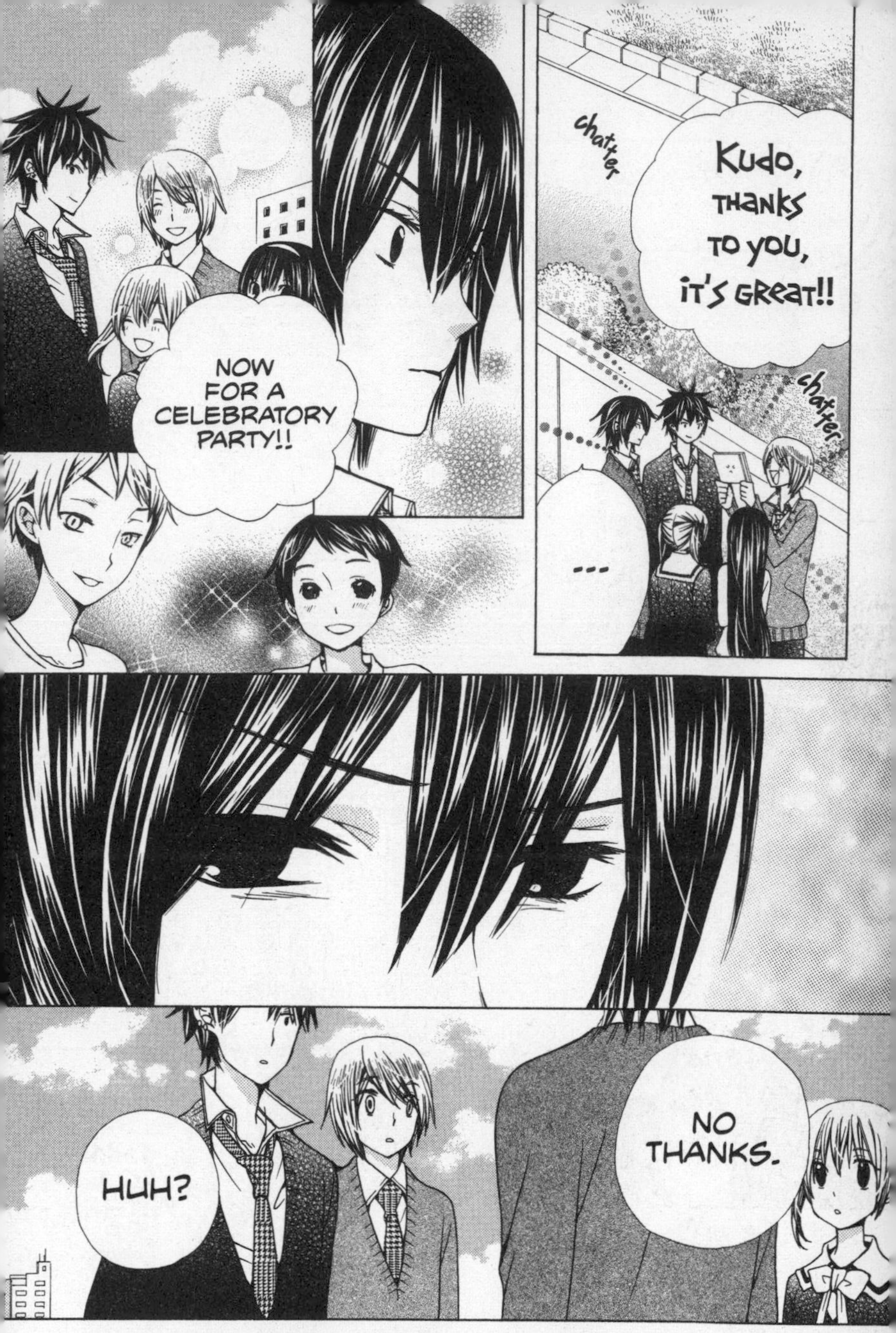
chatter
Kudo, thanks to you, it's great!!
chatter
...
NOW FOR A CELEBRATORY PARTY!!
NO THANKS.
HUH?

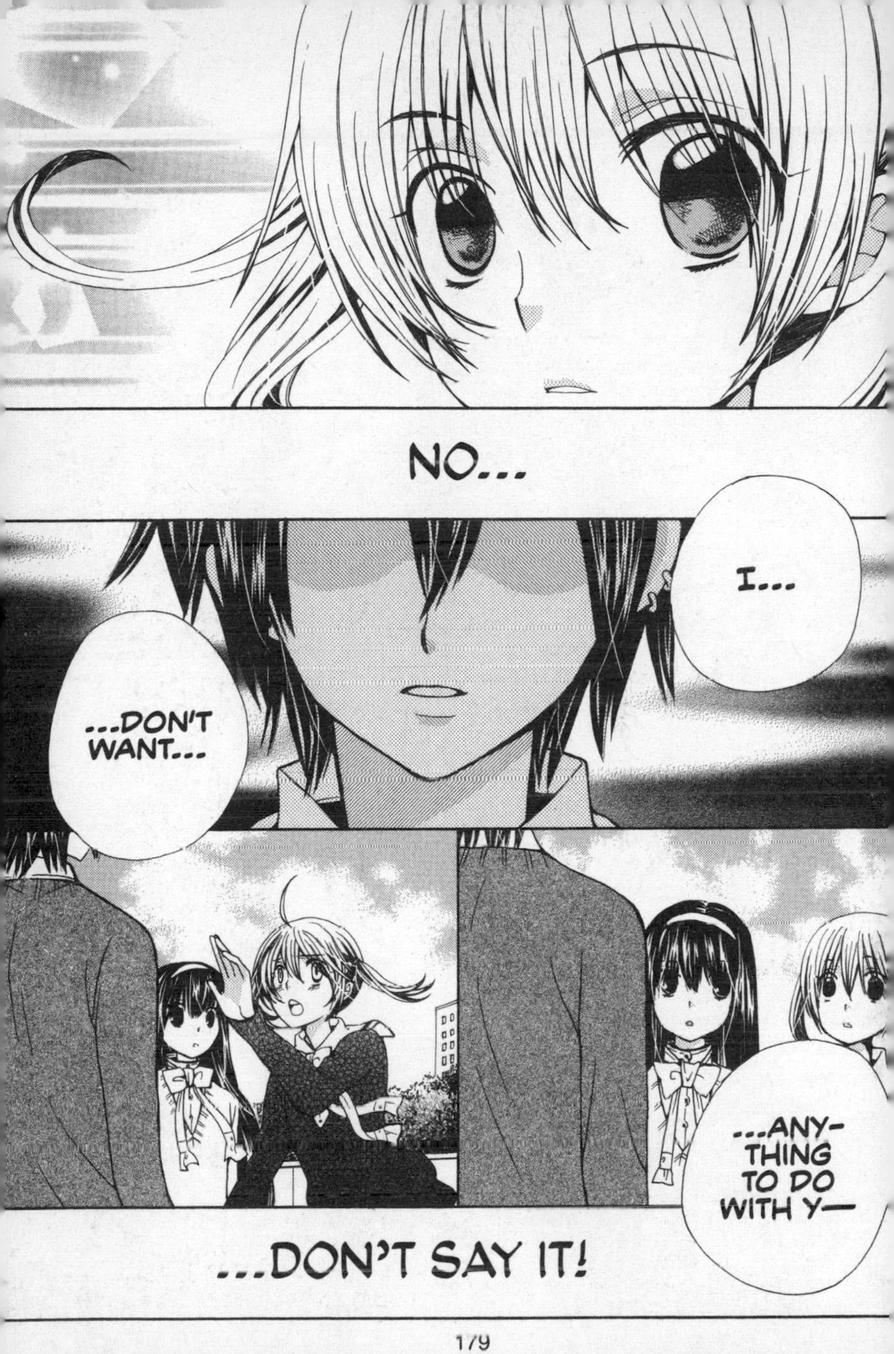
NO...
I...
...DON'T WANT...
...ANY-THING TO DO WITH Y—
...DON'T SAY IT!

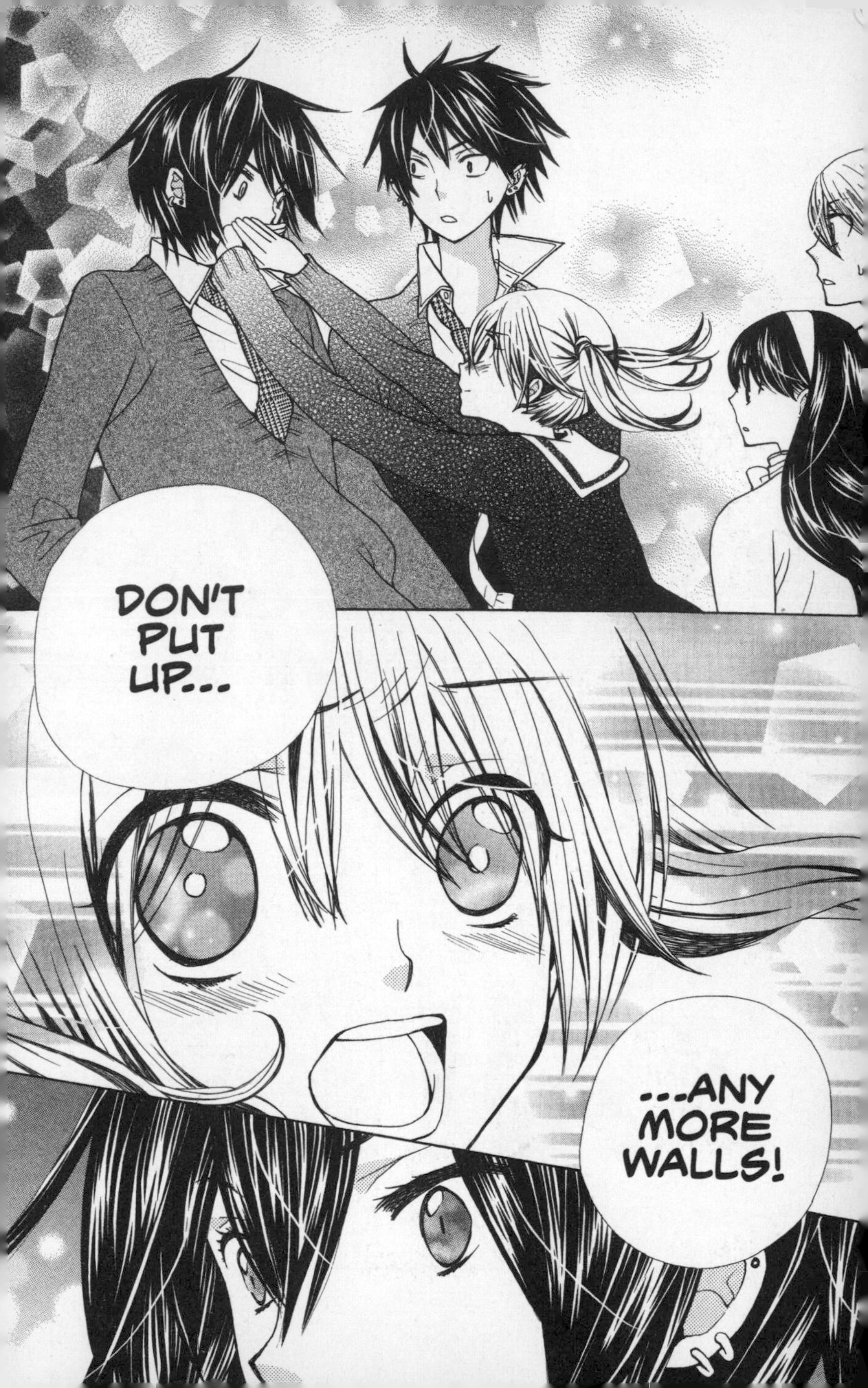
DON'T PUT UP...
...ANY MORE WALLS!

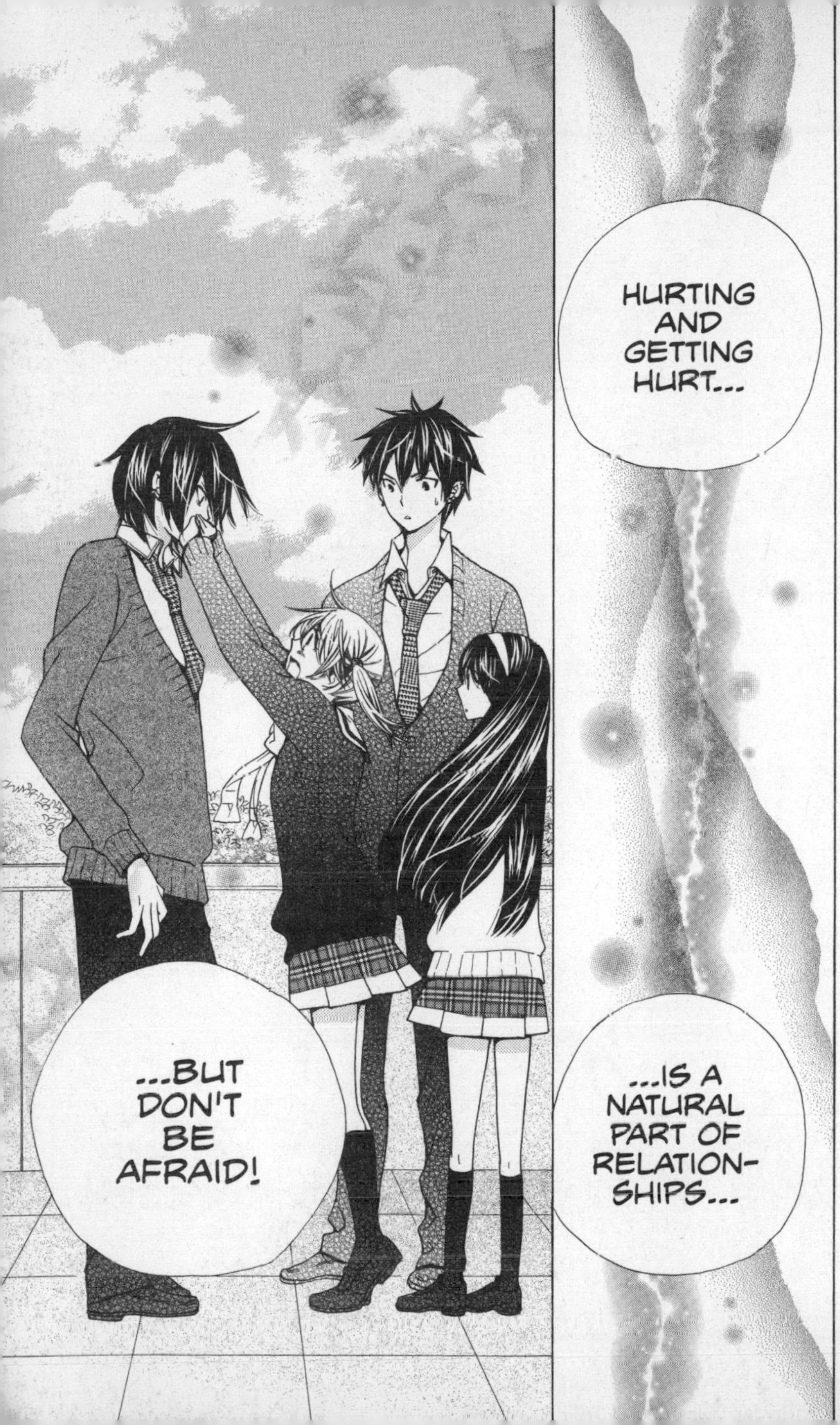
HURTING AND GETTING HURT...
...IS A NATURAL PART OF RELATION-SHIPS...
...BUT DON'T BE AFRAID!

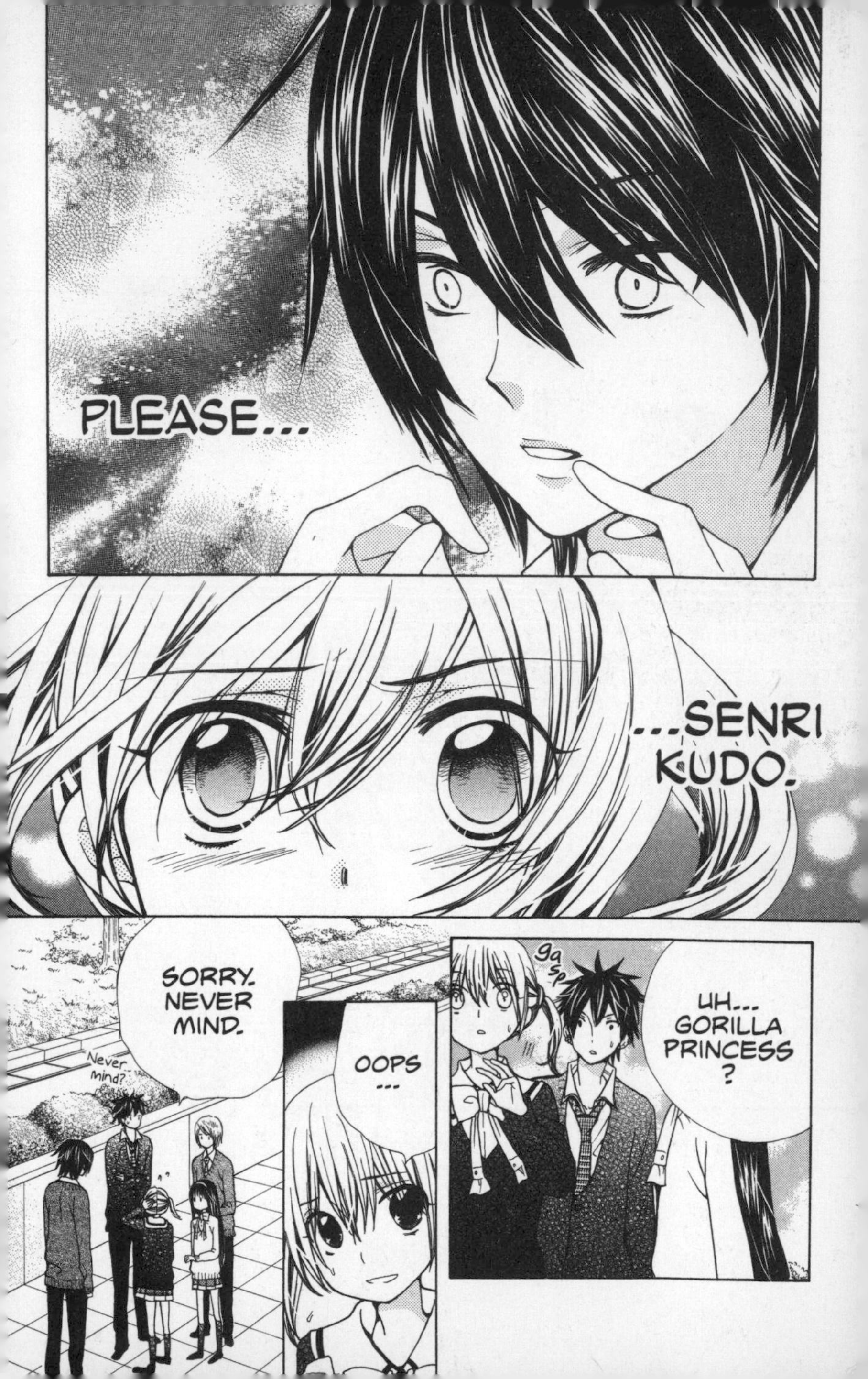
PLEASE...
...SENRI KUDO.
gasp
UH... GORILLA PRINCESS?
OOPS...
SORRY. NEVER MIND.
Never mind?

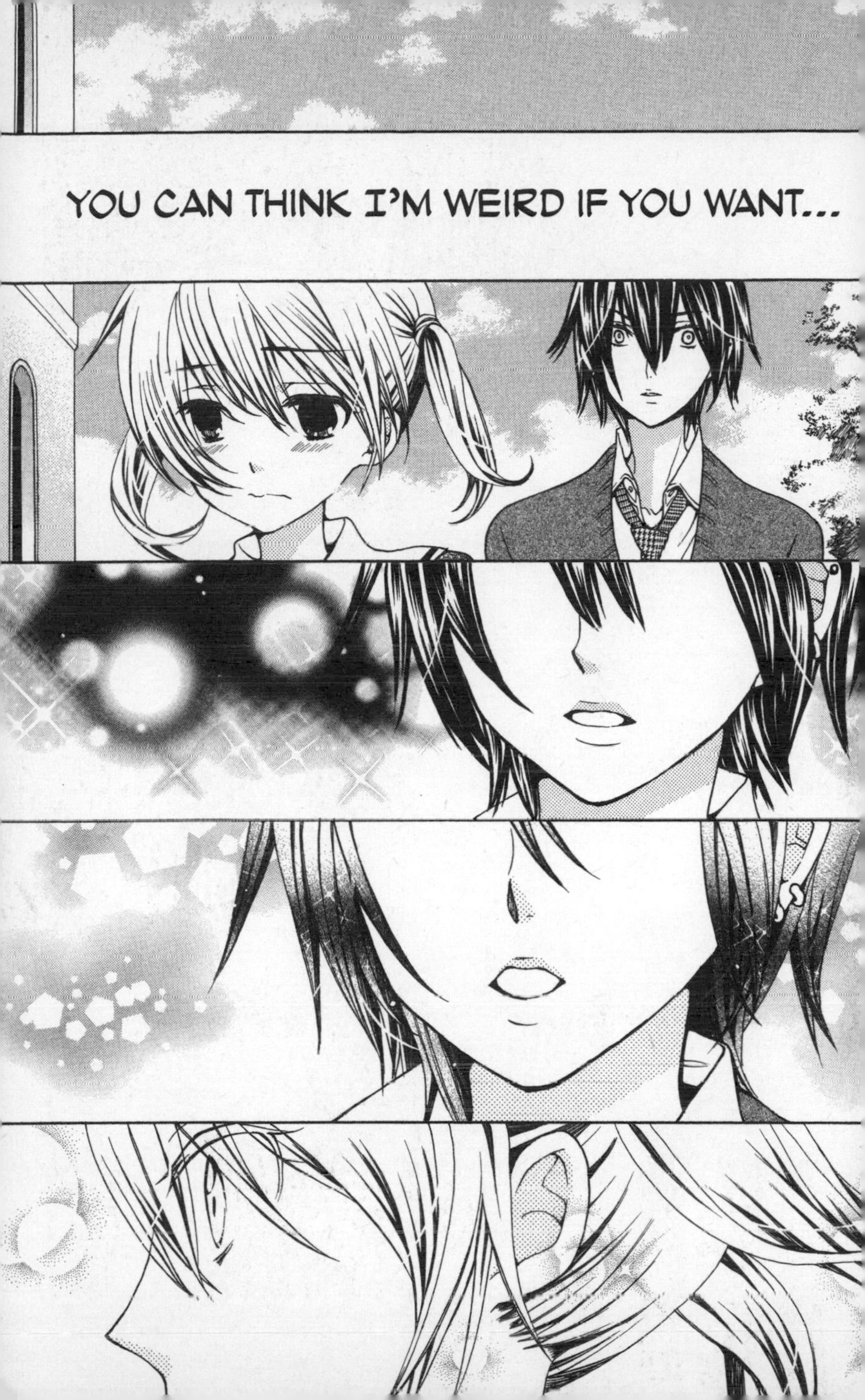
YOU CAN THINK I'M WEIRD IF YOU WANT...

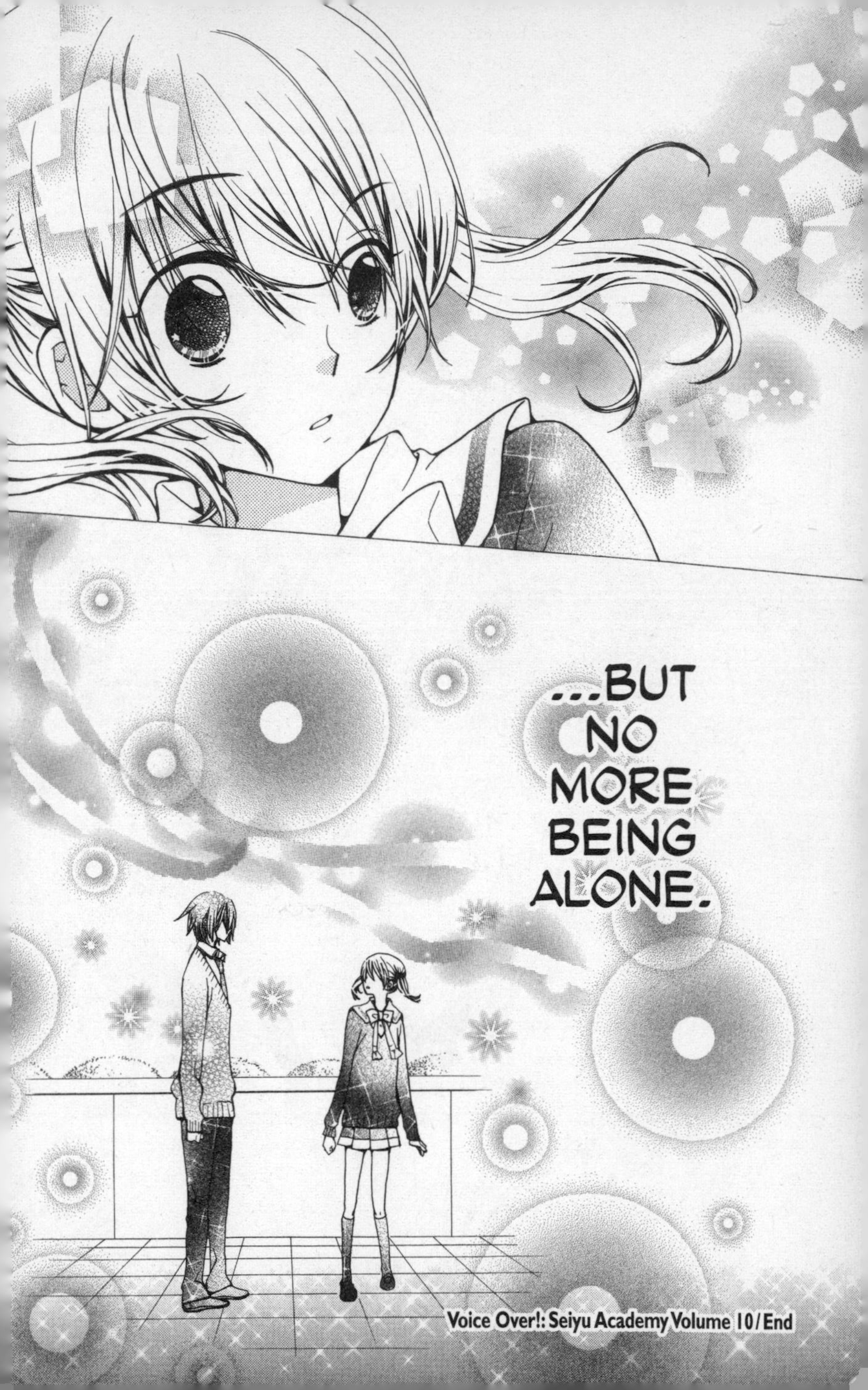
...BUT NO MORE BEING ALONE.
Voice Over!: Seiyu Academy Volume 10/End

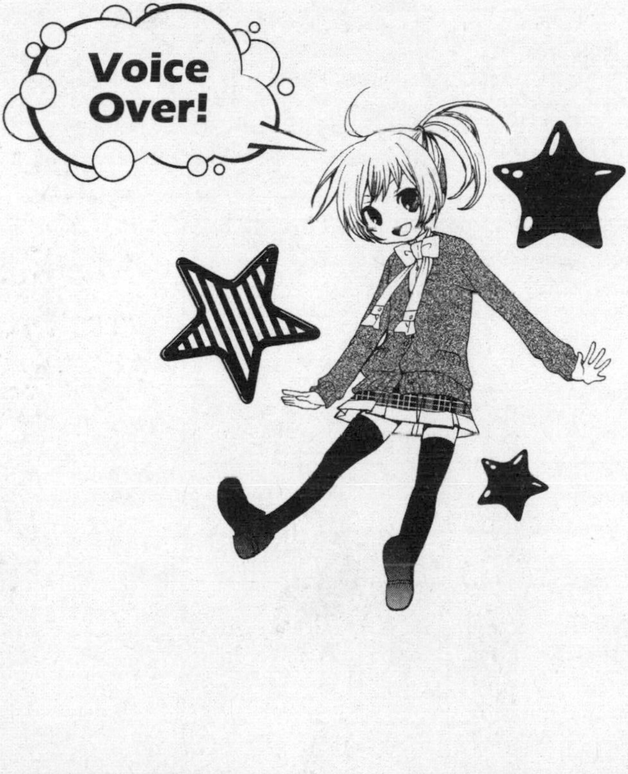
Voice Over!

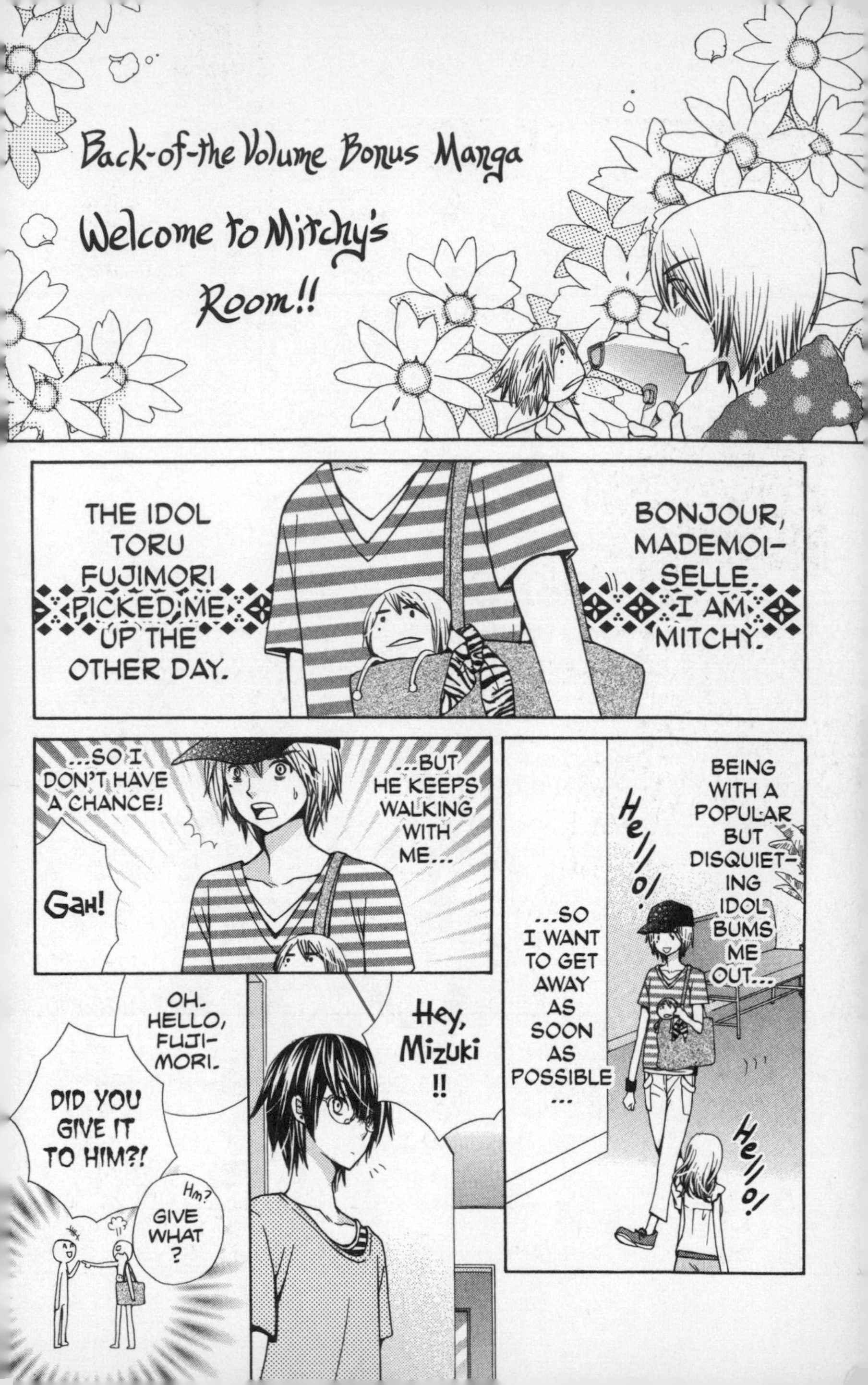
Back-of-the Volume Bonus Manga
Welcome to Mitchy's Room!!
BONJOUR, MADEMOISELLE. I AM MITCHY.
THE IDOL TORU FUJIMORI PICKED ME UP THE OTHER DAY.
BEING WITH A POPULAR BUT DISQUIETING IDOL BUMS ME OUT...
Hello!
...SO I WANT TO GET AWAY AS SOON AS POSSIBLE...
Hello!
...BUT HE KEEPS WALKING WITH ME...
...SO I DON'T HAVE A CHANCE!
Gah!
Hey, Mizuki!!
OH. HELLO, FUJIMORI.
DID YOU GIVE IT TO HIM?!
Hm?
GIVE WHAT?

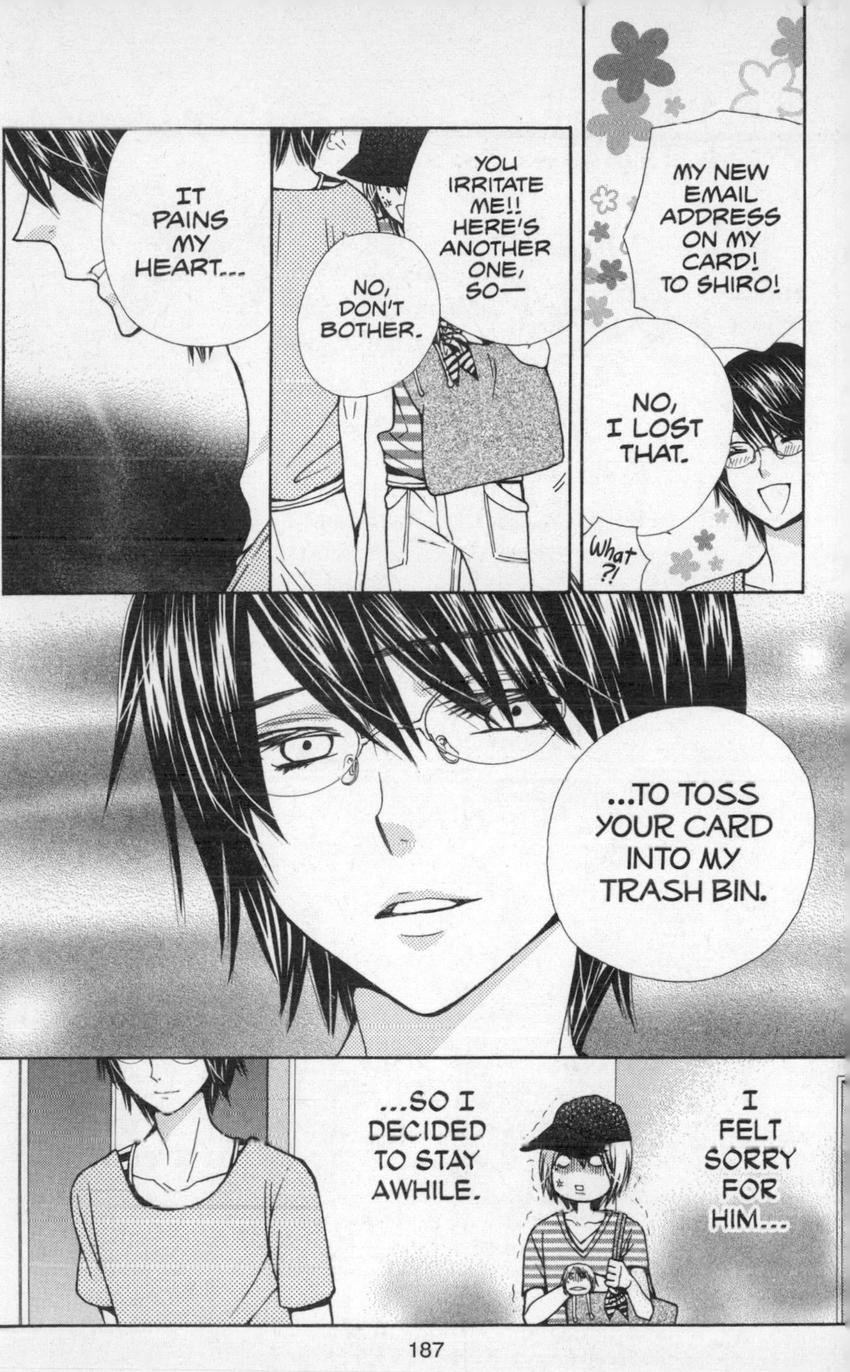
MY NEW EMAIL ADDRESS ON MY CARD! TO SHIRO!
NO, I LOST THAT.
What?!
YOU IRRITATE ME!! HERE'S ANOTHER ONE, SO—
NO, DON'T BOTHER.
IT PAINS MY HEART...
...TO TOSS YOUR CARD INTO MY TRASH BIN.
I FELT SORRY FOR HIM...
...SO I DECIDED TO STAY AWHILE.

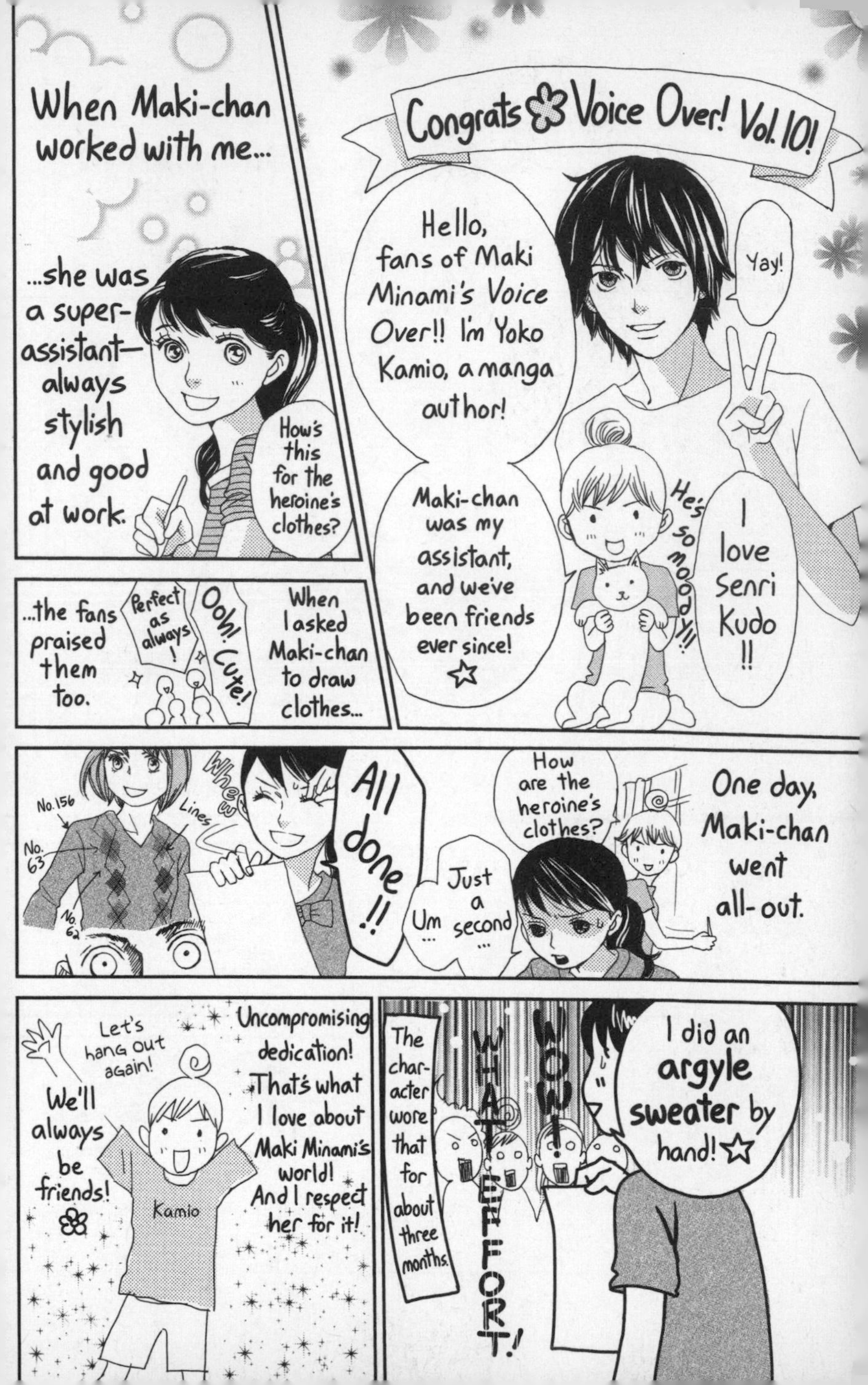
Congrats Voice Over! Vol. 10!
Hello, fans of Maki Minami's Voice Over!! I'm Yoko Kamio, a manga author!
Yay!
Maki-chan was my assistant, and we've been friends ever since! ☆
He's so moody!!
I love Senri Kudo !!
When Maki-chan worked with me...
...she was a super-assistant—always stylish and good at work.
How's this for the heroine's clothes?
When I asked Maki-chan to draw clothes...
Ooh! Cute!
Perfect as always!
...the fans praised them too.
One day, Maki-chan went all-out.
How are the heroine's clothes?
Just a second...
Um...
All done!!
Whew
Lines
No. 156
No. 63
No. 62
I did an argyle sweater by hand! ☆
WOW!
WHAT EFFORT!
The character wore that for about three months.
Uncompromising dedication! That's what I love about Maki Minami's world! And I respect her for it!
Let's hang out again!
We'll always be friends!
Kamio

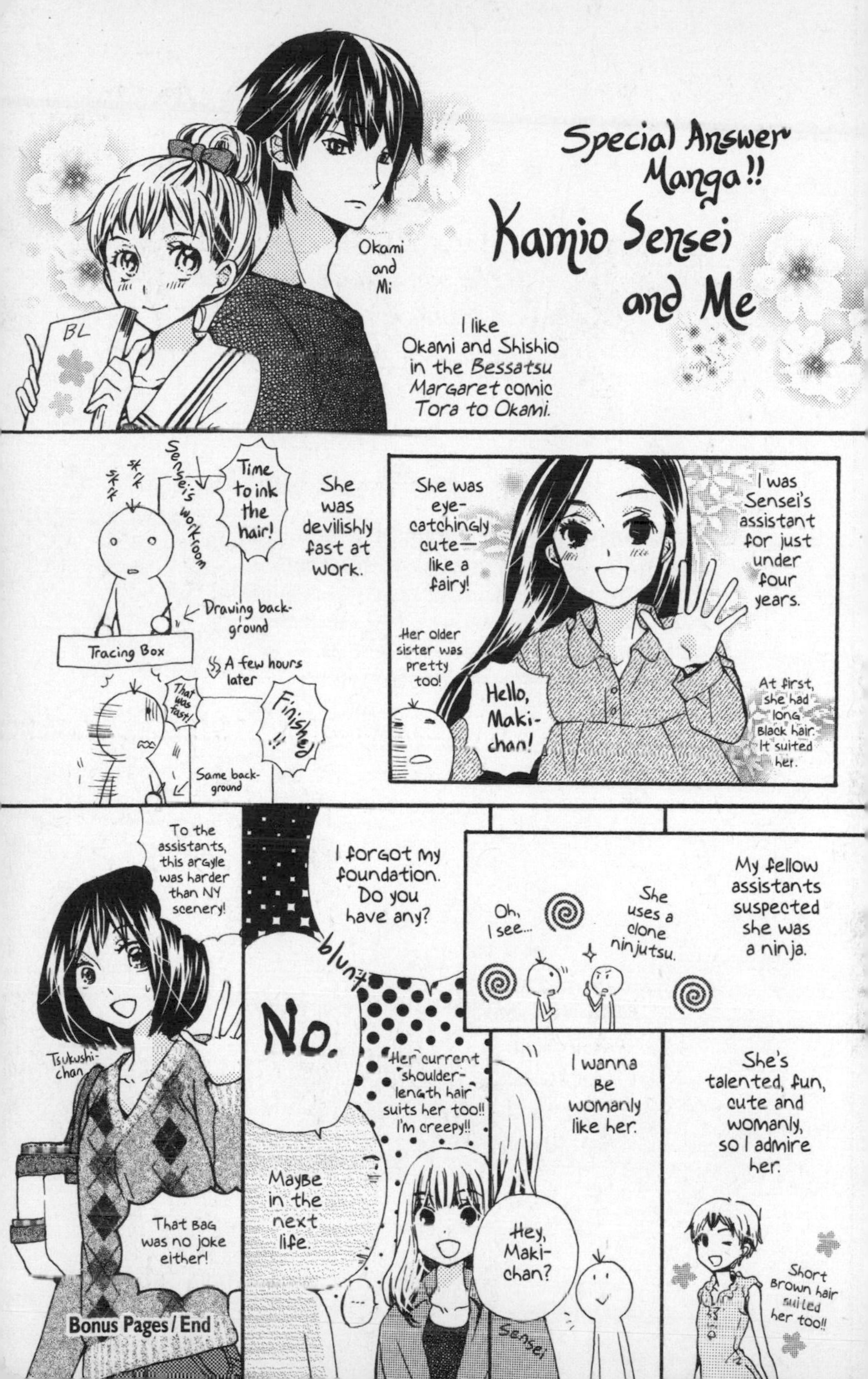

Special Answer Manga!!
Kamio Sensei and Me
Okami and Mi
I like Okami and Shishio in the Bessatsu Margaret comic Tora to Okami.
I was Sensei's assistant for just under four years.
At first, she had long black hair. It suited her.
Hello, Maki-chan!
She was eye-catchingly cute—like a fairy!
Her older sister was pretty too!
She was devilishly fast at work.
Time to ink the hair!
Sensei's workroom
Drawing background
Tracing Box
A few hours later
Finished!!
That was fast!
Same background
My fellow assistants suspected she was a ninja.
She uses a clone ninjutsu.
Oh, I see...
She's talented, fun, cute and womanly, so I admire her.
Short brown hair suited her too!!
I wanna be womanly like her.
Hey, Maki-chan?
Sensei
I forgot my foundation. Do you have any?
blunt
No.
Her current shoulder-length hair suits her too!! I'm creepy!!
Maybe in the next life.
...
To the assistants, this argyle was harder than NY scenery!
Tsukushi-chan
That bag was no joke either!
Bonus Pages / End

Maki Minami is from Saitama Prefecture in Japan. She debuted in 2001 with *Kanata no Ao* (Faraway Blue). Her other works include *Kimi wa Girlfriend* (You're My Girlfriend), *Mainichi ga Takaramono* (Every Day Is a Treasure), *Yuki Atataka* (Warm Winter) and *S•A*, which was published in English by VIZ Media.

VOICE OVER!
SEIYU ACADEMY
VOL. 10
Shojo Beat Edition

STORY AND ART BY
MAKI MINAMI

TECHNICAL ADVISORS
Yoichi Kato, Kaori Kagami, Ayumi Hashidate,
Ayako Harino and Touko Fujitani

Special Thanks
81produce
Tokyo Animator College
Tokyo Animation College

English Translation & Adaptation/John Werry
Touch-up Art & Lettering/Sabrina Heep
Design/Yukiko Whitley
Editor/Pancha Diaz

SEIYU KA! by Maki Minami
© Maki Minami 2012
All rights reserved.
First published in Japan in 2012 by HAKUSENSHA, Inc., Tokyo.
English language translation rights arranged with
HAKUSENSHA, Inc., Tokyo.

Printed in the U.S.A.

Published by VIZ Media, LLC
P.O. Box 77010
San Francisco, CA 94107

10 9 8 7 6 5 4 3 2 1
First printing, April 2015

www.viz.com

www.shojobeat.com

This is the last page.

keeping with the original Japanese comic format, is book reads from right to left—so action, sound fects, and word balloons are completely versed. This preserves the orientation of the iginal artwork—plus, it's fun! Check out e diagram shown here to get the hang f things, and then turn to the other de of the book to get started!

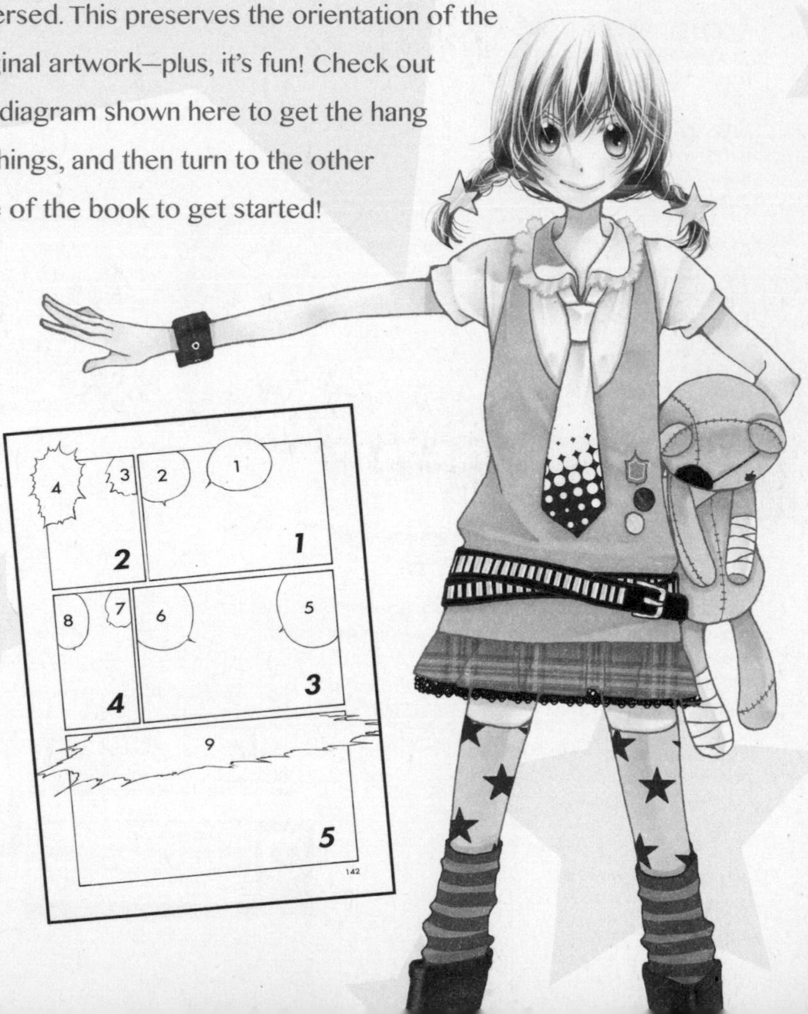
1
2
3
4
1
2
5
6
7
8
3
4
9
5
142